Where the PRESIDENTS Were Born:

The History and Preservation of the Presidential Birthplaces

LOUIS L. PICONE

Schiffer Publishing Ltd

4880 Lower Valley Road • Atglen, PA 19310

Printed in China

Designed by Danielle D. Farmer
Cover Design by Bruce M. Waters
Edited by Rosemarie Flood
Type set in Bauer Bodoni Blk Cn/ Slimbach/Zurich BT

ISBN: 978-0-7643-4079-6
Printed in China

Schiffer Books are available at special discounts for bulk purchases for sales promotions or premiums. Special editions, including personalized covers, corporate imprints, and excerpts can be created in large quantities for special needs. For more information contact the publisher:

Published by Schiffer Publishing, Ltd.
4880 Lower Valley Road
Atglen, PA 19310
Phone: (610) 593-1777; Fax: (610) 593-2002
E-mail: Info@schifferbooks.com

For the largest selection of fine reference books on this and related subjects, please visit our website at **www.schifferbooks.com**
We are always looking for people to write books on new and related subjects. If you have an idea for a book, please contact us at proposals@schifferbooks.com

This book may be purchased from the publisher.
Please try your bookstore first.
You may write for a free catalog.

In Europe, Schiffer books are distributed by
Bushwood Books
6 Marksbury Ave.
Kew Gardens
Surrey TW9 4JF England
Phone: 44 (0) 20 8392 8585; Fax: 44 (0) 20 8392 9876
E-mail: info@bushwoodbooks.co.uk
Website: www.bushwoodbooks.co.uk

All text and images are by the author unless otherwise noted

Note that changes in visitor information may occur. Please be sure to visit varied websites, etc. for new or updated information.

Dedication

For mi famiglia,
Francesca, Vincent & Leonardo

Contents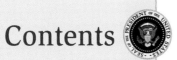

Acknowledgments

First and foremost I thank my beautiful wife, Francesca. While I always thought authors who started off by thanking their spouses were a little hokey, I now know exactly what they had in mind. This book took two years to research and write, which invariably meant that many hours spent working on the book were *not* spent doing something else I should have been doing. Without her endless support and eternal patience while I sequestered myself in my office, toured historic sites, or prattled on about the presidential birthplaces, the dream of writing this book could not have become a reality.

Secondly, I thank my boys Vincent and Leonardo for accompanying me on visits to the presidential birthplaces. Sometimes they are attentive and engaged, other times silly, bored or bewildered, but regardless, they always make me smile and they are the best travel buddies I could ever ask for.

Before I dole out my next round of thanks, I first want to take a quick sidebar to tell a story. My father is a great man, but over the years, has become a very difficult person for whom to buy gifts. My mother, a wonderful woman for the record, is also difficult to buy gifts for, but she is gracious enough to insist that her children do not need to get her anything (although we always do anyway). My Dad, on the other hand, makes no such claim. After years of videos that went unwatched and unopened (perhaps because he still hasn't figured out the DVD player), and books that went unread (he does know how to read, so not sure what the story is there), I had a revelation – road trips! I come from a family that loves to travel. At every family gathering, we inevitably talk about where we have been, where we are going, and where we are going after that. I'm guessing if you bought this book with the intention of visiting all of the presidential birthplaces, then you know what I am talking about and our families would get along just fine. So a few years ago I gave him the gift of a "Birthplaces of America" road trip for Christmas, with stops around the Chesapeake Bay and the Outerbanks of North Carolina that included the birthplace of our country (Jamestown), the birthplace of aviation (Kitty Hawk) and, of course, the birthplace of George Washington and James Monroe.

Shortly after returning, I started to write this book and the rest, excuse the pun, is history. On that maiden trip were my Mom and Dad, my oldest son, Vincent, and my niece, Mary. The road trip immediately became an annual tradition, but the second trip was admittedly a thinly veiled excuse to load up the car to see where the presidents were born. By year three, the veil came off and the trip was now an unabashed excuse to see presidential birthplaces, but since I still flipped the bill, it was still technically a gift! And on the latest adventure, my youngest son, Leonardo, was old enough to make the arduous journey along with my wife, Francesca, which increased the enjoyment while inversely decreasing the amount of elbow room in the minivan, which was a fair trade-off. We are also lucky to have enough nieces and nephews to fall just one short of fielding a baseball team and from this pool, one lucky child is selected each year to join the trip, some more willingly than others. With good humor they all pile into the minivan, which is soon knee deep in fast food wrappers, to drive hours to see sites both historic and obscure. So for braving the 100 degree heat to tour James K. Polk's birthplace replica in Pineville, North Carolina, for spending over an hour lost in Barboursville, Virginia, searching for Zachary Taylor's birthplace marker without once suggesting we give up the hunt (we never did find it, but as you will read it was not our fault), for waking up at 3 a.m. and packing sandwiches to journey to Summerhill, New York to see Millard Fillmore's birthplace, thank you Mom, Dad, Francesca, Vincent, Leonardo, Danielle, Maggie, Mary, and Olivia for the memorable trips full of laughs and presidential birthplaces, sometimes simultaneously. To those nieces and nephews who have yet to accompany us, Katrina, Rayona, Zev, and Ami – pack your bags, because your time will come!

And to the rest of my family, thank you for the support, encouragement, proofreading, and suggestions (both solicited and otherwise!).

Thank you to my father-in-law and renowned artist Mel Leipzig for being so generous with his time and talent to assist with this book.

I also owe a huge debt of gratitude to my editor, Rosemarie Flood. She has an eagle eye for detail and found more mistakes than I should admit to. She also has an incredible talent of transforming my clumsy text into historical prose for which I am very grateful.

To the people who dedicate their time to studying and preserving the presidential birthplaces, I tip my cap to you all, but to the following I owe a special debt of gratitude. Thanks to Ray Crider, concierge at the Boar's Head Inn in Charlottesville, Virginia, and Anna Berkes, Research Librarian at Monticello, for information regarding the ultimate fate of the Thomas Jefferson birthplace replica. Thanks to Michael Fleetwood from Franz Haas Machinery, current owners of the land where James Madison was born. Thank you to Bill Thomas, president of the James Monroe Memorial Foundation, for the personal interview and for his commitment to memorializing the birthplace of the fifth president. From the President James K. Polk State Historic Site, thanks to Scott Warren (Historic Site Manager II), Courtney Rounds (Site Interpreter II), Robert Dreher (Maintenance Mechanic II), and Sarah Allen (Intern, UNCC) for the detailed information including ownership history of the eleventh president's birthplace. For additional information about Polk's birthplace, thanks to Michael Hill, Research Branch Supervisor at the North Carolina Office of Archives and History. Thank you Jean and Sara, guides at the Franklin Pierce Homestead in Hillsborough, New Hampshire, for being more than generous with your time and patience for my incessant, and often redundant, birthplace questions. Thanks to Bud Barkdoll from the Franklin County Historical Society for providing historical information and personal recollections about the James Buchanan birthplace cabin when it stood in Chambersburg, Pennsylvania, from 1925 through 1953.

Thank you LaVon Shook (Official Historian) and Eric L. Peters (Customer Service Representative) from the Ohio State Fairgrounds. Mr. Shook is a fountain of information about the Ulysses S. Grant birth cabin during the period it stood at the fairgrounds from the 1890s until 1936 and was kind enough to provide a personal tour of the site where the home once stood. Thanks to Katie Martin from the Village of Moreland Hills for information about the James Garfield birthplace and replica. Thanks to Director Patrick Finan and volunteer Bill Jones from the William McKinley Birthplace Home and Research Center in Niles,

Ohio, for the detailed information about the sometimes bizarre saga of the original birthplace of our twenty-fifth president. Thank you to Linda Bugbee, daughter of Mr. Jesse F. Waldron, who was lucky enough to actually have lived in the Richard Nixon birthplace home in Yorba Linda, California, and gracious enough to share her insights on the experience. Thanks to Joan Johnson, president of the Reagan Birthplace for the photograph and kind offer to open the birthplace to me off-hours. For information about the birthplace of George Herbert Walker Bush and the 1997 ceremony held in his honor, thanks to Edie Clifford, librarian for the Milton Historical Society. Thanks to Martha Berryman from the Clinton Birthplace Foundation, Inc. for the abundance of information about the history of President Clinton's first home and his experiences growing up in Hope, Arkansas. And thanks to David Coleman, Manager and Guest Relations Officer at the Kanucha Bay Resort for providing information about the replica of Bill Clinton's first home that was built on the resort grounds in Okinawa, Japan, in 2000. From the Yale-New Haven Hospital, where George Walker Bush was born, thanks to Susan Dee, Hospital Archivist for information about the history of the hospital and what it was like in 1946 when our forty-third president was born within its walls.

For photographs of the birthplaces, thanks to Peggy L. Dillard, Director of Library and Archives at the Woodrow Wilson Presidential Library, Ellen Harris from the Lillian G. Carter Nursing Center (birthplace of Jimmy Carter), Bill Urbin from the Franklin D. Roosevelt National Historic Site and Stacy Bandelier, Graphics Supervisor for the Missouri State Parks for a photograph of the Harry S Truman birthplace. Thanks to Liz Lindig, Program Assistant from the Lyndon B. Johnson National Historical Park and Chris Nordyke, Director of Marketing at the Richard Nixon Foundation. Thanks to Dave Rimington for the photograph of the Gerald R. Ford Birth Site and Gardens. And a special thank you to E. Elanie Pichay and Alvin Fejarang for photographs of the Ka'piolani Hospital where both Barack Obama and Elanie's beautiful niece were born. An extra special thank you to photographer extraordinaire Mary Baldwin and my fabulous cousin, Nicole Sage Kayes, for saving the day with the eleventh hour photographs of Jimmy Carter's birthplace.

And to the rest of park rangers, tour guides, and historians who have provided invaluable historical information and context, whom I either neglected to mention or never got your name, thank you, too. And, of course, thanks to all of the good people at Schiffer Publishing, including Pete Schiffer, Jennifer Savage, and Dinah Roseberry for giving a first time author an opportunity and for their superb efforts in putting this book together.

Finally I would like to thank my kid brother, and fellow presidential birthplace traveler, Joseph. In addition to providing several of the photographs, I also owe him for the inspiration to learn more about the leaders of this great nation. Several years ago, my son, Vincent, showed him a food-stained placemat that featured pictures of all of the presidents. His Uncle Joseph proceeded in rattling off all of the presidents, in order, from Washington to Obama. As I listened in awe, verifying his flawless memory against the Dollar Store placemat, I knew that I had a lot to learn about the American presidents.

Introduction

We don't like birthplaces very much. We resist them. Usually they're much changed and don't tell us much about the individual.[1]

~National Park Ranger, 1997

I will start by saying that I do like birthplaces very much and I respectfully disagree with the National Park Ranger quoted above. I find presidential birthplaces fascinating and I know there must be others like me, so perhaps it would be best to start off this book by explaining why.

From Abraham Lincoln to Zachary Taylor and everyone in between, the birthplaces of these great men who went on to serve the nation's highest office deserve to be celebrated. Good, bad, or mediocre, each of these men once led the greatest country in the world and where they started that journey is significant. We would not be the nation we are today if not for each and every one of these men. In addition to being a critical piece of presidential history, the story of the birthplaces is the story of America itself. The first six presidents were born on plantations or large farms from well-to-do families from the time where only the wealthy rose to positions of influence and power. Starting with Andrew Jackson is the trend of presidents from not-so-noble beginnings as the elite began to lose their stranglehold on the office. From Jackson to James Garfield, including Jefferson Davis, nine of the next fifteen presidents were born in simple log cabins. Instead of seeing this as a detriment, these men capitalized on their humble beginnings to appear more accessible to the common voting man.

As America moved west, so did the presidential birthplaces – from the original thirteen states into Kentucky and Ohio, until we had presidents born coast-to-coast and then finally outside of the continental forty-eight. Preservation and recognition efforts first began years after the Civil War, when America's healing proved that our democracy would endure, and as a country, we could afford to look back and celebrate those who led us through the tumultuous years. In the early part of the twentieth century, as the country prospered, the preservation efforts expanded. Private and government funds poured into lavish recreation and memorialization projects. When America struggled in the Great Depression and in times of war, these projects took a back seat to more pressing matters. Preservation efforts stalled while funds were diverted to more critical needs and often the neglected homes fell into disrepair. When the nation began to get back on its feet, the condition of these birthplaces reflected the state of the country itself as funding was once again directed towards preserving these historic sites. In the twentieth century, as the nation became more aware of its historical significance in the world, we began to recognize the presidential birthplaces earlier and earlier in the careers of these great men.

Almost every presidential birthplace is recognized in one way or another and each has an interesting and unique history with some truly fascinating stories to tell. The few exceptions are our most recent presidents, George Walker Bush and Barack Obama, but hopefully this wrong will be righted in the not-too-distant future. These preservation efforts have varied and the degree by which a birthplace is memorialized does not always match the greatness of the man. For instance, the birthplace of James Buchanan, often considered our worst president, is honored with a thirty-one foot stone pyramid within a state park and his birth cabin has been preserved on display at a nearby university. Meanwhile the only recognition of the birthplace of Thomas Jefferson, founding father and the author of the Declaration of Independence, is a roadside marker on a littered industrial road off of the main highway.

Unlike battlefields and homes where a famous individual lived later in life, birthplaces are obviously not considered significant at the time the historic event occurred. It is only many years later that people begin to take note of these buildings, and even then recognition is gradual, as these men have evolved from local politicians or military leaders to our nation's leaders. Would a town recognize the birthplace of a mayor, state senator, or army general? Probably not. A senator or vice president? Maybe. By the time that these men have achieved a title that warrants their past life to be reviewed and preserved, their place of birth had most likely changed hands and been altered. For some of the homes, the historical significance is recognized too late and the structure is long gone. While that may seem like an insurmountable hurdle, it is not always the case. Replicas have been built to re-create and sometimes, improve upon, the original.

Another reality is that presidential birthplaces are becoming less interesting. Gone are the days of log cabins and plantation homes. Modern leaders are born in hospitals, making the presidential birthplaces less historic and more sterile. One day we will have a president born in a hospital and brought home to a condo and it's difficult to envision the historians of the future faithfully recreating and furnishing a unit within a condominium complex. ("If you look to the left you can see the historic 52-inch flat-screen TV.") Also the days of scouring through hand-written archives, yellowed newspapers, and noisy and overheated microfiche, are fast disappearing. Computerization and the Internet have all but guaranteed that historical information will never be lost again.

I first became interested in the subject after visiting George Washington's birthplace home. The tour guide was a pleasant elderly woman decked out in colonial garb. As she stood outside of the "birthplace" home, she explained to the group how the tour of the home would be handled, that we would walk in as a group and then were free to walk upstairs, no flash photography, no running, no gum chewing – the standard litany of rules. However, what she did not explain was exactly what we would be looking at. Noting this omission, I finally asked if this was the actual birth home of President Washington. She answered with a curt "No" and quickly changed the subject without any further explanation. That moment piqued my curiosity and prompted me to do additional research on the home, which led to the discovery of a fascinating story. Thinking that with forty-four men holding the highest office in the land, including the sole President of the Confederate States of America, Jefferson Davis, there must be more interesting stories out there. And I found, as will you, that indeed there were.

I hope you enjoy reading this book as much as I have enjoyed writing it.

Thank You,
Louis Picone

THE COLONIAL
Presidents

1.
George Washington

Wakefield, the inaccurate memorial house at the George Washington Birthplace National Monument in Westmoreland County, Virginia. *Photo credit: George Washington Birthplace National Monument, National Park Service*

Vital Birthplace Information

Birthplace	Westmoreland County, Virginia
Name	Popes Creek, Wakefield
President's birthday	February 22, 1732
How long in the home	3 1/2 years
Life of the home	Before 1718 to December 25, 1779
Style	Plantation home
Still in existence	No
Ultimate fate	Destroyed by fire
Commemoration	George Washington Birthplace National Monument
Open to the public	Yes
Cost	Free
For more information	www.nps.gov/gewa
Replica exists	Yes, at birthplace
Significance	First presidential birthplace to be memorialized (1815)
Closest birthplace	James Monroe, 4.1 miles

What you will find there today:

The birthplace is a National Monument consisting of 560 acres and administered by the National Park Service. The original house is long gone; however, the National Park Service does an impressive job at creating a memorial, being that they have few authentic artifacts to work with. What stands there today is a replica that was later determined not to resemble the original home. More significant is the footprint of the original home in which Washington was born.

Address/Directions:

1732 Popes Creek Road
Colonial Beach, Virginia 22443

If you are using GPS, you can search by attraction for George Washington Birthplace National Monument. The birthplace is off of Route 3, about thirty-eight miles east of Route 95 or about eight miles west of Montross. You will see signs when you start getting close.

History

George Washington was born near the banks of a small creek that flows into the Potomac River in the northern neck of Virginia. Before Europeans landed in the New World, Native Americans inhabited the land. As European colonists moved beyond Jamestown to settle within Virginia, the Popes Creek area remained under control of the Powhatan Confederacy led by Chief Opechancanough until the middle of the 1600s. The Confederacy was a group of Native American tribes joined by a common language and land. During these years, the Popes Creek area was used for the harvesting of oysters.[1] By the 1650s the Powhatan Confederacy had ceded control over this land and the first European to inhabit Westmoreland County was Henry Brooks. In 1653, Brooks settled on the land, although he did not formally patent the property until four years later in 1657, and then again the patent was reissued five years later on March 18, 1662. This 1662 deed defined the boundary of the Brooks Tract...

> ...on the northwest side to a marked corner hiccory with a creeke that divideth this land and the land now in possession of Daniel Lisson on the northeast side with the potomack river on the southeast side with the Creeke dividing this land from the land of Colo. Nathaniel Pope to a marked red oake on the southwest side thence with a line of marked trees running west and northwest 60 poles northwest half a point more westerly 140 poles to the aforementioned marked hiccory and place.[2]

Starting in 1655, two years before his first patent, Brooks began to sell off his land. In February of 1657, he deeded a 100-acre parcel on the bank of Popes Creek to his daughter, Lydia, and her husband, Lawrence Abington.[3] The plantation became known as the Abington Tract. It dwindled over the years; however, the site of the George Washington birthplace remained under the ownership of the Abington family until 1718.

In 1657, about the same time that Henry Brooks sold the land to the Abingtons, John Washington, great-grandfather to the first President of the United States of America, first set foot on American soil. John was in his mid-twenties and once in America he met Nathaniel Pope. In 1656, Nathaniel Pope had also purchased land from Henry Brooks on the east bank of Popes Creek, hence the creek's name. John Washington became friends with Colonel Nathaniel Pope, and more than just friends with his daughter, Anne. Soon John and Anne were married, and for a wedding gift, Colonel Pope gave the young couple 700 acres of his property. Over the next fifty years, the Washington family expanded their land holdings as the property was passed down through generations.[4]

The Washington family's holdings crept closer and closer to the eventual birthplace property. Finally in 1718, Augustine Washington, son of Lawrence Washington, and grandson of John Washington purchased the land on the western banks of Popes Creek from the Abington family.[5] By this time there already existed a small structure that was built prior to 1718. From 1722 through 1726 Augustine greatly expanded this structure into a mid-sized plantation home. A local undertaker completed the work for the first three additions for the price of "5,000 pounds of tobacco."[6] At a time when people named their homes, Augustine dubbed his abode "Popes Creek."

Augustine married Jane Butler in 1715 and they had four children; however, only two, Lawrence and Augustine Jr., lived to adulthood. Augustine Jr., called Austin by his parents, was the first Washington to be born at Popes Creek in 1720. Jane died in 1729; however, Augustine did not remain single for long, quickly remarrying the 23-year-old Mary Ball. At approximately 10 a.m. on February 22, 1732, their first child, and perhaps the most famous American in history, George Washington, was born in the home on Popes Creek. The Washington family went on to have two more less notable children in this home. In 1735, they left Popes Creek and moved to their home on Little Hunting Creek (Mount Vernon).[7]

Augustine died in 1743 and most of his property went to his two sons from his first marriage, Lawrence and Austin. A year earlier, Augustine had given the Popes Creek plantation to Austin after his return from ten years studying in England. George Washington would often come to visit the home after his father's death to see his older stepbrother, including frequent well-documented visits from 1748 through 1753. During the years Austin owned Popes Creek, the home was expanded; he transformed the footprint from a rectangle to a *U*-shaped structure by adding to the ends of the home. Austin was also active in civic life in Westmoreland, serving as a colonel in the militia and in the House of Burgesses from 1754 to 1756. When Austin died in 1762, the home was passed on his son, William Augustine, and, in 1770, the new owner renamed the property from Popes Creek to "Westfield." During the years William Augustine owned the home, a small addition was made to the northern wing.[8]

On Christmas day in 1779, the birthplace of our nation's first, and perhaps greatest, president burned to the ground. William Augustine was out on an afternoon ride and returned to find the roof of the home ablaze. The suspected cause of the fire was a stray spark from the chimney that ignited a pile of cotton. The home was never rebuilt and William Augustine moved to a new residence a mile away, which was built in part using bricks salvaged from the Washington birthplace home. At this time, George Washington presumably had other things on his mind. He was encamped at Morristown, New Jersey, during one of the worst winters on record in the midst of the Revolutionary War.[9] After the home was destroyed, the property was neglected and fell into a further state of disrepair. The site became known as "Burnt House Point," a name that appears in several legal documents.[10]

The Popes Creek property remained in the Washington family until the 1850s; however, the birth site was never rebuilt upon. In the early 1800s, the property was owned by George Corbin Washington, United States Congressman and George Washington's grandnephew. On October 13, 1813, he sold a portion of the land, not including the birthplace, to John Gray, a transaction that would later be the root of a controversy regarding the true location of the birthplace. George Corbin Washington died on July 17, 1854, and the land was passed on to his son, Lewis William Washington.[11]

Two years later, in 1856, Lewis William Washington offered to donate the land of the birthplace home and the family burial site to the state of Virginia. His gift of approximately sixty acres came with the condition that an iron fence must be erected around the site and a "modest, though substantial tablet" be erected.[12] For two years the state contemplated the offer and the estimate of $2,000 it would take to accommodate the demands and in 1858 the terms were accepted. Governor of Virginia Henry A. Wise visited the site and Lewis William Washington pointed out the exact location of the birthplace.[13] However in the confusion of the Civil War, the contract was not acted upon and the land reverted back to the Washington family.[14]

Lewis William Washington owned the property until he died in 1871, and his son, Major James Barroll Washington, became a joint-owner of the land. During these years, plans to accept the property shifted from the state of Virginia to the federal government. Finally, on May 22, 1882, the donation of the birthplace was official when Major James Barroll Washington donated the historic land to the United States of America.[15] Thus after being in the Washington family for 164 years, the birthplace of our nation's first leader was now passed to the government for posterity. This purchase is significant in birthplace history, as it is the first time any level of the United States government had appropriated funds to memorialize a presidential birthplace.

Preservation

One could imagine that a country so young would not be focused, as we are today, on nostalgia and preservation. From the American Revolution and the Continental Congress through the Civil War, this country was more concerned with preserving its own existence than celebrating and commemorating the founding fathers that laid the groundwork for this great republic. For this reason, it is not wholly surprising that it took sixteen years after the death of George Washington for someone to finally take note of his birthplace.

That someone was George Washington Parke Custis, adopted grandson of the president. His father, Custis, was son to Martha Washington from her first marriage and adopted by George Washington.

An interesting side note:

George Washington Parke Cutis's daughter, Mary Anna, would go on to marry Robert E. Lee, whose father "Light Horse Harry" Lee briefly owned the James Monroe birthplace in 1799.

George Washington Parke Custis was understandably enamored with his adoptive grandfather, George. Imagine a *Star Trek* fanatic today – his house is decorated with memorabilia, he knows every episode inside and out, and occasionally puts on a Starfleet uniform complete with authentic phaser gun to impress his friends. This was George Washington Parke Custis, except his fixation was George Washington, not Captain Kirk or Mr. Spock. Sometime in 1815, Custis and a few of his friends traveled to Popes Creek to memorialize George Washington's birth site. There they placed a commemorative stone with the simple inscription: "Here the 11th of February, 1732, GEORGE WASHINGTON was born." The date of February 11 was the

old-style date used before 1752. Afterwards the birth date was recognized as February 22, 1732. The stone was placed near the ruins of the chimney on what Custis assumed to be the birth home.[16] He also noted the presence of fig trees that he surmised to have been planted by the Washington family.

Over time, treasure hunters broke off pieces of the marker, and whatever wasn't destroyed, was moved around by farmers who had used the Washington land. By the time the land was turned over to the state of Virginia in 1858, the commemorative stone was broken into three pieces. Twelve years after that, in 1870, it was nowhere to be found.[17]

This marking is more significant than it may appear at first glance, not just for the George Washington birthplace, or even for presidential birthplaces, but also for all birthplace commemorations. According to Seth Bruggeman in his book *Here, George Washington Was Born: Memory, Material Culture, and the Public History of a National Monument*, this is the first of its kind in America. Outside of the nativity of Jesus Christ at Bethlehem, birthplaces had not been previously recognized as significant.[18]

When the state of Virginia had first planned to accept the property from Lewis William Washington, they did so with the intention of creating a memorial. However, after the Civil War, and throughout the years of reconstruction, either because of politics or other priorities, nothing was done. On May 22, 1882, the federal government took ownership of the project and the historic land. Prior to this acquisition, Congress had approved $3,000 of funding in 1879[19] and $30,000 in 1881 to purchase the land and erect "a monument to mark the birthplace of the Father of (t)his Country;"[20] however, it was fifteen years before the project was completed. Due to its remote location, a wharf had to first be built at Popes Creek to sail in the materials on the Potomac. In 1896, a fifty-foot obelisk of Vermont granite was erected. The monument was similar in appearance, but a tenth the size of the infamous Washington Monument in nearby

Washington, D.C. The monument was to be constructed on the site of the birth home, but without the 1815 commemorative marker to reference, the chimney remnants and fig trees were used as a landmark.

In the 1920s, Josephine Wheelright Rust led a group of "public spirited citizens" to create a more appropriate tribute to George Washington. Mrs. Rust was a distant cousin of George Washington and a direct descendent of Colonel Nathaniel Pope and John Washington. Her vision was a reconstructed birth home and plantation so visitors could step back in time to experience what the property was like at the time of Washington's birth. On June 11, 1923, she held a meeting in her home and officially formed the Wakefield National Memorial Association "to rebuild the home in which George Washington was born, to restore the neglected graveyard of his ancestors, and to make Wakefield a place of pilgrimage for all those who venerate the name of Washington."[21] They allotted themselves nine years to finish the task to coincide with the 200-year anniversary of Washington's birth.[22] This goal was met. Through both public and private contributions, the organization raised about $185,000. They also persuaded John D. Rockefeller Jr. to purchase 267 acres surrounding the birth site for $115,000, which was also donated to the federal government. [23] The organization has since been renamed the George Washington Birthplace National Memorial Association and is still active at the site to this day.

In January 1926, Josephine Rust and a group of association trustees met with President Calvin Coolidge at the White House to share their plans for the site. With the president's support, Congress authorized the Wakefield National Memorial Association to build "a replica of the house in which George Washington was born." President Calvin Coolidge signed the bill into law on June 7, 1926.[24] Having no drawings of the home from when it existed or schematics of its construction, building a "replica" was a tall, if not impossible, task. The group had only a description of the amount of rooms and chimneys in the home, similar to a real estate ad that reads, "Four bedrooms, two and a half bath, etc."

The home was to be erected on the believed site of the actual birth home; however, there was a slight problem since a fifty-foot monument already occupied the location. Three years later, when the nation was sunk into the Great Depression, continued federal funding was hotly debated in Congress. An agreement was finally struck when it was determined that funding would continue as long as the home was transferred to the federal government upon completion. Desperate for funds, the Wakefield National Memorial Association agreed. On January 23, 1930, $65,000 was granted to move the monument (to its present location at the entrance to the site) and to build the replica home. That same day the birthplace grounds were granted status as the George Washington Birthplace National Monument.[25]

The Wakefield National Memorial Association hired Edward W. Dunn Jr. as the architect and J.J. Jones and Conquest, a contractor from nearby Richmond, Virginia, to build the home for $45,000. Work started on December 12, 1930, and a memorial home that resembled a typical Georgian residence of the period was completed in the summer of 1931.[26] On June 22, 1931, Josephine W. Rust signed the deed to transfer the land and buildings over to the federal government. Four days later, with her vision completed, Josephine W. Rust suddenly died on June 26, 1931. The next month,

the house and grounds were made open to the public. Almost a year later, on May 14, 1932, the National Park Service took custody of the 367 acres.

At the same time that plans for the Wakefield replica were being developed, Henry Woodhouse made a controversial announcement. Woodhouse had gained notoriety as an aviation expert at the dawn of the era of flight. In the early years of the twentieth century, he founded the aviation magazine *Flying* with the assistance of Robert J. Collier (who would coincidently play a large part in preserving Abraham Lincoln's birthplace). By 1930, Woodhouse was best known as the president of the Ariel League of America and he used his wealth to purchase real estate and pursue his interests, which included George Washington. In the late 1920s, he combined these passions when he purchased large parcels of Washington's ancestral lands with the intentions of building a zeppelin airport on the grounds. He also obtained a large amount of historical artifacts relating to the family of the first president. One of these artifacts was a deed dated October 13, 1813 from "Page 656 of the Deeds and Wills Book No. 35 of Westmoreland County, VA." In this document, George C. Washington sold some of the property to John Gray; however, he withheld the land "on which the house stood in which George Washington was born."[27]

Woodhouse interpreted the evidence he gathered to point to Bridges Creek, not Popes Creek, as the true birthplace. This alternate location was over a mile away from Popes Creek where the monument stood and the replica was being planned. On January 6, 1930, his dispute was published in the *New York Times* and the controversy lingered for about a year. Eventually, it was determined to be an error in the translation of the deed and the *New York Times* later reported his "view elicits no support from any one who is familiar with conditions at Wakefield."[28]

While the Woodhouse controversy died down, the peace did not last for long. In 1936, a true bombshell was discovered when excavations at the birthplace grounds exposed another foundation, which provided strong evidence that the memorial home was built about 100 feet away from actual location. One could only imagine that there were many people who wished this discovery was never made after so much time, effort, and expense went into the recreation. As if an incorrect location was not bad enough news, the unearthed foundation was shaped like a "U" which contradicted the traditional rectangle shape of the replica home. After analysis, the new find was marked and reburied. Not knowing how to handle this discovery, the new building was called "Building X."[29]

This was an awkward find for both the national monument site administration as well as the federal government. For the site, the question was how to present and explain both the memorial home and Building X to the tourists. For the federal government, the nagging question was exactly what the heck had they just paid for. The National Park Service would spend over thirty years trying to come to grips with this realization as they pondered how to convey this message to the visiting public. The mysterious Building X moniker persisted for several decades, long after most people involved knew that it was actually the birth home. In 1966, the mistake was first made public in newspaper articles across the country.[30] Two years later, in 1968, Building X was officially given a name when the National Park Service declared that the foundation was here on in to be known as the birth site of George Washington.[31]

This site was again re-excavated in 1974. Perhaps someone hoped it would no longer be there and it would turn out Building X was really just a bad dream. Unfortunately, this did not happen. Today, this foundation is marked with crushed oyster shells.

The site of the George Washington birthplace in Westmoreland County, Virginia. The house is long gone, but the footprint is marked with crushed oyster shells

Visitor Information

Each year, about 100,000 people visit the birthplace of George Washington.[32] The park is open daily from 9 a.m. to 5 p.m. Even today it still appears that the National Park Service has not quite figured out how to tell the story of the two homes, so now that you know the real story, listen closely while the guides tell you about the Wakefield replica.

2.
John Adams

The John Adams birthplace in Quincy, Massachusetts.

Vital Birthplace Information

Birthplace	Braintree (now Quincy), Massachusetts
President's birthday	October 30, 1735
How long in the home	26 years
Life of the home	Approximately 1650 to present
Style	Saltbox
Still in existence	Yes
Commemoration	Part of the Adams National Historical Park
Open to the public	Yes
Cost	$5.00
For more information	www.nps.gov/adam
Replica exists	No
Significance	Oldest presidential birthplace still in existence
Closest birthplace	John Quincy Adams, 75 feet

What you will find there today:

At over 360 years old, the John Adams residence is the oldest original presidential birthplace in existence. The home, which is a stone's throw from the John Quincy Adams birthplace, is part of the Adams National Historic Park, run by the National Park Service. Throughout the book, I will point out restoration projects that may not seem like the best use of taxpayer funds; however, I strongly believe the National Park Service does an amazing job in preserving our nation's historical treasures.

Address/Directions:

133 Franklin Street
Quincy, Massachusetts 02169

The best way to see the home, and the only way to view the interior, is to take the bus tour starting from the National Park Visitor Center in downtown Quincy. The address for the Visitor Center is 1250 Hancock Street in the Galleria at Presidents Place.

History

The history of the John Adams birthplace dates back to shortly after the Pilgrims first landed at nearby Plymouth Rock. In the 1600s, William Needham owned the property where the birthplace now sits a few miles outside of downtown Boston. At the time, the land was within the northern part of the town of Braintree. William was a patriot, serving in the Billerica Militia during the French and Indian War. Around 1650, the first home on this property was built at the foot of Penn's Hill along Coast Road, which wound all the way from Boston to Plymouth. By 1681, the home was owned by Joseph Pennimen. In this year, what was to become the John Adams birthplace home was built using some of the original structure from the William Needham home of 1650. Years later, when the Adams Chapter of the Daughters of the American Revolution were renovating the home in 1896, a brick was found in the southeast corner of the foundation stamped with the date 1681. The home has nine rooms and eight-foot ceilings, which were high for the time. In the back room was built a large fireplace that would have been the center of activity during the cold Massachusetts winters. The home is a "saltbox" structure, typical for Massachusetts in the 1600s, so called because it is shaped like the box that salt was packaged in at the time.[1]

John Adams' father, John Sr., purchased the house and six to seven acres of land in 1720 from Joseph Pennimen. John Sr. considered land a good investment and later expanded his property to 188 acres. He was a religious man and a prominent member of the Braintree community, serving as the Deacon of the First Parish Church as well as town constable and a lieutenant in the local militia. To earn his living, he split his time between farming and shoemaking.[2]

Fifteen years later, on October 30, 1735, in the "front chamber nearest the street," our second president, John Adams, was born to Deacon John, forty-four, and his wife Susanna, twenty-six.[3] As John grew into a young boy, he spent formative time in his birthplace, being home schooled and observing his father performing his civic and religious duties. The spacious property included farmland, marsh areas, meadows, and wooded areas, which were perfect for a young adventurous boy like John to spend hours exploring. As a young man, John left Quincy to matriculate at Harvard, and then returned to his birthplace after graduation to practice law.[4]

When Deacon John died in 1761, John's brother, Peter Boylston Adams, inherited the birth home while John inherited the home next door (eventual birthplace of John Quincy Adams), also owned by John's father. John Adams eventually bought his birth home from his brother in 1774, giving John Adams the distinction of being the first president to own two presidential birthplace homes at the same time.[5] For the next six years, his widowed mother lived in the home until her death in 1780. After her passing, the home was rented to several different tenants over the next two decades, becoming the first presidential birthplace to ever serve as a rental. In 1803, John Quincy Adams purchased the home as well as his own birthplace next door, thus giving him the distinction of being the second, and last, president to own two presidential birthplace homes at the same time.[5]

In 1810, John's fifth and youngest child Thomas Boylston Adams moved into the home, and remained until 1818. After Thomas left the birthplace, it was again a rental, housing various tenants over the years. By 1885, the home was vacant and the surrounding land was sold off in parcels, shrinking the birthplace property. The home remained empty for more than a decade, until the Adams Chapter of the Daughters of the American Revolution took an interest in preserving this historic home.[6]

Preservation

In 1896, Charles Adams Jr., the great grandson of John Adams, gave the Adams Chapter of the Daughters of the Revolution permission to restore both birth homes and to use the John Adams birth home as their headquarters. The Daughters spent a year completing the restorations, decorating the homes as they appeared in colonial times. On June 17, 1897, the doors were swung open to the public, welcoming a "large crowd of people from [Quincy] and surrounding towns" who had come to see the historic homes.[7]

The cost of this restoration was a whopping $515.49. Part of the expense was painting the home red, which was believed to be the color of the home at the time of John Adams' birth, but later determined to be inaccurate.[8] During these years when the home was open to the public, the property remained in the possession of the Adams family heirs. For over 150 years members of the Adams family owned the home; however, this reign came to an end in 1940 when they donated the historic home to the city of Quincy. Ten years later, the property was turned over to the Quincy Historical Society.

The next year, an unfortunate incident occurred at the birthplace when members of the Quincy Historical Society came to open the home one February morning in 1951 to find the front door wide open. The members entered and found that the place had been ransacked! Vandals had broken in and jumped on the bed leaving their muddy footprints. At first they may have thought this to be a mischievous act, but would have soon realized it was much more serious when they found that the vandals also "slashed [Adams'] portrait and smashed [Adams'] nose from a marble bust."[9] Perhaps these hoodlums were not fans of the Alien and Sedition Acts, because they left the John Quincy Adams' birthplace untouched.

After the vandalism, peace returned to the birthplace home throughout the 1950s. On December 19, 1960, the home received the honor of being designated a National Historic Landmark. At the time, locals affectionately referred to the pair of birthplace homes as "the little red houses" and the price of admission was a bargain at one house for 30¢ or 2 for 50¢. That price included a visit to the museum on the ground floor and even got you a peek upstairs, which today is off limits for visitors. At the time, both homes were managed by the city of Quincy, and the custodian who maintained the homes was living in the John Adams birthplace.[10]

The John Adams birthplace had its share of prominent visitors over the years. On July 15, 1925, while serving as president, Calvin Coolidge and his wife, Grace, visited the home on a trip made in honor of the White House photographers. The president made himself right at home and reportedly sat in John Adams' easy chair while snacking on soda and donuts![11] On June 9, 1967, first lady Lady Bird Johnson visited the home where the second president was born.[12] Lady Bird was no stranger to presidential birthplaces, and during the 1960s, she visited no less than six birth homes (also John Quincy Adams, James Polk, Herbert Hoover, Eisenhower, and Lyndon B. Johnson), perhaps more than any other first lady.

The birthplace was added to the National Register of Historic Places (National Register Number #66000129) when it was created on October 15, 1966.[13] In 1979, both birthplaces were deeded back to the Adams family so they could donate the homes to the National Park Service on May 1. Along with the John Adams retirement home, Peacefield, the birthplaces became an important addition to the Adams National Historic Site.

The following year began a six-year reconstruction project which would cost the taxpayers $175,000. Research conducted by the National Park Service had led historians to believe the home was in actuality white, not red as previously believed. The home was painted white; however, once again additional evidence was discovered that indicated the home was not white, but in fact unpainted. So the paint was removed, which is how the home appears today. The home was decorated with authentic period pieces to resemble how it would have looked when John Adams lived there. There are no original pieces in the home that were owned by the Adams family, as they are all located in Peacefield. Today, the birthplace home is now approximately a third original materials with the remainder having been replaced or rebuilt over the years.[14]

Visitor Information

Don't just stop at the birthplace of John Adams; make sure you visit the birthplace of his son John Quincy and the "Old House," also known as Peacefield, where John Adams spent his final years. This is an unusual National Park site in that it is not open year round. The birthplaces are only open from mid-April to mid-November, so make sure you check the National Park Service website for dates and times before you go. Reservations are strongly suggested – ever since the HBO mini-series *John Adams* premiered, the tour has been a hot item. Visitation has climbed steadily, tripling over the last ten years to approximately 250,000 people annually. The *John Adams* production has amazing historical special effects. When watching the film, note the birthplace homes and the wide open spaces around them and then compare that with the busy streets of today. Also, now that you've seen where John Adams was born, make sure to stop at the United First Parish Church, walking distance from the visitor center, to see where he is buried.

3.
Thomas Jefferson

Vital Birthplace Information

The birthplace of Thomas Jefferson on Virginia Highway 250.

Birthplace	Goochland County (now Albemarle County), Virginia
Name	Shadwell
President's birthday	April 13, 1743
How long in the home	10 years (birth – 1745, 1752-1770)
Life of the home	1737 to February 1, 1770
Style	Farmhouse
Still in existence	No
Ultimate fate	Destroyed by fire
Commemoration	Historic marker
For more information	explorer.monticello.org
Replica exists	Not anymore
Significance	First presidential birthplace to be destroyed (1770)
Closest birthplace	Zachary Taylor, 13 miles

Address/Directions:

Across the street from:
2422 Richmond Road
Charlottesville, Virginia 22911

To get there, take exit 124 Virginia Interstate 64. Take Route 250 driving east. After .9 mile, the marker will be on the right, directly across from "Floor Fashions of Virginia, Inc." If you see Vdot Way, you have gone too far.

What you will find there today:

The birthplace of Thomas Jefferson is commemorated with a white historic marker erected by the Virginia Department of Historic Resources in 2001, which bears the following inscription:

W-202 SHADWELL, BIRTHPLACE OF THOMAS JEFFERSON. Thomas Jefferson – author of the Declaration of Independence, third President of the United States, and founder of the University of Virginia – was born near this site on 13 April 1743. His father, Peter Jefferson (1708-1757), a surveyor, planter, and officeholder, began acquiring land in this frontier region in the mid-1730s and had purchased the Shadwell tract by 1741. Peter Jefferson built a house soon after, and the Shadwell plantation became a thriving agricultural estate. Thomas Jefferson spent much of his early life at Shadwell. After the house burned to the ground in 1770, he moved to Monticello, where he had begun constructing a house.

History

Thomas Jefferson was born in Goochland County, Virginia, today known as Albemarle County, which at the time was part of the "Blue Ridge frontier of Virginia."[1] Peter Jefferson, future father of the third president, was one of the first settlers of this vast wilderness area. Peter and his first cousin by marriage, William Randolph, had served together as magistrates and militia officers, and by 1736, they were both purchasing plots of land in the area. As they eagerly gobbled up acres, they inadvertently stepped on each other's toes. Peter had his eyes on 1,000 acres on the Rivanna River, but when he went to purchase the land, he found that William had beat him to 400 acres of this property only two days earlier. William Randolph was willing to part with his land, but he had a price. So on May 18, 1736, William deeded 200 of these acres to his best friend for... a bowl of punch! Reading the deed, try to imagine the reaction of the Goochland county clerk:

By deed dated May 18, 1736 William Randolph Jun. Esq. of the County of Goochland conveyed to Peter Jefferson, Gen't. of the County of Goochland, in consideration of "Henry Weatherborne's biggest bowl of Arrack punch to him delivered," one certain tract or parcel of land containing two hundred acres, situate, lying and being on the north side of the North Anna in the parrish of Saint James in the County of Goochland aforesaid and is bounded as followeth, to-wit:

Beginning at a corner black oak on the north side of the hive, thence north 23 degrees west 102 poles; thence north 64 degrees west 116 poles on the said line to a double hickory on the River shore the Sandy falls; thence down the river according to its meanders 332 pols to the beginning, and contains by estimation 200 acres be the same more or less.

Together with all houses, orchards, gardens, fences, woods, ways, waters, water courses and all other appurtenances to the same belonging or in any wise appertaining and all the state, right, title use, property, interests, claim and demand whatsoever, of the said William Randolph.

This deed provides: That William Randolph, his heirs, shall and will at any time within the space of 7 years next after the date of the these presents at the reasonable request of the cost and charges in the law of said Peter Jefferson, his heirs and assigns, make, do and execute all such further and other deeds of conveyance necessary in the law for the better and more perfect assuring of the above granted land and premises in appurtenances.

So just what is Arrack Punch? Batavia Arrack, the main ingredient in Arrack Punch, is an alcoholic drink from South Asia made from fermented fruit grain, and sugarcane. Mix in Jamaican rum, loaf-sugar, and hot water and you have Arrack Punch. Henry Weatherbone worked at the Raleigh Tavern in Williamsburg, Virginia, and apparently, he made a damn good bowl of the stuff.[2] This property eventually contained the birthplace of Thomas Jefferson.

The next year, 1737, Peter Jefferson built a one and a half-story weatherboard farmhouse on the property. With the help of several servants, Peter cut the lumber and the wooden pegs used as nails for the home.[3] The house had a central hall and four square rooms. Since no house was complete without a name, Jefferson called his "Shadwell" after the London parish where his wife, Jane Randolph, was born. Three years later, Peter began to cultivate tobacco on his 1,400-acre Shadwell farm.

In this house, on April 13, 1743, our third president and Peter's third child (and first son), Thomas Jefferson, was born. He lived in Shadwell for two years and then returned when he was nine. Peter Jefferson died on August 17, 1757. Being the oldest son, but not yet of age (he was only fourteen), Peter left the land to his son, Thomas, upon his twenty-first birthday. He also inherited about thirty of his father's slaves. In 1764, Thomas took ownership of his inheritance and he continued to live in the home.

Tragedy struck Shadwell on February 1, 1770, when the home burned to the ground. All of his books were lost in the fire, at the time valued at $1,000 as were his personal letters, law books, and information regarding the home itself. The only item salvaged was Jefferson's fiddle.[4] The fire gave the Shadwell home the unfortunate distinction of being the first presidential birthplace to be destroyed and lost forever to history.

Jefferson retained ownership of the birthplace property, although after the house burned, he moved to nearby Monticello. Soon he had other things on his mind, like the American Revolution.

By 1794, Jefferson owned four plantations, including Shadwell and Monticello. He would rotate crops among the plantations until 1799. Again, with other things on his mind, like being the third President of the United States, Thomas turned to other priorities and leased the land to his overseer William Page, for a cost of $1 per acre. In 1813, Thomas Jefferson gave 775 acres of Shadwell property to his grandson, Thomas Jefferson Randolph.[5]

Ownership is spotty over the next century. It is documented that what remained of the dwelling was torn down in the 1840s. Thirty years after that, Shadwell was sold at an auction. By 1912, the Shadwell estate was owned by New York Congressman Jefferson M. Levy.[6] He had also owned Monticello at the time and is credited with saving the historic home for future generations. By 1945, when excavations were going on to locate the birth home foundation, a family by the name of Smith owned the land.

Preservation

The St. Louis Historical Society erected the first historic marker at the birthplace in 1923 or 1924. The simple stone marker reads:

Here Was Born Thomas Jefferson, April 13, 1743, Lover of Liberty.

The marker, which looks more like a tombstone, was placed in a grove of trees besides an old foundation; however, years later it was determined that this structure dated to the 1800s, the century *after* Jefferson's birth.[7]

In 1926, a historic marker was placed at the Shadwell estate that read:

Peter Jefferson acquired the land in 1735, and built the house about 1737. Thomas Jefferson was born here, April 13, 1743. He lived here, 1743-1745 and 1752-1770. The house burned in 1770, and Jefferson then moved to Monticello.[8]

Note the date of 1735 is not correct, as the deed is from 1736. The marker stood for seventy-five years until it was replaced with the current one erected in 2001.

In 1941, the Thomas Jefferson Memorial Foundation funded an architectural excavation of Shadwell to determine exactly where the birth home was located. The foundation chose architect Fiske Kimball to lead the effort and located the foundation of several buildings.[9] There had always been a debate about the upbringing of Thomas Jefferson, as well as several other presidents. He was often considered to be from humble beginnings, not quite the log cabin roots of other presidents, but still the belief was that he had hailed from a simple backwoods home. Fiske Kimball was convinced of the opposite extreme, that Jefferson was born in a mansion. The truth lies somewhere in between. On this first excavation, a 32- by 56-foot foundation was unearthed. Fiske felt this structure too small to be the birthplace and concluded it must have been the slaves' quarters.[10]

Based upon the Fiske Kimball's findings, a group of individuals founded the Jefferson Birthplace Memorial Park Commission in 1945. Led by William Sobieski Hildreth, a local banker and community leader who was active in the Thomas Jefferson Memorial Foundation, the commission was tasked with purchasing the birthplace land and creating a replica of the Shadwell birth home. At the time, the land was owned by a family named Smith who agreed to sell the historic property. Given his experience in the matter, the foundation commissioned Fiske Kimball to help determine exactly where he was born.[11] At the time, it was unknown if Jefferson was born at Shadwell or at Tufton, which lie on the other side of the Rivanna River. Unbeknownst to Kimball, he had already discovered the birthplace four years earlier.[12]

In November 1945, Frank K. Houston, president of the Thomas Jefferson Memorial Foundation had grand plans for the birthplace when he wrote the *New York Times* suggesting that Shadwell would be the ideal location for the permanent home of the newly chartered United Nations. He wrote:

Adjacent to the birthplace is a large acreage of rolling and beautiful county, which could no doubt be secured [for the permanent home of the United Nations].[13]

Obviously, his pitch was not successful, but it is interesting to see the vision for Shadwell in the post war years.

The Thomas Jefferson Birthplace Memorial Park Commission funded another excavation again in 1954, this time led by Roland Wells Robbins.[14] Robbins was an "historical investigator" who, ten years earlier, had located Henry David Thoreau's cabin at Walden Pond. By driving metal rods, which he called his "steel fingers," gently into the ground he was able to locate the foundation and other artifacts.[15] In early 1955, he discovered another site about 100 feet from the "slave quarters" that Fiske Kimball had found four years earlier. Here he found fireplace remnants and other relics that dated from the same era of the Shadwell dwelling. Based on this evidence, he concluded that this site was the birth home.[16]

The Thomas Jefferson Birthplace Memorial Park Commission had raised over $150,000 and was so convinced of Robbins' findings that they went ahead and funded the recreation of the birth home.[17] In 1959, they hired architect Floyd Johnson and R. E. Lee and Sons, Incorporated, a construction company from Charlottesville to create the replica.[18] Johnson originally did not have much information to go by outside of the foundation and an inventory listing furnishings and out buildings from the Albemarle County historical records. Then Fiske Kimball found a document in the Monticello archives that he believed might have been a plan of the birthplace, possibly written by

Peter Jefferson, Thomas' father. Johnson was by no means convinced that this artifact was the real deal; still, it was better than nothing, so he used it as a guide to design a house that "represents generally a Piedmont Virginia plantation house of the eighteenth century." He admitted that "it [was] in no sense a reconstruction," but rather it was a historic "representation," consisting of two stories, six rooms, an *A*-frame steep-pitched roof, painted neutral white, and filled with furnishings from the period.[19] The home was completed in 1960 and furnished with period pieces, both donated and purchased by the birthplace commission. The re-created birthplace was officially opened to the public on Saturday, July 1, 1961. Visitors were welcome five days a week, Wednesday through Sunday, from 9 a.m. to 5 p.m. and admission was free.[20]

In 1963, the home and mortgage were transferred to the Thomas Jefferson Memorial Foundation. Doubts quickly began to creep in about the authenticity of the location. Experts soon realized that instead of being built on the site of the birthplace home, the representation was more likely located on a colonial dumping ground. Things quickly went downhill for the birthplace replica. In 1964, the home did not reopen to the public and the furnishings were sold or returned to their donors. Three years later, the home and property were sold to the Ednam Forest Corporation and the home was moved about ten miles away to where the Boar's Head Inn is now located.[21] The building still exists today. It is located on the drive into the main resort on the right and is a rental used by local businesses.[22]

In June 1991, a team of archeologists led by William Kelso began another excavation to definitively locate the original birth home. By mid-September of that same year, the archeologists had determined that the site that Kimball had believed to be the slave's quarters fifty years earlier was actually the original birth home. Based on the findings in the cellar, the archeologists believed that the home was made of wood and brick, but the number of floors in the home is unknown.[23] Today the Shadwell property is owned by the Thomas Jefferson Foundation, which also operates Monticello.

Visitor Information

Of the thousands of people that visit Monticello each year, be one of the handful that also drive the few extra miles to stand at the site of his birth. A word of warning, if you are traveling with other people who may not be as enthusiastic as you are about the presidential birthplaces, this may be the first of many times you hear the words "we traveled all this way for this?" Don't worry, you will soon get used to these words; however, in this case they have a point. A historic marker may suit Benjamin Harrison or Warren G. Harding, but does seem inadequate for the Founding Father who penned the Declaration of Independence. Thomas Jefferson is undoubtedly the most important president whose birthplace is only designated with a simple historic marker. He is consistently ranked in the top five and is the only one in the usual top ten that does not have a major historical attraction at his birthplace (Washington, Lincoln, both Roosevelts, Truman, Wilson, Eisenhower, Reagan, Polk and Jackson).[24]

Of course visit Monticello, but if you have some extra time, you should also visit the nearby Michie Tavern. Not much happened there – it was an old tavern that was moved seventeen miles to get some of the tourists as they leave Monticello, but it is an interesting thirty-minute tour.

4.
James Madison

Vital Birthplace Information

Birthplace	Port Conway, Virginia
Name	Conway House
President's birthday	March 16, 1751
How long in the home	Briefly
Life of the home	About 1720 to the 1930s
Style	Small plantation home
Still in existence	No
Ultimate fate	Fell into the Rappahannock River
Commemoration	Historic marker
Open to the public	Yes
Cost	Free
For more information	www.haas.com
Replica exists	No
Significance	First president to be born outside of his paternal home
Closest birthplace	James Monroe, 12.9 miles

The James Madison birthplace in Port Conway, Virginia.

What you will find there today:

Close to the birth site is a historic marker on the north side of the Rappahannock River, by the James Madison Memorial Bridge, which joins Port Royal to Port Conway. It stands in front of the Emmanuel Episcopal Church. The marker, which was erected by the Virginia Historic Landmarks Commission in 1971, reads:

EP 8 BIRTHPLACE OF MADISON
At this place, Port Conway, James Madison, Fourth President of the United States and Father of the Constitution, was born, March 16, 1751. His mother was staying at her paternal home, Belle Grove. Four hundred yards east when her son was born, Madison's father, James Madison Senior, lived in Orange County; the President had his home at Montpelier in that county.

Address/Directions:

The birthplace marker is located 4 miles north of Port Royal, Virginia on the James Madison Parkway (US Route 301) in Port Conway, Virginia.

History

James Madison was born in a small home on a plantation owned by his maternal grandparents, known as "Belle Grove." The plantation had been owned by his ancestors since 1670 and was first mentioned in a deed in 1678.[1]

The small home where the president was born was known as Conway House. Francis Conway, James Madison's grandfather, built the home in the 1720s on the grounds of Belle Grove, which was located in what was then Port Royal (now Port Conway) on the northern bank of the Rappahannock River.[2] James' parents, James Sr. and Eleanor (Nelly) Rose Conway Madison, did not live in Conway House. They were residents of Montpelier in Orange County, Virginia, near Zachary's Taylor's birthplace. In March 1751, they were visiting Nelly's mother and stepfather in Port Conway when Nelly was expecting a child. On March 16, 1751, she delivered a son, James Madison, who is the last president from the original Founding Fathers of the United States of America. This is significant in birthplace history as Madison is the first president to be born outside of his parent's home.

Several years later, John Hopkins took ownership of the property and birth home. In 1770, John Hopkins gave Belle Grove to his daughter and her husband, John Bernard, as a wedding gift. Twenty years later, in 1790, a second, more prominent, plantation home, also known as Belle Grove, was built on the estate. The property, including both homes, stayed in the Bernard family until 1839 when they sold to Carolinus Turner. Almost a hundred years later, in 1930, the property was purchased by Mr. and Mrs. John Hooker from Winnetka, Illinois.[3] Around this time, the original birth home was destroyed forever when it fell into the Rappahannock River.

Preservation

On August 1,1892, a bill was passed in Washington, D.C. to set aside $1,000 to "mark by a suitable column the birthplace of James Madison."[4] Progress was slow, and ten years later, this project had still not been completed. By 1901, the home was up for sale.[5]

In 1929, there began another effort to memorialize the James Madison birthplace, this time by the newly formed Caroline Chamber of Commerce representing Caroline County, Virginia. At the time, the restoration of the George Washington birthplace was in the works and the construction on the "replica" birth home was about to begin. The Chamber of Commerce discussed building a bridge over the Rappahannock River connecting Port Conway and Port Royal. This bridge, now known as the James Madison Memorial Bridge, is located 400 yards from the site of James Madison's birthplace home. The Chamber also proposed building a memorial to James Madison in an attempt to capture some of the tourism about to stampede to the George Washington birthplace. After fundraising and a public awareness campaign, a small monument was erected to mark the birthplace of James Madison. At this point the home was still standing, but not for much longer.[6]

In the 1930s, in the midst of the Great Depression, the home deteriorated and fell into the Rappahannock River. The loss was without fanfare and was not mentioned in local papers.

In the middle of the 1950s, a feud erupted over bragging rights to the birthplace when the chairman of the Caroline Board of Supervisors, C.A. Holloway, claimed that Port Royal, south of the Rappahannock River, was the rightful location of James Madison's birth. Historians claimed an erroneous author was the basis of Holloway's statement, but regardless, he requested that the sign marking the birthplace be moved across the river.

Adding to the confusion was that in 1751, at the time of Madison's birth, Port Conway was known as Port Royal. The Sheriff of Port Conway told reporters, maybe not fully in jest, that if anyone is seen removing the sign, they were to be arrested. Fortunately for Port Conway, strong evidence came from Madison himself who was quoted as saying his birthplace was "on the north bank of the Rappahannock River, at Port Conway, opposite the town of Port Royal on the 5th of March, 1751 (old style date)."[7] No arrests were known to have been made.

In 1971, the Virginia Historic Landmarks Commission erected a marker about .2 miles from where the home had stood. At the time, the site was unmarked since the marker that was erected in the late 1920s stood no more than a decade. Two years later, on April 11, 1973, the Belle Grove plantation was added to the National Register of Historic Places (National Register Number #73002029). The Belle Grove mansion, which was built in 1790, was perhaps the driving force of the landmark status, although being on the same property as the presidential birthplace home obviously didn't hurt.[8]

In 1987, Belle Grove was put on the market with a $1.8 million dollar price tag for the historic 400-acre plantation.[9] The next year, the property was bought by Franz Haas Machinery of America, Inc., an Austrian company with offices in Richmond that builds the equipment used to make sweets such as "wafers, cookies and crackers, ice cream cones, waffles and pancakes, and wafer sticks." As of this writing, they still own the historic property.[10]

In recent years, what may be the foundation of the birthplace home has been unearthed on the banks of the Rappahannock River.[11] To date, this discovery has yet to be verified.

Visitor Information

Located on the northern side of the Rappahannock River on the James Madison Parkway (US Route 301), the birthplace marker stands right in front of the Emmanuel Episcopal Church. Built in 1859, the church was damaged by Union troops in the Civil War. After the war, funds were raised to restore it and in 1987, the Emmanuel Episcopal Church was added to the National Register of Historic Places. For a bite to eat after visiting the birthplace, head south on the James Madison Parkway until it turns into A.P. Hill Boulevard. At the intersection with Tidewater Trail (Route 17) is Horne's Restaurant. Opened in 1960, today you can get their special homemade meatloaf and an old fashioned milkshake made in their "antique multimixers."[12]

5.
James Monroe

The James Monroe birthplace monument in Westmoreland County, Virginia.

Vital Birthplace Information

Birthplace	Westmoreland County, Virginia
President's birthday	April 28, 1758
How long in the home	16 years
Life of the home	Approximately 1752 to approximately 1918
Style	Farmhouse
Still in existence	No
Ultimate fate	Destroyed over time
Commemoration	Historical monument
Open to the public	Yes
Cost	Free
For more information	www.monroefoundation.org
Replica exists	Not yet
Significance	Earliest president with preservation/recognition still in progress
Closest birthplace	George Washington, 4.1 miles

Address/Directions:

**4460 James Monroe Highway
(State Route 205)
Colonial Beach, Virginia 22443**

The birthplace marker is located 4.5 miles north of Route 3. If you are traveling north, the marker will be on the right.

What you will find there today:

On the north side of State Route 205 is a memorial obelisk that stands about twelve feet tall that reads:

Birthplace of James Monroe
April 28, 1758
July 4, 1831
Fifth president of the United States 1817- 1825
Governor of Virginia 1799 and 1811
Proclaimed the Monroe Doctrine December 2, 1823
Declares the Americas no longer subject to European colonization
The marker was dedicated on November 12, 1993

Behind the obelisk is a small podium that reads:
James Monroe
1758 – 1831
Soldier • Patriot • Statesman
This marks the birthplace of James Monroe, April 28, 1758
Westmoreland County, Virginia
Attended college of William & Mary; Officer, Continental Army, American Revolution; Married Elizabeth Kortright, 1786;
US Senator; Minister Plenipotentiary to France and then to England;
Represented the United States in Spain;
Governor of Virginia;
Signed treaty of Louisiana Purchase;
Negotiated to acquire Florida; Secretary of State;
Secretary of War;
Fifth U.S. President, 1817-1825; Promulgated Monroe Doctrine, 1823;
Died July 4, 1831, Buried Hollywood Cemetery; Richmond, VA.
Placed by the Virginia Daughters of the American Revolution
April 24, 2004 Mary Jane Irwin Davis, State Regent
Presented 26 April 2008 by the Virginia Daughters of the American Revolution
Bana Weems Caskey – State Regent 2007-2010
Patricia Hatfield Mayar – Honorary State Regent • State Regent 2004-2007
Sine Die

On the street in front of the memorial is another historic marker that reads:

JP 6 BIRTHPLACE OF MONROE
In this vicinity stood the Monroe home where James Monroe, fifth president of the United States, was born, April 28, 1758. His father was Spence Monroe and his mother, Elizabeth Jones. He left home at the age of sixteen to enter William and Mary College and later he left college to enter the army.

Virginia Conservation Commission 1947

The actual birth home foundation is marked with wooden posts. In the middle of these posts is yet another marker that was dedicated on April 22, 1989. A visitor center is the newest addition at the birthplace location.

History

The birthplace of the fifth president is located in Westmoreland County, Virginia, only a few miles from where George Washington was born. In the first half of the 1600s, Native Americans, known as the Powhatan Confederacy, inhabited the land. By the 1640s, settlers began to encroach upon the Indian territory, and in 1648, the first local government of Northumberland County was established. That same year, Andrew Monroe became one of the first land patent holders in the region. The Monroes arrived in the New World from Fowlis, Scotland in 1637 and settled in Virginia after spending more than a decade in Maryland. Like many ancestors of our early forefathers, Andrew Monroe began acquiring large parcels of land. Starting with a modest 200 acres in 1650, he quickly added 440 more acres in 1652 and then another 280 acres in 1666. This last parcel gave him all of the land between Monroe Creek and the mouth of Monroe Bay. By this time, Northumberland County had been divided, and the Monroes resided in Westmoreland County. Andrew farmed tobacco on his land and was also active in civic life. When he died in the 1680s, he left behind a wife, Elizabeth, and five children. Much of his land went to his son Andrew Monroe II, including the tract from Monroe Creek to Monroe Bay.[1]

After Andrew died, Elizabeth remarried a neighbor, Edward Mountjoy "before 23 February 1686/7."[2] Edward also owned a considerable amount of property near the Monroe estate. On February 20, 1693, Elizabeth and Edward deeded a portion of this land to Andrew Monroe II.[3] This acreage included the land west of Monroe Creek that would eventually become the birthplace of the fifth President of the United States. Andrew continued to acquire and sell acreage over the next several years. The site of the birthplace changed hands during this time; however, it remained in the Monroe family, transitioning to Andrew's brother, William, by 1713.[4]

William had two sons Andrew III and William II and his intention was for the land to be split evenly between them upon his death. Andrew III died before his father, but not before he had a son of his own, Spence. So when William died in 1737, the land was split between his grandson, Spence, and his son, William II. Spence inherited the northern property and William II the southern portion.[5]

Spence Monroe married Elizabeth Jones of King George County in 1752. In addition to being a farmer, Spence was also a carpenter, and after his marriage, it is believed that he built a one and a half-story frame house complete with two chimneys for his new bride. In 1839, an engraving of the home appeared in a New York publication, *The Family Magazine.* This rendering is the only known image of the Monroe birthplace and has played a critical part in recent reconstruction efforts.[6]

Six years after the marriage, the couple had their second child, a son, James Monroe, on April 28, 1758. James would go on to fight in the American Revolution and serve his county as the fifth President of the United States. For the next sixteen years, James lived in the home his father built, until 1774 when he left to study at the College of William and Mary. Once he left, he never again lived in the home of his birth. That same year, both of his parents died. The property was divided between James and his younger brother, Spence Junior, with the birth home going to James. Later, records indicate that James eventually owned all of his father's estate. Shortly after James began his studies, the college was shut down due to the Revolutionary War in 1776. James enlisted in the Third Virginia Regiment and eventually rose to the title of lieutenant colonel. After the war, James moved to a farm in King George County.[7]

In 1783, James Monroe sold all of his Westmoreland land (550 acres) to Gawen Corbin, who held the property for sixteen years. On April 1, 1799, Corbin sold 850 acres to Henry "Light Horse Harry" Lee, which included the original 550 acres as well as over 300 more acres he had acquired. "Light Horse Harry" was a former Governor of Virginia, a cavalry officer in the American Revolution, and perhaps most notably, father of the Confederate General Robert E. Lee. Harry may have been trying to flip the property for a quick profit since eight months later, on November 26, 1799, he sold to Isaac Pollock from Washington, D.C.[8] A little over a month after selling the Monroe birthplace, "Light Horse Harry" would utter the classic phrase that he is best remembered by. Speaking to both houses of Congress after the death of George Washington in Philadelphia on December 26, 1799, "Light Horse Harry" called our most revered president, "First in war, first in peace, and first in the hearts of his countrymen."

The new owner, Isaac Pollack, did not hold it for much longer than Lee, selling it in 1801 to Marcia Burnes, a philanthropist from Washington, D.C.[9] Marcia's father, David Burnes, had owned much of the land on which the capital of Washington, D.C. was built. From the sale of her father's land she amassed an incredible amount of wealth and had become known as "the Heiress of Washington City."[10] In 1802, on her twentieth birthday, Marcia married U.S. Congressman John Peter Van Ness and the property was transferred to him, and it remained with the Van Ness family for forty-five years until John's death in 1847. During this time, James Monroe had risen from Minister to the Court of Saint James (Britain) under Thomas Jefferson to the President of the United States from 1817 to 1825. On July 4, 1831, James Monroe died in New York City, making him the third of the first five presidents to die on Independence Day (Adams and Jefferson both passed away on July 4, 1826).

A trustee held the birthplace property until 1849, when all 862 acres were sold for only $3,000 to Thomas Ditty and Joseph Harvey of Westmoreland.[11] Harvey sold the land in 1853 to George Bourne and Henry Kingsberry, shipbuilders from Kennebunkport, Maine. Four years later, in 1857, the property was sold to three local men, Joshua and Thomas Reamy of nearby Stafford County and Randall Sutton of Westmoreland. When the Reamys and Sutton owned the home, it was a hundred years old and in an advanced state of disrepair. It had been partially dismantled and severely dilapidated.[12]

By this time, the property was known as Monroe Hall, an unincorporated community in Westmoreland County that included the birthplace site. On August 12, 1868, the Reamys and Sutton sold the land to Henry Gouldman for a little over $4,000. Three days later, Gouldman turned around and sold to Robert Bell and Samuel Baker for $6,000 for a quick $2,000 profit! Bell and Baker kept fifty acres for themselves and sold the remaining land, which included the birthplace, to George J. and Mary E. Haines of Washington, D.C.[13]

Haines cleared the land and subdivided it into smaller parcels to sell. The birthplace property, now reduced to an eighty-four-acre parcel, was sold to Moses Watts and Samuel Stewart in 1874. Both Watts and Stewart were listed as "colored" in tax records, which is astonishing considering less then a decade after the Civil War African-American people would own the land of former slave owner and president, James Monroe. For years, the original Monroe structure had been deteriorating, and by 1850, it was no longer worthy of noting on tax assessments and deeds, although there still remained the foundation, some bricks, and a dilapidated chimney. After almost 160 years, these bricks would be put to use.[14]

Samuel's Grandson, the Reverend Cornelius Stewart was a soldier in World War I. After returning in 1918, he removed the foundation and bricks to use in local buildings including the New Monrovia Baptist Church.[15] Over the next few years, souvenir hunters slowly took whatever bricks weren't used for the church. From over 800 acres, Charles Edward Stuart purchased a parcel of now only six acres, including the birth site in June 1929 for $4,800. At the time, plans were in motion for the George Washington birthplace re-creation and Stuart thought that he might be able to cash in on the purchase. Stuart contacted the Department of the Interior to ask if they were interested in purchasing the land, but was told that the federal government had no interest in the dead president's birthplace.[16] Stuart owned the site until 1941 when he found a willing buyer in the Monroe Birthplace Monument Association, an organization formed five years earlier with the mission of purchasing, preserving, and memorializing the birthplace site.

Preservation efforts first began in 1923.[17] The efforts are still underway...

Preservation

The Rodney Dangerfield of Presidential Birthplaces, James Monroe's birthplace has been fighting to get respect since before the Great Depression! Since 1941, when the site was first purchased for the expressed purpose of preservation, the numerous false starts and dead ends in memorializing this historic site reads like a soap opera. The James Monroe birthplace is unique amongst the early presidents in that history is happening now and the preservation efforts are going on as this is being written.

The first attempt to purchase the birthplace was made in the winter of 1923. The president's granddaughter, Rose Gouvernor Hoes, and a group of about twenty people formed the Society of the Descendents of James Monroe to buy the house from the Reverend Cornelius Stewart. The society was concerned that the remains of the home were being removed so quickly that soon there would be nothing left to buy.[18] By 1929, enough of the bricks and foundation had been removed that it was no longer apparent where the home had once stood; however, it was believed that a locust tree marked the location of the birth home.[19] Despite this clue, the original site was so obscured that local preservationists were forced to make an attempt to locate the birthplace site.[20]

In 1927, Rose Gouvernor Hoes and her son, Laurence Gouvernor Hoes (the president's great grandson), founded the James Monroe Memorial Foundation (JMMF) and purchased historic items that once belonged to James Monroe in hopes of memorializing their famous relative. At the time, the only property they could obtain with connections to the president was his law office in Fredericksburg and they wasted no time restoring the offices and creating a museum, which was opened to the public the following year. Twenty years after the organization was founded, it was incorporated in the state of Virginia in 1947. The group remained on the sidelines as far as the birthplace was concerned for the next fifty or sixty years; however, its first President, Laurence Gouvernor Hoes, was always personally involved in the James Monroe birthplace restoration efforts. Led by its current president, Bill Thomas, the JMMF is now in charge of the birthplace reconstruction and commemoration effort. Hopefully, the stars are now aligned and the fifth president will soon have a worthy birthplace memorial.[21]

In 1936, another group was formed to commemorate the fifth president, the Monroe Birthplace Monument Association (MBMA), comprised of concerned citizens from the northern neck area. In 1937, the first president, Mrs. Rubenette Lee Fleet, began a public appeal for funds to purchase the site "and develop it into a suitable memorial to that great American patriot and world renowned statesman" and, appealing to the women of the region, sought to "do belated justice to the name and fame of the great and good son of Elisabeth Jones Monroe."[22] She started with an immediate goal of $3,875 with the ultimate goal of $15,000 to purchase approximately 100 acres and received encouragement when sitting president, Franklin Roosevelt, wrote to commend her on her efforts.[23] On May 4, 1938, the Virginia State Senate approved $10,000 towards the effort. Virginia State Senator Robert O. Norris, who sponsored the bill, spoke in support of the funding:

> It would seem fitting that his birthplace should be converted to a national shrine for the people not only of our country, but for all those of the Western Hemisphere for which his [Monroe] doctrine applies.[24]

By 1941, the MBMA had raised the $15,000 to purchase the property from the Stuarts as well as surrounding land from three other landowners.

For eleven years, the only notable accomplishment was a historic marker that was erected in 1947 by the Virginia Conservation Commission. Finally, in 1952, things began to happen when Laurence Gouvernor Hoes took the helm of the project and worked with the MBMA (a year earlier Hoes had suggested merging both organizations, but members rejected the idea).[25] Architect Milton L. Grigg designed a tribute that included a memorial building, a statue of Monroe, a library, offices, gardens, and more. Plans for the "Pan American Park" were grand, but perhaps too much so.[26] By 1956, after a road system was built to support the memorial, the plans quickly fizzled. By 1958, the Monroe Birthplace Monument Association was under fire for not filing the necessary annual reports and disbanded. Even though they were no longer a legal entity, they still technically retained ownership of the land, something that would prove problematic in the years to come.[27]

In the 1960s, local historian Virginia Sherman located what she believed was the site of the birth home, but an extensive archeological dig was required to confirm. She urged both county and state officials to proceed with an excavation.[28] However, by 1971, the birthplace was an embarrassment – the land had become an illegal dumping ground and the county had closed access and even removed the roads that led to the site and the historical reference from its county maps (In 1986, the road VA 209 was officially decommissioned).[29]

In 1972, the county began to petition for ownership of the land, with the goal to have a monument erected in time for the 1976 bicentennial.[30] The problem was that although it had been defunct for fifteen years, the land (as mentioned earlier) was still technically owned by the Monroe Birthplace Monument Association.[31] By 1973, the red tape had been cut and the property was transferred to the Westmoreland County Historical Preservation Corporation and immediately they commissioned an excavation to determine the exact location of the birth site.[32] However, they quickly appeared to have buyer's remorse. By late 1974 into 1975, they were trying to give the land away to the federal government to use as a National Park Site. There were already several sites within the National Park System dedicated to presidential birthplaces, including JFK and George Washington only five miles away, but the offer was declined. The National Park Service cited lack of funds and lack of historical significance since there wasn't even a house on the property.[33]

Unable to donate the land to the federal government, the historical society moved forward with the excavation.[34] In early 1976, the Virginia State Landmarks Commission, led by Keith Eggloff, began to dig.[35] Three months later their efforts were rewarded when they found a 20 foot by 58 foot foundation and convincing evidence that it was indeed the birth site.[36] The site was quickly added to the Virginia Historic Landmarks Commission register in January 1977, and it took another two years for the site to be included on the National Register of Historic Places (National Register Number #79003095) in 1979.[37] Unfortunately, the euphoria was short lived. After finding the birth home, the site still remained unopened to the public for another decade.

Hoping the federal government had a short memory, again the land was offered to the National Park Service in 1984 and again, the offer was declined. A decade earlier it was turned down due to lack of funds and lack of historical significance. With the economic malaise of the 1970s behind the country, lack of funds was no longer the primary issue, but the tract of land with no birth home was no more historically significant than it was ten years earlier. Summing up the sentiment of the National Park Service, chief historian Dr. Edwin Burns said, "There is a loss of integrity in the site – no house".[38] Next, the offer was made to the Association for the Preservation of Virginia Antiquities (APVA).[39] At first they were interested and planned to build a monument to commemorate the historic site, but the deal quickly got tangled in red tape and fell through.

As if out of desperation to make some sort of progress on memorializing the site, another historic marker was erected in 1987. The next year, a private citizen, Dorothy Samson, showed interest in obtaining the land and developing a re-created home and farm. She quickly grew frustrated with the county and withdrew her offer as she became convinced that the commission "was not interested or even concerned with preserving the Monroe Birthplace".[40] The decade did end on a high note when the corners of the birthplace were marked with wooden posts and a marker was placed in the middle of the site. The plaque chronicles the life of service by our fifth president, and in a ceremony on April 22, 1989, county and state politicians and historians dedicated the marker. Also in attendance was Virginia Sherman, who located the birth home over twenty years earlier.

The new decade of the 1990s brought renewed attempts to get the National Park Service to take over the site, but again, to no avail (can't say they didn't try!). On November 12, 1993, the Westmoreland Board of Supervisors dedicated a historic marker. The obelisk, which still stands, is easy for passers by to see from the highway, but it is not located exactly on the birth site, which sits about 300 feet away.

By 1999, Westmoreland County restarted efforts to recognize one of their favorite sons (it's tough being born in the same county as George Washington!). In 2001, the county paid the Warren T. Byrd Landscape Architects $35,000 to develop plans for the memorial, and in October, the proposal was completed. These plans were more modest than those from the early 1950s, with the focus on authenticity, returning the land to its mid-eighteenth-century appearance. With the plans approved, the difficult stage of fundraising was again underway.[41]

In 2004, the Virginia Federation of Garden Clubs planted a garden at the birthplace dubbed the James Monroe Birth Site Garden. Located at the garden is a plaque that reads:

James Monroe Birth Site Garden sponsored by the Virginia Federation of Garden Clubs, Inc. Funded in part by a 2003-2005 grant from National Garden Clubs, Inc. and Principal Financial Group.

By 2005, things appeared promising. Attention was paid to making sure every bureaucratic "i" was dotted and "t" crossed.[42] On April 4, 2005, their diligence was rewarded when a ninety-nine year lease was granted to the James Monroe Memorial Foundation. The JMMF, started by Laurence Gouvernor Hoes in 1927, has been led since the 1990s by only its third president, Bill Thomas. Also included

in the organization are several descendents of James Monroe.[43]

Excavation efforts in the new millennium have been led by James Monroe's *Alma mater*, the College of William and Mary and several archeologists from the 1976 excavation have also been involved. In the spring of 2008, a $500,000 visitor center was completed. A dedication ceremony was held on April 26, 2008, and was attended by "a slew of dignitaries, proclamations, and hereditary and historical societies."[44] On that day the Virginia Daughters of the American Revolution also unveiled a small historic marker. However, keeping with the seventy-year struggle, the visitor center remained unopened for months due to confusion over who was responsible for staffing it.[45] These problems have since been resolved and the visitors center is now open.

Currently, both private and public funds are being secured and red tape cut to reconstruct the birthplace based on the 1845 etching.[46] The estimated cost of construction ranges from $700,000 to $1,000,000. If you would like to donate to these efforts, please visit the JMMF website for more information.

Visitor Information

I first visited the James Monroe birthplace immediately after leaving the George Washington birthplace. While it may not be fair, one can't help but make the comparison between the fifty-foot obelisk at the Washington birthplace and the twelve-foot model at Monroe's birthplace. However, I look forward to returning once the re-creation is completed to see when James Monroe's birthplace finally gets the memorial it deserves. The Visitors' Center is open on weekends from Memorial Day to Labor Day from 11a.m. to 4 p.m. There is no cost for admission, but to help fund the birthplace replica, donations are appreciated.

6.
John Quincy Adams

The John Quincy Adams birthplace in Quincy, Massachusetts.

Vital Birthplace Information

Birthplace	Braintree (now Quincy) Massachusetts
President's birthday	July 11, 1767
How long in the home	18 years total (1767- 1783, 1805-1807)
Life of the home	1663 to present
Style	Saltbox
Still in existence	Yes
Commemoration	Part of the Adams National Historical Park
Open to the public	Yes
Cost	$5.00
For more information	www.nps.gov/adam
Replica exists	No
Significance	First president to be born on the same street as an earlier president
Closest birthplace	John Adams, 75 feet

Address/Directions:

141 Franklin Street
Quincy, Massachusetts 02169

Just like John Adams' birthplace, the best way to see the John Quincy Adams birthplace, and the only way to view the interior, is to take the bus tour starting from the National Park Visitor Center, located at 1250 Hancock Street in the Galleria at Presidents Place in downtown Quincy.

What you will find there today:

The John Quincy Adams birthplace, which is next to his father and second president John Adams' birthplace, is part of Adams National Historic Park, run by the National Park Service.

History

John Quincy Adams was born in the town of Northern Braintree (now Quincy) located several miles outside of Boston, Massachusetts. Gregory Belcher, an original settler of Northern Braintree, first owned the birthplace property. In 1663, Belcher built a small one-room home with a fireplace for his son, Samuel Belcher, possibly as a wedding gift. In 1679, Samuel died, leaving the home to his oldest son, Gregory. In 1716, Gregory built what was to become the birth home of our sixth president, incorporating elements of the original 1663 structure. This home was built in the saltbox style, almost identical to the John Adams birth home, with the exception of a lean-to in the rear of the home. Rafters visible in the attic indicate that the lean-to was added after the original 1716 construction.[1] In 1744, Deacon Adams, John Adams' father, and John Quincy Adams' grandfather, purchased the home and its nine and a half acres for the tidy sum of 500 pounds. It was only seventy-five feet from the John Adams birthplace and the small swath of land between the two homes was the perfect location for the Adams' family outhouse.[2]

When Deacon Adams died in 1761, the home was left to his first son, John Adams. John and his wife, Abigail, moved into the home after their marriage in 1764 and converted the kitchen to his law office, later adding a side door to allow clients and visitors to enter directly into his office.[3] It was in this home that John Adams planned his successful defense of the British soldiers in the Boston Massacre.

In 1765, the Adams had their first child in the home, Abigail, nicknamed "Nabby." Two years later, on July 11, 1767, their second son, John Quincy, was born in the "east front chamber" of the home.[4] In this home Abigail home schooled young John Quincy. The Adams also had a front seat to the events leading up to the American Revolution as British soldiers and American militia marched past the home along the Old Coast Road. During the war, soldiers trained in the farm's fields and refugees were sheltered in both birthplaces.[5]

Next to the birth of the future president, the most notable event to take place in this home was in 1779, when John Adams, along with Samuel Adams and James Bowdon, wrote the Massachusetts Constitution. This document is the oldest written Constitution still in use in the world today. Much of the language of this document is similar to the United States constitution to which John contributed to almost a decade later.[6]

In 1783, when the family moved to Europe, the Adams family rented out the home to various tenants, including an African-American family. From 1800 to 1804, the pastor of the First Congregational Society, Reverend Peter Whitney, rented the home.[7] Whitney, the author of several books, including *History of the County of Worcester*, and his son officiated at John Adams' funeral in 1826.

In 1803, John Quincy purchased both birthplaces. This is the only the second time in history that a president has owned two Presidential Birthplaces at the same time. John Quincy lived in his birth home on what is now 141 Franklin Street from 1805 through 1807. Again the home would be rented until 1885. From 1885 through 1896 the home was vacant.[8]

Preservation

In 1896, Charles Adams Jr., the great grandson of John Adams, gave permission to the Adams Chapter of the Daughters of the American Revolution to restore both birth homes. Additionally, he granted permission to use the John Quincy Adams birth home as the headquarters for the Quincy Historical Society, formed in 1893.[9] The patriotic women spent a year completing the restorations, decorating the homes as they appeared in colonial times. On June 17, 1897, the doors were opened to the public and "large crowd of people from [Quincy] and surrounding towns" came to see the historic homes.[10]

This restoration cost a total of $1,650 and included a new roof and a fresh coat of red paint, which was believed to be the color of the home at the time of the sixth president's birth. As with the second president's birth home, this color would later prove inaccurate. In addition to interior and exterior restorations, the home was also raised two feet to be in line with the current level of Franklin Street. After the restorations were complete, the doors were opened to the public. Additional work was done on the home in 1923 when a new split cedar shingle roof was installed. The home remained in the possession of the Adams family until 1940, when it was donated along with the John Adams birthplace to the city of Quincy, Massachusetts. The two birthplaces remained a package deal in 1950; they were both turned over to the Quincy Historical Society. In that same year, restorations were also completed to the joists beneath the floor.[11]

The John Quincy Adams birthplace had several important visitors throughout the years. On July 15, 1925, Calvin Coolidge and his wife, Grace, visited the home accompanied by Melville E. Stone from the *Associated Press*. President Coolidge, who was a distant relative of John Quincy's mother, Abigail Adams, "studied numerous prints and old pictures which covered the walls, gazed at the planked ceiling with cross beams and walked up a creaky flight of stairs to take a look at the four-posted canopy bed, covered with patch quilts."[12] On June 9, 1967, sitting President Lyndon Baines Johnson's wife, Lady Bird, visited the saltbox home where John Quincy Adams was born.[13]

On December 19, 1960, the home was designated a National Historic Landmark and it was placed on the National Register of Historic Places (National Register Number #66000128) upon its creation on October 15, 1966.[14] When restorations were done in the late 1800s, the two homes were both painted red, the traditional color of barns and farmhouses. The homes became affectionately known to locals as "the little red houses" and had become a popular attraction; open from 10 a.m. to 5 p.m. daily. The price of admission was even waived for "school and other children's groups."[15] The city continued to manage the property until 1977, when it was turned over to the Quincy Historical Society, which was so critical in the restoration efforts eighty years earlier.

On May 1,1979, both the John Adams and John Quincy Adams birthplaces were turned over to the National Park Service to become part of the Adams National Historic Site. The following year began a six-year reconstruction project which would cost the taxpayers $175,000. Research conducted by the National Park Service had turned up evidence that Abigail had wanted the home painted a "stone" color. This was assumed to be off-white, so the home was repainted to its present color using paint and techniques from the eighteenth century. Today, approximately half of the home consists of original material. Like the John Adams home, the John Quincy Adams home was adorned with authentic period pieces donated by families from Quincy. The home was restored to resemble what it is believed to have looked like when John Quincy lived in the home; however, without benefit of photographs for either home, the National Park Ranger admitted it's a "best guess."[16]

Visitor Information

Obviously, it is unlikely that anyone would visit the John Quincy Adams birthplace without visiting his father, John Adams', birthplace, so no need to state the obvious. However, there is also a lot of non-Adams history also to be explored in Quincy. The town was originally settled as part of North Braintree in 1625 and Quincy has had a proud ship-building history. It was here that James J. Kilroy, a ship inspector at the Fore River shipyard, wrote "Kilroy is here" along with a silly cartoon in chalk on the ships after completing his inspections. That mysterious phrase went "viral" in World War II until it was seen all over the world. It is also at Quincy's Dennison Airport that Amelia Earhart earned her chops as a pilot. In addition, Quincy is the home of the first Dunkin' Donuts and the first Howard Johnsons, which started as a drug store and soda fountain shop in 1925.[17]

7.
Andrew Jackson

Andrew Jackson's birthplace marker at Andrew Jackson State Park in Lancaster, South Carolina.

Vital Birthplace Information

Birthplace	Waxhaws area of South Carolina… Or is it Union County, North Carolina?
President's birthday	March 15, 1767
How long in the home	9 years
Life of the home	Before 1767 to after 1784
Style	Log cabin
Still in existence	No
Ultimate fate	Lost to time
Commemoration	Andrew Jackson State Park
Open to the public	Yes
Cost	$2.00 adults and age 15 or younger free
For more information	www.southcarolinaparks.com/ park-finder/state-park/1797.aspx
Replica exists	No
Significance	First log cabin president and first birthplace controversy
Closest birthplace	James Polk, 21.7 miles

Address/Directions:

**Andrew Jackson State Park
196 Andrew Jackson Park Road
Lancaster, South Carolina 29720**

The entrance to the Andrew Jackson State Park is right by the junction of Route 5 and U.S. 521 near the border of North Carolina.

What you will find there today:

In South Carolina, a stone monument marks the birthplace within Andrew Jackson State Park. It contains the following inscription: "I was born in So Carolina, as I have been told, at the plantation whereon James Crawford lived about one mile from the Carolina Road X of the Waxhaw Creek – Andrew Jackson to J.H. Witherspoon, August 11, 1824." Jackson said in his last will and testament that he was a native of South Carolina. This stone stands upon the plantation whereon James Crawford lived. Near the site of the dwelling house, according to the Mills map of 1820.

The "X" is shorthand for crossing. On the reverse side it simply reads: Birthplace of Andrew Jackson Brave, truculent, noble, able, honest. This marker erected by Catawba Chapter Daughters of the American Revolution Rock Hill, South Carolina November 1928 D.A.R.

On the left side of the monument is a circular "U.S. Geological Survey Benchmark" marker attached in 1936 that notes the altitude at 582 feet.

There are two other identical historic markers in South Carolina (both #29-9) that let travelers know they are approaching the birthplace location. One is at the intersection of Old Church Road and Charlotte Highway (U.S. 521) and the other at the intersections of Charlotte Highway (U.S. 521) and Andrew Jackson State Park Road; both locations are entrances to the Andrew Jackson State Park. The identical signs read:

Seventh President of the United States. Near this site on South Carolina soil Andrew Jackson was born on March 15, 1767, at the plantation whereon James Crawford lived and where Jackson himself said he was born. Erected by the Waxhaws Chapter – Daughters of the American Revolution 1967.

In Jackson's "other birthplace" in North Carolina is an eight-foot-tall stone marker built on what was believed to be the site of Andrew's Uncle George McKemey's home. The stone marker is located about a mile and a half away from the South Carolina marker and it is here that North Carolinians claim is the location of the true Andrew Jackson birthplace. *It bears the inscription:*

Here was born March 15, 1767, Andrew Jackson, Seventh President of the United States. Erected by the North Carolina D.A.R. 1910. These stones were part of the original cabin.

To get to the marker, turn right as you leave the Andrew Jackson State Park in Lancaster, South Carolina. At the first intersection, turn right onto East Rebound Road. In about a mile, you will cross Old Church Road and continue onto a dirt road. After a few feet on the dirt road you will be in North Carolina. Continue for about half a mile, past the Mount Zion Baptist Church on the left until you reach the marker.

There is also a marker on NC 75 (South Main Street) at the intersection with Rehobeth Road in Waxhaw that reads:

L-11 ANDREW JACKSON
Seventh president of the United States, was born a few miles southwest of this spot, March 15, 1767.

This marker was erected in 1938.
If you haven't guessed by now, this is going to be an interesting story….

History

It took only seven presidents to have a birthplace location controversy, and the Andrew Jackson controversy has more twists and turns than a roller coaster.

Originally, the Cherokee, Catawba, and the Waxhaw Indian tribes inhabited the land where Andrew Jackson was born. Of course, they were displaced when first the European settlers came in the middle of the 1700s from Northern Ireland. The Jacksons date back to 1765 when Andrew Sr. and his wife, Elizabeth Hutchinson, first arrived from Ireland. The Waxhaw region straddles North Carolina and South Carolina and the Jacksons lived in Mecklenburg (now Union County) on the North Carolina side. Two years later, with his wife only days away from having their third child, Andrew Jackson Sr. tragically died, becoming the first father who did not survive to see his son, and future president's, birth. He had hurt himself clearing land several days earlier and the injury proved fatal.[1]

According to legend, friends and family carried the body in the bitter cold on a horse-driven sled to the Old Waxhaw Presbyterian Church for the funeral. Perhaps to fight off the cold or maybe to celebrate the life of their fallen friend, the group began to drink and drink… and they kept drinking until they were rip-roaring drunk. The inebriated funeral procession apparently never noticed that their load had gotten a little lighter. Eventually, the pallbearers realized that the body of Andrew Jackson Sr. had rolled off the sled into a stream a few miles back.[2]

After the funeral, the grief stricken widow, Elizabeth Hutchinson Jackson, went to stay at her sister and brother-in-law George McKemey's home, also in Mecklenburg (yet another point of confusion is that the family name is also cited as McKamie, McAmey, McKenney, and McCamie – for sake of this writing, I will stick to the most oft-used name of McKemey). The McKemeys had purchased the land in 1766; however, it is unclear whether the cabin resided in North Carolina or South Carolina. It is also unknown if she intended to visit or if she was forced to stop when she went into labor to deliver her son, Andrew Jackson. Shortly after her stay at the McKemey's home she moved a mile and a half away to stay with another sister and brother-in-law, James and Elizabeth Crawford. The Crawfords lived on a plantation in the Waxhaw region of South Carolina (but paid taxes to North Carolina). When Andrew Jackson was nine years old, he left his uncle's home to live with James Crawford's brother, Robert, at his farm. There, Andrew grew into a young man on this farm, living there until he left for school in Nashville at the age of seventeen.[3]

With all of this moving in the waning days of her pregnancy, the actual birthplace of Andrew Jackson is a key piece of the mystery. Did the grieving pregnant widow have her son at the McKemey home and afterwards bring her newborn child to the Crawford's cabin? Or did she leave the McKemey home while she was still pregnant to have her son at the Crawford cabin? Andrew Jackson never questioned his birthplace as South Carolina; however, there are conflicting reports of him both citing the Crawford and the McKemey home as the site of his birth.

The second key piece of the controversy is the borderline of the states, then and now. The Crawford cabin was clearly in South Carolina, but the exact location of the McKemey home is not so clear. In 1767, North and South Carolina were still colonies and not yet states and the boundary was along the road that connected Camden, South Carolina, to Salisbury, North Carolina. Today, this road is primarily in South Carolina. The current marker at what is believed to be the McKemey residence is only 300 yards from the border in an area that was part of South Carolina in 1767 and North Carolina after 1813. In addition, it's probably a safe bet that the Jacksons, McKemeys, or the Crawfords couldn't care less about which side of the border they lived on at the time.

As if North and South Carolina battling over the birthplace wasn't enough to deal with, other locations including Virginia, Pennsylvania, and Ireland also briefly tried to claim Jackson as one of their own. Another theory put forth is that Jackson was born at sea, while his parents were sailing from Ireland to America.[4] In 1858, a *New York Times* article claimed that Andrew Jackson was actually born on the estate of James Strode. At the time the Strode home was in Berkeley County, Virginia, but this now falls within West Virginia. The argument over whether this would have constituted a Virginia or West Virginia birthplace would have been an interesting one, but the facts are loose in the Strode home theory.[5] To make the claim fit Jackson's birth date, it was revised to "about 1764 or '65" however, this theory still seems to pop up every fifty years or so. It appeared in the October 1902 issue of the *West Virginia Historical Magazine* in detail and was again brought up in 1967.[6] Regardless, all of these non-Carolina claims have since been rebuffed.

The question of Jackson's birthplace was first asked when he ran for president in 1828; however, the dispute was a tepid one since Jackson himself claimed it was South Carolina. There are several existing written records from Mr. Jackson supporting that belief including personal letters, his will, and his famous proclamation against South Carolina nullification in 1832, a response to South Carolina's declaration that federal taxes were unconstitutional. In it he declared to South Carolinians, "Fellow-citizens of my native State!"[7] Nor did anyone else raise this question during his lifetime. Jackson died on June 8, 1845 with the lifelong belief that he was a South Carolinian. The Waxhaws straddled South Carolina and North Carolina and Jackson believed he was born on the South Carolina side, but the exact location was never known. One thing is known – after six presidents of elite New England or southern plantation upbringings, Andrew Jackson was the first of the log cabin presidents. Born from humble beginnings on the eve of the American Revolution, he was to rise to this highest office in the land.

A few weeks after his death, Samuel Hoey Walkup, who would one day become a colonel of the 48th North Carolina Infantry Regiment, made a speech at a Fourth of July ceremony in which he claimed that Andrew Jackson was born in North Carolina. Walkup based this assertion on Jackson's younger cousin, James Faulkner, who stated that one night,

while together at the McKemey cabin, Jackson told him that they were in the home where he was born.[8] The controversy simmered for fifteen years at which time, thanks to James Parton, it began to boil over. The most popular biographer of his time, Parton published a three-volume biography of the seventh president titled *The Life of Andrew Jackson* in 1860. The renowned author would once again revisit the subject when he wrote an abbreviated version of the Jackson biography only two months before his death in 1891.

Using, among other sources, Faulkner's claim, James Parton concluded that Andrew Jackson was not born in South Carolina, as Jackson himself believed, but rather across the state line in Union County, North Carolina, at the home of his Uncle George McKemey. Parton also cited Mrs. Sarah Lessley Lathan, whose mother delivered Andrew Jackson and often told her daughter that the event occurred at the McKemey cabin.[9] Several other biographies had been published in the same time frame, all in contrast to Parton, claiming South Carolina as Jackson's birthplace, but the controversy had taken hold.

For several decades following the book, Parton's claim was accepted and North Carolina had the undisputed honors. That was until 1902, when Augustus Caesar Buell of Philadelphia introduced another twist. Buell was also a prominent biographer and his dispute was not of the McKemey birthplace, but rather of the location of the home in 1767. Parton believed it to be North Carolina, but Buell believed it to be a fraction of a mile into South Carolina.[10] Two years later, in 1904, Buell would publish his own account of the seventh president, *History of Andrew Jackson, pioneer, patriot, soldier, politician, president.* In it he wrote:

> **Jackson was born in 1767. At that time the exact boundary-line between the two colonial Carolinas was debatable; at least it had never been subjected to scientific delimitation. But the spot where the McCamie cabin stood was, in 1767, under the unquestioned – or rather the tacitly admitted – jurisdiction of the colony of South Carolina. Therefore, Jackson was born in that Colony.[11]**

Or in other words, when Jackson was born, the cabin was in South Carolina. However in 1794, the state lines were drawn, and this changed. Buell went on to write that the new boundary lines...

> **...located the McCamie cabin about eighty rods north of the line in what was then (1794) Mecklenburg County, but since set off in what is now Union County, North Carolina. Therefore, Jackson, though born in the colonial South Carolina of 1767, was also born on soil that became part of the state of North Carolina in 1794.[12]**

South Carolina was later supported by the *Report of the Historical Commission of South Carolina* made to the South Carolina Legislature by Dr. A. S. Salley in 1908. Perhaps it was no surprise when Salley concluded in his thirty-two page report that Jackson was born in South Carolina. What he did claim that had little previous support was that his birth took place not at the McKemey cabin, but at the home of James Crawford.[13]

Despite this mounting evidence, popular opinion remained with North Carolina as the rightful birthplace. According to an article in *The New York Times* in 1922, "with extraordinary unanimity, encyclopedias and biographers state that Jackson was born in North Carolina."[14] In the time of Jackson, the congressional directory stated that he was born at the George McKemey homestead in Mecklenburg, North Carolina, and moved that same year to the Waxhaw settlement in South Carolina.[15] This remained unchallenged until February 23, 1922, when South Carolina Congressmen William F. Stevenson again raised the question of his birthplace. Stevenson, who was born in North Carolina, must not have been very popular with his constituents when he argued that Andrew Jackson was actually born in South Carolina. He told his peers:

> Mr. Chairman and gentlemen, it is an old controversy, but recently I have discovered that in the last edition of the Congressional Records, the permanent one, the myth that Andrew Jackson was born on the McKemey Plantation in North Carolina has been engrafted on our Congressional Directory, and I desire to controvert that proposition and once and for all place before the Congress and this country the evidence as to the birthplace of Andrew Jackson.[16]

In 1925, Congress tried to put the issue to rest once and for all by passing a special resolution to update the congressional directory, which was compiled by Ansel Wold and contained biographies of all members of Congress since 1774.[17] Legislators from both states presented their case. While in the midst of these proceedings, a startling discovery was made. In November 1927, a letter was discovered in a trunk in an attic of a home in Craddock, Virginia. The home belonged to Thomas C. Benthall, a passenger agent of the Old Dominion Steamship Company. The letter dated March 4, 1820 and written by Andrew Jackson himself to Benthall's great uncle Thomas Watson of Baltimore, stated that he was born in South Carolina. Jackson had sent the letter from his Hermitage homestead in Nashville, Tennessee, in response to a question about his birthplace.

> I do myself the pleasure to inform you that I was born (as stated by the author of the work you have mentioned) in the State of South Carolina on the 15th of March, 1767.

The work mentioned by Jackson is Samuel Putman Waldo's Memoirs of Andrew Jackson from 1819.[18]

Despite this new piece of evidence, Congress was still unable to come to a conclusion about the birthplace. In 1929, they declared an indecision and the directory was subsequently revised to cite the possibility of either state claiming the honor, stating that Jackson was "born in such obscurity March 16, 1767 that two states have claimed his birthplace, though he himself stated that he had been told it was in the Waxhaw settlement of South Carolina."[19]

Preservation

The battle to recognize and preserve the Andrew Jackson birthplace plays out like a heavyweight fight for the undisputed championship belt of presidential birthplace bragging rights. Perhaps a dual would be a more appropriate analogy for Mr. Jackson, but since I don't know much about fencing, I'll stick with boxing!

In the first round, North Carolina came out swinging. When James Parton first kicked off the birthplace controversy and evidence began to mount that Andrew Jackson may have actually been a North Carolinian, the Mecklenburg County Chapter of the Daughters of the American Revolution quickly pounced by erecting a historic marker on the site in 1858 to bolster their claim. The current monument, built from stone from what is believed to be the original George McKemey home, was erected in 1910 by the North Carolina Daughters of the American Revolution on what is believed to be the site where the chimney once stood. The eight-foot-tall stone bears the inscription:

Here was born March 15, 1767, Andrew Jackson, Seventh President of the United States

Erected by the North Carolina D.A.R. 1910

These stones were part of the original cabin.

Soon after, a white tablet was posted at the Waxhaw, North Carolina train station to let visitors know as soon as they arrived that Andrew Jackson was one of their own.

Andrew Jackson's North Carolina birthplace marker in Union County.

The tablet read:

> Andrew Jackson, former President of the United States and general of the American forces in the War of 1812, was born six miles southwest from this station. The Jackson birthplace site has been marked and a little park has been laid off around it by the Daughters of the American Revolution.[20]

Despite the marker, many citizens of South Carolina still shared the sentiment written in the *Spartanburg Herald* on May 2, 1911, that dismissed the North Carolina claim as "founded principally on the imagination."[21] Still, North Carolina's early grab proved convincing, and by 1922, North Carolina was the accepted birthplace of our seventh president. The congressional directory listed Andrew Jackson as having been "Born at the George McKenney homestead in Mecklenberg [sic] County, N.C." The fact that Andrew Jackson himself believed he was born in South Carolina did not sway the northern state.[22]

In round two, South Carolina started to fight back to reclaim the birthplace of the seventh president. Again, it was the Daughters of the American Revolution that took up the challenge, only this time it was the Catawba Chapter, from Rock Hill, South Carolina. With the assistance of the South Carolina Archives, the site of the Crawford log cabin was located only a stone's throw from the North Carolina border. Just like baseball, birthplaces can also be a game of inches. At the time, the property was owned by T. Y. Williams, a lawyer who had served in the South Carolina House and Senate. He proudly granted permission to have the monument erected on his land, although had he not, he would have had a tough time in his next re-election campaign. To mark the site, a six-foot tall, three-ton stone from Lancaster County was used. E. B. Blakeney donated the boulder and J. J. Sassi from Rock Hill did the stonework and lettering. The marker was completed in November 1928.[23]

The unveiling ceremony was held the next year on May 24, 1929, and the local paper invited South Carolina citizens to attend if they "want to hear some REAL HISTORY."[24] T.Y. Williams was master of ceremonies and he started with an invocation by Reverend Fred T. Grier. Then the crowd sang a few patriotic songs, including "The Star Spangled Banner," and once the audience was feeling suitably patriotic, South Carolina Democratic Congressman William F. Stevenson, who seven years earlier had first raised the debate in Congress regarding Jackson's birthplace, addressed the crowd. Several other speakers followed and then J.J. Sassi and members of the Catawba Chapter of the Daughters of the American Revolution

were introduced. However, the most honored guests were Mrs. J. C. Symmes and her daughter Mrs. M. A. Candler, Andrew Jackson's great-great and great-great-great granddaughters.[25]

Finally, the crowd got to see what they came for when the white cloth was pulled off of the boulder. Included on the inscription was a reference from a letter Andrew Jackson had sent Lancaster native James H. Witherspoon in August 1824. Witherspoon had written Jackson asking him where he was born and Jackson responded:

> I was born in So Carolina, as I have been told at the plantation whereon James Crawford lived about one mile from the Carolina road X [short hand for crossing] of the Waxhaw Creek, left that state in 1784, was born on the 15 of March in the year of 1767.[26]

Badly bruised, but not yet knocked out, North Carolina answered back in round three with a few weak jabs. In 1938, the state of North Carolina erected another marker on Route 75. The language of the marker casts a wide net and can be applied to either state, stating that Jackson "was born a few miles southwest of this spot."

All judges scored round four for South Carolina. In 1951, the state of South Carolina moved to further memorialize Andrew Jackson by creating a park in Lancaster that included the birthplace marker. The state set aside $15,000 for the park and the next year $11,500 of that sum was used to purchase about 350 acres.[27] The land was purchased by Lancaster County and it was promptly turned over to the state for development and establishment as Andrew Jackson State Park in 1953. On the land was a sign directing visitors to the historic site that read:

> To Birthplace of Andrew Jackson – The place where he himself said he was born one fourth of a mile from here.[28]

The new state park in South Carolina resurrected the old debate, which in spite all of the markers erected on both sides of the border, was still unanswered. In 1961, the General Assembly of North Carolina appropriated $12,500 to answer the burning question. The next year they hired historian Max Harris to conduct the analysis.[29] After completing his research, he produced a "fat study… that concluded the evidence pointed in both directions."[30]

Over the next few years, claims would continue to be made by both states and in 1965 a proposal was made to donate the land between the two sites to the federal government to research and erect an Andrew Jackson Memorial. A target date was set for the 200th birthday on March 15, 1967. The federal government ultimately decided they would stay out of this dispute and declined the offer. That same year, the Waxhaws Chapter of the Daughters of the American Revolution sought to further bolster South Carolina's claim when they erected two identical historic markers at the entrance roads into Andrew Jackson State Park.[31]

In later years, the argument would be taken from the halls of government to the gridiron. In 1979, high school football teams from Union County, North Carolina and Lancaster, South Carolina faced off to settle the argument once and for all. On August 17, 1979, the dispute was finally settled and the winner was North Carolina by a score of 36-6.[32] An annual "Andrew Jackson Festival" was also held around this time. Somehow parades, arts, crafts, and a flea market were the new weapons of choice to determine the "bragging rights to the birthplace of Andrew Jackson."[33]

As if the football victory was not conclusive, in 1981, the North Carolina legislature again appropriated money for an exhaustive study, this time $61,050. Seven archeologists were hired to excavate the sites and the price tag eventually rose to $80,000. The next year, Christopher E. Allen published the results, reaching the same inconclusive conclusion as Max Harris had twenty years earlier for a seventh of the price.[34]

The argument continued throughout the next decade. In 1986, the post office released a series of stamps commemorating the presidents and chose to honor their birthplaces by issuing cancellation stamps from the historic locales. This was simple enough for the rest of the presidents, but not for Mr. Jackson. In the end the post office was diplomatic and issued a cancellation stamp reading "Garden of the Waxhaws, NC/SC," but ultimately sided with South Carolina by issuing it from a South Carolina zip code.[35]

In 1991, perhaps the boldest and definitely the costliest claim was made by North Carolina when a $593,000 museum and memorial was proposed on the North Carolina side of the border.[36] North Carolina's attempt to outspend South Carolina into submission was defeated the next year when explosive evidence was found. The knockout blow was delivered when a map of the North Carolina/South Carolina border from 1820 was found. Prominent North Carolina historian Wylie Neal wrote to a Florida company requesting a series of historical maps. Neal had devoted a lot of his time trying to prove Jackson was born in North Carolina, but Jackson was not on his mind when he requested the maps. Instead, he was trying to see General Charles Cornwallis' route through the Carolinas. One of the maps he received was of Lancaster County surveyed by J. Boykin in 1820 and, much to his surprise, on the South Carolina side were the words "Gen. A Jackson's Birth Place." Regarding the discovery, Neal said:

> And here I get this map looking for something else, and lo and behold there it is right in South Carolina.[37]

He knew enough that the battle was over, and in February 1992, he threw in the towel, conceding the honors to South Carolina, "until someone can show me better evidence, the dispute is over."[38]

Whether the map marks the Crawford or the McKemey cabin is not clear, but after settling the state, there doesn't seem to be any Crawfords or McKemeys left to continue this battle. From time to time, North Carolina still puts up a weak argument, but their false bravado now sounds like a fan of a last-place baseball team talking trash to a New York Yankee fan. My Dad is a proud Mets fan, so he knows what I'm talking about.

Visitor Information

While evidence seems conclusively to point to South Carolina, hedge your bets and make sure to visit both the marker in North Carolina and the state park in South Carolina. The Andrew Jackson State Park is open year round from 8 a.m. to 6 p.m., with longer 9 a.m. to 9 p.m. hours during daylight savings time. On the grounds is a small museum to learn more about the man and the region unto which he was born. In addition to visiting the birthplace, you can also go fishing, boating, camping (for $18.10 per night) or hike one of the two one-mile loops, the Crawford Trail and the Garden of the Waxhaws Trail.

8.
Martin Van Buren

Birthplace	Kinderhook, New York
President's birthday	December 5, 1782
How long in the home	14 years
Life of the home	1759 or earlier to 1926
Style	Tavern
Still in existence	No
Ultimate fate	Torn down
Commemoration	Historic marker
For more information	www.cchsny.org
Replica exists	Yes, private residence in Lake Mohawk, New Jersey
Significance	First president born in a state (the first seven were born in the colonies)
Closest birthplace	Franklin Roosevelt, 46 miles

The birthplace of Martin Van Buren in Kinderhook, New York.

Address/Directions:

46 Hudson Street
Kinderhook, New York 12106

The site is located a quarter of a mile east of the intersection with US 9.

What you will find there today:

At the birth site is a historic marker on the front lawn of a modern private home. This is not the home of President Van Buren.

The marker matter-of-factly reads:
New York
BIRTHSITE
Martin Van Buren, Eighth President of the United states, was born on this site December 5, 1782.
State Education Department

History

The Van Buren family immigrated to America from the village of Buren, Holland, in 1631. Like many Dutch at the time, they came to settle in the Hudson Valley in New York. For 150 years, the Van Burens lived on this land and Abraham Van Buren, Martin's father, made his living as many of his ancestors did, through farming. However, through the generations, the Van Buren property diminished along with the family stature. By 1782, Abraham Van Buren was a freehold farmer in the town of Kinderhook, New York, and to make extra money, he also ran a tavern in his home. This was one of the first taverns in the village and the building dated back to 1759. The building had one and a half stories, a steep roof and two front doors.[1]

In this tavern, on December 5, 1782, Abraham's wife, Maria Hoes, had a son, Martin Van Buren. The boy who would one day become perhaps the first mediocre President of the United States spent much of his youth on this farm and tavern. In addition, the home was used as the town meeting place and it was where citizens came to vote.[2] At age 14, Martin Van Buren left Kinderhook for New York City, where he embarked on a legal career as an apprentice to a local attorney, Mr. Sylvester.[3]

The house was partially torn down in the late nineteenth century. By the 1920s, the structure had become an eyesore. After local residents complained, whatever was left of the historic home was completely torn down in 1926.[4] When it was being demolished, the initials MVB were found carved into one of the beams in the cellar.

The home that currently sits at the site was built in 1956.[5]

Preservation

Perhaps overshadowed by the Lindenwald estate, the home where Martin Van Buren spent his final years also in Kinderhook, there has been little recognition for the birthplace of the eighth president. For over 130 years after his presidency, the location was unmarked. Finally, sometime after 1974, an undated marker was erected by the New York State Education Department.

While the original may not have been shown much respect, a replica of the birth home was built in Lake Mohawk, New Jersey, in 1939. The house was part of a series of historical replicas created by the Arthur D. Crane Company; however, this was not a museum for Martin Van Buren, but rather part of a new development of residential homes. Years earlier, in 1926, the same company had built Lake Mohawk by damming a beautiful mountain valley in Sparta, New Jersey. The company had a flair for the historical and created a replica of Powder Horn Green from Williamsburg, Virginia. Around the green, they built replicas of historic homes. For the Van Buren home, the architect Robert T. Crane used photographs and other historical records to make the recreation as authentic as possible. The home boasted all of the modern amenities for summer occupancy near the shores of Upper Lake Mohawk. In the summer of 1939, two women from Brooklyn, New York, Miss Cora M. Florence and Miss Eleanor A. Thomson, purchased the home.[6] Today, the Powder Horn Green is still a pleasant neighborhood. While there is no marker at the Van Buren replica, there is an island in the middle of the cul-de-sac that features an American flag and at the base is a marker that reads:

Daughters of the American Revolution. Dedicated by N.J. State Society June 15, 1935.

Visitor Information

I scored the Martin Van Buren hat trick by also visiting the Martin Van Buren National Historic Site and nearby gravesite when I dragged, or should I say, was "willingly accompanied" by my wife and sons, Vincent and Leonardo, in the summer of 2008. At the National Historic Site is the president's thirty-six-room mansion dubbed Lindenwald, the home to which he retired after his presidency and the best source of Martin Van Buren information in Kinderhook. The mansion and Visitor Center are seasonal, so make sure you check the National Park Service website for the visiting hours before you go. Less that a mile from the birthplace you can also see Van Buren's final resting place. He lies in a gravesite marked by an obelisk in the Reformed Church Cemetery. Just follow Hudson Street north and the cemetery is on the right. When visiting the site of the birth home, please remember the home at the site is not the original. What is there now is a private residence and you should respect the privacy of the current owners.

9.
William Henry Harrison

Berkeley Plantation, birthplace of William Henry Harrison, in Charles City County, Virginia.

Vital Birthplace Information

Birthplace	Charles City County, Virginia
Name	Harrison's Landing, Berkeley Plantation
President's birthday	February 9, 1773
How long in the home	17 years
Life of the home	1726 to present
Style	Georgian mansion
Still in existence	Yes
Commemoration	Berkeley Plantation
Open to the public	Yes
Cost	Adults $11.00, children ages 6-12 are $6.00
For more information	www.berkeleyplantation.com
Replica exists	No
Significance	Visited by more United States presidents than any other birthplace (13)
Closest birthplace	John Tyler, 7 miles

Address/Directions:

12602 Harrison Landing Road
Charles City, Virginia 23030

Located halfway between Richmond and Williamsburg off Route 5 in Charles City, Virginia.

What you will find there today:

The historic Berkeley Plantation is located on about 1,000 acres, 450 of which are used as a working plantation. William Henry Harrison was perhaps the least significant president, if due to nothing else than serving less than any other Commander in Chief. But despite this distinction, the home he was born in perhaps saw more history than any other presidential birthplace. From the original settlers to the founding fathers and the Revolutionary War to the Civil War, Berkeley Plantation was at the center of many of the major historical events that have shaped this nation. When the home was designated a National Historic Landmark it was listed as "Berkeley – Benjamin Harrison V Birthplace." The birthplace of a president was not even enough to get top billing in this home, taking a backseat to his father and signer of the Declaration of Independence. In actuality, being the birthplace of William Henry Harrison is not even the second or third most important event that happened here, since it is eclipsed by the first Thanksgiving and its Civil War significance.

In front of the house is a historic marker that was erected in 1928 by the Conservation Development Commission that reads:

NO 7V BERKELEY AND HARRISON'S LANDING
A short distance south. The place was first settled in 1619 but was abandoned. It was repatented in 1636. Benjamin Harrison, signer of the declaration of independence, lived here. His Son, William Henry Harrison, President of the United States, was born here, 1773. In July-August 1862, General McClellan had his head-quarters at Berkeley while the Army of the Potomac was here.

Look closely at the date on the back of the marker; instead of 1928, it reads 1298.

History

The history of the William Henry Harrison birthplace began thousands of miles away in England in the early years of colonizing North America. At the beginning of the 1600s, the New World was being settled by businesses across the Atlantic. One such interest was the London Company, which, in 1607, established Jamestown, the first permanent settlement in America. Twelve years later, on February 3, 1619, another parcel of land was granted by the London Company to five partners, Sir William Throckmorton, Sir George Yeardley, George Thorpe, John Smith, and Richard Berkeley. The land grant consisted of 8,000 acres on the banks of the James River that was to be known as the "Berkeley Hundred."[1]

Prior to the arrival of the colonists, the Powhatan Confederacy, a group of American Indians united under Chief Opechancanough, occupied the land on the banks of the James River. As the settlers continued to arrive, the Powhatan Confederacy was pushed up north towards the Potomac River. At the beginning of October in that same year, the Good Ship Margaret set sail from Bristol, England. The ship's Captain was John Woodlief and along with him were thirty-seven colonists setting out to establish the Berkeley Hundred settlement. After the two and a half month journey, the ship landed at Jamestown, Virginia, on December 4, 1619. Upon disembarking, Woodlief pulled out the company charter and read aloud:

IMPR Wee Ordane that the day of our ships arrival at the place assigned for plantacon in the land of Virginia shall be yearly and perpetually kept holy as a day of thanksgiving to Almighty God.[2]

Luckily for the crew, Captain John Woodlief was better at sailing than he was at spelling!

The group soon left Jamestown to venture into the Virginia wilderness to settle "The Town and Hundred of Berkeley."[3] Upon arrival, they began to establish their community by constructing a storehouse and assembly hall. On the first anniversary of the ship's landing, December 4, 1620, the people of Berkeley kept their word and celebrated their "thanksgiving to Almighty God." Thus, a year before the pilgrims landed on Plymouth Rock, the first Thanksgiving was celebrated, not in Massachusetts, but in Virginia at Berkeley Plantation.[4] The debate still continues to this day.

George Thorpe, one of the original partners, arrived at Berkeley the following year to relieve Captain John Woodlief who was managing the settlement.[5] These first months were rough and several settlers did not make it. In an attempt to curb the high mortality rate, Thorpe developed a medication to improve the colonists' health. He brewed a corn and maize concoction and prescribed two servings daily and the treatment proved effective. This gives Berkeley another historical first, distiller of the country's first bourbon whiskey.[6]

The settlement prospered and soon grew to ninety people; however, all was not well at Berkley. The Powhatan Confederacy was growing angry as the settlers continued to encroach upon their land. On March 22, 1622, this anger culminated with a coordinated attack throughout the Virginia Colony led by Chief Opechancanough. When the dust settled on this Indian massacre, nine of the Berkeley settlers, or ten percent, were dead. Soon after this attack, Berkeley Plantation was abandoned.[7] This also marked the end of the short-lived Berkeley Thanksgiving tradition, which is why Massachusetts residents were able to claim it as their own.

Berkeley Plantation remained deserted for fourteen years. In 1636, the land was purchased and re-patented by seven London merchants: Captain William Tucker, William Harris, Maurice Thompson, George Thompson, Thomas Deacon, Cornelius Boyd, and Jeremiah Blackburn. After several years, ownership of the plantation passed to John Bland, also a merchant from London. Bland lived at Berkeley with his son, Giles, who gained notoriety for his role in the 1676 uprising known as "Bacon's Rebellion" to protest the friendly policy towards the Native Americas. For his participation, Giles was hanged for his crimes. After the punishment, the Colonial Governor of Virginia, Sir William Berkeley, confiscated the plantation.[8]

Fifteen years after Bacon's Rebellion, in 1691, Benjamin Harrison III purchased Berkeley Plantation. The Harrisons were one of the first families of Virginia, settling in the colony in 1630. He renamed the property "Harrison's Landing," a name that would stick until after the Civil War.[9] In 1726, his son, Benjamin Harrison IV, built the original mansion that still stands today. The home was constructed in the Georgian style and over the door was placed a stone with the date of 1726 and the initials of Benjamin and his wife, Anna. This home is now believed to be the oldest three-story brick house in Virginia and the first with a pediment roof.[10]

On December 13, 1730, the Harrisons had a son, Benjamin V, who would go on to serve as a Virginia delegate to the Continental Congress from 1774 through 1777. However his most notable achievement occurred in 1776 when he was one of the original fifty-six men to sign the Declaration of Independence. After the war, he served three terms as Governor of Virginia. Due to his accomplishments, the National Historic Register lists the property as the "Benjamin Harrison V Birthplace," implying that his birth was the most notable event to occur in the home. I respectfully disagree. In my estimation, the most notable event occurred on February 9, 1773, when William Henry Harrison was born in Berkeley Mansion. William Henry would one day serve his country, albeit briefly, as the ninth President of the United States.[11]

In 1781, in the waning days of the Revolutionary War, turncoat Benedict Arnold stormed the plantation in search of Benjamin Harrison V. By signing the Declaration of Independence, Harrison had committed treason against the British and Arnold was out to capture him for his crime. The Harrisons, including young William Henry, fled for their lives. Finding the home vacated, Arnold instead plundered the plantation and burned the family portraits on the front lawn. Once the coast was clear, the Harrisons returned and William Henry Harrison continued to live in the home until leaving for Philadelphia, Pennsylvania, to study medicine in 1790. The next year, Benjamin V died and left the home to William's older brother, Benjamin VI. He renovated the home in the Adam style and added small interior stairs around 1800.[12]

In 1840, when he ran for the President of the United States, William Henry Harrison set several campaign firsts. Interestingly enough, he was the first to actually campaign on his own behalf. Before him, stumping for the job was considered beneath the dignity of the office. Another groundbreaking first was the campaign slogan when the now infamous "Tippecanoe and Tyler too" broke the ice for catchy campaign phrases. However, his most significant contribution as far as presidential birthplaces are concerned was that William Henry Harrison was the first candidate to downplay his regal origins, a practice that would be frequently copied over the next hundred years or so. Harrison was the first man born from wealth since Andrew Jackson paved the way to the presidency for those of humble roots and he really had to stretch to portray himself as a rags-to-riches success. To do this, he created the myth of the William Henry Harrison log cabin. He distributed handkerchiefs emblazoned with a picture of a log cabin and also placed hundreds of log cabins around the country, implying they were replicas of his birthplace.[13] To further impress visitors as well as woo votes, live raccoons were placed on the roof and hard cider was served inside.[14] His "log cabin and hard cider" campaign proved effective as he defeated Martin Van Buren's reelection bid to be elected the ninth president of this great nation.

In 1841, after winning the election, William Henry Harrison visited the plantation and sat in his boyhood room to write his inaugural address. He must have spent plenty of time in the room, because his address was the longest in history, clocking in at 105 minutes. At almost seventy, Harrison wanted to show the audience that he had the stamina to be president. That may explain the long speech, but why he delivered it without a coat on a freezing winter day is anybody's guess. Harrison fell sick from the ordeal, and weeks later he earned the dubious distinction of being the first president to die in office. The next year in 1842, the Harrisons relinquished their beloved plantation after succumbing to financial problems.[15]

During the early stages of the Civil War, in 1862, the plantation served as a supply base and camp for the Union Army of the Potomac after their retreat from the Battle of Malvern Hill. On July 3, 1862, General George McClellan began to move his Union soldiers onto Harrison's Landing. The soldiers camped out on the sprawling plantation and the general moved into the mansion, which served as his home and headquarters.[16] Twice Abraham Lincoln visited the home to meet with his general. During the time McClellan was stationed at Berkeley Plantation, another historic event occurred. With the aid of his bugler, Oliver Willcox Norton, Brigadier General Daniel Butterfield, commander of the Third New York Brigade, wrote the simple "Taps" to mark the end of a day. From across the James River, confederate soldiers heard the haunting melody and started using the tune to honor their fallen soldiers, a military tradition that continues to this day.[17] During these weeks, the birthplace home was also used as a Union hospital. On August 16, after six weeks on the plantation, the Union soldiers left the plantation to join with General John Pope's army in Northeastern Virginia.[18]

One of the soldiers encamped at Berkeley that summer of 1862 was a 12-year-old Scotsman drummer boy named John Jamieson. Forty-five years later, in 1907, he would return after purchasing the home and 14,000 acres at a bank auction in New York City for $24,000. By that time, the once-stately manor and the rest of the buildings on the plantation had fallen apart and farm animals roamed freely throughout the historic mansion. Jamieson did not do much to help the state of the buildings, and by 1915, the home was again in disrepair. In 1927, upon John's death, his son, Malcolm Jamieson, inherited the plantation, including William Henry Harrison's birth home.[19]

Preservation

On October 25, 1913, six years after John Jamieson purchased Berkeley Plantation, the Virginia Society of the Colonial Dames first recognized the home when they placed a marker at the birth site. Mortimer Harrison, great grandson of the ninth president, made an address at the unveiling ceremony.[20]

When Malcolm Jamieson inherited the estate in 1927, the home was in shambles. Reflecting back years later, he said simply, the home was "horrible looking."[21] The once-stately mansion was "painted barnyard red, infested with rats and other vermin, and reeking of the manure piled knee-deep in the basement."[22] However, when he first arrived at Berkeley Plantation in 1929 from New Jersey, he was able to look past the sordid state to recognize the historic value of the plantation home. Malcolm immediately began to restore it. He spent all winter scrubbing the red paint off the home. Four years later, he gained a partner and a wife when he married Grace Eggelston. The couple divided up the work, Grace toiling on the inside and Malcolm focusing on the outside. After completing the restorations, the home was opened to visitors in 1938.[23]

In 1954 a historic sign was erected that read:

V-7 BERKELEY PLANTATION OR HARRISON'S LANDING: A short distance south, it was first settled in 1619, when the first Thanksgiving was held here. The present mansion, built in 1726, was the birthplace of Benjamin Harrison, signer of the Declaration of Independence, and President William Henry Harrison. During July and August 1862, it was the headquarters of General McClellan. The bugle call "Taps" was composed here then by General Butterfield.

Another monument was dedicated in June 1969 solely to commemorate the site where "Taps" was first played. This monument was donated by the Virginia Department of the American Legion.[24] On November 11, 1971 the site was designated a National Historic Landmark (National Register Number #71001040).

Berkeley has always attracted presidents including the first ten who all dined there. William Henry Harrison's grandson, Benjamin Harrison, and our twenty-third president was not born in Berkeley; however, he visited the plantation once. But as the Black Sheep Republican in the family, he was apparently not welcomed with open arms.[25] In more recent times, it has been used to deliver campaign speeches. On November 6, 1988, Dan Quayle visited while stumping with George Herbert Walker Bush, and on November 20, 2007, President George Walker Bush spoke to about 500 people to call on Americans to perform more community service.[26] Berkeley Plantation has been host to thirteen American presidents (including Abraham Lincoln), more than any other presidential birthplaces.

On President's Day, February 16, 2009, a ceremony was held by the U.S. Mint at the mansion to commemorate the minting of the William Henry Harrison dollar coin, the ninth in the series of presidential dollar coins.[27] Today, the home is still owned by the Jamieson family (Malcolm and his wife passed in 1998 and 2000 respectively). They receive no federal or state subsidies and are supported through visitor's admission, events on the grounds, and 500 acres of land that is used by farmers.[28]

Visitor Information

Berkeley Plantation is open year round every day from 9:30 a.m. to 4:30 p.m. with shorter hours from January through mid-March (10:30 a.m. to 3:30 p.m.). The only way to see the home is with a guided tour, which lasts about an hour and starts with a film shown in the basement that gives an excellent overview of all of the historical highlights of the home. After visiting the home, make sure to leave yourself plenty of time to wander around the historic plantation grounds.

10.
John Tyler

"Greenway", the home in which John Tyler was born in Charles City County, Virginia.

Birthplace	Charles City County, Virginia
Name	Greenway, Marlie
President's birthday	March 29, 1790
How long in the home	31 years total: 23 years from 1790 to 1813 and 8 years from 1821 to 1829
Life of the home	Approximately 1776 to present
Style	Plantation home
Still in existence	Yes
Commemoration	Historic marker
Open to the public	No
For more information	www.charlescity.org
Replica exists	No
Significance	Earliest presidential birthplace still being used as a private residence
Closest birthplace	William Henry Harrison, 7 miles

What you will find there today:

John Tyler's birthplace is currently a private residence and not open to visitors. In front of the home is a roadside historic marker that reads:

No. 10-V GREENWAY
This was the home of John Tyler, Governor of Virginia, 1808-1811. His Son, John Tyler, President of the United States, was born here March 29, 1790.

As with his neighbor, William Henry Harrison, the Conservation Development Commission erected Tyler's marker in 1928 and President John Tyler also receives second billing to his father.

Address/Directions:

**John Tyler Memorial Highway
(Virginia Route 5)
Charles City, Virginia 23030**

The John Tyler birthplace is seven miles east of the William Henry Harrison birthplace on the north side of Virginia Route 5.

History

John Tyler was born on a Virginia plantation a mile north of the James River. Amazingly, Tyler was born only seven miles away and off the same road as his predecessor, William Henry Harrison, illustrating what an exclusive club the early presidents belonged to. Imagine you and your neighbor some day becoming back-to-back presidents!

The plantation home where John Tyler was born "was a comfortable, well-finished genteel residence of six rooms."[1] The home stood one and a half stories and was built in the Williamsburg style, traditional for the day and unremarkable except for its historic occupants. Behind the home were several buildings that created a courtyard effect. It was built circa 1776 by John Tyler Sr. who served in the Continental Army and later as governor of Virginia. His plantation was originally known as "Marlie" and the story goes that John's youngest sister, Anne, who was born in 1778, insisted on calling the home "Greenway" after the plush green surroundings, and the new name stuck.[2] Fourteen years after the home was built, on March 29, 1790, the Tylers had a son, John, who would one day become the tenth President of the United States.

In 1802, John Tyler began to study at the College of William and Mary in Williamsburg and by 1805 his brother, Wat Tyler, joined him at the school. John Tyler Sr. wanted to be able to comfortably pay for his children's education and may have also wanted to be closer to his sons. The school was only about twenty-five miles east on Route 5, but in 1802, that was a much longer journey than it is today. One major asset Tyler Sr. had was his land holdings, so in 1805, he decided to part with them to help make ends meet. The notice to sell Greenway appeared in the *Richmond Enquirer* on September 15, 1805, under the heading "For Sale on Private Contract" and it gives a clear picture of the home where John Tyler grew up:

> **Greenway contains five hundred acres, well improved. On it is a genteel, well-furnished dwelling-house, containing six rooms, all wainscoted, chair-board high, with fine dry cellars the full length of the house, which is 56 feet; also every other building which a reasonable person could wish or desire, to wit: a handsome study, storehouse, kitchen, laundry, dairy, meat-house, spring-house, and an ice-house within the curtilage; a barn 40 by 34 feet, two granaries, two carriage houses, 20 stalls for horses, a quarter for house servants; a handsome pigeon-house, well stocked; and several other houses for slaves; a well of water (so excellent that I can drink with delight after returning from a mountain circuit), a large, fertile garden, abounding with a great variety of shrubs, herbs, and beautiful flowers, well enclosed. The buildings new and well covered with shingles.[3]**

In addition to Greenway, John Tyler Sr. also put two other plantations, Mons Sacre and Utopia, up for sale. As an incentive to sell them all, Tyler offered to throw in "thirty or forty slaves and stocks of every kind" as a package deal if someone would buy all three.[4] Tyler went on to give more information than was probably necessary:

> **It may now be enquired, why I should, in an advanced stage of life part with an estate so convenient and agreeable in all**

> **respects. In the first place, in a little time I shall be compelled by the unerring voice of nature to "quit this mortal coil," and it is right I should so adjust all my matters as to leave nothing for litigation after my death. My years of regret will be, therefore, but few on that score. And lastly I am desirous of obtaining a situation more convenient and cheap for the education of my sons, which the savings from a narrow, parsimonious salary, and the profits arising from a much neglected estate, in consequence of my attention to public duties, can never support.[5]**

Despite pouring out his soul, the sale did not happen and John Tyler Sr. would keep Greenway for the rest of his life. In 1808, John Tyler Sr. became governor of Virginia and must have had many of Virginia's most distinguished citizens visit Greenway. One such recorded visit was from Thomas Jefferson.[6]

In 1813, John Tyler's father passed away and the future president married Letitia Christian. John's oldest brother, Wat Tyler, inherited Greenway; however, he did not want to keep the plantation, nor did the newlyweds want to live there. The Tyler's sold the home to William Douglas.[7] In the fall of 1821, John and Letitia had a change of heart about Greenway. By this time, the home was owned by John Minge, and he agreed to sell John Tyler his birthplace home for $7,000.[8] For eight years, John Tyler lived there, during which time he served as governor of Virginia. In 1829, he sold the Greenway estate for good to move several miles away to Sherwood Forrest, the home he would keep for the rest of his life.[9] This home is about three miles east on Route 5 and privately owned by descendents of President Tyler. The grounds are open to visitors and the home available for tours.

In May 1932, Greenway was once again in the hands of the Tyler family, when Dr. Lyon Gardiner Tyler, son of the former president, purchased both Greenway as well as another of his ancestor's estates, Mons Sacre, at public auction for $25,050.[10] Lyon was born at Sherwood Forrest and went on to be a successful author and president of The College of William and Mary. In case you are thinking that the numbers don't add up for a man born in 1790 to have a son alive in 1932, consider that John Tyler had a presidential record fifteen children with two wives. Lyon was number thirteen and was born in 1853, when the president was sixty-three years old. He would go on to sire two more children, the last at the age of seventy.

Lyon Tyler did not last long at the estate and after about a year and a half, the home was again put up for auction on Monday October 15, 1933. This time a lumberman, F.H. Avery, purchased the home and 725.7 acres along with another plantation (Gunna, 390.33 acres) for $26,500. He estimated the property would yield 3,000,000 feet of cordwood and railroad ties.[11]

By 1969, the home was again a private residence owned by Cyrus Beale. Ten years later, the listed owner, Betsy Beale Gunter, was struggling to pay her taxes on the sprawling 1,200-acre estate, so she put Greenway up for sale for $1,300,000.[12] She used Stevens and Company from Chancelorville, Virginia to handle the real estate transaction. The estate was sold on September 21, 1979 to a West German (before the fall of the Berlin Wall) family partnership, Heinrich Harling, K.G. from Eversen. The Harlings were international timber magnates with interests in North and South America and Europe and they purchased the historical landmark for $1,006,000, considerably less than the asking price.[13] Amazingly, the same realtor also handled the sale of the Zachary Taylor birthplace Montebello on the same day! Another coincidence is that Montebello was also sold to Europeans (investors from England).[14] Two foreigners buying National Landmarks is perhaps a sign that the late seventies were not the high point of American landmark preservation history.

Today, the home is still standing and is privately owned. This is significant in that John Tyler is the first president whose birthplace is still a private residence and not opened to the public. The next presidential birthplace with the same circumstances is the home in which George Herbert Walker Bush was born, 134 years after John Tyler.

Preservation

On October 27, 1913, the Society of the Colonial Dames in Virginia placed a marker at the birth site of John Tyler. Judge George L. Christian of Richmond, a descendent of John Tyler's wife Letitia Christian, made an address at the unveiling ceremony.[15] Christian said the Dames came "to this sacred spot, and placed here a memorial to commemorate the deeds and virtues of this truly great, and good Virginian; one who climbed to the top-most round of the ladder of fame in America, and who won every step of that ascent by his genius, his manly virtues and his steadfast fidelity and devotion to truth, to principle and to duty."[16]

In 1928, the Virginia Conservation and Development Commission erected the current marker. In 1969, the birthplace received two important recognitions: On September 9, the estate was placed on the Virginia Landmarks Register (File # 018-001), and just two months later, on November 17, it was added to the National Register of Historic Places (National Register Number #69000336).[17]

The "Greenway" birthplace marker in front of the home where John Tyler was born in Charles City County, Virginia.

Visitor Information

Please remember the John Tyler birth home is a private residence, so you should respect the privacy of its owners. While the John Tyler home is not open to visitors, Sherwood Forrest, where the president spent his final years, is nearby and available for tours. The drive along the John Tyler Memorial Highway (Virginia Route 5) is a pleasant one that takes you through an important swath of American history. I visited in 2010 after leaving Berkeley Plantation along with my Mom, Dad, son, Vincent, and my fifteen year old niece, Maggie. Despite being at the birthplace of the man who signed into law the annexation of Texas, only my father and I were impressed enough to get out of the car while the rest of our group opted to enjoy the ambiance from the comfort of the minivan.

11.
James Knox Polk

The monument erected by the Mecklenburg Chapter of the Daughters of the American Revolution in 1904 at the birth site of James K. Polk in Pineville, North Carolina.

Vital Birthplace Information

Birthplace	Pineville, North Carolina
President's birthday	November 2, 1795
How long in the home	11 years
Life of the home	Before 1795 to approximately 1920
Style	Log cabin
Still in existence	No
Ultimate fate	Torn down
Commemoration	President James K. Polk State Historic Site
Open to the public	Yes
Cost	Free
For more information	www.nchistoricsites.org/polk/polk.htm
Replica exists	Yes
Significance	First president undisputedly born in North Carolina
Closest birthplace	Andrew Jackson, 22 miles

Address/Directions:

**12031 Lancaster Highway
Pineville, North Carolina 28134**

The James K. Polk Birthplace is located at the corner of Polk Street and Main Street in Pineville, North Carolina.

What you will find there today:

The President James K. Polk State Historic Site showcases a reconstructed home built on the original location where James K. Polk was born when his parents worked the 150-acre farm. Today, the twenty-one acre site includes a visitor center that features a film and commemorates the man and his presidency, and a museum. In addition to the birth home, the State Historic Site features authentic reconstructions of a stand-alone kitchen and barn. Also on the site is a stone monument erected by, you guessed it, the Daughters of the American Revolution in 1904. The monument reads:

HERE STOOD THE HOUSE IN WHICH WAS BORN NOVEMBER 2, 1795 JAMES KNOX POLK
President of the United States 1845-1849
Erected by the Mecklenburg Chapter of the Daughters of the American Revolution 1904.

At the entrance to the park is another historic marker that reads:
L 78 James K. Polk 1795 – 1849 Eleventh President of U.S. born nearby in a house no longer standing. Land & reconstructed buildings now a State Historic Site.

The Division of Archives and History erected this marker in 1990.

History

The original inhabitants of the area of Mecklenburg County, North Carolina were the Catawba Indians. In the 1760s, European settlers first came to the region, mostly from Northern Ireland. The town was later renamed Pineville in the 1850s due to the large pine trees that shadowed the area. One of the first inhabitants of the area was Thomas Polk who was soon followed by his brother Ezekiel, who would become the grandfather to our eleventh president. Ezekiel's son, Samuel, married Jane Knox on Christmas Day in 1794, and as a wedding gift, Ezekiel gave the young couple a 150-acre farm in Mecklenburg County, North Carolina. Most likely, Samuel Polk, with the help of his relatives, built a log cabin on his property where he lived with his bride. The cabin was a large two-story home. Upstairs was a loft and downstairs was split into two rooms with three doors to create a cross breeze.[1]

It was in this home, on November 2, 1795, that James Knox Polk, the first of ten Polk children and future President of the United States, was born. At about the time the Polks started having children, they added onto the home to accommodate the expanding family, quickly filling up the space as they went on to have four more children in the log cabin. Over the years, they also expanded their farm from 150 to 426 acres, which was used primarily to grow cotton. During the years, the Polks lived in Mecklenburg County; Sam was active in civic life, serving as militia captain and road caretaker. Sam owned four slaves so he had a vested interest as a member of the slave patrol.[2]

Eleven years after James's birth, the family left North Carolina in 1806 to head for the Duck River Valley in Tennessee and James K. Polk never returned to the site where he was born. Three years after leaving Mecklenburg County, in 1809, Samuel sold the homestead to his neighbor, David Morrow for a good price of about $2,500. The home, and all or part of the property, changed hands several times over the years. In 1812, the Thomas and Andrew Spratt purchased the homestead. They held the deed for nine years until selling to William Cook in 1821.[3]

In 1849, the home was purchased by Nathan Orr and was in a bad state of deterioration. In 1851, part of the home was moved to the barnyard to use as shelter for the farm animals. Throughout the remainder of the nineteenth century, the home was owned by several people as it continued to deteriorate. In 1859, Orr sold the homestead to James Hennigan for $2,000. The home again changed hands when it was sold to S. Younts in 1876 and A. Rhyne in 1892.[4]

By 1900, not much more than the foundation still remained, and around 1920, whatever was still left of the home was torn down.[5] The last private owner of the property was John S. Miller, who purchased the home around 1903. By the time he sold the land in 1964, he owned twenty-one acres that included the birthplace site.[6]

Preservation

The birthplace was first recognized in 1904 when the Daughters of the American Revolution paid nearly $100 to erect a fifteen-foot rubble stone pyramid at the site of the birth home.[7] Two historians, J.B. Alexander and Captain W.E. Ardrey, presided over the unveiling ceremony on September 26, 1904, before a crowd of 400 people. The speakers praised their hometown hero with quotes like :

Here upon this spot was born one of the great men of earth. He came of a great race of people. They were diamonds unpolished, but diamonds of "the first water."[8]

At the time, the property was still actively used as farmland.

On January 10, 1936 the North Carolina Highway Historic Marker Program started and one of the first markers, numbered L1-1, was placed at the Polk Birthplace. This marker was later replaced in 1956, and again in 1990 with the one that still stands today. In the middle of the 1950s, James Stenhouse, an architect from Charlotte, North Carolina, started a "one-man campaign" to create a more appropriate memorial for the eleventh president.[9] In 1957, Stenhouse, along with the Mecklenburg County Historical Association and the State Department of Archives and History began efforts to purchase the home site. They received support in 1963 when a bill was introduced in the North Carolina State legislature approved a bill to allocate $67,000 to restore the James K. Polk birthplace.[10] The next year, in 1964, the state of North Carolina used part of those funds to purchase the land from John S. Miller for $28,775 to create the President James K. Polk State Historic Site. The state received permission from the Mecklenburg Chapter of the Daughters of the American Revolution to relocate the monument to make room for a historic reproduction of the birthplace on the original site.

In 1966, construction started on the birthplace replica, using materials from a cabin from the same period that was located about three miles away on Providence Road. Thanks to Governor David Lowry Swain, who attended school with Polk's younger brother Marshall Tate, there is an account of what the original cabin looked like. In 1849, he made a drawing of the home; however, this was forty-three years after the Polks lived in the home so its accuracy is debatable.[11] In 1867 Swain gave a speech that provided additional direction used in the reconstruction, in which he said,

The re-created birth home of James K. Polk in Pineville, North Carolina.

The house pointed out to me was of logs, had never been weather-boarded, and was much dilapidated. It was formed by two pens, one about 20 by 16. The other about 12 by 16, making a structure 32 by 16, with a single roof and brick chimney at the north end, and stood about 200 yards south of Little Sugar Creek.[12]

After two years of construction, the restored two-bedroom crude log cabin birthplace was completed in 1968. The home was officially dedicated in a ceremony held on May 20, 1968. In attendance was the mayor of Pineville, C.H. McCoy, the North Carolina governor Dan Morroe and the first lady of the United States, Lady Bird Johnson. About 3,500 people were in the audience to hear Mrs. Johnson speak of the familiar theme of rising from humble beginnings to become President of the United States. After her speech she was presented with a key to city. Mayor McCoy said that this was the first time the key to the city has been given out in the ninety-six years that Pineville had been incorporated and then jokingly added that it was the only key in town.[13]

In a separate ceremony on December 6, 1968, sixty-four years after the initial dedication ceremonies, the monument and new visitor center were rededicated. The main speaker that day was Professor Hugh T. Lefler from University of North Carolina-Chapel Hill and the South Mecklenburg High School Band entertained the crowd.[14]

Visitor Information

Each year, about 13,000 people visit President Polk's birthplace and the site also plays host to the occasional wedding. The park is open Tuesdays through Saturdays from 9 a.m. to 5 p.m.. On Sundays and Mondays, the park is closed. Admission is free; however, donations to help maintain the site are welcome. When I visited in July 2011, our guide, Robert, gave a very informative tour of the birth home and detached kitchen. There are frequent special events at the President James K. Polk State Historic Site so make sure to check the calendar on the park's website before you go.

12.
Zachary Taylor

Vital Birthplace Information

Birthplace	Barboursville, Virginia
Name	Montebello
President's birthday	November 24, 1784
How long in the home	6 weeks
Life of the home	Before 1874 to unknown
Style	Plantation guesthouse
Still in existence	No
Ultimate fate	Lost to time
Commemoration	Historic marker
For more information	www.orangecovahist.org
Replica exists	No
Significance	Last president born in an unexpected location (the only other is Andrew Jackson)
Closest birthplace	Thomas Jefferson, 13 miles

The birthplace of Zachary Taylor in Barboursville, Virginia. *Courtesy of Joseph F. Picone*

Address/Directions:

Highway 33 and Old Montebello Drive
Barboursville, Virginia 22942

Montebello is about two miles east of the intersection with Route 20.

What you will find there today:

At the birthplace location is a historic marker erected in 1929 that reads:

D 20 MONTEBELLO
Here was born Zachary Taylor, twelfth President of the United States, November 24, 1784. Taylor, commanding an American army, won the notable battle of Buena Vista in Mexico, 1847.

When I visited in March 2010, the sign was nowhere to be found. I later discovered that it was removed for construction.

History

In 1784, Colonel Richard Taylor and his wife, Sarah Dabney Taylor, sold their home in Hare Forest near Culpepper, Virginia. Expecting their third child, the Taylors set out with their slaves to find a new home for the growing family. At the end of their first day on the road, they stopped for the night at the home of Sarah's stepmother's sister, Valentine Johnson, and her husband, William. The Johnson family lived on a plantation called Montebello in Orange County, Virginia, and the Taylors stayed in a small log guesthouse. During the night, someone from the Taylor party became very sick with the measles. They had only planned on staying one night, but ended up quarantined in the home for six weeks. During that time, on November 24, 1784, Sarah gave birth to the future hero of the Mexican War and president, Zachary Taylor.[1] Zachary Taylor was born with the presidency in his blood, being that his second cousin, James Madison, also held the highest office.

Colonel Taylor soon left his family to journey on ahead with his slaves to establish a new home in Springfield, Kentucky. Finally, the rest of the family, including baby Zachary, also left Montebello.[2] There are two additional sites within Orange County, Virginia, that have also claimed to be the birth site, Hare Forest and Bloomingdale; but Montebello is widely accepted as the true nativity scene.

Over the years, the property changed hands several times. In 1934, the owner of Montebello was Leslie B. Gray, a lawyer from New York City and a descendent of Zachary Taylor.[3] In 1947, Mr. and Mrs. J. Barbour Rixey purchased the estate.[4] They remained the owners for over thirty years until September 21, 1979, when they sold the 273-acre property for about $425,000 to Geoffrey Wollard and his wife and two teenage children. Wollard, an English farmer, also owned 660 acres in Cambridgeshire, England, and spent about a month each year in Virginia. Two years after purchasing the home, he spoke of how much he enjoyed his American home:

We love this place so much, when we are in England, we think of this.[5]

Taylor's birthplace was sold on the same day as the John Tyler birthplace, Greenway, by the same realtor, Stevens and Company from Chancelorville, Virginia.[6] There is uncertainty regarding the actual home in which President Taylor was born, since there were several guest cabins on the property at the time. Perhaps due to being an obscure president in the state better known as the birthplace of Washington, Jefferson, and Madison, not much effort has been made to solve it. In the 1970s, there was a guesthouse on the property and newspapers wrote in no certain terms that the home was "considered to be the birthplace of Zachary Taylor"[7] and also called it "the house where Zachary Taylor is said to have been born."[8] It is also possible that the home no longer exists and the exact location is unknown. On the property, there are the remains of a brick chimney that may, or may not, be from the birthplace cabin.[9]

Preservation

The first recognition of the birthplace of Zachary Taylor, albeit the wrong one, took place at the start of the twentieth century when, on July 10, 1900, the Montpelier Chapter of the Daughters of the Revolution unveiled a bronze tablet affixed to large rock at Hare Forest. A large crowd attended the ceremony presided over by Mr. John G. Williams. After singing "America," a prayer was offered by Revered P.L.B. Cross. Next, Revered Charles J. Hill delivered an address about the life and character of the twelfth president. The ceremony climaxed when Zachary Taylor's granddaughter, Miss Sarah Wood of Winchester, Virginia, pulled the veil to reveal the marker. Amid thunderous applause, the crowd got their first look at the marker which simply read:

On this site Zachary Taylor President of the United States was born Nov 24, 1784.

The crowd sung "The Star Spangled Banner" to conclude the formal ceremony, which was followed by a "delightful basket picnic in a pleasant grove near by".[10] While Hare Forest has been widely ruled out as a candidate for the birthplace honor, the marker remains.

In 1929, the Virginia Conservation and Development Commission erected the historic marker on US 33 East in front of Montebello, which still stands today.

Visitor Information

In March of 2010, I set out to visit Montebello. Together with my traveling companions; we entered Barboursville in the early evening and anticipated a quick visit to stop by the historic marker. The road weary crew was in good spirits, but the mood slowly soured as we spent more than an hour driving up and down US 33 trying to locate the exact birthplace location. Finally, I put my ego in the glove compartment and stopped in nearby Gordonsville for help. The gentleman I approached was friendly and eager to assist, but when I asked him if he knew where Zachary Taylor was born, he politely misinformed me that Taylor was born in Tennessee, but James Madison was born up the road! The site he was referring to was James Madison's home, Montpelier, which was not his birthplace, but his well-intended mistake does illustrate how locals are not exactly brimming with pride over their famous son. Even the Orange County website makes no mention of the Presidential Birthplace. After I returned home, I called the Virginia Department of Historic Markers and found out that the sign had been taken down. This was actually news to them as they were not aware that the marker was missing; however, my call was effective. When my brother, Joseph, visited two months later, the sign was back up and appeared to have been freshly painted. To all future visitors, you're welcome!

13.
Millard Fillmore

The historic footprint of Millard Fillmore's birthplace in Summerhill, New York.

Vital Birthplace Information

Birthplace	Locke (now Summerhill), New York
President's birthday	January 7, 1800
How long in the home	Several years
Life of the home	1799 to 1852
Style	Log cabin
Still in existence	No
Ultimate fate	Torn down for firewood
Commemoration	Historic marker and pavilion
Open to the public	Yes
Cost	Free
For more information	www.nysparks.state.ny.us/ parks/157/details.aspx
Replica exists	Yes, at Fillmore Glen State Park
Significance	First Presidential Birthplace replica not located on original location
Closest birthplace	Martin Van Buren, 187 miles

What you will find there today:

The actual site of the birth of the nation's thirteenth president is in the town of Summerhill, New York, on the appropriately named Fillmore Road. At the time of Fillmore's birth, the town was known as Locke. At the site is a quaint steel pavilion donated by the Nucor Corporation, a flagpole, and some picnic tables. The main attraction is the actual footprint of the birthplace log cabin that Fillmore was born in, which is marked and located on the side of a small hill. At the roadside, about 100 feet from the cabin site, is a historic marker that reads:

Millard Fillmore 13th President of the United States, was Born in a log cabin in the Adjacent Field Jan 7, 1800.

The New York State Education Department erected the marker in 1932.

About five miles away is a replica of the log cabin in which Millard Fillmore was born. The cabin is located near the entrance of the also appropriately named Fillmore Glen State Park in nearby Moravia, New York. The park used to be a camp for Franklin Roosevelt's Civilian Conservation Corps (CCC) in the 1930s.

Address/Directions:

Fillmore Road
Summerhill, New York 13092

The birthplace is located a half mile northwest of Route 135.

History

At the end of the 1700s, Nathaniel and Phoebe Fillmore were living in Bennington, Vermont, when a land promoter convinced them to pack up and move to more fertile land in the New York Finger Lakes region. The adventurous couple settled on a farm in the town of Locke (today known as Summerhill) in Cayuga County, New York. There the Fillmores built a small log cabin with one door and one window.[1] Shortly after arriving, Millard Fillmore, the first president to be born in the nineteenth century, was born on January 7, 1800. He was the first of four consecutive United States presidents born in a log cabin, five including Jefferson Davis. The Fillmores did not stay long in the cabin. It appears the land prospector was a shady character because, in the following years, Nathaniel Fillmore lost the home over "an inadequate survey and uncertain titles."[2]

Fillmore would later describe his birthplace as "completely shut out from enterprises of civilization and achievement."[3] Over 200 years later, Millard would be amused to learn that not much as changed.

The cabin was still in existence throughout most of Fillmore's presidency. Sadly, in 1852, the final year of his presidency, when the cabin should have been preserved for the ages, it was instead torn down and the lumber was used for firewood.[4]

Preservation

In the 1860s, it was believed that Millard Fillmore was born in Vermont in his parent's home about two miles from Bennington. A cousin that lived nearby the purported birth site even corroborated the story. In 1868, the home was reported to be a battered old red-wooden farmhouse "well known in the vicinity as 'The old Dimmick Stand.'"[5] The town went as far as to memorialize the site, before being forced to acknowledge their error and have the recognition removed.[6]

In December of 1929, the town of Summerhill offered the birthplace land to the federal government. At the time, the birthplace of George Washington was being rebuilt, so New York Republican Representative John Taber (1880-1965) must have thought it would be a good time to present the offer. He also proposed a $35,000 appropriation to build a memorial to the former president. Perhaps being only six weeks into the Great Depression, or maybe because Millard Fillmore was no George Washington, the proposal never got off the ground.[7]

Even at the time this donation was offered, the precise location of the birthplace cabin was still a mystery. While the general location was known, the exact site of the historic cabin was not. That mystery was solved in May 1931, when Marquis de Lafayette French, an 83-year-old resident of Antwerp, New York, pointed out the historic location to the Cayuga County Historical Society. As a boy, French had played at the site and he was able to recognize the location from the landscape and nearby trees.[8]

The next year, the New York State Education Department erected a historic marker on the road about 100 feet from the site. This marker still stands today.

In 1965, the Millard Fillmore Memorial Association (formed two years earlier) honored the town's most famous son by building a replica of the birthplace cabin. They strived to construct the replica as authentically as possible by using native materials from a similar cabin from the same era. What was not authentic was the location. The home was built in Fillmore Glen State Park, about five miles from the original birth site.

The re-created Millard Fillmore birth cabin at Fillmore Glen State Park in Moravia, New York.

Visitor Information

On a spring day in 2010, I took the three-hour drive to the historic site with my father. My Dad is one of only two people I know who would agree to drive three hours to see a historic marker of what many consider one of our nation's worst presidents (the other is my brother, Joseph). The site is well marked and easy to locate, and if you see the Empire State Nudist Park, you are getting close! When we visited, nobody else was at the site, except for the bugs. Logging was taking place across the street, although on that Saturday morning the site was quiet. After spending some time at the birthplace, we drove to nearby Fillmore Glen State Park at 1686 State Route 38 in Moravia to see the historic recreation. Filled with period pieces and made from authentic-era lumber, one can imagine it was not easy being born in the heart of winter in this section of upstate New York.

14.
Franklin Pierce

Lake Franklin Pierce in Hillsborough, New Hampshire, beneath which lies the birthplace of Franklin Pierce.

Vital Birthplace Information

Birthplace	Hillsborough, New Hampshire
President's birthday	November 23, 1804
How long in the home	Several weeks
Life of the home	Before 1804 to 1926
Style	Log cabin
Still in existence	No
Ultimate fate	Submerged beneath Lake Franklin Pierce
Commemoration	None
Open to the public	Yes
Cost	Free
For more information	www.psnh.com
Replica exists	No
Significance	Only Presidential Birthplace that requires scuba gear to visit
Closest birthplace	Calvin Coolidge, 70 miles

Address/Directions:

**Off the Franklin Pierce Highway (Route 31/9)
Hillsborough, New Hampshire 03244**

From the east or west, take Route 9 and the road is renamed Franklin Pierce Highway as you enter Hillsborough. Lake Franklin Pierce will be to the south of the highway. From the north take Route 31 and from the south take Route 202 or Route 123. All of these roads will intersect with Route 9.

What you will find there today:

The Franklin Pierce birth site is submerged beneath Lake Franklin Pierce. The maximum depth of the lake is about thirty feet and you may want to bring your fishing pole as it is fully stocked with bass, pike, perch, catfish, and more.

History

In 1735, the Massachusetts Governor Jonathan Belcher issued a land grant in southern New Hampshire that included the present town of Hillsborough. The parcel was about six square miles and was the seventh of nine land grants that were intended to form a defense against Indian attacks. Shortly after the original grant, Colonel John Hill purchased the land and named the parcel Hillborough. The "s" was later added when the town was incorporated on November 4, 1772.[1]

At that time, Benjamin Pierce lived across the state line in Massachusetts. Pierce was a patriot who took on the British in the battle of Bunker Hill and served with General George Washington during the Revolutionary War. An interesting note: The marker in front of the Pierce Homestead incorrectly states, "The Pierce Homestead was built in 1804 by Benjamin Pierce, a *general* in the American Revolution..." The truth is that Benjamin Pierce was not a general in the American Revolution, as he never rose beyond the rank of Ensign during the war. After the war, Ensign Pierce got a job surveying land for Colonel Stoddard in Cheshire County, and in 1786, this new job first took him to New Hampshire. On his return home, he passed through the town of Hillsborough. Pierce liked what he saw and decided it was the place to settle and raise a family.[2] He moved from Massachusetts to New Hampshire and began to purchase land, starting with 50 to 100 acres, and eventually amassing more than 700 acres.[3]

The original parcel was off of Keene Road near the North Branch River and today the stretch of road by the lake is known as the Franklin Pierce Highway. There was an existing log cabin on the property that belonged to a Pennacook (or Penacook) Indian, which Benjamin Pierce purchased for $50. The Pierces lived in the home and also used it as a tavern.[4] In the winter of 1804, Benjamin Pierce was wrapping up final construction on a larger homestead for his family, also in Hillsborough. However, whether by plan or providence, on November 23, 1804, Franklin Pierce was born in the original log cabin. Franklin was Benjamin and Anna Kendrick's seventh of nine children and he would one day become the fourteenth President of the United States and the only born in New Hampshire. Shortly after his birth, the family moved into the new home, which was also used as a tavern by the Pierces. Today, this home is known as the Franklin Pierce Homestead and is open to visitors.

The birth cabin was later destroyed and the site is now submerged beneath Franklin Pierce Lake, which will make the Franklin Pierce birthplace preservation chapter the shortest of this book.[5] In 1926, the Jackman Dam and Power Plant was built to provide power to New Hampshire residents, flooding the North Branch River and creating the 519-acre Jackman Reservoir and burying the birthplace. At least the dam and reservoir were later renamed Lake Franklin Pierce and Lake Franklin Pierce Dam respectively to honor the President's birthplace. The dam is owned and run by Public Service of New Hampshire (PSNH). According to local legend, the foundation of the birth home can be seen poking above the waterline when the lake is low.

Preservation

Franklin Pierce is the first president with an unmarked and unacknowledged birthplace, unless you consider the name of the lake. The next is George W. Bush, born 142 years later.

Visitor Information

I visited in summer of 2010 and started with a tour of the Franklin Pierce Homestead, where the Pierces moved just weeks after Franklin's birth. This is the best place to learn about the president and the town, since you will not learn much about him staring at a lake. One gets the feeling that historians and preservationists may be a little ashamed of this fact as the brochure uses vague language that may lead those less informed than you to mistake the home for the birthplace, "the Pierce Homestead was built in 1804 by Benjamin Pierce the year his son Franklin was born."[6] Regardless, the home is an important piece of Pierce history as it remained in their family until it was donated to the state of New Hampshire in 1925, when it was restored to its early nineteenth-century appearance. The hours listed on the website may not be accurate, so call before visiting.

My guides were knowledgeable and generous with their time, spending over an hour and a half with me, and only me, since I was the lone guest touring the home that day. Historians may regard Pierce as one of our lesser presidents, but don't tell that to the guides at the Pierce Homestead who praised his high regard for states rights, his ability to preserve the Union, and of course, his good looks! My persistent questions focused more about the birth home, and as the only person on the tour, I was a little difficult to ignore. However, with few historical records of the birth home, there was just not much to say and they did their best to steer my attention back to the Franklin Pierce era toaster and tableware. As the tour was wrapping up, I couldn't resist asking one last time (as if they were hiding something from me). "Do you know anything else about the birthplace?" Having already answered the question five times, she once more flatly replied, "No, but I know that's what you really want!"

It was a blazing hot summer day, so after leaving the Homestead, my first stop was the nearby Corner Store for an ice cold Moxie before visiting the lake. Lake Franklin Pierce is surrounded by a lot of private property and is not easily accessible, so getting a good look at the right area is not easy. On the east side take Barden Hill Road to Mountainside Drive, a dirt road that ends at a small beach called Mountainside Drive Beach. Walk out onto the pier and gaze slightly southwest. On the west side the best viewing is from the private Breezy Point community. Between those two points is the Antrim-Hillsborough county line, near where lies the submerged Franklin Pierce birth cabin.[7]

15.
James Buchanan

Buchanan's Birthplace State Park in Cove Gap, Pennsylvania. *Courtesy of Ralph Picone*

Vital Birthplace Information

Birthplace	Cove Gap, Pennsylvania
Name	Stony Batter
President's birthday	April 23, 1791
How long in the home	6 years
Life of the home	Approximately 1780 to present
Style	Log cabin
Still in existence	Yes
Commemoration	HOME: Authentic birth home at inauthentic location BIRTHPLACE: Stone pyramid monument at Buchanan's Birthplace State Park
Open to the public	Yes to both places
Cost	Both are free
For more information	www.dcnr.state.pa.us/stateparks/parks/buchanansbirthplace.aspx
Replica exists	No
Significance	Largest memorial to one of the worst presidents
Closest birthplace	Zachary Taylor, 150 miles

Address/Directions:

Buchanan's Birthplace State Park is located near Cove Gap, Pennsylvania, between McConnellsburg and Mercersburg along PA Route 16. From U.S. Route 30 take PA Route 75 south and follow the signs to Buchanan's Birthplace State Park.

What you will find there today:

The birthplace is within the Buchanan's Birthplace State Park, Pennsylvania's smallest state park at only 18.5 acres. The highlight is the birthplace marked by a 300-ton stone pyramid, thirty-one feet tall with a thirty-eight square-foot base. The actual cabin is a few miles away on the campus of Mercersburg Academy.

History

Near the end of the American Revolution, a businessman named John Tom built a trading post in Cove Gap, which was located on a traveling route through the Allegheny Mountains. This location was considered the edge of the American frontier, and travelers heading west frequented his trading post. He called the post "Tom's Trading Place" and it included two cabins he built, one used as a residence, the other to store merchandise. The trading post also featured barns, stables, rooms for weary travelers, a store, and an orchard. To help him manage the business, he hired an assistant James Buchanan Sr., from County Donegal, Ireland, in 1783.[1]

By the late 1780s, John Tom's business was struggling and he found himself on the brink of financial ruin. To help pay his debts, Tom sold the trading post to James Buchanan Sr. in 1789, who renamed it "Stony Batter" after his ancestral home in Northern Ireland. Shortly after the purchase, he married Elizabeth Speer. On April 23, 1791, the second of eleven children, James Buchanan was born in their log cabin.[2] James would one day become the fifteenth President of the United States of America and the only one from the state of Pennsylvania. As a young boy, James would play in the woods and legend has it his mother tied a small cowbell around his neck so he wouldn't get lost.[3] The Buchanans operated Stony Batter for six years after James' birth, until moving to 17 North Main Street in Mercersburg. Construction on this new home began in 1796 and the property was later converted to a hotel. It is now a private residence.

In 1865, a local businessman, Mr. Daniel Miller Bowles (a.k.a. D.M.B.) Shannon purchased the birthplace land and the following year sent a letter to invite the former president to visit. Politely declining, Buchanan captured his sentiments in his response dated July 7, 1866 when he wrote:

> **I am pleased to learn that you have purchased the place where I was born. It is a rugged but romantic spot, and the mountain and mountain stream under the scenery captivating. I have warm attachments for it and for Mercersburg; but do not expect, at least for the present, to pay you a visit.**[4]

The Shannon family retained ownership of the historic property until 1906.

Preservation

Harriet Lane, niece and first lady to the fifteenth president, tried to purchase Stony Batter starting in the early 1880s, but the Shannon family was fully aware of the historical value and drove a hard bargain on the asking price. During these negotiations, the first public effort to mark the birthplace was made in 1893 when a bill was introduced by the Pennsylvania legislature to purchase the home and build a memorial. State Representative John Cessna of Bedford County requested $5,000. Of that sum, $150 to $200 was to purchase the land and the rest to build the memorial.[5] The bill did not pass into law, but even if it had, it is unlikely the Shannon family would have sold for what they must have perceived as a paltry sum.

The Shannons knew they were sitting on a historic piece of land and continued to ask a premium price. Harriet Lane realized that she might not be able to complete the purchase in her lifetime, so when she wrote up the terms of her will in 1895, she set aside $100,000 for the James Buchanan Monument Fund to create a birthplace memorial consisting of "a huge rock or boulder in its natural state, except that proper surfaces or tablets should be prepared or provided for necessary inscriptions."[6] She designated four trustees to complete her request; however, by the time she died on July 3, 1903, only two remained, Lawrason Riggs, a lawyer from Baltimore, and E. Francis Riggs, a banker from Washington, D.C. (Calderon Carlisle and William A. Fisher had died). They worked three years before arriving at terms to purchase the land from the Shannons (Daniel died in 1900 and his wife in 1903, leaving the estate to their four children, Oliver, William, Virginia, and Antoinette). Finally, on July 18, 1906, they completed the purchase of Stony Batter for $3,000, which included 18.5 acres of mountainous land. Work on the pyramid memorial, designed by Wyatt and Nolting, a Baltimore architectural firm, began the following year on October 12, 1907.[7] Creating this 300-ton monument was no small task. The original crew of twenty men ballooned to thirty-five and a small railroad was created to bring supplies to the location. By the end of winter, the memorial was complete and the property was transferred from Lawrason Riggs to the Pennsylvania General Assembly in 1911, formally establishing the Buchanan's Birthplace State Park.

The birthplace site had become a permanent memorial to the man many consider the country's worst president, but the birthplace cabin was still on its journey towards posterity. In 1850, Mr. Jacob McCune purchased the 20- by 25-foot log cabin in which Buchanan was born. At the time, Buchanan had become well known, recently completing a four-year term as United States Secretary of State, and McCune may have wanted a building with both practical and historical value. Of course, no presidential birthplace story can be complete without a birthplace controversy, and James Buchanan is no exception.[8] While it is generally accepted that the birthplace cabin was purchased in 1850, early newspaper articles provide conflicting evidence. In 1880, it was reported that McCune had purchased the cabin "between fifty and sixty years ago," which would date the cabin to 1820 to 1830 – a little early to conclude that the log cabin was a relic that should be preserved.[9] Government documentation does cite the 1850 date, which is generally accepted.

After purchasing the presumed birth cabin in 1850, McCune carefully numbered the logs, broke them down and then rebuilt the cabin at 128 South Fayette Street in Mercersburg, exactly as it stood in Cove Gap. McCune was a weaver by trade, and he converted the birthplace into his workshop. Several years later, James Buchanan was speaking at a nearby hotel before he became president. He reportedly concluded his speech by escorting the audience outside to see the cabin in which he was born. Learning the lesson from William Henry Harrison, he knew his humble beginnings were an asset, not a detriment, and he leveraged his log cabin roots to his advantage.[10]

sure to note that the tenants were "a colored family" in 1902 and "a Negro family" in 1925.[13]

By 1925, the home had passed from the McCune family to Charles Grove, a barber, when it caught the attention of Dr. John M. Gelwix from Chambersburg. Gelwix was a "company surgeon for the Cumberland Valley Division of the Pennsylvania Railroad" who felt that the historic home should be preserved – and that he could make a profit from it.[14] Regardless of his motives, if not for John Gelwix, the Buchanan birthplace log cabin would not likely still be here for us to see today. Although in an advanced state of disrepair, Grove claimed that, except for the roof, the home was completely original.[15]

In 1925, Dr. Gelwix, along with his wife, Mary, and their associates, Frank A. and Florence D. Zimmerman, formed the Stony Batter Antiques Exchange, Incorporated. Through this corporation they purchased 11 North Second Street near the Hotel Washington in Chambersburg for $7,200 and then they bought the birth home from Grove for about $1,000.[16] The home was broken down and the logs were moved twenty miles away to Chambersburg,

Buchanan's Birthplace State Park in Cove Gap, Pennsylvania. *Courtesy of Ralph Picone*

In 1866, after Jacob McCune passed away, his son, Reverend R. Lewis McCune, purchased the home. Reverend Lewis also obtained another Buchanan relic, the log cabin building once known as "the Latin School" where young James Buchanan had studied. The new log cabin was appended to the birth home to enlarge the structure to a two-room, two-story home. McCune took good care of the structure, and in 1880, it was reported to be "in an excellent state of preservation."[11] The home was rented out to various families over the next several years, including Civil War veteran, John Rodgers and his wife, in 1886.[12] The home began to deteriorate, and by the start of the twentieth century, local interest had completely abated. It continued to be rented out and fall further into decay. Due to the predominately African-American population, the neighborhood became known locally as "Little Africa" and the newspapers made

Pennsylvania. The schoolhouse that was appended to the birthplace cabin while it was in Mercersburg was removed and not included when the home was reassembled in Chambersburg. In front of the home a bronze plaque was erected that read:

The cabin in which James Buchanan, 15th President of the United States was born, April 23, 1791, and which was moved from Stony Batter to Mercersburg 1850 and to this site 1925.

Another historic marker was also erected in the vicinity of the original birth site at Cove Gap that read:

James Buchanan President 1857-1861.
Born Apr. 23, 1791, a half-mile from here. The home

itself was moved to Mercersburg in 1850, and in 1925 to Chambersburg, where it may still be seen.

Over the next eighteen years, the cabin was used as a gift shop. From 1925 through 1933, the cabin was managed by Mrs. Dorothy Sutliff and followed by Mr. Riddle until 1935. By this time, the store was known as the Buchanan Gift Shop and was run by Mrs. Ellen Sutliff. In 1943, the gift shop closed and the home became the headquarters for the local Girl Scouts of America.[17] In January 1947, the Girl Scouts were evicted when the Stony Batter Antiques Exchange, which was still run by Dr. Gelwix, sold the home and property to Arthur V. Rock and his wife, Florence J. Rock, for $12,000.[18] The Rocks already owned a nearby sandwich shop that adjoined the cabin property. One month later, on February 1, 1947, John D. Lippy, an author from Gettysburg, Pennsylvania, signed a two-year lease with the Rocks to convert the cabin into a museum.[19] Lippy already ran two other museums in Gettysburg, the Wills House, where Lincoln stayed the night before delivering his Gettysburg address, and the Dobbin House, which today is run as the Historic 1776 Dobbin House Tavern. On March 20, 1947 at 3 p.m., John Lippy remotely launched the grand opening of the President James Buchanan Cabin Museum from radio station WCHA, broadcasting from Gettysburg. The free museum and gift shop, stocked with mementos of the president's life from Lippy's personal collection, unfortunately did not last long.[20] By the end of 1949, Lippy was in bad health and relinquished the home back to Mr. Arthur V. Rock. Shortly afterwards, it was being used as the Democratic Party headquarters, and by 1953, it was again up for sale.

Through the efforts of Dr. Charles S. Tippetts, headmaster for the Mercersburg Academy, the historic home was purchased for $300. For the last time the home was moved, this time back to Mercersburg. The log cabin was placed on the campus of the Mercersburg Academy, which is where it still stands today.[21]

In 1991, on what would have been James Buchanan's 200th birthday, about 100 people gathered at the birthplace marker to rededicate the site. A sign was also unveiled on Interstate 81 directing tourists to the birthplace site.[22]

The site in Chambersburg, Pennsylvania where the James Buchanan birth cabin stood from 1925 until 1953. Today the location is a parking lot next to the Clinical Hypnosis Center.

Visitor Information

One of the great things about visiting presidential birthplaces is that many of them are off the beaten path. The James Buchanan birthplace is not easy to get to and there are no other major tourist attractions in Mercersburg. So, if you've been to this one, consider yourself a true aficionado. The monument is impressive and the state park is tranquil and rustic.

In 2010, I visited Chambersburg with my father to see the infamous site where the birthplace cabin stood for almost three decades. Unfortunately, there is no marker at 11 North Second Street to let passersby know of its historic significance, but rather there is a small parking lot between a residential building and a former firehouse that is now the site of the Clinical Hypnosis Center. If you do visit, make sure you stop by the Franklin County Historical Society located a block away at 175 East King Street. It is located in an old jail that was listed on the National Register of Historic Places in 1970. Tours are available of the jail, and at the Historical Society, you will find a helpful staff. When we visited, we had the good fortune of meeting Bud Barkdoll who located a treasure trove of information about the birthplace cabin in Chambersburg and also shared stories about seeing the cabin as a youth.

WESTWARD EXPANSION

16.
Abraham Lincoln

The 56 steps at Abraham Lincoln's birthplace in Hodgenville, Kentucky. Cue "Gonna Fly Now."

Vital Birthplace Information

Birthplace	Hodgenville, Kentucky
Name	Sinking Spring
President's birthday	February 12, 1809
How long in the home	2 years
Life of the home	1808 or 1809 to after 1816
Style	Log cabin
Still in existence	Maybe
Ultimate fate	A mystery
Commemoration	Abraham Lincoln Birthplace National Historical Park
Open to the public	Yes
Cost	Free
For more information	www.nps.gov/abli
Replica exists	Maybe
Significance	First president born outside of the original thirteen states
Closest birthplace	Jefferson Davis, 123 miles

Address/Directions:

Sinking Spring Farm
2995 Lincoln Farm Road
Hodgenville, Kentucky 42748

The birthplace is located off US 31E, 1.3 miles from KY 61.

What you will find there today:

The authentically un-authentic Lincoln log cabin is housed within a Romanesque granite and marble structure that sits atop a hill in rural Kentucky. One feels like Rocky climbing the fifty-six steps (one for each year of the president's all too short life) to reach the birthplace. The site is managed by the National Park service and resides on 116.5 acres.

History

Neither the first nor the last log-cabin president, Abraham Lincoln is no doubt the most famous – and the one most often associated with the humble log-cabin beginnings. However, the Lincoln birthplace log cabin is perhaps one of the greatest conundrums of all of the presidential birthplaces. While it is possible that not one single log in the cabin is authentic, this reproduction is entombed and revered as if it were the real thing.

The farm where Abraham Lincoln was born had been the center of several land exchanges in the quarter century before Thomas Lincoln, Abraham's father, purchased it in 1808. The transactions that preceded his ownership would become critical when the Lincoln's legal right to the property was challenged two years after purchasing it.

In 1783, the Sinking Spring farm was part of a 30,000 acre land grant from the commonwealth of Virginia to William Greene. In February 1786, William Greene sold half of this grant to Joseph James, who in turn sold it to Richard Mather, an investor from New York with plans to subdivide and sell the property for a profit. On May 1, 1805, he sold over 300 of the 15,000 acres to David Vance. Now this is where things really start getting tricky. David Vance then sold the property to Isaac Bush, but David Mather still held a lien on the property. At this time, both David Vance and Isaac Bush had an outstanding debt to Richard Mather.[1]

Meanwhile, several miles away in Elizabethtown, Kentucky, Thomas Lincoln, carpenter and future father to Honest Abe, purchased a 230-acre farm and married Nancy Hanks. The Lincolns, looking for additional land to farm, came across Sinking Spring, which was owned by Isaac Bush at the time. The Lincolns liked what they saw and Bush sold them the sprawling 348 acres on Nolin Creek on December 12, 1808, for all of $200, or less than 58¢ an acre![2] Now there were three people that owed money to Richard Mather, but whether intentionally or just out of sheer confusion, none of this debt was being paid.[3]

At the time they moved onto the farm, the Lincolns already had a one-year-old daughter, Sarah, and Nancy was expecting her second child. The first order of business for Thomas was to build a home for his growing family and he chose a site on top of a hill near the actual Sinking Spring, the source for the household water, on the southwest corner of the farm. The log cabin he built was believed to be about 16 by 18 feet and, as typical of the time, it would have had a dirt floor, one chimney, one door, one window, and only one room.[4]

On February 12, 1809, about three months after moving into the home, Nancy gave birth next to the fire. Her second child, Abraham Lincoln, was named after his grandfather who was killed by Indians in May 1786. Abraham Lincoln is known for his humble beginnings and most people believe the he was born into abject poverty; however, the fact is that his family owned two farms totaling almost 600 acres. Abraham Lincoln who would become the sixteenth President of the United States, was the first born

outside of the original thirteen colonies (Kentucky entered the Union in 1792).

For two years, Nancy kept the home and cared for the family while Thomas farmed the land, although he found the rocky terrain and red clay of Sinking Spring difficult to cultivate. By 1811, the title dispute with Richard Mather finally forced Thomas Lincoln out of Sinking Spring, so he packed up his young family and moved about ten miles northeast to Knob Creek. Maybe $200 wasn't so great of a deal after all!

Richard Mather filed a suit in September 1813 to collect the debt owed to him by Thomas Lincoln, David Vance, and Isaac Bush. David Vance could not be found; however, Thomas Lincoln and Isaac Bush both attempted to pay off their debts. Perhaps frustrated with the length of time that had already passed, Richard Mather would not accept payment and the court ruled in his favor. He now wanted his land back, and in 1816, he got just that. For his troubles, he was able to sell the land at a commissioner's sale to John Welsh for $87.74 in December 1816.[5]

Years later, the home was owned by Harry Brother (until 1840), and it was during this time that his son, Jacob S. Brother, later claimed that the birthplace cabin was destroyed. On September 8, 1903, Jacob made the following statement to Jonathan Todd Hobson, an author writing a book about Lincoln:

> **My name is Jacob S. Brother. My father's name was Henry, but he was generally known as "Harry." I was born in Montgomery County, Kentucky, March 8, 1819. In the year 1827, when I was eight years old, my father purchased the old farm on which Abraham Lincoln was born, in Kentucky. He purchased it off Henry Thomas. We lived in the house in which Lincoln was born. After some years, my father built another house almost like the first house. The old house was torn down, and, to my knowledge, the logs were burned for fire-wood. Later he built a hewed log house, and the second old house was used as a hatter-shop. My father followed the trade of making hats all his life. The pictures we often see of the house in which Lincoln was born are pictures of the first house built by my father.[6]**

Subsequent historians have found inconsistencies in this statement, which is perhaps not surprising since Jacob S. Brother was eighty-four at the time he made it and was recalling events at least sixty-three years earlier. Records show that Brothers only owned the house from 1835 to 1840 and was evicted for failure to pay for the home. Regardless, the statement is a valuable piece of the puzzle and, interestingly, the National Park Service's comprehensive Administrative History makes no mention of this claim.

Several years later, the Creal family purchased the 110 acres, which included Sinking Spring and the site of the birthplace cabin and the more recent Henry Brother cabin.

Preservation

The first effort to locate and preserve the birthplace cabin was made in 1860 when Abraham Lincoln was in the midst of a presidential battle with the fate of the union hanging on the outcome. At that time, the historical and financial significance of the property and birth cabin, assuming it still existed, were better understood. In the spring of 1860, the Creal family claimed to have moved the remains of the birth home to a nearby farm owned by Dr. George Rodman. It is possible that if a cabin was indeed moved, it may have been the cabin that was built by Henry Brother in the 1830s. George and his brother Dr. Jesse Rodman, associates of the president, were interested in owning his birth cabin. A local resident, Lafayette Wilson, and a partner, James Dyer, claimed to have had disassembled a cabin on the Creal farm and moved the logs a mile away to be used as a "spring house."[7] These logs were later used as building material for a two-story cabin, according to an interview with Lafayette Wilson in 1906. With forty-four years passed since the Lincolns lived in the log cabin, the credibility of whatever it was that Wilson and Dyer moved, assuming they moved anything, is questionable. The farm with the rebuilt cabin was later purchased by the family of John Davenport, who claimed to have lived in the Lincoln birth cabin starting in 1875.[8]

In contemporary literature, the National Park Service begins to refer to the structure that appeared after 1860 as "the symbolic home." According to the National Register of Historic Places:

Without question, the authenticity of the Lincoln cabin is a debatable matter.[9]

However, in 1860, the authenticity of the cabin was not in doubt. Perhaps the first authenticated attempt to recognize the historic site was in 1865 when artist John B. Rowbotham traveled to Sinking Spring to draw the birthplace. He was hired by a Cincinnati publication to complete the artistic rendition for an upcoming book by Joseph Barrett titled *Life of Lincoln*. All he found were a few stones that may have been the chimney.

It would be another twenty years before the government first made an attempt to preserve the birthplace. On July 12, 1886, Representative Thomas Robertson, from Kentucky, presented House Resolution No. 200 to set aside $10,000 "to erect a granite shaft, on the Creal plan."[10] The bill did not pass. House Representative John Lewis decided to try for a $100,000 appropriation (H.R. 8589) ten years later in April 1896. This amount would not only purchase the land, it would also cover the cost of a National Soldiers' Home near Sinking Spring. This did not pass either. In 1904, an unsuccessful bill was proposed in the Kentucky house to appropriate $10,000 to convert the land into a park.[11] By 1908, private efforts to memorialize the birthplace were in motion when bill HR 20435 was proposed by Illinois Representative Marin B. Madden to pledge $100,000 towards the effort. The sum was reduced to $50,000, but still could not pass through Congress. It appears the public supported the efforts, but was not willing to open their wallets to push it forward.[12]

With no government funding to preserve the birthplace materializing, American entrepreneurs seized the opportunity. On November 23, 1894, Alfred W. Dennett and Reverend James W. Bigham purchased the 110-acre Creal farm for $3,000. Dennett was a successful businessman from New York who owned several restaurants across the county. He was also a religious man and his "Dennett's" restaurants clearly reflected his faith – the walls were adorned with bible verses and he required his waitresses to attend daily prayer services. By the 1890s, he had made millions, and had given much of his money to charity. Bigham, his partner, was an African-American Methodist minister from Crittendon.[13]

Although professing admiration for the sixteenth president, their primary motive was the almighty dollar. The two had already entered into several business ventures together to help raise money for missionary causes.[14] After purchasing the land, Dennett then set out to find the birthplace cabin so it could be restored to its original location. In August 1895, Dennett gave Reverend James Bigham "orders to have the old cabin in which the great president first saw the light reconstructed out of its original logs."[15] Instead of reconstructing a cabin, the Reverend Jim chose to buy the cabin from John Davenport. Thirty-five years earlier, Davenport claimed to have purchased the Lincoln log cabin from the Creal family.

With the land and home reunited, Dennett created "Lincoln Spring Farm" and "Lincoln Birthplace" to attract tourists to the historic property. Several miles away, in Louisville, soldiers from the Grand Army of the Republic (GAR) were soon to be encamped. Dennett saw these soldiers as potential customers and planned to build a hotel to attract them to the historic home site. Unfortunately, only a few hundred soldiers and tourists trickled in and his grand plans never materialized. Seeking an alternate source of income from his new assets, Dennett put Reverend James W. Bigham in charge of the birthplace cabin to see if it could generate income outside of Kentucky.[16]

Shortly afterwards, Dennett also purchased what he claimed was the birthplace cabin of Jefferson Davis. The possibilities for promotion with the two former Civil War leaders' birthplaces side by side were endless! Or at least they thought they were. They first tested the waters on this dynamic duo at the 1897 Tennessee (Nashville) Centennial Exposition. The cabin was broken down and the 143 logs were carted to Nashville, where they were reassembled and displayed alongside the Jefferson Davis cabin in the amusement section along with "a giant seesaw and a phantom swing."[17] After Nashville, Dennett and Bigham continued to show their log cabins around the country at fairs and expositions, repeatedly breaking down and rebuilding the log cabins. Soon enough the logs were mixed together and Dennett and Bigham no longer knew, or probably really cared, which was which. Their bigger concern was that thirty-two years after the Civil War, the juxtaposition of these two cabins side by side was not as attractive and profitable as they anticipated.[18] After losing money on several exhibitions, the logs were stored in a rented warehouse below a restaurant in the Bowery on the lower east side of Manhattan, New York.

There the logs stayed until 1901 when Dennett rented them to promoters Elmer "Skip" Dundy and Frederic Thomson. The pair had planned to showcase the Lincoln birthplace logs, but when they visited the basement to see what they rented, they found not one but two disassembled log cabins and learned that they had both the Abraham Lincoln and Jefferson Davis homes in their possession. The business partners seized upon the opportunity and sent them both to Buffalo, New York for the 1901 Pan-American Exposition. Dundy and Thomson were already showcasing their new carnival ride called "A Trip To The Moon" and the two cabins fit nicely into a display called "Old Plantation." While this may sound genteel, the racist exhibit of the "South be'fo' de Wah" that featured "150 Southern Darkies" would have horrified the Great Emancipator![19] On September 6, 1901, President William McKinley was a guest of the expo and attended an afternoon reception at the Temple of Music building, about 2,000 feet from the Lincoln and Davis birthplace cabins. The president was shaking hands with members from the audience when an anarchist, Leon Czolgosz, pulled a gun and shot him two times. Eight days later, the president was dead.

After the expo, the Jefferson Davis and Lincoln cabins were returned to New York City, but many of the logs were lost in transit. In 1902, the partners entered into a long-term lease with an older amusement park, "Sea Lion Park," at Coney Island. The next year, it was reopened as "Luna Park", *luna* being the Latin word for moon, with "A Trip To The Moon" as the star attraction. Perhaps not quite as popular, the Lincoln Cabin was also put on display at Coney Island. Even in 1902, the Lincoln Log Cabin had gained an almost mythic notoriety. While in storage, rumors surrounded the true whereabouts of the logs. It was reported that Lincoln's son, Robert Todd Lincoln, purchased the logs for $10,000 and they were also spotted in Chicago and New York City. The truth was much more mundane. After running its course as a carnival attraction, it was disassembled and packed away beneath the amusement park.[20]

In 1903, the cabin was taken out of storage for a fundraiser on March 24 for the Beecher Memorial Fund, held at the Plymouth Church at 75 Hicks Street in Brooklyn, New York.[21] One of the attractions at the fundraiser was a Lincoln impersonator, but the undisputed star of the event was the cabin itself set up in the church parlor. Then a "startling discovery" was made: Dundy and Thomson revealed that, during the past years, logs from the Jefferson Davis cabin had become "thoroughly grafted" with the Abraham Lincoln cabin and what they had was now "half Lincoln cabin and half Davis cabin."[22] After the fundraiser, the hybrid cabin was again put in storage at Coney Island. It was around this time that doubts first began to appear in print that this carnival attraction could be the real thing. The *Boston Evening Transcript* asked the question in April 1903:

> Does any sane man believe that a pioneer cabin built of green logs more than ninety-four years ago would still be preserved?[23]

And when a suspicious newspaperman asked James Bigham, the man who purchased the cabin in 1895, if the log cabin was *really* the log cabin in which Abraham Lincoln was born, Bigham defiantly replied:

> Lincoln was born in a log cabin, weren't he? Well one cabin is as good as another![24]

Meanwhile Dennett's plans to profit from Sinking Spring farm – first a park and later a home for Civil War soldiers – had not worked out as he had hoped. These unsuccessful ventures were followed by failed attempts to sell it to the federal government and the Illinois

Central Railroad Company. With debts from his New York creditors mounting, Dennett transferred the farm to David Crear (also seen as Greer and Grear) in April of 1899.[25] Crear was from New York and was the treasurer of the Christian Missionary Alliance and he believed he could use the farm for missionary purposes. Dennett had also been interested in missionary work; however, the transfer was probably motivated more to hide his assets than charity. While Crear held the property, Dennett continued to work on transferring the land to the federal government.[26]

By March 1902, David Crear had fallen delinquent on his taxes. The land was advertised for sale and offers flooded the office of the Sheriff of Hodgenville.[27] A week after the land was put on the market, David Crear came up with the money for the back taxes. The home was taken off of the market and Crear was able to hold onto the farm for another three years, although it was now clear that the birthplace was not in the right hands.[28]

As Dennett's financial state began to deteriorate, so did his mental state. In 1901, he was $92,000 in debt and declared bankruptcy. He lost all of his money in mining investments and had "no assets except a suit of clothes worth $20."[29] Penniless, he was reduced to selling bibles to make a living. In April 1904, he was arrested after he was "found wandering in the Piedmont Hills [section of San Francisco] with a pillow slip around his head yelling "Glory! Glory!""[30] He got deeper into trouble when he attacked two men in the prison where he was being held and was "placed in an insane ward" and examined by the "lunacy commissioner."[31] Four years later, in January 1908, Alfred Dennett died at the age of seventy-two.[32]

When Dennett was committed, the birthplace logs were transferred to David Crear. However, the birthplace property was another story. With Dennett's creditors still trying to get what they were owed, the validity of the transfer of the Lincoln farm was challenged in a Larue County court. In May 1905, Judge Jones ruled that the transfer of property to David Crear was not valid and the land was to be sold to pay Dennett's debts.[33] Shortly after the verdict, the county placed an advertisement, "on Aug 28 the Lincoln Farm was to be sold between the hours of ten and two from the court house steps at public out-cry and to the highest bidder."[34]

A small crowd gathered on that Monday afternoon at 12:30 to bid on the birthplace of perhaps our greatest president. Starting at $1,500, the price gradually increased to $3,600 when the auctioneer finally pounded the hammer and there were no higher bids. The new owner was Richard Lloyd Jones, sent to Hodgenville to purchase the farm on behalf of Robert J. Collier, publisher of *Colliers Weekly*.[35] Collier had read about the neglected state of the property a year earlier and felt that the birthplace of one of our greatest presidents deserved much better. On April 18, 1906, Collier and his fellow-minded friends formed the Lincoln Farm Association to "make Lincoln's humble birthplace a national shrine… and dedicate it to the American people as the abiding symbol of the opportunity with which democracy endows its men."[36] The association was headquartered at 74 Broadway in New York City and the first president was Joseph W. Folk, Governor of Missouri. The board of directors included prominent Americans William Jennings Bryan, William Howard Taft, the Archbishop of Baltimore James Cardinal Gibbons, August Belmont Jr. (builder of the Belmont racetrack) and Mark Twain (listed under his birth name Samuel L. Clemens). Collier officially transferred the birthplace property from himself to the association on June 19, 1906.[37] Now that the association owned the land, the first task was to raise money to preserve the property as a National Park. Twain even published a plea for funds in the *New York Times* on January 13, 1907, in which he declared "his birthplace is worth saving." Donations were collected in increments of 25¢ to $25.[38] School groups called "Lincoln Leagues" were established to collect small change. And, in June 1907, New York philanthropist and nature lover Mrs. Russell Sage donated a single gift of $25,000.[39] All told the group raised $350,000 from about 100,000 people.

In February 1906, the Lincoln Farm Association began a search for the birth cabin. Leveraging the power of *Colliers Weekly,* a plea was made for the return for the cabin. In the February 12 issue, it was written that the cabin was being held "intact in a cellar in Stamford, Connecticut, for ransom."[40] While this made good print, the only truth was the logs were stored in a cellar. Three years earlier, when the cabin was removed from Coney Island, the 200 to 250 logs, a door, a window, and some floor boards were moved about twenty-five miles away to the basement of the Poppenhusen Mansion in College Point, Long Island. The Lincoln Farm Association tracked down the rightful owner, David Crear, and negotiated a purchase price of $1,000.[41]

The logs were removed from the Poppenhusen Mansion basement on February 21, 1906, and transferred to a storage house in New York City. For the trip, the logs were draped in flags and along the way, men removed their hats and children sang hymns when the logs passed by them. After being unloaded in New York, the logs remained in storage for four months.[42]

In June 1906, a detail of the Kentucky Militia commanded by Captain Neville S. Bullitt was dispatched to New York to retrieve the birth cabin logs and escort them back to Kentucky with honors. On June 5, the cabin logs were again draped in flags and began their procession home. Once again, school kids lined up to salute and grown men solemnly paid their respects in the presence of the sacred relics. The logs continued their tour through Philadelphia, Baltimore, Harrisburg, and Indianapolis until returning to Kentucky on June 12. The cabin was rebuilt without a roof in Louisville's Central Park; however, souvenir hunters became such a concern that an armed guard had to be posted at the cabin to keep it from getting picked to pieces.[43] Brass bands welcomed the cabin back to Kentucky and the celebration was dubbed "Home-coming week."[44]

Afterwards, the logs were put away for safe storage and the Lincoln Farm Association hired the Hodgenville law firm of Williams and Handley to determine their authenticity. They used affidavits from locals, including Judge John C. Creal and Lafayette Wilson, who claimed to have moved the logs in 1860. After reviewing the statements, the Lincoln Farm Association was satisfied beyond a doubt that the logs were the true remnants of the Lincoln birthplace.[45]

Now that the birthplace property and cabin were in the hands of the Lincoln Farm Association, the next step was settling on a suitable memorial. The selected design was submitted by John Russell Pope, who also designed the Jefferson Memorial, National Archives Building, and Yale University. Lack of funding would alter the original plans for a two-story memorial to be completed by the president's 100th birthday in 1909. The memorial was downsized to a single story and Norcross Brothers from Louisville was hired to do the construction for $237,101. In addition, plans were changed to merely break ground on his 100th birthday.[46]

To commemorate the groundbreaking, a ceremony was held on February 12, 1909 to lay the cornerstone and officially kick off construction of the memorial. The cornerstone was suspended in mid air, held by a derrick hovering over the festivities. At 1 p.m., the ceremony began. Six speakers were featured, but the main event was the incredibly popular President Theodore Roosevelt,

in what would be one of his last trips made as president.[47] Also at Hodgenville that day were Richard Lloyd Jones, Kentucky Governor Augustus E. Wilson, Robert J. Collier, and Joseph W. Folk. Invited, but not able to attend due to poor health, was 92-year-old Mrs. Ben Hardin Helm, Abraham Lincoln's only living sister-in-law. It was a miserable cold and rainy day, but that did not stop 12,000 people from coming to see what the *Gettysburg Times* called "America's Bethlehem."[48] Roosevelt was escorted by Union and Confederate veterans from Louisville and made a twenty minute speech, referring to Lincoln as "one of the two greatest Americans."[49] While not known for his humility, still one can only assume he was not referring to himself as the other!

The newspapers noted a "notable absence of negroes in the crowd," however, one dignified African-American honored guest was Mr. Isaac T. Montgomery, a former slave owned by Jefferson Davis.[50] Montgomery placed copies of historic documents, including the United States Constitution and the Emancipation Proclamation, into a box in the ground. At 2:45 p.m., the cornerstone was lowered on top of the time capsule and "the president applied the first trowelful of mortar to hold the cornerstone in place."[51] The cabin was in Hodgenville for the ceremony, but several months later, it was moved to Louisville to protect it from the elements, vandals, and souvenir hunters.[52] The same year of the 100th birthday cornerstone ceremony, Jonathan Todd Hobson published *Footprints of Abraham Lincoln: Presenting Many Interesting Facts* which contained Jacob S. Brother's statement claiming that the Lincoln birth cabin was actually destroyed over seventy years earlier. If true, this would mean that the centerpiece of the quarter-million-dollar memorial was a fraud; however, the accusation did not cause a stir at all.

In the fall of 1911, the memorial was finished. For the last time, the log cabin was disassembled and put back together again inside the memorial. However, when the cabin was rebuilt, it was discovered to be too big for the memorial. This was a problem, but since the memorial was made of granite and the cabin was made of wood, there was only one practical solution, so the logs suffered one last indignity and were cut to make the cabin fit. The Lincoln Farm Association clumsily reduced the cabin size from 16 by 18 feet to 12 by 17 feet and at least eleven logs were replaced.[53]

The dedication ceremony was held on November 9, 1911, starting with an invocation delivered by Rabbi H. G. Enslow and a benediction by Archbishop Thomas S. Byrne. President William Howard Taft, who was also on the Board of Trustees of the Lincoln Farm Association, was the main speaker before the crowd of 3,000 people. Also stepping up to the dais that day were Kentucky Governor Augustus E. Wilson, Missouri Governor Joseph M. Folk, Idaho Senator William E. Borah, and Major General and former Commander of the Grand Army of the Republic, John C. Black.[54] The ceremony included an official transfer of the deed from the Lincoln Farm Association to the state of Kentucky; however, this did not go as planned. The National Park Service's comprehensive Administrative History simply states:

> **The plan of Governor Wilson of Kentucky, to accept and maintain the Park for that State, apparently did not bear fruit.**[55]

Since the donation to the state did not work out, efforts began at the federal level when, on June 3, 1912, Kentucky Representative Ben Johnson introduced H.R. 25074 to accept the home as a donation. The bill was shot down in 1912 and an identical version S.

602 was also introduced in the Senate by Idaho's William E. Borah; however, with the same results. The pair was not discouraged. Borah again introduced the bill on April 9, 1913[56] and the next year Johnson brought forth H.R. 12802, both to no avail. After a year off, it was Senator Borah's turn in 1916 when he introduced H.R. 8351; however, this time the stars were aligned. After four years of relentless effort, Johnson and Borah and the whole country were rewarded when President Woodrow Wilson signed the bill into law on July 18, 1916.

On September 4, 1916, in what must have seemed like déjà vu to many people, another ceremony was held for the Lincoln Farm Association to officially donate the area, but this time to the federal government. President Wilson saw fit to personally visit the birthplace for the dedication ceremony on a warm pleasant day with 25,000 in attendance. The festivities were kicked off with an invocation made by the President of Center College in Danville, Kentucky, Dr. William Canfield. The next speaker was Confederate Soldier General John B. Castlemen, who claimed Lincoln saved his life after he was captured by the Union. After several more speakers, Robert Collier announced the formal presentation of the deed and Missouri Governor Joseph Folk, President of the Lincoln Farm Association, handed the paper to Secretary of War Newton D. Baker. Finally, President Woodrow Wilson was handed the microphone to praise the sixteenth president and accept the gift on behalf of the nation.[57]

If at the time there were any doubts to the authenticity of the log cabin, they were not evident in the quotes from some of the many speeches made that day:

Lincoln was born in yonder little cabin.

How eloquent this little house within the shrine is of the vigor of democracy!

This little hut was the cradle of one of the great sons of men.

It is peculiarly appropriate that the legal title to Mr. Lincoln's birthplace should rest in the Nation itself.[58]

Nor did the federal government conduct independent research to confirm that either the land or the cabin was actually where Lincoln was born.[59]

The site was dedicated as the Abraham Lincoln National Park with the condition that "there shall never be any charge or fee" to see the historic birthplace.[60] Robert Jones was named commissioner and John Cissell, grandson of John Creal, was named custodian. Cissell served in this role for over forty-two years until his retirement on January 1, 1949. The site remained under the War Department's jurisdiction until 1933, when it was transferred to the Department of the Interior. For the first decade under the War Department, the site was neglected and fell into disrepair. It was not until 1926, when a new entry road was constructed that there was any significant funding provided for the site.[61]

In 1948, Ron Hays, an insurance investigator from Grosse Pointe Park, Michigan, shocked the world when he published an article in the September 5 edition of the *Abraham Lincoln Quarterly* titled "Is the Lincoln Birthplace Cabin Authentic?" He claimed that the cabin may have been a promotional stunt of Dennett and Bigham and was not the real deal. In his research he cited the

statement of Jacob S. Brothers made forty-five years earlier. None of this was truly news to the National Park Service; however, they had long been in denial or apathetic to the true origins of whatever it was within the walls of the memorial.[62]

The National Park Service officially acknowledged the controversy in 1956 when, as part of the "Mission 66" project, where many National Parks were restored and refurbished, interpretative signs at the Lincoln birth site were reworded to indicate that the "National Park Service considers the cabin of debatable authenticity."[63] This must have been a difficult time for the National Park Service, since they were simultaneously dealing with how to address the Washington birthplace dilemma.

The "symbolic cabin" located at the Abraham Lincoln Birthplace National Historical Park and once purported to be the original Abraham birth cabin in Hodgenville, Kentucky. *Photo credit: Abraham Lincoln Birthplace National Historical Park, National Park Service*

Over the years, many important world leaders continued to visit the site to pay homage to America and one of its greatest citizens. In 1923, Lloyd George, former British Prime Minister who led the United Kingdom during the First World War, visited the birth cabin and was greeted by several hundred locals.[64]

On Flag Day, June 14, 1936, another United States president, Franklin Roosevelt, visited the Lincoln birth site. The popular president did not speak; however, a crowd of over 50,000 still came out to greet him. After his visit he made a statement, and in the midst of the Great Depression, his words were telling when he said:

I have visited the cabin in which Abraham Lincoln was born… I have taken from this cabin a renewed confidence that the American spirit is not dead.[65]

Indeed, it was not.

In what had now become a right of passage, yet another president, this time Dwight Eisenhower, visited the park on April 23, 1954. At the birthplace, the president participated in a Boy Scouts ceremony and spoke curiously about Lincoln:

You can find no instance where he stood up in public and excoriated another American. You can find no instance where he is reported to have slapped or pounded the table or struck a pose as a pseudo-dictator or of an arbitrary individual.

If he had something or someone particular on his mind whom he was comparing Lincoln to, the reporters of the day were dumbfounded.[66]

In recent years, the authenticity of the birth cabin was challenged using modern scientific techniques when the History Channel featured the cabin in the show *History's Mysteries*. They took core samples and were able to determine the age of the cabin. If anybody still believed this was the real thing, the History Channel scientifically proved that the logs dated to the 1850s, forty years after Lincoln's birth and twenty years after the Jacob Mather claim that the log cabin was the built by his father, Harry.

The question of whether the logs within the marble behemoth are the real deal is not the only controversy regarding Lincoln's birthplace. Whether he was actually born at Sinking Spring has also been subject to debate over the years. Shortly after the completion of the birthplace monument, two additional locations in Kentucky claimed birthplace honors, including Beechland in Washington County and Elizabethtown – the two homes Thomas and Nancy lived in prior to moving to Sinking Spring. Despite the fact that Abraham Lincoln would have had to be born up to three years earlier did not phase locals who claimed rights to the true birthplace.[67] More recently a book was written in 2003 called *The Tarheel Lincoln,* in which Jerry Goodnight explored an almost century-old theory that Abraham Lincoln was the illegitimate son of Abraham Enloe and born near Bostic, North Carolina. The premise is that Nancy Hanks was a teenage servant to Mr. Enloe and bore his child in a scandalous affair. He also claims that Lincoln himself was aware of his true parentage.[68]

Despite the controversies, the Lincoln log cabin has endured as a symbol of the ability of a man born into poverty to ascend to the highest office in the country, at one of the most pivotal points in America's history. Regardless of the authenticity of the structure or the accuracy of the perception of Abraham Lincoln's financial status, the symbol remains.

Throughout the years, replicas of the iconic birthplace have been built in many interesting locations. In 1923, Thomas S. Murdock built one for wealthy heiress and Lincoln fanatic Miss Mary Bowditch Forbes so she could "house her extensive collection of artifacts and documents." The fake birthplace cabin was erected in the backyard of her mansion in Milton, Massachusetts, which is the actual birthplace of George Herbert Walker Bush (born in 1924, one year after the cabin was built). More compelling is that the cabin was built behind what is today the Forbes House Museum at 215 Adams Street, less than 1,000 feet away on the same street from the house where Bush was born![69]

In 1930, a log cabin replica was also built near Hollywood, California, for the D.W. Griffith film *Abraham Lincoln*.[70] In 1959, American G.I.s stationed overseas built another in Frankfurt, Germany, in front of "Amerika haus,"[71] an American cultural center that "was part of the American military government's efforts to familiarize the German population – by means of 're-education' – with western ideals of democracy and human rights after twelve years of Nazi domination."[72] What more symbolic way to celebrate freedom, than the birth cabin of man who is most credited with ending slavery in America?

Not only a national symbol, the Lincoln log home has also become a part of our popular culture. It has been celebrated in stamps, toys, and my son has not one, but two Lincoln log cabin banks. It was also featured on a redesigned penny in 2009. But the most enduring homage to the sixteenth president's birth cabin is undoubtedly "Lincoln Logs." In 1916, the year President Wilson accepted the birthplace cabin, John Lloyd Wright, twenty-four-year-old son of famous architect Frank Lloyd Wright, watched builders move timber for the Imperial Palace Hotel and thought that miniature versions of those same building logs would make a great kid's toy. Two years later, Lincoln Logs was on the market and they have remained a popular toy ever since.[73]

Visitor Information

The Lincoln birthplace is opened every day at 8 a.m. to 4:45 p.m., with expanded hours from Labor Day through Memorial Day when it closes at 6:45 p.m. The cabin has always been a popular tourist spot, and today, over 200,000 people visit the Lincoln birthplace every year.[74]

I was one of those visitors in the summer of 2008 after visiting the birthplaces of the Ohio presidents. Driving to the National Historic Site, I did not know what to expect. This was before I started writing this book so I hadn't done any research beforehand. Of course I knew that Lincoln was born in a log cabin and after visiting the birthplaces of the Ohio seven, I expected a subdued birthplace memorial to the Great Emancipator. Needless to say, subdued is not a word that anyone would use to describe this memorial. I was stunned when I pulled in to the parking lot and saw a structure that would fit much better in ancient Rome or Greece than rural Kentucky!

1.
Jefferson Finis Davis
The Only President of the Confederate States of America

The 351 foot monument at the birthplace of Jefferson Davis in Fairview, Kentucky.
Courtesy of Joseph F. Picone

Vital Birthplace Information

Birthplace	Fairview, Kentucky
President's birthday	June 3, 1808
How long in the home	2 years
Life of the home	1804 to 1886
Style	Log cabin
Still in existence	No
Ultimate fate	Torn down
Commemoration	Jefferson Davis State Historic Site
Open to the public	Yes
Cost	Free
For more information	parks.ky.gov/findparks/histparks/jd
Replica exists	Yes
Significance	Tallest birthplace monument (351 feet)
Closest birthplace	Abraham Lincoln, 123 miles

Address/Directions:

**258 Pembroke-Fairview Road
(State Highway 158)
Fairview, Kentucky 42221**

The Jefferson Davis birthplace is located off of Route 80/68. From either direction, take the Jefferson Davis Highway and turn south on to Pembroke-Fairview Road (State Highway 158). The birthplace is on the immediate left.

What you will find there today:

The birthplace of the only President of the Confederate States of America is within the Jefferson Davis State Historic Site. On the site is a dramatic 351-foot concrete monument similar to the one dedicated to our first president in Washington, D.C. Reopened in 2004, you can take an elevator to the top to see an amazing view of southern Kentucky. There is also a 3,600-square-foot interpretive visitor center and of course, a gift shop where you can purchase hard to find "War Between the States" items. For the children, there are the standard park picnic grounds and a playground. The monument is opened from May through October.

On the grounds is a historic marker that reads:
Here the only President of the Confederate States of America was born June 3, 1808, the son of Samuel and Jane Cook Davis. The family moved to Mississippi during his infancy.

Marker # 57 erected by the Kentucky Department of Highways.

Above the entrance to the obelisk is a plaque that reads:
Jefferson Davis Monument S.F. Crecellius, Engineer G.R. Gregg, Contractor 1917-1924
Elevator Installation By American Elevator & Machine Co Louisville Kentucky.

History

At the end of the 1700s, settlers began to arrive in Kentucky, attracted from the east by the excellent farming land. Samuel Emory and Jane Cook Davis were two of those early pioneers, when they first came to Kentucky in 1793. Samuel Emory was a captain with the Georgia infantry in the Revolutionary War, and for his service, he was awarded a 600-acre tobacco plantation in what was then known as Christian County (now Todd County). There, the couple built a "double-pen log house," held together with "hand-wrought nails and wooden pegs." Compared to other birthplace log cabins, the Davis home was a spacious four rooms, painted yellow and including a large porch and the first glass windows in the area.[2] After the land proved poor for farming, Samuel found another way to earn a living. Just like Martin Van Buren and Franklin Pierce's fathers, Samuel Davis also doubled his home as a tavern. He called his establishment the Wayfarer's Inn, which catered to both man and beast.[3] On June 3, 1808, the couple had a son, Jefferson Finis Davis, who would one day become the only President of the Confederate States during the brief secession of the Civil War. Davis was born only seven months earlier and in the same state as his Civil War rival, Abraham Lincoln. Also like Lincoln, Davis only lived in his birthplace home for two years. In 1810, the Davis' left Kentucky for the deeper south of Bayou Teche, Louisiana.

The house remained on the property for the next seven decades. In 1875, Davis visited his birthplace for the first time since leaving as a child. It was a decade since the Civil War had ended and local newspapers reported that the sixty-seven year old Davis "is still strong and erect. His face; however, is a sad one and tells the story of the fate of the confederacy."[4]

In 1885, a tract of land, which included the Jefferson Davis birthplace home was purchased by Captain Lewis Clarke, a "prominent tobacco man, and several other gentlemen." They were all "follower[s] of the Lost Cause" and the purchase was made on behalf of the Bethel Baptist Church to build a new house of worship.[5] The leaders at the church wanted to ensure that they had the former CSA President's blessing, so as a ceremonial gesture, the home was deeded to Jefferson Davis with the precondition that he in turn would "donate it to the church for a building site." He kept his end of the bargain and, on March 10, 1886, the land officially changed hands. By this time, the "old log cabin was going rapidly into decay," so it was broken down to make room for the Bethel Baptist Church.[6]

The construction was quick, and by November 1886, the church was completed. Jefferson Davis was invited to attend service at the newly constructed Bethel Baptist Church to help christen the new house of worship. The dedication service was held on November 19, 1886, and was Jefferson Davis' last visit to the site of his birth.[7] He spoke eloquently when he said:

It is with heart full of emotion that I thank you for commemorating the spot of my nativity by building this temple to the True God. In reply to the question why I am not a Baptist I would only say that my father who was a much better man than myself was a Baptist. I left this place during my infancy, and after an absence of many years revisited it on a previous occasion. On both visits I have felt like saying, "This is my own, my native land." I see around me now in this beautiful house of worship, the most gratifying use to which the spot of my birth could be devoted. It speaks highly for this community that the most commodious and handsome of all its buildings belongs to God. It shows your reverence and love for your Creator. I rejoice to hear of the continued progress and prosperity of my old home. I am not here for the purpose of making a speech nor would I mar the effect of this solemn dedication, nor of the beautiful and eloquent sermon to which you have listened, by attempting one. I came only to tend to you formally the site on which this building stands. May He who rules the heavens bless this community individually and collectively and may his benediction rest upon this house of worship always. I thus leave it with you. More than this it would be improper for me to say.[8]

The Bethel Baptist Church built at the original location of the Jefferson Davis birthplace cabin in Fairview, Kentucky. This photograph was taken from the top of the birthplace monument. *Courtesy of Joseph F. Picone*

In yet another similarity to his nemesis Abraham Lincoln, these words sound much like the Gettysburg Address, in that it was a brief speech about how a speech could not do the moment justice.

As a token of his appreciation, Davis presented the church with a silver salver and chalice. Within the walls of the church the following words were engraved in stone:

JEFFERSON DAVIS,
OF MISSISSIPPI, WAS BORN
June 3, 1808,
ON THIS SITE OF THIS CHURCH
HE MADE A GIFT OF THIS LOT
March 10, 1886,
TO BETHEL BAPTIST CHURCH,
AS A THANK-OFFERING TO GOD

On August 23, 1900, the church was struck by lightening and burned to the ground. Not much survived the fire, but two items that were spared were the engraved stone and the silver salver and chalice. Shortly afterwards, another church was built at the same location, and it is that second structure that stands today on the site of the Jefferson Davis birth cabin.[9] In 1908, on what would have been the 100th birthday of the CSA President Jefferson Davis, church services were held and a dinner was served in his honor.[10]

Preservation

Before the log cabin was removed from its original site to make way for the church in 1886, an engraving was made of the homestead and a copy was presented to Jefferson Davis.[11] Now that the image had been appropriately recorded, W.B. Brewer of Fairview carefully marked the logs before breaking down the log cabin.[12] About a decade after the cabin was removed Alfred W. Dennett and the Reverend James Bigham claimed to have purchased the Jefferson Davis birth cabin. The purchase of the actual birth cabin logs is consistently described as "alleged" and while no articles can be found confirming the authenticity, none can any be found disputing it either. The two had recently purchased what they claimed to be the Abraham Lincoln birth cabin and must have thought that by owning the birth cabins of both Civil War presidents they would have a guaranteed tourist attraction on their hands. From the previous chapter focusing on the Abraham Lincoln birth cabin, the reader will recognize the parallel journey also taken by the Jefferson Davis cabin over the following twenty years. The first venue the pair chose to show off their new attraction was the Tennessee (Nashville) Centennial Exposition in 1897 where the birth cabins were displayed side by side in the amusement park section of the expo.[13]

After the expo, both cabins were broken down and the logs were stored in a rented warehouse below a restaurant in the Bowery on the lower east side of Manhattan, New York. There the logs stayed until 1901 when promoters Elmer "Skip" Dundy and Frederic Thomson came along. Dundy and Thomson were business partners and wanted to showcase their amusement park ride "A Trip To The Moon" at the 1901 Pan-American exposition in Buffalo, New York. As an added attraction, the pair rented the Lincoln birth cabin from James Bigham to put alongside their carnival ride. When they went to the basement to retrieve the logs, they found they got more then they bargained for when they discovered not one, but two disassembled log cabins. It was only then that they learned that they had in their possession both the Abraham Lincoln and Jefferson Davis homes. Taking advantage of their discovery, both cabins were brought to Buffalo. Together they were included in the "Old Plantation" exhibit, which was placed on the Midway, two doors down from "A Trip To The Moon." The official description for the "Old Plantation" pulled directly from the *Official catalogue and guide book to the Pan-American Exposition* best highlights the irony and overt racism in this exhibit, "presenting a veritable Old South Plantation, representing the "South be'fo de Wah," introducing 150 Southern darkies in their plantation song and dances. Old Uncles and Aunties, formerly slaves, living in the genuine cabins in which Abraham Lincoln and Jefferson Davis were born, also other historical cabins from the Old South."[14]

After the singing and dancing former slaves vacated the Confederate leader's birthplace, the cabins were again taken apart. By this time, nobody knew which logs belonged to which cabin. They were carted back to New York, and to add to the confusion, many logs were lost in transit and never arrived. The next year, Dundy and Thomson rebuilt just one cabin to put on display at their newly acquired amusement park, "Sea Lion Park" at Coney Island in Brooklyn, New York.[15] As if the defeat in the Civil War was not bad enough, Lincoln trumped Davis one more time when the reassembled logs were billed as the birthplace of Abraham Lincoln with the fact that some logs were from Jefferson Davis' birthplace simply ignored. This can be seen as adding insult to injury, but the truth is that after the Buffalo Exposition, the only reason anything is known about the Davis logs is because of the demand and reverence for his rival Abraham Lincoln's cabin. Dundy and Thomson may have wanted to forget that some of the logs were actually from the Jefferson Davis birthplace, but this was an inconvenient truth that would not remain a secret for long.

After the 1902 season, the logs were packed away until the following spring. On March 24, 1903, the logs were again on display, this time as part of the "Beecher Memorial Fund" charity event at the Plymouth Church at 75 Hicks Street in Brooklyn, New York. When the cabin was put on display the cat was finally let out of the bag when a "startling discovery" was made. Dundy and Thomson conceded that what was really inside the church included not only logs from Abraham Lincoln's cabin, but also remnants of the Jefferson Davis cabin. They confessed that after years of being a traveling duo, logs from the two cabins had become "thoroughly grafted" and the resulting mutation was now "half Lincoln cabin and half Davis cabin."[16] This is especially ironic since the first pastor at the Plymouth Church and memorial fund namesake was Henry Ward Beecher, brother of Harriet Beecher Stowe (*Uncle Tom's Cabin*) and fervent abolitionist!

After the embarrassing revelation, the attraction was again packed up and stored away. Again, the Jefferson Davis logs appeared to have been forgotten. In February 1906, what was now solely believed to be the Lincoln log cabin materials were purchased for the Abraham Lincoln birthplace memorial being built in Hodgenville, Kentucky. The 200 to 250 logs, a single door, one window, and some floorboards were located in the basement of the Poppenhusen Mansion in College Point, Long Island. After the purchase, the materials were moved into storage in New York City and then in June they were carted to Louisville, Kentucky.

When the logs arrived in Louisville, they were rebuilt, roofless, in Louisville's Central Park for a homecoming celebration. Even though some logs had been lost over the years, the cabin that stood in Louisville was still much bigger than it should have been since it contained materials from two homes. After a week, the oversized cabin was again broken down and put away in safe storage. The Lincoln Farm Association, in charge of the Lincoln Birthplace Memorial, hired a law firm to confirm the logs authenticity. Displaying the cabin in Coney Island was one thing, but now a lot of money was about to be spent to memorialize these logs and people wanted to be sure it was the real deal. While the law firm reported back that the logs were the true remnants of the Lincoln birthplace, the mystery is that the excess logs from Louisville in 1906 were no longer around when the cabin was rebuilt inside the Lincoln Birthplace Memorial five years later.[17] What happened to those excess logs is unknown to history. This mystery can be viewed as the lost Jefferson Davis cabin, but truthfully the logs were so mixed up that it's a long shot that there was anything authentic about what was pulled out of that Poppenhusen Mansion basement.

While controversy has surrounded the Abraham Lincoln cabin, the real irony may be that one or two of those logs that make up the "Abraham Lincoln Birthplace" may actually belong to his arch nemesis, Jefferson Davis. Kind of like finding out that a relic believed to be from the Holy Cross actually belonged to Judas Iscariot!

While what may or may not have been the Jefferson Davis birthplace was sitting in storage in Louisville, Kentucky, the first attempt at preserving the birthplace property was proposed by an aged Confederate General Simon Bolivar Bruckner at a reunion of the Orphan's Brigade of the Confederate Army of Glasgow, Kentucky on September 12, 1907. Dr. C. C. Brown of Smith's Grove had first conceived the memorial and he asked Bolivar to champion the idea at the reunion, which would take a full decade to come to fruition. Shortly after the proposal, Bruckner formed the Jefferson Davis Home Association, which included Dr. Brown, to purchase the home site and build a memorial.[18] The group visited the birth site in on Saturday, September 28, 1907. By this time the original 600-acre farm had been subdivided into smaller lots and the birth cabin site was located on a nine-acre parcel. The group toured the surrounding property and set their sights on seven parcels totaling twenty acres. Some homes and cottages existed on the property, but the residents were eager to sell "their places at a reasonable price," however the group was careful to note that they "did not wish to disturb in any way [the] house of worship."[19] After seeing that the land was obtainable, they did what all good birthplace associations must do, raise money. The group knew their target audience and they believed that donations would pour in from "Confederate veterans and southern sympathizers."[20] The group put a hold on the land, which was set to expire on April 27, 1909. This may have seemed within their reach at first, but as the due date approached, the group was short of their goal and was in danger of losing the option. Many times in history leagues of dedicated patriotic women have spearheaded efforts to preserve presidential birthplaces. While the ladies did eventually prove critical in preserving the Jefferson Davis birthplace, the primary champions in bringing about a monument to Davis were aging and fiercely loyal Confederate Soldiers. Short of funds, General Bennett H. Young from Louisville donated the necessary money to purchase the twenty acres of land for $7,052.[21] On a rainy June 3, 1909, the "Jefferson Davis Memorial Park" was officially established and dedicated. Unfortunately, General Young, who had been critical in obtaining the birthplace land, was ill and unable to attend.[22]

In 1914, Simon Bolivar Bruckner passed away. Over the next several years, many more Confederate Generals, still loyal to their leader, took the baton to lead the Jefferson Davis Home Association or contributed greatly to its purpose. General George W. Littlefield donated $48,000 to the effort, or almost twenty percent of the total cost, and General W.B. Haldeman, commander of the Orphan's Brigade, led the Association when the monument was completed.[23]

By 1917, the Jefferson Davis Home Association had raised approximately $150,000. With sufficient funds in hand, the next order of business was choosing the design for the monument. Colonel S. F. Crecellius, an architect from Georgia, was selected for the task. He came up with an obelisk, similar to the Washington Monument, sitting atop a base of Kentucky limestone. C. G. Gregg of Louisville, Kentucky was selected to complete the project with a price tag of $75,000. Ground was broken on June 17, 1917, at a site nearby the church, which marked the actual birthplace site. A year later, the monument was half way completed at 175 feet when America entered the First World War. Construction was halted in October 1918 as America's boys and resources were dedicated to the efforts in Europe.[24] Even though the construction crew had laid down the tools, progress was made on the birthplace memorial when in 1920, Kentucky General Assemblyman V.M. Williamson brought forth legislation to accept and maintain the monument after its completion.[25]

After waiting for several years, the Jefferson Davis Home Association made a decision. Instead of the original 350-foot target, only another five feet of concrete would be added and the monument would be reduced to 180 feet. The cost had already run to almost $100,000 and funds were nearly exhausted. In addition, it had been over fifty-five years since the end of the Civil War and veterans were quickly becoming an endangered species and soon there would be no Confederate soldiers left.[26] With the new plan, work resumed in August 1921, and a date was set of June 3, 1922 for the official unveiling.

Immediately, a storm of protest erupted over the plan to cap of the monument at half its original size. This was seen as an affront to the Southern gentleman Jefferson Davis. It was bad enough he lost the war, but to cut his memorial to half its original size was the last straw and Confederate Veterans were outraged. Now it was time for a group of patriotic women to take the lead, and thankfully, the United Daughters of the Confederacy accepted the challenge. They vowed to raise $20,000 to pay for the completion of the monument as originally planned.[27] To accomplish this goal they sold "souvenir certificates at one dollar each."[28] On August 27, 1921, John H. Leathers, Treasurer of the Jefferson Davis Home Association announced to the joy of the Confederate veterans that the monument would be built to its full height of 351 feet.[29]

In January of 1922, the Kentucky assembly appropriated an additional $15,000 to pay for the installation of a steam elevator. With the infusion of funds, work was able to resume temporarily. However, by June 1922, construction again stopped with the tower standing at 216 feet.[30] After over a year, the money collected by the United Daughters of the Confederacy saved the day and work again resumed on August 15, 1923. This time, it did not stop until it was completed.[31]

As the monument was nearing completion in December 1923, an unfortunate incident occurred. Lest we forget what this man symbolized to many people, the Ku Klux Klan was permitted to burn a cross at the top of the still-incomplete monument.[32]

The 351-foot monument was finally completed in 1924. The site was officially dedicated in a ceremony on June 7, 1924. While the population of Fairview was only about 100 people in 1924, 10,0000 came out to celebrate Jefferson Davis. The governors of Kentucky and Tennessee took part in the festivities and Union and Confederate veterans were able to put their differences aside to honor the Southern leader. General W.B. Haldeman, then President of the Jefferson Davis Home Association, "delivered an inspiring address."[33] All eleven states that had made up the Confederate States of America were represented at the ceremony. As seen throughout presidential birthplace history, dedication ceremonies have added meaning when there includes a familial link to the former president. If organizers have not been able to get the Man of Honor himself, then spouses, children, siblings, and grandchildren have stood in and have been treated as the most-honored guests. This was no exception on that summer day in 1924 when grandson and namesake Jefferson Hayes Davis, an army major from Colorado Springs, was in attendance. And while perhaps not the most honored guest, the most interesting attendee had to have been Jesse James Jr., son of the notorious train robber and murderer of the Wild West. At the ceremony, the monument and park were officially presented to the State of Kentucky. The presentation was made by Colonel Robert J. McBryde and accepted by Kentucky Governor William Jason Field.[34] Three years later to the day, the "Jefferson Davis Memorial Park" became part of the Kentucky State Park system.[35]

To oversee the Jefferson Davis Memorial Park, a seven-member board was formed. The group met for the first time shortly after the June 7 dedication, and the first order of business was to create a replica of the birthplace home.[36] This idea had been conceived years earlier with the plan for the building to also serve as the caretaker's home.[37] Again, C.G. Gregg was called upon to lead the construction. The exterior of the replica was built to exactly resemble the clapboard cabin that Jefferson Davis was born in, while the inside was more modernized and included restroom and visitor services. On October 17, 1924, a dedication ceremony was held for the opening of the birthplace replica.[38]

This birthplace replica remained open to the public until as late as 1963.[39] Since then, it has gone through modifications and additions. Today, it is used as the park ranger's home and is no longer open to the public.

A replica of the Jefferson Davis birthplace cabin at the Jefferson Davis State Historic Site in Fairview, Kentucky. Today the structure is used as the park ranger's residence. *Courtesy of Joseph F. Picone*

At the time of the dedication, in 1924, the monument contained an empty shaft. Later a steam elevator was added and in 1929, it was converted to an electric elevator. This apparently was reason enough to celebrate, so another dedication ceremony was held. In 1967, still another dedication ceremony took place to mark the 150th anniversary of Kentucky statehood, and in 1973, the monument was added to the National Register of Historic Places (National Register Number #73000849). In 1977, after the monument had been "ravaged by time and lightening," a massive renovation project was undertaken to restore the obelisk. A special framework was constructed to fit the top of the monument and a helicopter lifted it on top of the monument and is now on display at the birthplace site.[40] The monument again underwent renovations in 1988 and 1997.

Visitor Information

At the visitor center, there is a short film about the political life of Jefferson Davis and the construction of the memorial monument. The gift shop and visitor center are open year round from 9 a.m. to 5 p.m., but the monument is only open from May 1 through October 31 (also 9 a.m. to 5 p.m.). The best time to visit may be June for the annual Jefferson Davis birthday festival where the highlight is the crowning of "Miss Confederacy"![41] It is interesting to note how Davis and his birthplace have been portrayed over time. Newspaper articles leading up to the dedication in 1924 describe him glowingly as "a man of fine sense and sterling character,"[42] "a man of great and noble principles which he was true to the last," and "a pure life was his and there was no selfishness in it" (except for the slaves, of course).[43] Today, Jefferson Davis' legacy is more complex; however, the confederate's birthplace still attracts about 30,000 people a year. As a park superintendent was quoted in 2005, most of the visitors are "die-hard Southerners, simply because of the nature of the site; however, "every once in a while you get someone who comes in and asks why we have a monument to a traitor, but that's rare."[44]

17.
Andrew Johnson

Vital Birthplace Information

Birthplace	Raleigh, North Carolina
President's birthday	December 29, 1808
How long in the home	Unknown
Life of the home	About 1795 to present
Style	Kitchen
Still in existence	Yes
Commemoration	**HOME:** Mordecai Historic Park **BIRTHPLACE:** Historic Marker
Open to the public	Yes
Cost	Free
For more information	raleighnc.gov/mordecai
Replica exists	Yes, in Tennessee
Significance	Only president born in a kitchen
Closest birthplace	William Henry Harrison, 150 miles

The former site of Casso's Inn and the birth location of Andrew Johnson in downtown Raleigh, North Carolina at the corner of Morgan Street and South Wilmington Street.

Address/Directions:

Mordecai Historic Park
1 Mimosa Street
Raleigh, North Carolina 27604

The actual birth site is in downtown Raleigh on Morgan Street and South Wilmington Street.

What you will find there today:

The two-story kitchen where Andrew Johnson was born is in Mordecai Historic Park. Placed in front of the home is a plaque that reads:

Andrew Johnson, 17th President of the United States, was born in this house on December 29, 1808. At that time the house stood on Fayetteville Street.

At the actual birthplace site on Morgan and South Wilmington Streets in downtown Raleigh is a historic marker that reads:

H 6 ANDREW JOHNSON 1808-1875
President of the United States, 1865-1869. Born near here in a kitchen now located 1 mile N.E.

The Division of Archives and History erected the sign in the bicentennial year of 1976. It is located in front of the State of North Carolina Justice Building and across the street from the First Baptist Church.

History

In 1795, Peter Casso opened a stagecoach stop on the corner of Morgan and Fayetteville in Raleigh, North Carolina, which at the time, was still a sparsely populated settlement. The stop was called Casso's Inn, one of only two inns in Raleigh, and it was located on the perimeter of Union Square. At Casso's, patrons could get a room at the inn, a drink at the tavern, a meal at the restaurant and, of course, a visit to the cock-fighting pit. In 1808, Jacob and Mary Johnson both were employed at the inn, Mary as a weaver and Jacob as a horse keeper. The couple lived in a small two-story building that was used as the kitchen and was located behind the tavern and near the horse stables. December 29, 1808 was a special night at Casso's inn – there was a wedding party, but this was no ordinary couple. The bride was Peter Casso's daughter, Hannah, and she was marrying a successful merchant, John Stewart. Meanwhile, in the detached kitchen, Mary Johnson was in labor. That night, in a loft over the kitchen, she gave birth to the couple's third child and future president, Andrew Johnson. Legend has it that upon learning of the good news, Hannah Casso stepped away from her own wedding to pay a visit to the cabin to congratulate the family.[1]

Fifty-seven years later Andrew Johnson was sworn in as president when Abraham Lincoln was murdered. It was around this time that the birthplace was moved to East Cabarrus Street, between Wilmington and Blount Streets.[2] Strangers began to pour into the city to see where President Johnson was born, and Dr. Abraham Jobe from the U.S. Post Office knew the city better than anyone and was happy to oblige them. In his memoir he wrote:

> In visiting the old log house in which he was born, so many of them would split off small pieces to carry away that the house was pretty nearly destroyed during the first year I went there.[3]

While strangers may have been enthusiastic about the birthplace, the local citizens were not. Perhaps this was due to his Union loyalties while the pain of the Civil War defeat was still raw. The town of Raleigh was reluctant to embrace its famous son.

While it sat on East Cabarrus Street, the home began to fall into "a bad state of decay" and the local publication felt it necessary to point out that "for a long time it has been occupied by colored people."[4]

As for the original birth home site, today the Raleigh justice building is now located where Casso's Inn once stood.

Preservation

The home has been well traveled over the years. After the Civil War, the building was first moved several blocks away from Morgan and Fayetteville Street to nearby East Cabarrus Street.[5] There it stood for many years; however, the town had no interest in preserving the home. Sentiment began to shift shortly after the turn of the century. Despite Johnson's "failure to align himself with the South...in the war between the states", local residents began to call for saving the "little odd-shaped house" while there was still something left to preserve.[5] Finally, in July 1904, the Wake County Committee of the Society of the Colonial Dames purchased the home to donate it to the city of Raleigh. However, before turning it over, the patriotic ladies had the home moved to Pullen Park by the railroad tracks where it was "vulnerable... to locomotive sparks."[6] There the home stood for twenty-five years and slowly began to deteriorate.

In 1929, after the stock market crashed and the nation was suffering the Great Depression, the expected trajectory would have been for the home to further fall apart; however, Andrew Johnson's birthplace was initially able to buck the trend when the people of Raleigh banded together to restore the home in 1930.[7] Despite this effort, as the hard times continued, the home eventually fell victim as "hobos began to use it as an overnight lodging."[8] In an effort to save the home from complete destruction, WPA funding was used to move the house to the campus of the North Carolina State College of Agriculture and Engineering near the Raleigh Armory.[9] The home was jacked up, placed on a cart and wheeled to "a tree-shaded plot."[10] Finally starting to get the treatment it deserved, the home was "ensconced behind an old-fashioned picket fence."[11]

The home remained on the college campus until 1974 when it was once again moved one last time to Mordecai Historic Park. When the historians and architects dismantled the home to move it, they found that the home "differs radically...from the way it was when Johnson was born in it."[12] So when they rebuilt the home, they restored it to its original appearance. Today the home still stands in Mordecai Historic Park.

By 1940, there was a marker at the original birth location at the corner of Morgan and Fayetteville Streets. The current marker was erected in 1976.

Today, you can also find a mirror image replica of the birth home 280 miles away in Greenville, Tennessee, where the Johnsons lived after leaving Raleigh in 1826. The only noticeable difference is the chimney and downstairs window are on the left in the replica as opposed to the right side on the original. Nearby, a home in which Johnson lived during his later years is preserved as the Andrew Johnson National Historic Site and located diagonal to the National Park Visitors' Center on the corner of College and Depot Streets (but not part of the National Park Site) is the replica of the birthplace kitchen. The person responsible for this recreation is Andrew Johnson's great-granddaughter, Margaret Johnson Patterson Bartlett who worked at the National Park Site many years until 1976. In 1981, she felt that additional recognition was appropriate so she donated the money to create a replica of her great grandfather's birthplace. The home was first built on the campus of Tusculum College, where she had graduated in 1924 and where Andrew Johnson served as trustee from 1844 to 1875. A dedication ceremony was held on the campus grounds on November 24, 1981. Just like the real birthplace, the replica was also relocated – in 1999, it was moved to its current site outside of the Andrew Johnson National Historic Site.[13] In front of the home is a plaque that reads:

ANDREW JOHNSON BIRTHPLACE REPLICA 1999
The traditional story of Andrew Johnson's birth is held firmly in place by the preservation of a small historic structure located in Mordecai Park in Raleigh, North Carolina. That small building, probably built in the late 1700s, was part of a complex of buildings known as Casso's Inn, a well-known hotel of that period, located in Raleigh. This Inn

The home where Andrew Johnson was born, which was relocated several times before moving to its current location at Mordecai Historic Park in Raleigh, North Carolina in 1974.

A replica of the Andrew Johnson birthplace in Greeneville, Tennessee adjacent from the visitors' center of the Andrew Johnson National Historic Site.

was where Andrew Johnson's father worked as a stable keeper and his mother worked as a weaver. According to tradition, Andrew Johnson was born in the loft of the kitchen at the Inn. The story goes that on December 29, 1808 a wedding party was in progress at the tavern when the festivities were interrupted by news of the birth of a baby to the Johnsons. According to the same tradition, the bride went to the cabin at the back of the inn to visit with the baby and his mother. The building here is a replica of that birthplace of Andrew Johnson. It represents an important part the Andrew Johnson story and speaks of a man who began his life in very humble conditions and later became the seventeenth President of the United States of America.

Visitor Information

Raleigh is a beautiful, manageable city and the original birthplace location is located in the heart of the downtown area. The historic marker can be found right in front of the Justice Building and across from the First Baptist Church.

I visited in early 2010 on a cold winter day. As I stood admiring the sign and taking photographs, three men walked by. They were young professional types, perhaps a little past their prime, and were obviously curious as to what I found so interesting. For many years, the city kept their most famous son at a distance and it seems that times have not changed that much. As they walked past me, I could overhear their conversation. They looked at the sign, and then at me, and then again at the sign. Finally, one of the men incredulously asked his companions, "Who is Andrew Johnson?" After a brief pause, one of his friends hesitantly replied, "I'm not sure. I think he was president".

Mordecai Historic Park, where the birth home is located, offers tours Tuesday through Sunday. The park is not gated so the home is accessible even after park hours.

18.
Hiram Ulysses Simpson Grant

The birthplace of Ulysses S. Grant in Point Pleasant, Ohio.

Vital Birthplace Information

Birthplace	Point Pleasant, Ohio
President's birthday	April 27, 1822
How long in the home	A year and a half
Life of the home	1817 to present
Style	One room cottage
Still in existence	Yes
Commemoration	Grant Birthplace run by the Ohio Historical Society
Open to the public	Yes
Cost	$3.00
For more information	www.ohiohistory.org/places/grantbir
Replica exists	Not anymore
Significance	Only presidential birthplace home to be transported by boat
Closest birthplace	William Howard Taft, 27 miles

What you will find there today:

The Ulysses S. Grant birthplace is still in existence and is open to visitors. Today, the Ohio Historical Society manages the birth home. Inside the home are personal items that belonged to President Grant including the chest he took with him when he enrolled at West Point when he was only seventeen.[1]

In front of the birthplace is a two-sided historic marker erected by the Ohio Bicentennial Commission and the Ohio Historical Society in 2003. The marker reads:

Address/Directions:

1551 State Route 232
Point Pleasant, Ohio 45143

From the north or south, take US-52 to Route 232 East as soon as you enter Point Pleasant. The birthplace will be on your left after 1.3 miles.

Side A: **U.S. Grant Birthplace**
Hiram Ulysses Grant was born in this one-story, timber-frame home on April 27, 1822 to Jesse and Hannah Simpson Grant. The Grants settled in Point Pleasant the previous year, and Jesse took charge of the tannery located near the cottage. Now restored, the building remained in relatively good condition through the 1880s. In 1823, the family moved to Georgetown, Ohio, where Hiram lived until his appointment to West Point at age 17. Although reluctant to attend the Academy, Grant, now known as Ulysses Simpson Grant due to an error on the application, graduated in 1843 and was stationed at Jefferson Barracks near Saint Louis, where he courted his future wife Julia Dent, with whom he had four children, Frederick, Ellen, Ulysses Jr., and Jesse.

(Continued on other side)
Side B: **U.S. Grant Birthplace**
Grant served as quartermaster in the Mexican War (1846-1848), but resigned from the Army in 1854. He was living in Galena, Illinois, and working in the family's leather store at the outbreak of the Civil War in 1861. He volunteered for military service. Known as "Unconditional Surrender," Grant was appointed general-in-chief of Union forces by President Abraham Lincoln in 1864. His name recognition and lack of political ties made him the ideal candidate for the Republican nomination for the U.S. presidency. Grant was elected to two terms in 1868 and 1872. Despite Grant's character, his choice of cabinet appointments led to corruption in his administration. On July 23, 1885 at Mount McGregor, New York, Grant died just days after completing his acclaimed memoirs.

History

The village of Point Pleasant in southern Ohio was first laid out in 1822, and by the time that Ulysses Grant was born, eight years later, it had only grown to about fifteen to twenty families.[2] Within the village confines, Thomas Page opened a small store and tannery. One of his employees was Jesse Root Grant, originally from Pennsylvania. In 1821, Jesse moved into a one room, 16.5- by 19-foot timber cottage with a fireplace. The home was built four years earlier in 1817 and it was located near the mouth of Big Indian Creek at the Ohio River, only a short distance from the tannery. On June 24, 1921, Jesse Root Grant wed Hannah Simpson and his bride moved into the small cottage for which they paid $2 a month rent.[3] The couple got right down to the business of making a family and just over ten months later, in the early morning hours of April 27, 1822, a healthy 10-¾-pound baby was born. For almost a month, the future president did not have a name. They enlisted the help of their families and using suggestions from both sides, named the boy Hiram Ulysses Simpson Grant. In later years

he was better known as U.S. Grant, victorious general in the Civil War and our eighteenth president.

The Grants did not stay long in the birth home. The next year they moved to Georgetown, Ohio, and the brief time in his birthplace did not leave much of an impression on the future president. In Grant's 462-page autobiography *Personal Memoirs of U.S. Grant,* he summed up this period of his life in one sentence:

> **I was born on the 27th of June in 1822 at Point Pleasant, Clermont County, Ohio. In the fall of 1823, we moved to Georgetown…[4]**

After leaving the home, a lean-to kitchen was added instantly doubling the amount of rooms in the home! In 1865, after the Civil War had ended, a German family lived in the birth home of the country's most famous general.[5]

Preservation

Much like Lincoln's home, the Grant birthplace house and the property would take separate journeys until ultimately being reunited fifty years later. Less than a month after Ulysses S. Grant died, on July 23, 1885, the Grand Army of the Republic gathered in Cincinnati. The soldiers made a public proposal to purchase the home of their fallen hero.[6] Their idea to preserve the cabin did not come to fruition; however, three years later the home was purchased by a riverboat Captain named Mr. Powers in 1888. He had the lean-to removed and loaded the original structure onto a barge. The home was then floated down the Ohio River to Cincinnati. Once it was back on land, it was hitched to twenty-four horses and pulled to the corner of Elm Street and Canal Street. It is interesting to note that the marker that today stands in front of the home states that the cabin "remained in relatively good condition through the 1880s." Understanding that the home was uprooted and removed in 1888, the marker basically states that while the cabin was in Point Pleasant it was kept in good shape. After it left Point Pleasant, maybe not so much.

The cabin stood on display as part of the Ohio Centennial Exposition and was visited by thousands of people. After Cincinnati, the cabin toured around the country, settling in Goodale Park in Columbus for the centennial of the Northwest Territory in 1888 and later making its way to the Chicago World's Fair Exposition of 1893.[7]

Sometime afterwards, the historic cabin caught the attention of Henry Treat Chittenden (1834-1909), a millionaire showman from Columbus, Ohio, who made his money from real estate, railroads, and hotels. More significantly, he was also a friend of Grant and the captain of the "Squirrel Hunters" Brigade in the Civil War. Finally, he was a history buff and had served as vice president of the Ohio Centennial Exposition. He became interested in purchasing the birthplace cabin, but when he was given a price tag of $3,000, he first did an exhaustive study to confirm its authenticity. Once satisfied that the cabin was the real deal, he paid Captain Powers and had the building moved to the southeastern part of the Ohio State Fairground in Columbus, Ohio.[8] There the home stood for several years.

In 1896, Chittenden donated the home to the Ohio State Board of Agriculture. It was moved to another spot on the southeastern corner of the fairgrounds, and to protect it from the elements, an impressive brick and glass structure was built around it called the "Grant Memorial Building."[9] On September 4, 1896, the birth cabin and Memorial Building were dedicated. The ceremony started with a blessing by Reverend W.R. Parsons and then Ohio Governor Asa Smith Bushnell and Henry Chittenden both spoke before a crowd of 4,000 people. In addition, the Fourteenth Regiment Band played patriotic music for the appreciative crowd and the birth cabin received full military honors from Battery H of the Ohio Light Artillery.[10] The home stood in a prominent location near the 11th Avenue entrance outside of the "vehicles" building. Between the entrance and the cabin, in the shadow of the eighteenth president's birth home, was a man-made lake that was a popular spot for picnics.[11]

Over the years, two Ohio presidents visited the birth cabin. On September 2, 1897, William McKinley came to the State Fair; he had planned to come the year before for the grand opening, but his wife was sick so he postponed the visit. In late August 1912, William Howard Taft also visited the birth cabin for the Columbus Centennial celebration.[12]

Meanwhile, at the actual birthplace location in Point Pleasant, a memorial tablet was dedicated on October 2, 1907. U.S. Grant's son, General Fred Grant, accepted the honor. At the ceremony, the Ohio Governor Andrew L. Harris requested the "return to these grounds the house in which Gen. Grant was born".[13] This request went unheeded for almost three more decades.

On April 27, 1922, President Warren G. Harding spoke at the birthplace for the 100th anniversary of U.S. Grant's birth. This was Harding's first return to Ohio since his inauguration. With 20,000 in attendance to hear about President Grant, Harding instead chose to spend the lion's share of his speech discussing the post war atmosphere in Europe. Also coinciding with Grant's 100th birthday was the formation of a group of concerned citizens who worked to commemorate the birth site in Point Pleasant. The society cleared the land and planted trees at the birthplace and named the four-acre parcel "Grant Memorial State Park."[14] To help pay for the park, commemorative gold dollars and silver half dollars were minted, struck with a picture of the birth cabin.[15] However, the ultimate goal of the birthplace society, as well as the ambition of most of the citizens of Point Pleasant, was to get the cabin back. After thirty-four years, the citizens were getting inpatient. Prior to the President's visit one citizen was quoted:

We want it back. Here it belongs. We want to place it where is stood before and it shall be a shrine to the nation. What will people say when they come here…and discover that our most valuable treasure has been taken away from us?[16]

Unfortunately, the townsfolk would have to continue to wait.

In August 1926, the *New York Times* reported that the birthplace cabin was burned in Point Pleasant. A week later they retracted the article to a relieved nation when it was realized that the birth cabin was actually 120 miles away in Columbus, Ohio.[17] By this time, efforts were underway to have the original cabin returned, but apparently not moving fast enough. The next year, the people of Point Pleasant figured if they didn't have the original cabin, then they would build a re-creation and place it on the original birthplace location. While the real birthplace cabin was still standing inside the glass Grant Memorial Building on the capital grounds in Columbus,

Ohio, a dedication ceremony was held for the replica on October 29, 1927. In attendance was Ulysses Simpson Grant III, grandson of the eighteenth president and director of the Office of Public Buildings and Public Parks of the National Capital.[18]

In August 1930, 25,000 visitors, including several thousand aging Union and Confederate veterans converged upon Cincinnati for the annual Grand Army of the Republic gathering. The soldiers were greeted with a parade and patriotic speeches were made. The reunion culminated with a pilgrimage down the Ohio River to visit the birthplace of U.S. Grant. Forty-five years earlier, this group had discussed purchasing the home at their 1885 reunion; however, nothing had come of the proposal. Since the original cabin was still on the Ohio State Fairgrounds in Columbus, what the soldiers visited was the re-creation.[19]

By 1930, the original cabin was starting to show the wear and tear of being on the road for over forty years. Noting that it was deteriorating fast, Hugh Llewellyn Nichols, former Chief Justice of the Supreme Court of Ohio, led an effort to have it restored. He quickly raised over $100,000; however, the efforts slogged along as the country became mired in a Great Depression.[20] By the mid 1930s, the end was near for the cabin's time on the fairgrounds. Perhaps as a last farewell for the rundown old cabin, General John Joseph "Black Jack" Pershing paid a visit on May 11, 1935. Pershing was a veteran of many wars from battling Sioux and Apache Indians on the Western Plains to the Germans in World War I. On the day he came to pay his respects to General U.S. Grant's birthplace, he was accompanied by the First Brigade Assembly and First Regimental Drill Meet.[21]

The location where the Ulysses S. Grant birthplace log cabin once stood confined within the "Grant Memorial Building" on the Ohio State Fairgrounds in Columbus, Ohio. The site is now a parking lot that doubles as the Kiddieland Amusement Park. Standing on the location is the extremely helpful and knowledgeable Ohio State Fair Official Historian, LaVon Shook.

Finally, in 1936, the Point Pleasant citizens' long awaited wish was finally granted when the Grant Memorial State Park Society succeeded in retrieving the birthplace cabin.[22] The home was carefully taken apart on February 24, 1936, and after being loaded onto six trucks and placed on a towboat, it finally returned to the original location in Point Pleasant.[23] On October 4, 1936 a welcome home rededication ceremony was held and the birthplace was officially opened as the "Grant House Museum." However, the Grant Memorial State Park Society must have wished that they waited one more year when, in late January 1937, the Ohio River flooded and the home was submerged to its roof.

The Grant Memorial Building remained on the Ohio State Fairgrounds in Columbus for several more years. It was used for varied purposes until it was eventually torn down. Today, the site where the birth cabin once stood is in the middle of the paved "Kiddieland" amusement area within the Ohio State Fairgrounds. Unfortunately, despite the birth cabin of our eighteenth president having stood in this spot for forty years, there is no marker at the historic location.[24]

In 1978, the home was restored to look as it did back in the nineteenth century when baby Grant was born. However, with visitors never bursting through the doors and the economic woes of the 1970s and early 1980s, the cabin began to spin into a downward spiral. In 1981, the birthplace was closed due to lack of funds and did not reopen for four years. When it did, it was again hit by economic hardship. The birthplace had deteriorated and the Ohio Historical Society claimed they did not have the funds to make the necessary chimney, shingle, fence, gutter, and downspout repairs.[25]

In 1990, an agreement was entered between the state and the Ohio Historical Society for the Society to operate the birthplace; however, the troubles were not yet over. After portable toilets were removed, neighbors began complaining as visitors came knocking on their door asking to use the bathroom.[26] By the middle of the 1990s, the home was again largely neglected and visitation was down to about 5,000 people per year.[27]

In 1998, things started to turn around for the birthplace. After being relocated and exploited time and time again in the beginning of the century, and then ignored as it deteriorated throughout the latter half, the home was redeemed on August 6, 1998, when it was listed on the National Register of Historical Places (National Register Number #98001013). The National Park Service held a ceremony at the site in October of that same year. The recognition was largely due to Mary Campbell who had been trying for thirty-one years to have the site added to the register. By the time of the recognition, annual visitation had jumped to about 11,500.[28]

Five years later, in the spring of 2003, the Ohio Bicentennial Commission and the Ohio Historical Society erected and dedicated a historic marker.

Visitor Information

The home is opened April 1 through October 30 from Wednesday to Sunday. I visited in 2008 and took the brief, pleasant tour of the one-room home. Unaware of the earlier "portable potty" situation, I asked the woman who gave the tour if there was a public restroom for my son. Without knowing us at all, she allowed us to use her bathroom in her home next door and then gave my son a complimentary souvenir Steamboat pencil sharpener! Whoever she was, her kindness and generosity made this one of my most pleasurable birthplace visits ever!

19.
Rutherford Birchard "B.P." Hayes

Vital Birthplace Information

Birthplace	Delaware, Ohio
President's birthday	October 4, 1822
How long in the home	Approximately 1 year
Life of the home	Before 1822 to August 1910
Style	Brick home
Still in existence	No
Ultimate fate	Destroyed by fire
Commemoration	Historic marker
Open to the public	Yes
Cost	$2.85 per gallon of regular when I visited
For more information	www.bp.com
Replica exists	No
Significance	Only birthplace location currently occupied by a business
Closest birthplace	Warren G. Harding, 30 miles

Address/Directions:

**17 East William Street
Delaware, Ohio 43015**

The birthplace is in downtown Delaware on US 36/William Street, a half-block east of Sandusky Street.

The birthplace of Rutherford B. Hayes in front of a BP gas station on William Street in Delaware, Ohio.

What you will find there today:

A BP gas station now stands at the spot where President Rutherford B. Hayes was born. In front of the gas station is a historic marker with the following inscription:

THIS TABLET MARKS THE BIRTHPLACE OF RUTHERFORD B. HAYES
Nineteenth president of the United States
Born October 4, 1822
Placed by Delaware City Charter
Daughters of the American Revolution
November 1926

History

The Delaware Indians originally inhabited the area that is now Delaware, Ohio. The land was part of a land grant made to Moses Byxbe from Berkshire County, Massachusetts. Byxbe was a colonel in the Revolutionary War and was given the land grant as payment for his service in 1804, a year after Ohio joined the Union as our seventeenth state. Byxbe and Judge Henry Baldwin first laid out the town of Delaware in 1808.[1]

In 1817, Rutherford Hayes Jr. and his wife Sophia Birchard Hayes came to Delaware, Ohio from Vermont and upon their arrival, built a brick home on the north side of William Street (named after Judge Baldwin's brother, William Baldwin). The home was a sturdy two-story brick building with eight windows in the front and a gabled roof. It was beautifully finished in fine cherry and walnut woodwork and it had the distinction as the first brick building in town.[2] Rutherford and Sophia already had four children when she became pregnant with her fifth in 1822. As she entered her seventh month of her pregnancy, Rutherford took ill. On June 6, 1922 Rutherford Hayes Jr. died of typhus in his home. Three months later, on October 4 1822, Rutherford Birchard Hayes, the future president, was born in the home on Williams Street. The widow Hayes continued to live in the home with baby Rutherford for about another year until moving into another home in Delaware, Ohio.

In later years, the home was occupied by various businesses. In 1876, the year Rutherford B. Hayes was elected the nineteenth president, "J.S. Reichert Ware Rooms," a furniture store was being run out of the birthplace building. Historical records show this store had been in the birthplace location since at least 1866.[3]

In August of 1910, a fire broke out in the home. By the time the flames were finally extinguished, the birth home, and a piece of presidential history, was destroyed.[4] Rutherford B. Hayes is the third president to have had his birthplace destroyed by fire, but Hayes is the first since Thomas Jefferson (the other is George Washington). This string of sixteen birthplaces that were *not* destroyed by fire (including Jefferson Davis) is the longest in history.

A Standard Oil Company gas station was built on the birthplace location a decade later in 1920. It is at this writing a BP station.

Preservation

Unless the initials in the B. P. gas station mean "Birth Place" and not "British Petroleum" there hasn't been much of a preservation effort. In 1926, the Delaware Chapter of the Daughters of the American Revolution passed a resolution to memorialize the historic site with a bronze plaque. The next year, the D.A.R. gathered for the dedication ceremony. In 1955, the bronze plaque was attached to a stone tablet and landscaping was completed at the memorial, all paid for by the Standard Oil Company.[5]

Visitor Information

We visited in the summer of 2008, as we crisscrossed Ohio, snaking our way through the state's seven presidential birthplaces. By this point, my mother had gotten over the novelty of climbing out from the back of the minivan to see a birthplace marker so she stayed as my Dad, son Vincent, and utterly-confused niece, Danielle, got out to pay our respects. After visiting the birthplace and filling up the tank, we ate at Bun's Restaurant, which first opened in 1864, forty-two years after Hayes' birth.

20.
James Abram Garfield

The James Garfield log cabin birthplace in Moreland Hills, Ohio.

Vital Birthplace Information

Birthplace	Orange Township (now Moreland Hills), Ohio
President's birthday	November 19, 1831
How long in the home	28 years
Life of the home	1830 to after 1859
Style	Log cabin
Still in existence	No
Ultimate fate	Destroyed by fire
Commemoration	Historic marker and re-created birth home
Open to the public	Yes
Cost	Free
For more information	www.morelandhills.com
Replica exists	Yes, at birthplace
Significance	Last of the log cabin presidents
Closest birthplace	William McKinley, 44 miles

What you will find there today:

A replica of the log cabin birthplace of James Abram Garfield is located next to the Moreland Hills Police Station and Village Hall. It was built and opened in 1999. At the side of the road near the home is a two-sided Ohio Historic marker (number 15-18) stating on one side:

BIRTHPLACE OF JAMES A. GARFIELD.
20th President of the United States.
November 19, 1831
This was formerly Orange Township

And on the other,
James Abram Garfield, 20th President of the United States, was born here in 1831. His father died when he was two, but the family remained on the farm where James helped when he was not attending school. He continued to live here through his years as a driver and bowman on the canal and as a student at Geauga Seminary and Hiram Eclectic Institute (later Hiram College). He left here in 1859 when he was elected to the Ohio Senate.

The Moreland Hills Historical Society and the Ohio Historical Society erected the marker in 1990.

At the actual birthplace location, deeper into the woods, is a historic marker dedicated in 1931. At the spot is also an undated marker that reads:

THE CABIN
James A. Garfield was born in a cabin in the wilderness on November 19, 1831. The cabin was 20 feet by 30 feet, made of unhewn logs, notched and laid one upon another in what was called the "cob house" style. The height was 12 feet or more in front and 8 feet or more on the backside. The spaces between the logs were filled with clay or mud, making a warm home for winter and a cool one for summer.

Address/Directions:

4350 SOM Center Road
Moreland Hills, Ohio 44022

From US-422/I-271 take exit 28B for Harvard Road. After .4 miles turn right onto Harvard Road/Hiram Trail. After 2.4 miles turn right onto SOM Center Road and the birthplace (and Moreland Hills Town Hall and Police Department) will be on the left after .8 miles.

History

In January 1830, Abram and Eliza Ballou Garfield first settled in the little village of Orange Township (now Moreland Hills), Ohio, about fifteen miles outside of Cleveland in what was then a "poorly populated, fertile wilderness of old-growth forests."[1] The Garfields purchased Lot 10, in Section 3, Township 7, which was a fifty-acre plot of land, for only $2 an acre.[2] Abram's younger half-brother, Amos Boynton, had only recently settled in the area himself, so the Garfields temporarily moved into his little cabin. The crowded conditions must have helped motivate the men, because shortly after the arrival, Amos and Abram went to work on building a log cabin for the Garfield family, selecting a site "on an elevated mound, behind which was a little ravine."[3] The two men used a team of oxen to haul the timber from the forest for the 20- by 30-foot log cabin. The cabin had three windows, a ladder to a loft, a fireplace, and chimney. By the early spring of 1830, the cabin was completed and the Garfields moved into their new home and Abram began farming wheat on his land.

The following year, on November 19, 1831, the couple welcomed a son, James Abram Garfield, the last president to be born in a log cabin. When James was only seventeen months old, his father died of pneumonia and his mother raised him along with his siblings in this small cabin.

For twenty-eight years, James lived in this home until he was elected to the Ohio Senate in 1859.

The last time he returned to his birthplace was in 1880. He died the next year, on September 19, 1881, after being shot on July 2, 1881. The original log cabin was later destroyed by fire; however, the circumstances surrounding the fire are unknown. In 1929, the town of Moreland Hills was incorporated, and in the 1940s, the birthplace land was purchased for the Village Hall. At the time, there was no evidence of the birthplace cabin.[4]

Preservation

The first recorded recognition of the James Garfield birthplace was a gathering of old farmers and their families several months prior to his election in 1880. President Hinsdale of his *Alma mater*, Hiram College, made an address to the small crowd.[5] Over fifty years later, on what would have been James Garfield's 100th birthday, a more official ceremony was held when a marker was dedicated at the actual birthplace location.[6] The memorial boulder affixed with a bronze plaque, reads:

NOVEMBER 19, 1831
This boulder marks the site of the birthplace of James A.
Garfield the twentieth President of the United States
November 19, 1931
Presented by the Memorial Tablet Co. Mansfield, Ohio.

In 1936, a replica of the home was made and placed in the yard of the Garfield home in Mentor, Ohio, which is now a National Park Site.[7] The home was administered by the Lake County Historical Society and it was a much more rustic version of the replica that today is at Moreland Hills. The home at Mentor had a chimney on the left side and the front had a single window in the middle and a door to the right. This marks the first time that a replica was constructed at a different location prior to a permanent recognition being made at the original birthplace. In later years, the home was removed from the grounds.

A marker was erected in 1990, sponsored by the Moreland Hills Historical Society and the Ohio Historical Society, at the roadside in front of the birth site. Also, to honor the last of the log cabin presidents, the Moreland Hills Historical Society re-created the log cabin using descriptions of the original. In 1999, the "James Abram Garfield Memorial Cabin" was completed and opened to the public. At the dedication ceremony, Garfield family members were in attendance to honor their famous ancestor.[8]

This cabin differed significantly from the one created at Mentor sixty-three years earlier. The home in Mentor had a chimney on the left of the home and a single window to the left of the front door. In Moreland Hills, the chimney is on the right and there are two in front of the home, one on either side of the door. From the description included on a plaque on the front of the Moreland Hills cabin, it appears that the latter is the more accurate rendition.

In 1829 Abram Garfield, a farmer, and his wife, Eliza Ballou Garfield, built a log cabin, 20' x 30' described as having three windows, loft and ladder, fireplace and chimney. This cabin follows that description as nearly as possible. The Garfield's fourth child was born in that cabin, and became the last of our "Log Cabin presidents."

JAMES ABRAM GARFIELD
20th President of the United States of America
Born November 19, 1831 – Died September 19, 1881
James played in these woods, attended school nearby, helped his widowed mother on the farm and learned carpentry. He excelled as a student, became a college president, state senator, ordained minister, Brig. General serving in the Civil War, U.S. Congressmen and in 1880 was elected President of the United States of America.
The Moreland Hills Historical Society

On the left side of the cabin is another plaque, dated October 23, 1999, to thank the "Donors of Labors, Materials [and] Counsel for the James Abram Garfield Memorial Cabin." In front of the cabin is a charming statue of James Garfield depicting him as a boy growing up in the cabin.

The replica is located in front of the Village Hall and is visible from the road; however, this is not the actual location of the Garfield cabin. Behind the home is a trail that leads down to a stream. Crossing the stream will bring you to the actual birthplace location and the birthplace marker from November 19, 1931.

Visitor Information

The last of the log cabin presidents would probably not be too welcome today in this upscale community. From both directions on SOM Center Road (Route 91) there are large well-groomed homes and right down the road is the Chagrin Valley Country Club, a far cry from the rustic setting where James Garfield was born. The walk to the actual birthplace is through the wooded area and the trail can be slippery and muddy after it rains. Note there is also a handicapped drive to the actual birthplace accessible off of SOM Center Road.

As of this writing, the Moreland Hills Village Hall claims the Garfield birth cabin replica is open during summer months (June through September) on Saturdays only from 10 a.m. to 1 p.m., but my advice is call ahead to confirm. When I visited in summer 2010 during the visitor hours, the Village Hall and birth cabin replica were locked. To help support the birth cabin (and hopefully extend the visiting hours), you can purchase a personally inscribed brick, which will be placed on the pathway that leads to the Garfield log cabin replica. Visit the Moreland Hills Village Hall website for more information.

21.
Chester Alan Arthur

The replica of the home once believed to be the birthplace of Chester Arthur in Fairfield, Vermont. It was later determined to have been modeled after the second home in which Chester Arthur lived.

What you will find there today:

At the President Chester A. Arthur State Historic Site is a re-creation of the second home in which Chester Arthur lived; however, at the time the structure was built in 1953, it was believed to be a model of the birthplace home. Since then, historians have learned that this site was not the birthplace, but instead the second home in which Chester Arthur lived.

Address/Directions:

455 Chester Arthur Road
Fairfield, Vermont 05455

Take Route 36 to the town of Fairfield. At the intersection, go north and after about a mile, bear right. Continue five miles to the Chester A. Arthur State Historic Site.

History

Over 125 years before Barack Obama, the country of Chester Alan Arthur's birth was also a controversial topic of fierce debate from those across the aisle. Incomplete records, untruths, and the publication of a scandalous book brought Chester Arthur's legitimacy for the highest office into doubt. However, unlike Barack Obama, he chose to ignore rather than eventually address the accusations directly.

The story begins in 1828 when Chester Arthur's parents, William Arthur and Malvina Stone, moved to Fairfield, Vermont. They had previously lived across the border in Canada and then later in Burlington, Vermont. William recently had become an ordained Baptist Minister, and had moved to Fairfield to lead their forty-six-member congregation. The Arthurs moved into a one and a half-story frame "primitive cabin hastily erected in the village of

Fairfield."[1] The location of the home was listed as "Fairfield Center," although several sources gave different locations throughout Fairfield in later years, making his birthplace controversy one of country *and* county.

A year after moving into Fairfield, on October 5, 1829, the couple had their fifth child, and our twenty-first president, Chester Alan Arthur. This baby would one day become the northernmost-born president in United States history and the first to be born in a manse (the other two are Grover Cleveland and Woodrow Wilson). The next year, a more permanent parsonage was completed for the Arthurs and the family left the birthplace home.[2] After the Arthurs moved out, it may have later been used as a barn. Over the years, the structure succumbed to the elements, and by November 1886, when Chester Arthur passed away, the home was reduced to a "cellar that [was] partially torn down and filled with briars."[3] By 1903, the building had already been torn down.[4]

The controversy began after James Garfield won the presidential election in 1880 with Chester Arthur as his vice president. Shortly after the election, the Democratic National Committee hired a New York attorney Arthur P. Hinman to dig up dirt on the vice president elect. The Democrats did not believe that Chester was born in Fairfield, Vermont, nor did they believe he was even born in the United States of America. If they could prove their case, they could disqualify him from ever becoming president. Hinman figured the place to start was where Chester Arthur claimed he was born, so in December of 1880, he packed up and headed for Fairfield. He checked into the American House Hotel and began hanging around town, asking the locals, especially the old-timers, about the Arthur family.[5] After learning all he could from the Fairfield townsfolk, Hinman headed to Canada to continue his research.

Hinman concluded that Arthur was born in Dunham, Quebec, in Canada, not Fairfield, and was therefore not an American citizen.[6] He accused Arthur of traveling to Canada following his election as vice president in 1880 to see if there were any records or evidence of his birth. Finding none, he chose Fairfield, Vermont as his birthplace. He claimed that Arthur knew nobody would be able to prove otherwise and he was supported by the fact that his father was a preacher there around the time of his birth.[7] Hinman even went so far as to claim that the Arthurs did have a baby son while in Fairfield who had died as an infant and Chester Arthur had deviously appropriated his deceased younger brother's birth records.[8] In 1884, Hinman published his explosive allegations in his book *How a British Subject Became President of the United States.* The problem for Hinman and the Democratic National Committee was that even if their case could be proven, it was too late. By 1884, Chester Arthur had already been president for three years following the assassination of James Garfield.[9]

Arthur also provided fuel to the conspiracy theorists fire when he apparently lied about his birth year, claiming he was born in 1830, when he was actually born in 1829. Even his grave in Albany, New York, cites his birth date as 1830.

Preservation

The first effort to commemorate Chester Arthur's birthplace was made on November 23, 1900, when the Vermont House of Representatives proposed to erect a tablet to mark what was understood to be the actual location. At the time, P.B.B. Northrop, a producer of maple syrup, owned the land. Fortunately, Northrop donated the property to the state of Vermont to allow for the commemoration plans to proceed. Three years later, the memorial was ready. On August 20, 1903, a granite monument was placed at the site that read:

ON THIS SPOT STOOD THE COTTAGE WHERE WAS BORN CHESTER A. ARTHUR THE TWENTY-FIRST PRESIDENT OF THE UNITED STATES ERECTED BY THE STATE OF VERMONT.

A simple dedication ceremony was held, but bad weather and the remote location limited the turnout to "Franklin County people who could drive from nearby points."[10] Despite the sparse attendance, a litany of politicians and dignitaries spoke at the ceremony. Presiding over the event was former Congressmen Horace Henry Powers, and speakers included former Governor William W. Stickney and Abraham Lincoln's son, Robert T. Lincoln from Chicago, who served as Arthur's Secretary of War. The list goes on: Senator Redfield Proctor, Congressman D.J. Foster, Congressman Kittridge Haskins, and the principal speaker, Senator William E. Chandler, who had served under President Arthur as Secretary of the Navy. On that cold Vermont day, there may have been more speakers than people in the audience![11]

This marker still exists, making it the second oldest standing presidential birthplace historic marker, preceded only by Zachary Taylor's marker erected at Hare Forest three years earlier in 1900. Interestingly, in both cases, these markers recognized little-known presidents at a location that later proved to be inaccurate. In 1950, the state of Vermont purchased additional land surrounding the marker to accommodate a replica of the "birthplace home." Using a photograph from 1880 as a model, the re-creation was completed in 1953. Today, inside the home you can see the photograph; however, you may not recognize it. Fifty years after the president's birth, the home had become a downtrodden and ramshackle wooden shack, which bears little resemblance to the school-bus yellow manicured re-creation that stands there today. After 1953, historians determined that the re-creation was not built at the birthplace site, nor was it a replica of the birthplace home, but rather it was an accurate replica of the second home the in which the Arthurs lived during their time in Fairfield.[12]

In the early part of the twenty-first century, updated historic markers were placed in Fairfield to better reflect the ambiguity surrounding the actual birthplace site. In 2002, the Vermont Division for Historic Preservation erected a marker in front of the re-created home at the State Historic Site that reads:

21ST PRESIDENT OF THE UNITED STATES
Research indicates Chester Alan Arthur was born in Fairfield, Vermont, on October 5, 1829. When he was less than a year old his parents moved to a new parsonage built at this site. After graduating Phi Beta Kappa from Union College, he became a lawyer championing civil rights for blacks. Later, as Quartermaster General, he organized the provision of food & supplies to Union Civil War soldiers. On September 19, 1881, Arthur became president following the assassination of James Garfield. As president he advocated reducing tariffs and backed Civil Service reform, turning away from political patronage. Arthur died in 1886 and is buried in Albany, NY. This replica of the parsonage was built in 1954.

The Chester Arthur birthplace marker at the only intersection in Fairfield, Vermont.

Note the completion date of 1954 conflicts with the state's literature, which cites 1953. For some reason, precise dates seem to be a problem when it comes to President Arthur.

In 2003, the Vermont Division for Historic Preservation erected another historic marker at the center of Fairfield, which may have been the location of the birth home. This is the only intersection in Fairfield at North Road and Route 36. It reads:

BIRTHPLACE OF 21ST PRESIDENT
Although the exact location is debated, Chester A. Arthur was born on Oct. 5, 1829 in Fairfield. He became a New York lawyer and politician and was elected Vice-President in 1880. Upon the assassination of James Garfield, Arthur became President on Sept. 20, 1881. His administration was distinguished by the creation of the U.S. Civil Service, better relations with Central and South America, and the revival of the U.S. Navy. Arthur died Nov. 18, 1886. The State-Owned Historic Site is 5 miles northwest from here.

The marker is across from the Fairfield Country Store, but was erected at an odd angle, so if you are driving down Route 36 from the west you may miss it.

Visitor Information

The combination of a little-known president born at the most remote location of any commander-in-chief makes this a destination for only the most-dedicated birthplace collector. Throw in the short visiting hours and the roller coaster-like ride, if you visit Chester Arthur's birthplace, you are either a true aficionado or very, very lost.

When I visited in the summer of 2010, even my GPS started acting strangely. As I neared the home, I was serenaded with a chorus of "lost satellite... lost satellite... recalculating... recalculating," and it's little wonder since the home is literally at the end of the road – beyond the home, dirt picks up where the pavement ends – and when I finally *did* arrive, I was not surprised to find the parking lot across the street empty. There were two children playing in the front yard, but the large marker and flag assured me I was in the right place. Upon seeing me approach, the children quickly ran inside the home to sit quietly by their mother who also doubled as museum guide.

The home is filled with several placards of information about the twentieth president, the first three of which are completely dedicated to the birthplace mystery. In 2008, visitors' hours were cut from seven to two days a week due to budget issues, so the home is now open weekends only from early July through mid-October from 11 a.m. to 5 p.m. Each year about 400 people visit the home.[2] My brother, Joseph, visited two weeks before I did. When I signed the guest book, I noted only a handful of names were logged between our visits so obviously this is not a tourist hot spot. Be aware that only one person watches over the site, so if they are sick or otherwise unavailable, you may find the home closed. On my way up to northern Vermont, I stopped first at Calvin Coolidge's birthplace at Plymouth Notch. The friendly guide asked me where I was heading to and when I told her, she recommended I call ahead to make sure they were open. I followed her advice; however, the problem was that nobody answered. Not sure if that meant the home was closed or the guide was asleep; I took a chance and went anyway. When I arrived, I discovered why nobody answered – there was no phone! No computer either for that matter, but the most surprising omission was the missing gift shop! The house is probably not much more modern than the one the Arthurs lived in almost two centuries earlier.

On your way back to civilization, take a right on Dodd Street to visit the North Fairfield Baptist Church. It was on this site where the church stood that Chester Arthur's father preached. The original church was torn down and the current one was built around 1840.

22. & 24.
Stephen Grover Cleveland

A winter day at Grover Cleveland's birthplace in Caldwell, New Jersey.

Vital Birthplace Information

Birthplace	Caldwell, New Jersey
President's birthday	March 18, 1837
How long in the home	4 years
Life of the home	1832 to present
Style	Manse
Still in existence	Yes
Commemoration	Grover Cleveland Birthplace State Historic Site
Open to the public	Yes
Cost	Free
For more information	www.clevelandbirthplace.org
Replica exists	No
Significance	Only president born in New Jersey
Closest birthplace	Theodore Roosevelt, 23 miles

What you will find there today:

The Grover Cleveland birthplace is a State Historic Site administered by the New Jersey Department of Environmental Protection. The home is situated on 2.5 acres and is restored to how it appeared in 1837, the year the president was born in the back room. Many of the Cleveland family artifacts are within the home and displays tell the story of his political career and family life. The home contains the country's largest collection of Grover Cleveland artifacts and memorabilia, including his cradle and original family photographs. Each year about 5,000 people visit President Cleveland's birthplace.

Address/Directions:

**207 Bloomfield Avenue
Caldwell, New Jersey 07006**

There are several major highways in the vicinity of the Grover Cleveland birthplace including the Garden State Parkway, Route 23, Route 46, and Route 80. Follow signs to the town of Caldwell and the home is on Bloomfield Avenue/Route 506 across from Dunkin' Donuts.

History

The current town of Caldwell, New Jersey, is part of a larger piece of land that was first purchased from the Lenni Lenape Indians in 1702 by settlers moving west from Newark. The acquisition was known as the "Horse-Neck tract" because of its shape and later became known as the village of Horse-Neck. It encompassed modern day Caldwell as well as many of the surrounding towns. By 1740, the area of current Caldwell was home to about thirty-five families, but did not yet have a church, and for several decades visiting pastors, including Reverends Stephen Grover and James Caldwell, performed services. By the late 1770s, the townsfolk began efforts towards establishing a church of their own. Their work was rewarded on July 17, 1779, when in the midst of the Revolutionary War, the town of Horse-Neck gave a parcel of land to the First Presbyterian Church for a church for the parishioners, a manse for the minister, and a cemetery for the deceased.[1]

The Reverend James Caldwell, so integral a part of the establishment of the first church of Horse-Neck, was not to live to see its completion. In 1781, while serving as chaplain for the patriot army, Caldwell was killed under suspicious circumstances by an American sentry. In 1787, the parish was renamed in his honor, and in 1789, the town of Horse-Neck followed suit and was rechartered as the town of Caldwell, New Jersey.[2]

In 1788, the Reverend Stephen Grover was ordained as the initial pastor of the First Presbyterian Church and received an annual salary of $150. Three years later, in 1791, the church acquired an additional parcel of land. It would take over forty years, but eventually this land would be used for the manse, or home for the Pastor, which was erected in 1832. The home was a frame house, two stories in the main section with a single story kitchen and lean-to on the side. The home cost the First Presbyterian Church of Caldwell a tidy sum of $1,500. Today, this house is one of the two oldest homes in Caldwell.[3]

Reverend Stephen Grover remained as pastor at the church for forty-four years, living in the manse for the final two of those years. His tenure ended on May 11, 1834, when a new pastor, Reverend Richard Falley Cleveland, was ordained. The Reverend, his wife, Ann Neal, and their three children moved into the manse shortly afterwards (the Clevelands were well traveled, living in several cities along the east coast, most recently Portsmouth, Virginia). That same year, they had their fourth child, Richard Cecil, around Christmas, 1834. Just over two years later, on March 18, 1837, in the back bedroom of their home, the couple gave birth to their fifth of nine children, Stephen Grover. The boy, who would one day become the only man elected to two non-consecutive terms as president, was named after Reverend Cleveland's predecessor. The Clevelands had one more child in this home, their third daughter, Margaret Louise Falley, in 1838.[4]

During his time as pastor, the Reverend Cleveland and the church disagreed over wages. Cleveland was promised a $600 annual salary; however, the church claimed it could not pay him more than $450. The argument over finances soon spilled over to the quality of his sermons and eventually the parishioners actually took a vote on whether they liked his sermons or not. He won the vote, but saw the writing on the wall. The Reverend Richard resigned in the fall of 1840 and moved the family to another home in Caldwell for about a year, before moving on to Fayetteville, New York.

In 1841, the new pastor, Samuel L. Tuttle, moved into the manse followed by Isaac Newton Sprague (1850) and Charles T. Berry (1869). Berry was living in the home when Cleveland served his first term as president, and at the time, the birth room was being used as a library. During these years, the church expanded the manse several times as the congregation continued to grow. Berry was succeeded by Henry K. Denlinger (1894) and Nelson Chester (1899). Chester was in the manse when the president passed away in 1908 and was the last pastor to live in the birthplace home.[5]

Preservation

In 1881, when Grover Cleveland was mayor of Buffalo and running for Governor of New York, the historical significance of the birthplace home was first realized. Cleveland moved up quickly in politics, from mayor of Buffalo to President of the United States in only three years. In 1884, when Cleveland announced his candidacy for president, interest in the home began to intensify. At the time the Reverend Charles T. Berry was living in the home, and when a reporter showed up at the door he lamented, "I suppose I shall have numerous callers now."[6]

As his career rose, so did the understanding that the home should be preserved, possibly as a museum. In 1907, a small ceremony was

held to place a bronze plaque in the room Grover Cleveland was born in seventy years earlier. The plaque simply stated:

Here Grover Cleveland was born March 18, 1837.

Grover Cleveland did not attend the ceremony, nor did he return to his birthplace after his family moved to New York in 1841. However, from his writings, it is known that he regarded Caldwell warmly and was honored by the event. He wrote to the church in 1884:

Though I remember almost nothing of the village where

I spent a few very early days, I can sincerely say that the spot is dear to me as the place of his birth should be dear to every man.[7]

In the fall of 1907, Cleveland fell seriously ill after his health had been deteriorating for several years. That same year, his Caldwell birth home almost came to an end when a fire on Bloomfield Avenue nearly burned the president's residence to the ground. It was only due to the "hard work by the fireman and residents of the borough of Caldwell" that the building was spared.[8] The home would survive, but the president would not. The following year he suffered a heart attack and died on June 24, 1908.

One of the first people who suggested the birth home should be purchased for a memorial was Caldwell newspaper publisher William H. Van Wart. His efforts started to gain momentum when several executives from the life insurance industry began negotiations with the church to purchase the home in 1908. Insurance industry leaders held Grover Cleveland in high regard because "subsequent to his Presidential career, Mr. Cleveland had performed a national service in reforming and reorganizing the insurance business, public confidence in which had been shaken."[9] John H. Finley, who had become friends with President Cleveland when they both lived in Princeton, New Jersey, headed the effort to make the birthplace available to the public as a museum. More so than any other individual, Mr. Finley is responsible for preserving the Grover Cleveland birthplace for future generations to visit and enjoy. The president first met Finley when he became a professor at Princeton University in 1900 after moving there three years earlier. Finley had since become the president of the College of New York and editor at the New York Times; not surprisingly there exists an abundance of New York Times articles about the birthplace during these years. Not everyone from the church was thrilled with the idea of selling the manse, and negotiations dragged on for several years. Another proposal during this time was to turn the home into the headquarters of the local Democratic Club from Caldwell, Verona, Essex Fells, and Roseland, but church trustees objected and the plan fell through.[10] By 1912, the sale to Finley and his associates had enough support to complete the purchase. After the church board approved the sale by a vote of 15-2, they settled upon a purchase price of $18,000 and the home went under contract on March 9, 1912. The home had "become a bit dingy" and the association sought to raise another $25,000 to renovate and maintain it.[11]

Commemorative services were held on March 18, 1912, which would have been Cleveland's 75th birthday. Reverend Nelson B. Chester, the occupant of the manse at the time, conducted the services and John H. Finley was one of the speakers. While these annual services would continue for several years, the next year was a special one, as it included the opening of the manse to the public – a month prior to the 1913 ceremony on February 21, the coalition that administered the home incorporated the Grover Cleveland Birthplace Memorial Association "to honor and perpetuate the memory of Grover Cleveland."[12] The Association had grown to four officers (counting Finley), and thirty-nine trustees, including

local democrats such as $10,000 donor George Canfield, Caldwell newspaper publisher William H. Van Wart (who served as secretary), and August Belmont Jr. (builder of the Belmont racetrack). Belmont was perhaps one of the earliest supporters of presidential birthplaces, having also joined the Lincoln Farm Association seven years earlier to preserve Abraham's Lincoln natal home.[13]

The inauguration was a two-day ceremony including a service on Sunday, March 16, and an opening ceremony on Tuesday, March 18, on what would have been the 76th birthday of Grover Cleveland. In attendance that day was Cleveland's widow, Frances Folsom (who was by then Mrs. Thomas Jex Preston, having remarried a month earlier), and his children Esther, Marion, and Richard also attended. His other daughter, Ruth, after which the Baby Ruth candy bar was named, had died nine years earlier and his ten-year-old son, Francis Grover, was not written to have been in attendance. Several former cabinet members also attended. Caldwell pulled out all stops and showed its pride in their most famous son as local businesses shut down and Bloomfield Avenue was patriotically decorated and a parade marched before the house. The crowd for the event was one of the largest in Caldwell's history at that time. To start off the ceremony, first the check was turned over to George Canfield to formally purchase the home. Canfield wore two hats that day as both a member of the Grover Cleveland Birthplace Memorial Association and the chairman of the church treasury. Next, the key to the home was presented to Grover Cleveland's son, Richard. The family was led inside the home where perfume filled the air. Once inside, a bouquet of roses was handed to Esther, who years earlier had the distinction of being the only child of a sitting president to be born in the White House. She ceremoniously carried the roses into the room where her father was born seventy-six years earlier.[14]

The sitting President Woodrow Wilson, who coincidentally was also born in a Presbyterian manse in Staunton, Virginia, was also invited. Three days before the service, President Wilson declined "citing obligations he could not escape." Along with his regrets, he sent a brief message that was read at the ceremony. In it, he expressed his interest in the preservation efforts and his admiration for the former president:

I think it must be evident to everyone who has given attention to the matter that the feeling of the country, the feeling alike of admiration and affection, toward Mr. Cleveland grows warmer and warmer as years pass by. As we see him in perspective, he looms as one of our most notable figures in our long line of Presidents. I send these lines therefore as a sincere tribute of respect and admiration.[15]

Despite these kind words, while the former and current president had been acquaintances in Princeton, they were not known to have crossed party lines to develop a genuine friendship.

Theodore Roosevelt also sent his congratulations and well wishes to the Grover Cleveland Birthplace Memorial Association for the occasion, wishing them "all success in [their] efforts to secure the birthplace of Grover Cleveland." In his letter he referred to Cleveland as doing "more than any one man in the fight for sound and honest finance."[16] Honesty was the hallmark of the Cleveland presidency and he was often called the most honorable and honest man to serve office. Not a bad way to be remembered. We could use a few more like Grover Cleveland in the Garden State today.

A ceremony was held the following year, again presided over by John H. Finley who had become a regular fixture at all events surrounding the birthplace.[17] By 1915, the association proposed that the birthplace should be recognized and preserved as a National Memorial, free to the public. Their motives may not have been purely altruistic, as they also required the federal government pay for the annual maintenance costs. Despite the endorsement of President Wilson in 1916, the annual maintenance price tag of $500 was deemed too steep and the proposal failed.[18]

In the early part of the twentieth century, the Grover Cleveland home became a popular stop for presidential candidates; oddly enough, Republican candidates – one winner and one loser – came to visit the famous New Jersey Democrat's birth home. First in October 1916, Charles Evans Hughes, Republican candidate for president, took a break from the campaign trail when he stopped at the birth home in Caldwell. Hughes "thoroughly enjoyed his visit to the birthplace of Cleveland."[19] Two weeks later he would lose in a close election to Woodrow Wilson. Had he won, you would be reading much more about his birthplace in Glens Falls, New York. Next, in September 1928, Herbert Hoover visited Newark, New Jersey, while campaigning for the nation's highest office. He was greeted with a parade and his route took him on several stops including a 3:55 p.m. visit to the Grover Cleveland birthplace.[20] Of course, Hoover would go on to win the election and prosperity would reign over the United States... for almost a year.

In the 1930s, America was suffering in the Great Depression and the Grover Cleveland Birthplace Memorial Association was not immune to the hard times. By 1933, they were no longer financially able to support the birthplace home and were over $5,000 in debt. Having previously failed at the national level, this time they turned

to the state with an offer to donate the home to the government of New Jersey. The bill to accept the birthplace was introduced by Republican Assemblyman Alexander P. Waugh of Essex County in March 1933. The proposal was to have the transfer completed by what would have been the president's 99th birthday; however, the state would have to wait more than a year and a half.[21] The senate voted to accept the home on June 13, 1933, but the gift was delayed while the mounting bills were paid off since the state of New Jersey could not accept a property in debt.

In February 1934, at the suggestion of Dr. John H. Finley, New Jersey Governor Arthur Harry Moore established the Grover Cleveland Birthplace Association to help enable the state acquisition of the property. The association handled the finances and the museum collection. The twenty trustees serving without pay included Richard Cleveland, the son of the president, New York Times President Adolph S. Ochs, and of course, Dr. John H. Finley. At 4 p.m. on October 6, 1934, a ceremony was held to transfer the property to the state. Originally scheduled to be on the front lawn, poor weather forced the ceremony indoors to the Presbyterian Church. The Governor, Richard Cleveland, and the ubiquitous John H. Finley attended the ceremony. The home was now officially property of the state of New Jersey.[22]

Under the Works Progress Administration (WPA), $10,000 was allocated, in 1936, to restore the Grover Cleveland birthplace to how it looked the year he was born. (To help alleviate the nation's astronomical unemployment during the Great Depression, President Franklin Roosevelt created millions of jobs through work programs, including the WPA, under the New Deal.) Additional accolades came forty years later – on December 27, 1976, the home was placed on the New Jersey Register of Historic Places, and on November 16, 1977, it was also placed on the National Register of Historic Places (National Register Number #77000861).

After the home was turned over to the state, the new residents became the caretakers. These people would live on the second floor of the home while giving tours of the first floor during visitor's hours. This arrangement continued until 1995 when the caretaker moved to a nearby residence.

Visitor Information

Being the only president born in my home state, I take particular pride in having New Jersey's favorite son known as the most honest man to ever hold the office. Seeing the birthplace in Caldwell was a nice day trip I took with my young son, Vincent, in 2007. The staff was very pleasant and eager to inform and assist. One of the rooms included several toys from the period of Grover Cleveland's youth, which kept my three-year-old entertained, allowing me to see the home. Be aware that they do close for lunch, so do not plan to visit from noon to one o'clock in the afternoon.

New Jersey is known for its pizza and right across the street is some of the best around, Forte's Ristorante, so you may want to stop in for a slice after visiting the home. Also be aware that Grover Cleveland is not the only famous person to reside in Caldwell. Only a few miles away you can see the house where Tony Soprano lived, or at least the home where the exterior home scenes were filmed from the HBO series The Sopranos. You probably won't get whacked if you do a drive by, but do be considerate since the home is a private residence. For the true Soprano's aficionados, take a short drive to Holstens where the final scene of the series was filmed. Order the onion rings, but don't forget to keep your eyes on the bathroom door.

Back to the president, if you are looking for the cradle-to-grave Grover Cleveland experience, take the hour or so drive to Princeton, New Jersey, to see the gravesite of Grover Cleveland, his wife, and his daughter, "Baby" Ruth, in the Princeton Cemetery on Witherspoon Street. While in Princeton, drive past 15 Hodge Road to see the home where Cleveland lived after his presidency in 1897 until his death in 1908. Go around the corner to 72 and 82 Library Place to see two homes where Woodrow Wilson resided during his tenure at Princeton University. These years coincided with Grover Cleveland's residency, so imagine a former and future president living within a few minutes walk from each other. Note both presidents' former homes are now privately owned and not open to visitors, so please be considerate.

23.
Benjamin Harrison

Vital Birthplace Information

Birthplace	North Bend, Ohio
President's birthday	August 20, 1833
How long in the home	21 years
Life of the home	Before 1829 to July 25, 1858
Style	Log and frame farmhouse
Still in existence	No
Ultimate fate	Destroyed by fire
Commemoration	Historic marker
Open to the public	Yes
Cost	Free
For more information	www.northbendohio.org
Replica exists	No
Significance	Inspiration for William Henry Harrison's "log cabin and hard cider" campaign slogan
Closest birthplace	William Howard Taft, 18 miles

Address/Directions:

The historic marker that marks the Benjamin Harrison birthplace is at the corner of Symmes Avenue and Washington Avenue in North Bend, Ohio.

The birthplace of Benjamin Harrison in North Bend, Ohio.

What you will find there today:

In the midst of a suburban neighborhood in southwestern Ohio is a historic marker that reads:

Benjamin Harrison (1833-1901) was born here on a farm established by his grandfather, William Henry Harrison. A graduate of Miami University in Oxford, Harrison read law in Cincinnati and then moved to Indianapolis to practice. He became active in Republican politics before he served in the Civil War as a colonel of the 70th Regiment of Indiana Volunteers. In the 1880s, subsequent to his defeat for governor of Indiana, he served in the United States Senate, where he championed pensions for Civil War veterans, high protective tariffs, homesteading, and civil service reform. Harrison ran against incumbent Grover Cleveland in the presidential election of 1888, and received fewer popular votes, but carried the Electoral College. During his term as president, he convened the first Pan-American Conference, modernized the navy, and negotiated reciprocal foreign trade agreements. Harrison was re-nominated in 1892 but was defeated by Cleveland.

THE OHIO BICENTENNIAL COMMISSION
VILLAGE OF NORTH BEND
THE OHIO HISTORICAL SOCIETY
2003
47-31

History

The Benjamin Harrison birthplace was originally part of a massive land purchase made by John Cleve Symmes known as the Symmes Purchase. John Cleve Symmes was a judge from Trenton, New Jersey, and gave much of his resources to support the Continental Army during the American Revolution. When the war was over, Symmes, along with twenty-two partners, proposed to exchange the IOUs for one million acres in southwestern Ohio. Congress accepted the offer and the exchange was completed October 15, 1788. At the time, it was written that the land was "so infested by the Indians, that it was avoided by the whites."[1] The land grant was mismanaged from the start – surveys were inaccurate and the Symmes partners sold off parcels of land that were not included in the contract and, therefore, they did not own.

The area of North Bend was originally called Symmes because Judge Symmes managed the parcel. It was later renamed North Bend because of its location on the northernmost bend of the Ohio River.[2]

In 1795, William Henry Harrison married Judge Symmes' daughter, Anna. Thirty-four years later, in 1829, William Henry Harrison purchased a farm in North Bend, Ohio, the town founded by his father-in-law. After serving in public life for almost two decades, William Henry Harrison planned to retire on his farm; however, these plans would be short-lived. On the property was a small log cabin which stood about 300 yards off the bank of the Ohio River. Over the years, Harrison added to the home, and eventually, this small log cabin would become an expansive sixteen-room log and frame farmhouse. On the farm, the Harrisons grew corn which they used to distill their own whiskey.

William Henry Harrison and Anna Symmes had ten kids and right in the middle was child number five, John Scott Harrison. John Scott went on to marry twice and be a prolific father. He had three children with his first wife and ten with his second wife, Elizabeth Ramsey Irwin. His second child with Elizabeth Ramsey Irwin was Benjamin Harrison, born in North Bend on August 20, 1833. Benjamin would one day become the only man to follow in his grandfather's footsteps to become the President of the United States of America.

Benjamin grew up on the farm and attended school nearby. In 1840, when he was just seven years old, his grandfather, William Henry Harrison, ran for President of the United States and Benjamin Harrison's birthplace home became the centerpiece of his campaign. Trying to sell himself as having humble roots, William Henry often referred to his home in his "log cabin and hard cider" campaign, conveniently neglecting to clarify that his birthplace at Berkeley Plantation was a far cry from a log cabin and his home in North Bend was a sixteen-room mansion. Despite this misconception, the myth took hold and the North Bend home became forever linked to the election gimmickry, and the historical significance attributed to the home is most often associated with William Henry Harrison's campaign slogan and not Benjamin Harrison's birth.

The irony is that William Henry Harrison's birth was also overshadowed by other historical events that occurred at his Berkeley Plantation birthplace. With the possible exception of FDR, the Harrisons stand alone as the only two presidents whose birth is not the most historic event to occur in their birthplace. And in FDR's case, he was in the middle of all of the historic events that occurred at his Hyde Park birthplace during his presidency that overshadowed his birth.

Ten years after the campaign, when Benjamin Harrison was twenty, he married Caroline Lavinia Scott. The couple continued to live in the home at North Bend for a short time; however, the next year they moved to Indianapolis, Indiana. After William Henry Harrison's death in 1841, Anna Symmes Harrison continued to live in the home for another seventeen years. On July 25, 1858, tragedy struck when a fire broke out and flames engulfed the home. William Henry Harrison's son-in-law, Colonel W.H. Taylor, and his family were living in the home, and they were caught off guard and "barely escaped in their night-clothes."[3] When the smoke cleared, the home was destroyed. Almost nothing was saved and a treasure trove of presidential history from William Henry Harrison's brief tenure was lost.[4] The next year what was left of the home was torn down.[5] Understanding the historic significance of the home, some pieces may have been salvaged from the rubble; however, by whom and where these relics were located were unknown for 118 years. In October 1976, then North Bend Mayor Charles Lehring curiously commented that the "town has stored some of the door frames and windows in a barn somewhere."[6] Perhaps he was mistaken or misquoted, because current North Bend officials are unaware of their existence.

Preservation

On May 26, 2003, a small ceremony was held to dedicate the historic marker. About twenty people gathered at the site for the festivities. Speakers included member of the Ohio Historical Society and Ohio State Representative Steve Driehaus.[7]

Visitor Information

I stopped by the birthplace in May 2008 after visiting Grant and Taft's birthplace earlier in the day. Much like his presidency, Benjamin's Harrison birthplace is simple and unexciting, and you may find, like I did, that some of your less enthusiastic fellow travelers might choose not to get out of the car (their loss!). What is there now is a private residence and you should respect the privacy of the current owners. When visiting the site of the birth home, please remember the home at the site is not the original.

The birthplace is only a quarter mile from the final resting place of his grandfather, and our ninth President, William Henry Harrison. Stop by to pay your respects at Harrison Tomb State Memorial on US Highway 50 (also in North Bend). There you will also find the graves of John Cleve Symmes and Scott Harrison, the only person whose father and son were presidents.

25.
William McKinley

The William McKinley birthplace replica in Niles, Ohio.

Vital Birthplace Information

Birthplace	Niles, Ohio
President's birthday	January 29, 1843
How long in the home	9 years
Life of the home	Approximately 1837 to April 3, 1937
Style	Western Pennsylvania
Still in existence	No
Ultimate fate	Destroyed by fire
Commemoration	McKinley (re-created) Birthplace Home and Research Center
Open to the public	Yes
Cost	Free
For more information	www.mckinley.lib.oh.us
Replica exists	Yes, at birthplace
Significance	Only presidential birthplace to be cut in half
Closest birthplace	James Abram Garfield, 44 miles

What you will find there today:

At the birthplace location is a slightly larger than reality replica of the home where President McKinley was born.

In front of the home is a two-sided historic marker (Marker #17-78) erected by the Ohio Bicentennial Commission and the Ohio Historical Society in 2003. On the front it reads:

William McKinley Birthplace
One of seven native Ohioans to serve as president of the United States, William McKinley (1843-1901) was born at this site. The original house was moved from this site and ultimately destroyed by fire. The McKinleys lived here until 1852 when they moved to Poland, Ohio, where William attended the Poland Seminary. He briefly attended Allegheny College in Pennsylvania, but poor health and family financial strain forced him to return to Ohio. As an enlistee in the 23rd Ohio Volunteer Infantry during the Civil War, McKinley rose to the rank of major. After the war, he settled in Canton and practiced law. Elected to Congress in 1876, McKinley favored high protective tariffs, a policy he continued to support as President.

And the back reads:
As Governor of Ohio from 1892 to 1896, he introduced a comprehensive tax system that levied excise tax on corporations, improved state roadways, and enacted a law establishing a state board of arbitration. McKinley won the presidential election of 1896 convincingly. During his first term the nation was adopting imperialistic policies. The U.S. took possession of Puerto Rico, Guam, and the Philippines following the Spanish-American War (1898), and McKinley encouraged American interest in China and suggested the possibility of a canal linking the Atlantic and Pacific oceans. In part due to his economic policy and support of the gold standard, McKinley was elected to a second term. Six months after his inauguration in 1901, an assassin at the Pan American Exposition in Buffalo shot him. He died on September 14 from complications of the gunshot wounds.

Address/Directions:

40 South Main Street
Niles, Ohio 44446

From Route 80, take Exit 223 to Niles. Take Route 46 north for four miles into downtown Niles where it will turn into South Main Street. The McKinley Birthplace will be on your left.

History

In the early years of the nineteenth century, James Heaton settled the land that is now Niles, Ohio. Heaton was a businessman and had selected the area to build a blast furnace, which was perhaps the first west of the Alleghenies. Over the next thirty years, Heaton built up his business and soon was manufacturing the first bar iron in Ohio. His settlement became known as "Heaton's Furnace," and by 1834, it had become big enough to upgrade to Village status. James laid out the streets and named his new village "Nilestown" after a newspaper editor from Baltimore, *Hezekiah Niles.* For simplicity sake, the post office renamed the village to Niles in 1843.[1]

Today, Niles is home to over 20,000 people, but when the McKinleys – William Sr., his wife, Nancy Allison, and five children – first arrived in late 1837 or early 1838, the population was only about 300. William was an iron furnace manager and was able to find work at Heaton's furnace. To accommodate the sizable family, the McKinleys purchased a nice-sized home on 40 South Main Street from James Heaton. The style was similar to what was seen in Western Pennsylvania at the time, it had two stories with eight rooms and a 14- by 30-foot basement. It is unknown whether the McKinleys purchased an empty lot and built the home or if the home was already on the property.[2]

During those years, they added four more children, the first being Sara in 1840. Three years later, on January 29, 1843, William McKinley Jr. was born. He would one day become the nation's twenty-fifth president and the last to serve as a soldier in the Civil War. The McKinleys lived in the home for nine more years until they moved to Poland, Ohio, in 1852, so their children could receive a better education. After they moved, the home continued to remain in the McKinley family. William Sr.'s brother, James, owned the home for another seven years until 1859, at which time the home was sold outside of the family.[3]

Over the next decade, the home was owned and occupied by several different people. In 1870, a businessman, James S. Benedict, purchased the home, built an addition, converted the first floor into a general store, and rented office space in the building, with one of his tenants being an attorney. In Niles, the home became known as "Benedict Block." In 1886, the home was photographed, which is believed to be the first picture of the house.[4] The Benedict building was sold in 1890 to the City National Bank.[5]

While the McKinleys left Niles in the 1850s, his mother's family remained in the town. William McKinley visited Niles and his birth home several times, including while campaigning for the presidency in 1896 and again in 1899. During one of his visits, his mother showed him the room in which he was born.

On September 6, 1901, President William McKinley visited the Pan American Exposition in Buffalo and attended a reception at the Temple of Music building. While the president greeted guests and shook hands, an anarchist, Leon Czolgosz pulled a gun and shot him two times. Eight days later, the president was dead. Today, there is a marker at 30 Fordham Drive in Buffalo, New York, at the location of the fatal shooting. Only 2,000 feet away from the murder scene at the Temple of Music building, the Abraham Lincoln and Jefferson Davis birthplace cabins stood on display at the "Old Plantation" exhibit.

Preservation

Shortly after James S. Benedict sold the home in 1890, William McKinley was elected Governor of Ohio and people began to take note of the historic home. Instead of demolishing it to make room for the bank, a peculiar decision was made. In perhaps the strangest act ever perpetrated upon a presidential birthplace, the home was cut into two pieces. The home was sliced down the middle, separating the right and left portions of the building. One piece was moved to the rear of the lot on Franklin Alley and the other was moved across town to an amusement park called Riverside Park located on Salt Road in Mineral Springs. After the home was moved, a bank was built on the original site.[6] Interestingly enough, all three locations were billed as the "Birthplace of William McKinley" and postcards were produced to cite each structure's significance.

The half that remained in the rear of the lot was rented by several businesses over the years. One of the occupants was the fledgling company Harris Automatic Press Company, which rented two rooms in the birth home. Brothers Charles and Al Harris founded the company in 1895 and invented a device that automatically fed paper into the printing press. The first model for their automatic-feed printing press can now be seen in the Smithsonian in Washington, D.C.[7] Harris has come a long way since their start in the William McKinley birth home – today, this company is "an international communications and information technology company serving government and commercial markets in more than 150 countries. Headquartered in Melbourne, Florida, the company has approximately $5 billion of annual revenue and more than 15,000 employees".[8] Today, the location where this half sat is the parking lot for the William McKinley Birthplace Home and Research Center.

The other half of the home that was moved to Riverside Park was operated as a museum. Riverside Park was a trolley park opened in 1893 and owned by the Mineral Ridge-Niles Electric Railway Company. Trolley parks were established by trolley companies as a way to get workers and their families to ride the streetcars on weekends and were popular at the turn of the century as an affordable form of family entertainment. With the rise of the automobile, trolley parks began to decline, and today, there are less than a dozen still in existence.[9] The William McKinley home museum did see a rise in popularity after he was elected president in 1896, but Riverside Park then began a decline and closed in 1901, the same year the president was assassinated. After the park shut its doors, the home was rented until 1908, and then it was abandoned. The half-a-home then went quickly downhill. Soon every window was broken and it turned into "a shelter for tramps."[10] Vandals and souvenir hunters stole whatever was left in the home, including all but one of the walnut railings off of the staircase banister. By 1909, the home was almost in complete ruin.[11] Today, the site where the home stood is located beneath the Meandor Reservoir.

By the next year, the other half-a-home, which was moved to the back of the lot, was also vacant. The fate of the presidential birthplace did not look promising and its story may have ended then if not for the efforts of one woman, Miss Lulu Mackey. Miss Mackey was the Trumbull County court reporter and the first female member of the Trumbull County Bar Association. She was

also an entrepreneur who owned 200 acres at the corner of Route 422 and Robbins Avenue.[12] She thought the home would make a great centerpiece for a new housing development called "Tibbets Corners."[13] In November 1909, she purchased both halves and had them moved to her property about three miles away from the original site.[14] The pieces were then reconnected and restored as faithfully as possible. "Tibbets Corners" was renamed to "McKinley Heights," and today, the site where the home stood is the parking lot of the Pinetree Square shopping strip mall, where you can visit a Dollar General or the Urban Chiropractic Center.[15]

Miss Mackey, a collector of Americana and presidential memorabilia, opened the home as a museum in 1910 and filled it with historic items, including William McKinley's furniture and photographs. She also included memorabilia from other famous people from the Buckeye State. The museum was popular when it first opened and people gladly paid the admission price. However, by 1910, the wheels were in motion on another memorial to President McKinley located in Niles. One that would be more grand, more opulent, and more importantly, it would be free.[16]

On March 4, 1909, shortly after Ohioan William Howard Taft entered office, his first act as president was to sign a congressional act to build a birthplace memorial for William McKinley. The National McKinley Birthplace Memorial Association was formed to oversee this effort, led by William McKinley's boyhood friend, Colonel Joseph G. Butler.[17] In 1915, the design was awarded to McKim, Mead and White to build the Romanesque memorial building. The site chosen for the structure was a short walk from the original birthplace site on the location of his former schoolhouse.[18] On October 5, 1917, the building was finally completed and a dedication ceremony was held with President William Howard Taft in attendance.[19]

The 1917 opening of the McKinley Birthplace Memorial hurt attendance to the Birthplace Home Museum. From there, things began to go downhill. In 1920, the Chamber of Commerce accused Mackey of false advertising, since she was promoting the home as the site where William McKinley was born, when in actuality he was born three miles away. It may have just been semantics, but regardless, the bad publicity caused another dive in attendance from which it never rebounded. However, despite this setback, the home remained open and Mackey continued to charge an admission. She owned the museum until she died in 1934 at which time the memorabilia was moved out of the house and the building was abandoned.[20] This was also in the middle of the Great Depression when the nation and presidential birthplaces suffered immensely. Just like Andrew Johnson's birth home, hobos began to take refuge in William McKinley's birthplace.[21] On April 3, 1937, the home caught fire and was destroyed. The exact cause is unknown – one theory is that it was an electrical problem, but more likely, a hobo lit a fire to keep warm and accidentally set the home ablaze.[22] Regardless of how the fire started, the sad fact remained that after 100 years, the birthplace of William McKinley was gone forever.

Back on the original birth home site, the City National Bank was built in 1893.[23] Just like today, this bank went through a series of changes over the years. In 1905, the First National Bank

The site in Niles, Ohio where the William McKinley birthplace home burned to the ground on April 2, 1937. The home stood here from 1909 until its demise. At the time the site was known as "McKinley Heights," and today it is the Pinetree Square shopping strip mall.

purchased the building, and in that same year, it was changed to the Dollar Savings Bank. In 1918, it again changed, this time to the McKinley Federal Savings and Loan Company. The building was replaced in the 1940s with a more modern bank that stood until the 1993. Inside the bank, a plaque hung on the walls commemorating the birthplace location.[24] Today, this plaque is displayed in the William McKinley Birthplace Home and Research Center. When I visited, it was located on the wall to the left as you enter the main area of the Research Center. It reads:

THIS TABLET MARKS THE BIRTHPLACE OF WILLIAM MCKINLEY
TWENTYFIFTH PRESIDENT OF THE UNITED STATES
BORN JANUARY 29, 1943
DIED IN BUFFALO N.Y. SEPTEMBER 14, 1901.

In 1991, the McKinley Bank was purchased by National City Bank, but since they already had a bank in the area, in 1993, they closed the doors at the bank at the birthplace location. The McKinley Memorial Library saw this as an opportunity to obtain the birthplace property. The library worked out the deal between the National City Bank and the City of Niles – the bank donated the property to the city, and the city paid for the demolition of the existing bank. The deal was completed in 1995 and bank was demolished in 2000. In 2001, the city turned over the property to the McKinley Memorial Library.[25]

In June 2001, the library also bought an adjacent restaurant called Old Main Ale Chowder House for $140,000 to make room for the replica. The project was delayed as the costs to re-create the birthplace began to exceed estimations.[26] Ground was finally broken for the project on April 28, 2002. During construction, portions of the original foundation were unearthed so the replica was able to stay true to the location. It was built with the same dimensions of the original home, but space was added in the back to accommodate the Research Center.[27] The earliest photograph was from 1886 when the Benedicts owned the home, and shows an upstairs balcony. It was unknown if this was there when the McKinleys lived in the home; however, it looked nice so it was included in the replica. The home was completed the next year for a final cost of about $700,000, which was above and beyond the original budget estimates. However, if you visit the McKinley Memorial Library and the burial site in Canton, you will realize that no cost is too high when it comes to memorializing President McKinley! On May 4, 2003, a ceremony was held to dedicate the birthplace replica.

Visitor Information

The home is only open on Saturdays during the summer months from 11 a.m. to 4 p.m. and the tour gives you an excellent understanding of the history of the home, the early years of Niles and the president's life and family. The tour guide was extremely knowledgeable and helpful and I sincerely appreciated his patience and assistance. After leaving the home, turn left and walk down the street to see the McKinley Memorial Library, Museum, and Birthplace Memorial, which is fit for a Roman Emperor. If you plan your trip accordingly, you can take in a Mahoning Valley Scrappers baseball game. They are a Class "A" minor league affiliate of the Cleveland Indians and the field is located right behind the Eastwood Mall. Before the game, stop by the Brown Derby Roadhouse on 1231 Youngstown-Warren Road for delicious BBQ. The smell emanating from the restaurant is hard to resist and if you drive past with your windows down, you'll see what I mean. Get the full rack of BBQ ribs; just make sure you bring a hearty appetite.

26.
Theodore Roosevelt

Vital Birthplace Information

Birthplace	New York City, New York
President's birthday	October 27, 1858
How long in the home	14 years
Life of the home	1848 to 1916
Style	Brownstone
Still in existence	No
Ultimate fate	Demolished
Commemoration	Theodore Roosevelt Birthplace National Historic Site
Open to the public	Yes
Cost	Free
For more information	www.nps.gov/thrb
Replica exists	Yes, at birthplace
Significance	Shortest span between existence of original and replica (7 years)
Closest birthplace	Grover Cleveland, 23 miles

Address/Directions:

28 East 20th Street
New York City, New York 10003

The home is located between Park Avenue South and Broadway.

The re-created birthplace of Theodore Roosevelt on 28 East 20th Street in Manhattan, New York.

What you will find there today:

The Theodore Roosevelt birthplace is a National Historic Site administered by the National Park Service. The rebuilt home appears as it did when Theodore Roosevelt was born in 1858. On the exterior wall is a historic marker placed there by the Woman's Roosevelt Memorial Association in 1921. The marker reads:

THEODORE ROOSEVELT WAS BORN HERE OCTOBER 27, 1858
Birthplace reproduced by the Woman's Roosevelt Memorial Association
January 6, 1921

History

In the 1840s, Cornelius Roosevelt purchased two lots, #26 and #28, on East Twentieth Street in Manhattan, New York. At the time, the neighborhood was quiet, lined with trees, and a perfect place to raise a family in the city. In 1848, Cornelius had two New York brownstone homes built. The traditional four-story homes were wedding presents for his two sons, Robert and Theodore. Once completed, Robert and his wife moved into #28. In 1854, after Theodore married Martha Bulloch, he moved into #28 and Robert moved next door to #26. Theodore was a wealthy glass importer and banker, and a year after moving into the home, he began to grow his family. His first child born in the home was Anna in 1855. Three years later, on the evening of October 27, 1858, in the front bedroom on the second floor, an eight and a half pound future Rough Rider and self-proclaimed hero of San Juan Hill, Theodore Roosevelt, was born.

If you visit today, you can still see the original bed where he first saw the light of day. Young Theodore was a sickly child and his father built a gymnasium on a balcony appended to the back of the second floor for his son to exercise himself back to health. The family went on to have two more children in the home, Elliot in 1860 and Corinnie in 1861. The home was also where Theodore received his schooling, as the family employed private tutors for their children.[1]

Theodore Sr. was a wealthy philanthropist and was generally regarded as a genuinely nice person. One of his passions, which he passed on to his son, was an appreciation for the natural world. In 1869, he combined these passions when he signed the charter for the American Museum of Natural History in his living room. Today, the Roosevelt name is omnipresent throughout the museum.

In the fall of 1872, the well-to-do Roosevelts left for a yearlong tour of Europe and Egypt. When they returned in the autumn of 1873, it was to a new apartment across town at 6 West 57th Street. Theodore had spent his first fourteen years in #28 East Twentieth Street and the home remained in the Roosevelt family for almost another quarter century, until 1896.

In 1901, Theodore Roosevelt became the twenty-sixth President of the United States. During these years, the neighborhood where he was born had changed from residential to commercial, and the home went through several alterations. Throughout the next decade, business interests would trump nostalgia. No longer even recognizable as a home, the building was transformed into commercial property with the first three floors expanded with an addition that resembled large bay windows. The property barely resembled the original birthplace by 1916 when it was demolished to make way for a two-story café.

Preservation

In 1904, the Republicans of the Seventeenth Election District of the Twenty-Fifth Assembly District of New York were seeking office space in the home to meet. The group of Teddy Roosevelt devotees, led by Leo P. Glasel, named themselves the Roosevelt Club and rented a room on the fourth floor of the building they called a "Hallowed-Spot."[2] They were thrilled to receive a telegram from the president himself in which he said:

Permit me to extend my hearty congratulations on the occasion of the meeting of the club in the house where I was born.[3]

With the establishment of the club on October 12, 1904, the Roosevelt birth home preservation movement was now official. This is a significant shift in presidential birthplace preservation history, as for the first time, a grass-roots movement to commemorate the birthplace of a sitting president had taken hold.

At the time, a merchant was renting the birth room and the New York Republicans worked to make the room available to the public. On October 5, 1904, banners were displayed on the building,

speeches were made, and fans of the popular sitting president were allowed to make the pilgrimage to the birth room.[4] By the next year, the group was known as the Roosevelt Home Club and their stated mission was to purchase the birth home for $60,000, restore it with historic furnishings, and use it as a museum and political headquarters. Their unstated mission was to make a profit. The group numbered about 300 members including a veritable turn-of-the-century *who's who* with names such as Frick, Guggenheim, Thomas Edison, and the President of Harvard, Charles W. Elliot. On the president's 47th birthday, in 1905, a dinner was held in the birth room. In a speech at the event, former U.S. Senator John Mellen Thurston praised the president saying:

It is fortunate that we are led by a patriotic man, made in God's own image, Theodore Roosevelt.[5]

However, the organization quickly fell from grace, and within two months, the group was mired in controversy. Leo Glasel was accused of questionable financial dealings and was quickly ousted as president. He was replaced, in December 1905, with Roderick Regg, a young Republican lawyer and a fresh face for the organization, one distanced from the previous financial misdealing. Unfortunately for the club, the change in leadership was not enough to keep the scandal at bay. Nobody could account for the thousands of dollars in donations that had flowed in from its wealthy members, including Henry Frick's $10,000 gift. The group was also accused of misappropriation of funds, with much of the money not going to the purchase and preservation of the home as promised. To try to mend fences, the group traveled to Washington to meet with the President Roosevelt himself. "Mr. Roosevelt [was] said to have not been pleased."[6] Still, with enough funds to buy #28 East 20th Street, the Roosevelt Home Club completed the purchase in December 1905.

The club soon became a pariah with political figures now forced to disavow or explain away their association. Eight months later, in August 1906, the Roosevelt Home Club was falling apart at the seams. They had established Rough Riders Realty, but could not keep up with the payments on the property. Determining "that it cannot fulfill its mission," the Roosevelt Home Club decided to cut their losses and sell the home to businessman Herman Ronkow for $60,000.[7] Five months later, in January 1907, the club "which intended to preserve the property permanently as a clubhouse, but which only succeeded in getting into quarrels" finally dissolved.[8] Without an organization working to preserve the property, the home became a victim of the commercialization of the neighborhood. In 1916, the owner, businessman Gustavus L. Lawrence, chose to tear it down to make way for a two-story show room.[9] President Roosevelt was made aware of the impending destruction of his birth home and was first offered the chance to buy it, but he declined. For three years, the newly built structure served purely business purposes. Most thought preservation efforts had failed. Fortunately, as seen time and time again, a patriotic women's organization saw it differently.

On January 6, 1919, after leading the most adventurous life of possibly any president, Teddy Roosevelt died. Immediately after his death, two groups of concerned citizens were created with the sole purpose of memorializing this great man. The Roosevelt Permanent Memorial National Committee, led by Hermann Hagedorn, was formed only three days after his death and was later renamed the Roosevelt Memorial Association. Another group of patriotic women, led by Mrs. John Henry Hammond and Theodore Roosevelt's sister, Corinne (Mrs. Douglas Robinson), also joined forces to commemorate the president. The women organized fast and just over three weeks later, on January 29, 1919, the Woman's Roosevelt Memorial Association was incorporated in New York "to commemorate the life of Theodore Roosevelt by establishing and maintaining a permanent memorial in the City of New York."[10] That permanent memorial would be achieved by purchasing and razing the newly built commercial building and rebuilding and memorializing the original birth home. The women's organization did not envision the buildings as just a museum, but rather they anticipated the home would "be used as a national centre of Americanization and a school for citizenship" or a gathering place for patriotic organizations such as the Boy and Girl Scouts.[11]

The Woman's Roosevelt Memorial Association moved quickly. In November 1919, they made a $25,043.63 down payment on the $80,000 sale price and the home was theirs. In 1921, they demolished the existing structure and began to build a recreation of the birth home. They chose architect Theodate Pope, a member of the American Institute of Architects and one of the nation's first women architects, to design the home.

In January 1921, a ceremony was held to lay the cornerstone to kick off construction of the replica birthplace. General Leonard Wood, who served alongside Roosevelt with the Rough Riders, was the guest of honor when he laid the cornerstone and made the dedication address.[12] The nation was watching their efforts, and in April 1921, Vice President Calvin Coolidge wrote the women to "wish [their] patriotic efforts the success they so richly deserve."[13]

By 1922, the Woman's Roosevelt Memorial Association had grown to 700 members and the restoration was in full swing. The women conjured up all sorts of ideas for fundraisers, including balls, barn dances, and bazaars.[14] On April 7, 1922, they occupied the entire second floor of the Plaza Hotel for the "Roosevelt House Festival" where they held a bridge tournament, games, and an Easter hat sale.[15] For membership they charged adults $1.00 and only 25¢ for school children under sixteen years of age. Soon, their membership doubled to 1,400. Later that year, on what would have been the president's 64th birthday, the organization received a major boost when the Roosevelt Memorial Association provided a grant of $150,000. The Roosevelt Memorial Association was also formed in 1919 and was headquartered in Oyster Bay, Long Island (where the last home in which the president lived, Sagamore Hill, was located).[16] The two organizations worked side by side for over thirty years and officially merged in 1953 to become the Theodore Roosevelt Association. During those years of cooperation, the Woman's Roosevelt Memorial Association continued to have annual fundraisers for "The Roosevelt House." In 1939, a bridge party was held at the Roosevelt Hotel and was chaired by Theodore Roosevelt's grandniece, Mrs. Kenneth S. Walker.[17]

With the assistance of Theodore Roosevelt's widow, Edith, and his sisters, Annie and Corinne, the home was decorated to resemble the period that Teddy lived in the home. The Roosevelt women selected wallpaper, draperies, and donated many pieces of original furniture. Finally, in 1923, their work at the birthplace was completed. Next door, a museum and office were built where Theodore's Uncle Robert once lived.

On October 27, 1923, on what would have been the president's 65th birthday, a dedication ceremony was held to formally open the home to the public.

With impressive ceremonies, in the presence of as many persons as could crowd into the restored birthplace [about 300] of the late Theodore Roosevelt at 28 East Twentieth Street, was formally dedicated...as a shrine of American patriotism.[18]

Speakers broadcast the ceremony to hundreds more flag-waving spectators in the streets, five Army airplanes completed a flyby over the birthplace home, and letters from President Calvin Coolidge and former Rough Rider and Roosevelt friend, General Leonard Wood, were read, as they could not be in attendance. Acting New York City Mayor George Murray Hulbert (Mayor John Francis Hylan was suffering from a long illness) thanked the Woman's Roosevelt Memorial Association for creating "the house as a memorial to a great president and as a shrine of patriotism."[19] Also in attendance were James R. Garfield, son of the former president, and Roosevelt's Secretary of the Interior as well as Pennsylvania Governor Gifford Pinchot. On behalf of his father, Kermit Roosevelt graciously thanked everyone for the honor.[20]

The Roosevelt Memorial Association was able to obtain a 999-year lease on the birth home in 1929, thus securing the home for many, many, many, many generations to come.[21]

In 1962, a historic marker was placed on the building above the front door that reads:

LANDMARKS OF NEW YORK
Theodore Roosevelt Birthplace
President Theodore Roosevelt was born here on October 27,
1858, and lived here until he was 15. The house, a typical
brownstone of the 1840s, was restored in 1923 and opened
as a museum.
Plaque erected 1962 by the New York Community Trust.

With no mention of the building being a replica, you have to wonder if the New York Community Trust was aware that this was not the real birthplace building. Also there is an argument that can be made regarding how many years Roosevelt lived in the home. When his family left for the yearlong tour of Europe and Egypt, he was fourteen, and when he returned to his new home, he was fifteen, so technically, he only lived in his birthplace for fourteen years. Next time you're in Manhattan, impress your friends and point out these mistakes to your friends!

The next year, in 1963, the Theodore Roosevelt Association donated the birthplace to the National Park Service, officially establishing the Theodore Roosevelt Birthplace National Historic Site. Roosevelt's Sagamore Hill home was also donated along with approximately $500,000 to provide for the maintenance. That same year, the Theodore Roosevelt Birthplace National Historic Site was established. On October 15, 1966, the re-created home was added to the National Register of Historic Places (National Register Number #66000054).

In the mid-1970s, when New York was at a low point in its history, East Twentieth Street had given way to the dirt, grime, graffiti, and crime affecting much of the Big Apple at that time. The Theodore Roosevelt Association, determined not to let this historic landmark succumb to urban blight sponsored the "East 20th Street Revitalization Project" to clean up the block. Over the years, attendance at the birthplace has never been that impressive, considering its location in perhaps the busiest city in the country. According to National Park statistics, since 1964, annual attendance did not top 20,000 until the middle of the 1990s, and by the turn of the millennia, it was back below 20,000. Today, about 15,000 people visit every year.[22]

Visitor Information

The home can only be seen on a tour, which kicks off every hour from 10 a.m. to 4 p.m. on the hour, except at noon (Rangers have to eat lunch too!). It lasts about a half hour, but they leave you in a large room, which contains hundreds of Teddy Roosevelt artifacts and they let you hang out there as long as you'd like. The birthplace is located in lower Manhattan and there are many nearby sites that can be included in your visit. Around the corner is the infamous flatiron building on 175 Fifth Avenue at 23rd Street, which was the tallest building in New York when it was built in 1902. For a bite to eat, stop by Eisenberg's Sandwich Shop for a tuna salad on rye. This deli has been "raising New York's cholesterol since 1929."[23]

27.
William Howard Taft

The birthplace of William Howard Taft in Mount Auburn (now Cincinnati), Ohio.
Photo credit: William Howard Taft National Historic Site, National Park Service

Birthplace	Mount Auburn (now Cincinnati), Ohio
President's birthday	September 15, 1857
How long in the home	25 years
Life of the home	1840s to present
Style	Greek Revival
Still in existence	Yes
Commemoration	William Howard Taft National Historic Site
Open to the public	Yes
Cost	Free
For more information	www.nps.gov/wiho
Replica exists	No
Significance	Only presidential birthplace damaged in an earthquake (July 27, 1980)
Closest birthplace	Benjamin Harrison, 18 miles

What you will find there today:

The William Taft birthplace is a National Historic Site administered by the National Park Service. The site is located in an urban area outside of downtown Cincinnati. Its out-of-the-way location makes it unknown even to many locals; however, it is worth the trip.

Address/Directions:

2038 Auburn Avenue
Cincinnati, Ohio 45219

From the south, take I-71N to take Exit 2 (Reading Road and Eden Park Drive). Turn left at first stoplight onto Dorchester Avenue. At the top of the hill turn right on Auburn Avenue and go a block and a half to the Taft birthplace.

From the north, take I-71S to Exit 3 (Taft Road). In .75 mile, turn left onto Auburn Avenue and go .5 mile to the Taft birthplace.

History

Located a mile or two from downtown Cincinnati, Mount Auburn is currently a suburb of Cincinnati; however, when William Howard Taft was born, this was considered a separate town. The town of Mount Auburn was first mapped in 1837, and in the early 1840s, the Bowen family built a home at 60 Auburn Avenue (now 2038 Auburn Avenue) on 1.82 acres of land. The original home was a simple two story square brick building built in the Greek Revival style.[1]

That same year the house was built, Alphonso Taft came to Ohio with his wife, Louise. He was a successful lawyer and Yale graduate. Among his achievements, he is credited with being the cofounder of Yale's Skull and Bones society, which went on to include several future presidents in its ranks. Taft grew a successful practice and was soon upwardly mobile enough to leave the downtown area and purchase a home in the suburbs. On June 13, 1851, Alphonso and Fanny Phelps Taft purchased the home at 60 Auburn Avenue for $10,000. Alphonso immediately started renovating his new home – he modernized the plumbing, built a rooftop observatory, and also added three stories to the rear, making the bottom story the same level of the basement. When the work was done, the Taft home had a healthy eighteen rooms. Sadly, Fanny died in 1852, a year after they moved in; however, Alphonso would not remain a bachelor for long. The next year, he married Louise Torrey and on September 15, 1857, Louise gave birth to the future President of the United States and Chief Justice of the U.S. Supreme Court, William Howard Taft, in a first floor bedroom.[2]

The future president lived in the home until leaving for Yale University in 1874, and then returned after graduating four years later. While William Howard was away at school, in 1877, the house caught fire and was damaged. The Tafts turned lemons into lemonade and used the insurance money to make some enhancements to the home. Interior decorating was completed as well as structural changes to raise the ceiling height to eleven feet on the top floor. They also added an iron cornice around the home. In 1882, when Alphonso was appointed United States Minister to Austria-Hungary, he packed up and moved much of the family overseas. William Howard Taft stayed behind, but he did not reside in the home again. Instead, he moved out to make the house available to renters. Three years later, in 1885, Alphonso returned to live at 60 Auburn Avenue. In 1889, after thirty-eight years, the Tafts left the home for good.[3]

For the next ten years, the Tafts again became landlords, renting to several different families. In 1891, Alphonso died and Louise was no longer interested in owning the home. She put the home up for sale, but was unable to sell it until 1899 when Judge Albert C. Thompson purchased the house. The Thompsons owned and occupied the home until the judge's death in 1910, and during those eleven years, the neighborhood was urbanized and rezoned as larger properties were subdivided. Due to the rezoning, 60 Auburn Avenue was re-addressed as 2038 Auburn Avenue. The Thompsons made several alterations to the house, including replacing and expanding the porch. Two years after the judge's death, the home was sold to Colonel Ernest H. Ruffne, in 1912, the same year William Howard Taft lost his reelection bid to Woodrow Wilson for a second term as president. The home remained in the Ruffne family for twenty-eight more years until 1940. During these years, both the Colonel and William Howard Taft passed away – the Colonel died in 1937, Taft on March 8, 1930. After the Colonel's death, his daughter, Mrs. Louis K. Violet DeBus, put the home up for sale. In addition to being the birthplace of a former president, the home was now almost 100 years old and had historic value. In 1937, the William Howard Taft Memorial Association was incorporated and tried to purchase the home. After several attempts failed, the home was eventually sold on April 12, 1940 to Elbert R. Bellinger for $12,500. Along with his wife, Elbert lived in the adjacent home at 2030 Auburn Avenue and retained both properties for a time.[4]

The new owners entertained the notion of selling it to the William Howard Taft Memorial Association; however, their asking price was over double the value of the home. With the nation just emerging from the Great Depression and on the verge of World War II, the Bellingers sought other ways to profit from their new home. First the home was subdivided into seven apartments and rented out. Later, they considered a proposal to sell to local black undertakers to use as a funeral home, but ultimately this did not pan out.[5]

In 1951, the Bellingers moved into the Taft home. For the next seven years, efforts continued to purchase the Taft home for preservation. Bellinger was all too aware of the desire to purchase the home and his asking price was up to $75,000, more than double the appraised value of $35,000. Finally, in 1960, Elbert R. Bellinger made a deal which would allow him to live comfortably for the rest of his life and for the historic home to be preserved.[6]

Preservation

Around the time of William Howard Taft's death, in 1930, local civic minded people and admirers of the president began to understand the historic value of the home. In 1934, local women from the William H. Taft Elementary School PTA on Southern Avenue and the Mt. Auburn Civic Association joined forces to form the William Howard Taft Memorial Association. The association was incorporated on July 7, 1937 with a stated mission "to plan, promote, erect, and collect funds for a national memorial in honor of William Howard Taft and to insure its perpetuation."[7]

When Mrs. Louis K. Violet DeBus put the home up for sale after Colonel Ernest H. Ruffne's death, the William Howard Taft Memorial Association tried to purchase it. Mrs. DeBus was sympathetic to their efforts and she let her real estate agent, Mrs. Colter Rule, know that she was willing to work with the organization on a fair purchase price. Ultimately, the William Howard Taft Memorial Association could not negotiate the deal and the purchase did not materialize. Regarding the failed efforts, Taft's youngest son, Charles, pulled no punches when he said years later "the property could have been acquired if they tried, but they didn't know how to do anything."[8] The organization hoped the eldest son, Senator Robert A. Taft, could assist with the fundraising. However, in the middle of both an election cycle and the Great Depression, he felt it did not look good for him to raise funds to preserve his father's birthplace. For three years, the home was on the market; however, the William Howard Taft Memorial Association was unable to raise the asking price.[9]

In 1958, an effort was made to use the home as a museum as well as offices for a youth detention center located next door. Despite the close proximity, there were no realistic synergies with this plan and it ultimately, and probably for the best, did not come to pass. As the decade came to a close, progress was made, and in 1960, an agreement was finally reached. Elbert R. Bellinger leased the home to Charles Taft, youngest son of the president, for 100 years. The lease allowed Taft to purchase the home for $35,000 upon Elbert's death. Until then, the deal allowed Elbert to stay in the home with all expenses paid and a monthly stipend of $250 per month. He lived in his first floor apartment for another six years until his death on December 15, 1967. Years later, Charles would say, "It cost about $30,000 more than it would have if the ladies had been on the job."[10]

In 1961, the lease was transferred from Charles Taft to the William Howard Taft Memorial Association, and the home was now safely in the hands of preservationists. With Bellinger living in the home, the William Howard Taft Memorial Association surveyed the state of the house and found that it needed a lot of work. The National Park Service's first impression of the home was that it was a "beat up old building" and estimated it needed $92,500 in restorations.[11] The Taft family contributed almost $300,000 towards the restoration and ongoing maintenance. The Wood and Kock architectural firm was hired for the remodeling and carefully selected projects to "avoid disturbing Bellinger's use of his apartment."[12] Charles Taft used the newspapers to seek out locals who had information and pictures regarding his father's birth home.[13] And as the birthplace museum gained momentum, some big names lent their prestige to the effort. In July 1961, President John F. Kennedy and Supreme Court Chief Justice Earl Warren accepted spots as honorary chairmen joining former Presidents Hoover, Truman, and Eisenhower.

In April 1964, Secretary of the Interior Stewart L. Udall declared the home a National Historic Landmark. Later that year, on September 15 (what would have been President Taft's 107th birthday), a ceremony was held to celebrate the new historic designation. Charles Taft served as master of ceremonies and the only problem that afternoon was his Grandfather Alphonso's name was spelled incorrectly on the historic plaque. The typo was later corrected. Throughout the sixties, the restoration progressed as Charles Taft looked for additional sources of funding. By 1966, with his funding sources running dry and in need of $175,000, he turned to the federal government to take over the site. The nation had recently taken over the Herbert Hoover birthplace, so the Taft birthplace seemed a natural fit. On February 28, 1967, Ohio Senator Frank J. Lausche introduced a bill authored by Charles Taft for the "establishment of the William Howard Taft National Historic Site."[14] One of the major sticking points was that there was still someone living in the home; however, that problem would resolve itself when Elbert R. Bellinger passed away on December 15 of that same year. Using $35,000 borrowed by Charles Taft, the William Howard Taft Memorial Association purchased the home.

The National Park Service started to study the home as Congress also debated the practical and financial aspects of the acquisition. The research would conclude that the home was in poor condition; however, despite this assessment, on September 15, 1969, on what would have been William Howard Taft's 112th birthday, the House of Representatives passed the bill.[15] The Senate passed the bill nine days later, and in November 1969, both houses passed an amendment to include $318,000 for restoration. On December 2, 1969, Richard Nixon signed the legislation establishing the William Howard Taft National Historic Site.[16] It took another year until the title was officially transferred to the federal government on November 1, 1970. Charles Taft had worked on this for a long time, and his father would have been proud. Throughout the next two years the National Park Service staffed the site as restorations began. Finally, in the summer of 1972, the home was opened to the public.[17]

Restorations and funding battles continued for the rest of the decade as the home again fell into disrepair and suffered from a lack of interpretive facilities. Originally, the completion was scheduled to coincide with the 1976 bicentennial; however, that event came and went. By 1978, the cost estimate for restoration had increased tenfold to $3,153,000 with little progress yet made.[18]

Events would change on July 27, 1980, when the Taft birthplace was literally shaken at its foundation. An earthquake, registering 5.1 on the Richter scale, struck Cincinnati and damaged the home to the tune of $100,000. Analysis of the house concluded that the home was "in serious jeopardy unless corrective actions are taken soon."[19] Before the end of the year, emergency work was underway to stabilize the home. Perhaps the earthquake was a blessing in disguise as suddenly the funding issues began to dissipate and a steady stream of restoration dollars made its way to the site annually.

Another interesting transformation occurred during these years. William Howard Taft, who had previously been described as a lesser president of unspectacular achievements was now lionized as a man who "brought a special brand of conservatism, integrity, and respect to all the posts he held."[20]

In December 1982, the site was closed to the public while exterior and interior work restorations were completed and it remained closed for almost six years.[21] During that time, both of President Taft's remaining children passed away: Charles Taft on June 24, 1983 and his older sister, Helen, on February 21, 1987. By the time of his passing, Charles Taft had become the sole voice of the William Howard Taft Memorial Association. When he passed away, he took the Memorial Association with him, but a new association with close ties to the National Park Site emerged from the ashes. The Friends of the William Howard Taft Birthplace was created and became a powerful force for fundraising in the 1980s.[22]

By 1985, the exterior was completed and the National Park Service shifted focus to the interior. They sent a request out through the newspapers for donations or sales of period pieces to decorate the inside as authentically as possible. In the end, very few of the pieces were authentic to the home or actually owned by the Tafts.[23] The site reopened to the public on September 17, 1988, two days after what would have been Taft's 131st birthday. In January 2000, an impressive visitor center was added, including a Disney-like animatronic Charles Taft decked out in fishing gear welcoming you to the home.

Visitor Information

Each year about 17,000 people visit Taft's birthplace annually,[24] however, when I stopped by the National Park Site in 2008, we were the only visitors at the site. The site is open every day except New Years Day, Christmas, and Thanksgiving from 8 a.m. to 4 p.m. The only way to see the home is on a guided tour, which is run every thirty minutes.

28.
Thomas Woodrow Wilson

The birthplace manse of Woodrow Wilson in Staunton, Virginia. *Courtesy of the Woodrow Wilson Presidential Library, Staunton, Virginia.*

Vital Birthplace Information

Birthplace	Staunton, Virginia
President's birthday	December 28, 1856
How long in the home	Over 1 year
Life of the home	1847 to present
Style	Manse
Still in existence	Yes
Commemoration	The Woodrow Wilson Birthplace and Presidential Library
Open to the public	Yes
Cost	$12.00 adults (includes Presidential Library)
For more information	www.woodrowwilson.org
Replica exists	No
Significance	Last president born in a manse
Closest birthplace	Thomas Jefferson, 41.5 miles

Address/Directions:

**24 North Coalter Street
Staunton, Virginia 24401**

From Route 11/250 in downtown Staunton, turn east onto West Beverly Street. In about .2 miles, make the second left onto North Coalter Street. The birthplace will be on your left.

What you will find there today:

The Woodrow Wilson birthplace is the original home where the president was born. It is in pristine condition and part of the Woodrow Wilson Presidential Library. Along with Grover Cleveland and Chester Arthur, Woodrow Wilson was the third and last president born in a manse. The stories of the Wilson and Cleveland birthplaces are rife with similarity. Both were children of pastors at the First Presbyterian Churches of their towns. Both churches acquired land around 1800 and built a manse as their congregations expanded and both families left soon after the baby presidents were born in search of fatter paychecks elsewhere. Also like Cleveland, today, both homes have the original cribs used by the infant presidents.

History

On September 6, 1736, a patent for 118,491 acres of land in the Shenandoah Valley was issued to William Beverley by the Royal Lieutenant-Governor Sir William Gooch. This parcel was originally known as Beverley's Mill Place and was later renamed to Staunton, in tribute to the wife of Governor Gooch, Lady Rebecca Staunton.[1] For years there was no church in the town until 1804, when the First Presbyterian Church of Staunton was established. By 1845, the town and the church were growing and to meet the needs of the congregation, the First Presbyterian Church purchased additional land including the area atop a hill in Staunton's "Gospel Hill" district at the edge of the city facing the countryside. In January 1846, church minutes recorded that funding to build the manse on this newly acquired property was approved. The total cost for the manse was approximately $4,000, with $300 coming from a fair held by the women of the congregation in June 1846.[2]

The manse may have been built to attract its first occupant, Reverend Benjamin Mosby Smith. Two years earlier, he had rejected an offer for the position of minister at First Presbyterian Church, but now, with the manse a part of the deal, oddly enough he had a change of heart. After all, this was to be no ordinary house. The sizable manse had three floors, twelve rooms, four fireplaces, and center halls built in the Greek Revival style (the same style as his predecessor William Howard Taft's birthplace). According to the good Reverend's father, Reverend James Morrison, the home was to "be the best house in Staunton when it is finished. The lot on which it is to be built is one of the most beautiful situations in Staunton."[3]

The manse is strikingly familiar to the main building of Augusta Female Seminary, which was built in 1844. While it is unknown who designed the Wilson home, the similarity does open the possibility that the founder of the Augusta Female Seminary, the Reverend Rufus W. Bailey, also designed the Staunton manse. What *is* known is the builder of the manse, John Fifer of Augusta County. In 1847, the home was completed and the Reverend Benjamin Mosby Smith moved in with his family and several slaves. For seven years, this would be his home until a trade was arranged in December 1854, when Reverend Smith accepted a position of professor at the Union Theological Seminary and the Reverend Joseph Ruggles Wilson left his job as professor at the Hampden-Sydney College (in Prince Edward County, Virginia) to become the new pastor of Staunton's First Presbyterian Church. In March of the next year, Reverend Wilson moved into the manse with his wife, Jessie Woodrow Wilson, and their two daughters Marion, four, and Annie, two.[4]

The following winter, on the evening of December 28, Jessie went into labor. Shortly after the clock struck midnight, at approximately 12:45 in the morning, Jessie had her third child, her first son, and our twenty-eighth president (and the first Southerner elected to the office since the Civil War), Thomas Woodrow Wilson. Despite actually being born on December 29, Woodrow Wilson's birthday was always, and is always, celebrated on December 28.[5] What is less controversial is the location. The baby was born in the first room to the left as you walk in the front door and today you can still see the infamous bed he was born on. The family of five only lived in the home for a little over a year, leaving in early 1858. In Staunton, the Reverend Wilson earned $1,000 a year, so when he was offered $3,000 to move to another parish, the Wilsons packed up and moved to Augusta, Georgia.[6]

From 1858 through 1929, the manse was home to three succeeding pastors that presided over the First Presbyterian Church of Staunton. Woodrow Wilson was a frequent visitor to Staunton as his Aunt, Marion Woodrow Bones, lived in town; however, he did not return to his birthplace for over fifty-four years.[7]

In December 1912, after winning the election to become the twenty-eighth President of the United States, Woodrow Wilson was invited to his birthplace by the Reverend Dr. A.M. Fraser, a former classmate of Wilson's from Davidson College.[8] The town went all out to welcome home their favorite son. The route he took from the train station to the home was marked with garland and the still-novel electric lights.[9] The ceremonies included a reception at the manse, an "old Southern dinner" and a parade in his honor. The visit culminated with the president spending December 28, 1912, his 56th birthday, in the home where he was born.[10]

Reverend Fraser was the last resident to live in the manse, remaining until the home was sold to the Mary Baldwin College.[11]

Preservation

As seen with other birthplaces, it would unfortunately take the death of the president to initiate preservation efforts. This was no different for Woodrow Wilson who passed away in 1924. Shortly after his death, the trustees of Mary Baldwin College for Women attempted to raise $500,000 to honor Woodrow Wilson by building a memorial on the school campus, restore the chapel where he was baptized, and preserve the birthplace. In February 1925, the trustees met with the congregation of First Presbyterian Church to discuss their plans.[12] After obtaining approval, the Woodrow Wilson Birthplace Memorial Association was formed in June to raise the necessary funds. The group was chaired by the president of Mary Baldwin College, Edwin Anderson Alderman, and Franklin Delano Roosevelt served as a member of the advisory committee. Their efforts were launched on October 6, 1925, with a luncheon in Washington, D.C. at the Mayflower Hotel.[13] Despite the initial enthusiasm, fund raising went poorly and the original plan had to be scaled down; however, by June 1929, the group had raised the $30,000 purchase price for the birthplace.[14]

For nine years, the college owned the home, during which time efforts to preserve the birthplace were in progress. Once plans were solidified, the Woodrow Wilson Birthplace Foundation, Inc., was chartered in June 1938 to purchase and preserve the birthplace to be:

> ...dedicated to the aims and ideals and purposes for which Woodrow Wilson lived and died – that men of every nation and all times might have a fairer opportunity to enjoy the fruits of democracy and thus be the better enabled to attain the mental, moral and spiritual development intended for them by their divine creator.[15]

The foundation was led by Rose Frances Witz Whitney Hull, a former resident of Staunton and wife of the Secretary of State Cordell Hull. The group also included U.S. Steel chairman Edward R. Stettinius Jr. and prominent Virginians, Senators Carter Glass and Harry Byrd. In October 1938, the group purchased the birthplace home from Mary Baldwin for $25,000, of which $10,000 was appropriated by the state of Virginia.[16]

In 1940, the foundation began restorations to return the manse to its 1856 appearance. Ward Brown was hired as architect and R. Wilmer Bolling (Woodrow Wilson's brother-in-law) was hired for the project, which cost about $8,000. Additions that were added in 1900 were removed and furnishings were provided by Mrs. Wilson.[17] Finally, by 1941, seventeen years after the plans to purchase and preserve the home as a national shrine were first conceived, the birthplace was ready. To celebrate the opening of the home to the public, a dedication was held on May 4, 1941. For the ceremony, President Franklin Delano Roosevelt traveled to Staunton, calling the Woodrow Wilson birthplace a "shrine to freedom."[18]

Now that the home was in the hands of preservationists, the next order of business was the ongoing procurement of funds to maintain it. In September 1944, Mrs. Hull launched a drive to raise $100,000.[19] At the time of the announcement, they were already halfway there, as the Twentieth Century Fox Film Corporation had already donated $50,000.[20]

The Virginia Conservation Commission also commemorated Staunton's most famous son in 1950 when they erected two markers in the vicinity of the birthplace to let tourists know they are approaching the historic home. The first historic marker A-61 was erected on the Lee Highway (U.S. 11), just north of Staunton and south of the Woodrow Wilson Parkway (Virginia Route 275). If you are driving towards Staunton, the marker is on right. It reads:

BIRTHPLACE OF WOODROW WILSON US PRESIDENT 1913-1921
Three and one half miles south, on Coalter Street in Staunton, is the birthplace of Thomas Woodrow Wilson, 8th Virginia-born President. New Jersey Governor, 28th President (World War I). He was chief author and sponsor of the League of Nations. Born Dec 28, 1856, died in Washington, Feb 3, 1924. The birthplace is maintained as an historic shrine.

The second marker, A-62, is closer to the home at the southern city line at the intersection of Greenville Avenue (U.S. 11) and Ritchie Boulevard (Virginia Route 275). The marker is on the left if you are traveling north on Greenville Avenue towards Staunton. It reads:

One mile north, on Coalter Street in Staunton, is the birthplace of Thomas Woodrow Wilson, 8th Virginia-born President of the U.S., Princeton University President, New Jersey Governor, 28th President (World War I). He was chief author and sponsor of the League of Nations. Born Dec 28, 1856, died in Washington, Feb 3, 1924. The birthplace is maintained as an historic shrine.

In March of 1956, the Woodrow Wilson Birthplace Foundation launched a new fund drive to raise $595,000 to "enlarge and beautify" the birthplace.[21] In October 1959, the foundation honored Wilson's widow with a cake to celebrate her 87th birthday at the home her husband was born in 103 years earlier. By that time, the Woodrow Wilson Birthplace Foundation was under new leadership including Belle Baruch, daughter of Bernard Baruch, R.K. Serfass, and Lewis L. Strauss. Strauss had recently ended his term as chairman of Atomic Energy Commission and five years earlier had been the first chairman of the Herbert Hoover Foundation, which was formed to preserve President Hoover's birthplace.[22]

On October 27, 1960, in the waning days of his presidency, Dwight David Eisenhower visited the birthplace for the annual meeting of the Woodrow Wilson Birthplace Foundation. One person who was not in attendance that day was the president's widow, Edith Bolling Galt Wilson. The year 1960 was an election year and Edith was an ardent support of democrat John F. Kennedy:

I like President Eisenhower very much, but I am for Mr. Kennedy. I think it would be politically unwise for me to go under the circumsances.[23]

Eisenhower was unfazed and was able to make the day a thematic doubleheader when he also visited his mother's birthplace in nearby Mount Sidney. After his visit, he went to Mary Baldwin College to make a "non-political" speech before 5,000 people.[24]

On July 18, 1964, the year the Beatles came to America, the home was recognized as a Registered National Historic Landmark 1965 (National Register Number #66000926). Wilson's birthplace was included with ninety-five other sites, including John F. Kennedy's birthplace. More recently, in 2005, a $200,000 grant was awarded to the home from the US Department of the Interior "Save America's Treasures Program" to complete restorations in time for Wilson's 150th birthday in 2006.[25]

The home is still a source of pride in Staunton. For what would have been the president's 153rd birthday in 2009, 560 people gathered for the annual open house at the Victorian manse.

Visitor Information

To see the historic birthplace, you will need to take the informative tour that lasts about forty minutes. Visitor hours are 9 a.m. to 5 p.m. on Monday through Saturday and noon to 5 p.m. on Sundays from March through October. From November through February, times are 10 a.m. to 4 p.m. on Monday through Saturday and noon to 4 p.m. on Sundays. Next to the birthplace is the Woodrow Wilson Presidential Library. More of a museum than a library, its exhibits are well presented and filled with good information about the man and his presidency.

When I visited in March 2010, we stayed at the historic Stonewall Jackson Inn, which was built in 1924, has reasonable rates and is within walking distance from the Woodrow Wilson birthplace.

29.
Warren Gamaliel Harding

The birthplace of Warren G. Harding in Blooming Grove, Ohio.

Vital Birthplace Information

Birthplace	Blooming Grove, Ohio
President's birthday	November 2, 1865
How long in the home	16 months
Life of the home	1856 to after 1923
Style	Farmhouse
Still in existence	No
Ultimate fate	Lost over time
Commemoration	Historic marker
Open to the public	Yes
Cost	Free
For more information	www.ohiohistory.org
Replica exists	No
Significance	First president born after the Civil War
Closest birthplace	Rutherford B. Hayes, 30 miles

What you will find there today:

The birthplace marker is located on private property in front of a home that is not the original birthplace. The Ohio historic marker simply states:

Warren G. Harding, 29th President of the United States was born on this site November 2, 1865.

Harding Memorial Library Association and The Ohio Historical Society 7-17.

On the property is also a flag adorned with flowers and another small marker in front of it that reads:
Warren G. Harding Home Site

At first glance, this set-up looks more like a grave, but don't be fooled; Warren is actually buried about twenty-five miles away in Marion, Ohio. The birthplace markers were erected in 1977 (although the larger marker is dated 1978) and were jointly sponsored by the Harding Memorial Library Association and the Ohio Historical Society. They stand on the front lawn of a private home that is not the home in which the president was born.

Address/Directions:

**6297 Ohio Route 97
Blooming Grove, Ohio 44833**

The marker is .2 miles east of Williamsport-Blooming Grove Road (County Route 20) in Blooming Grove, Morrow County.

History

The Harding roots run deep in the Ohio village of Blooming Grove. Amos Harding first acquired the land where the future president was born in October of 1815 when he purchased 160 acres for $200 from John Maxwell. Both Amos and John Maxwell had migrated from Clifford, Pennsylvania. In the following years, more Hardings came to the village (then known as Corsica), including

111

Amos' son, Salmon, who helped map out the town. When Amos died in 1826, he passed the property on to his two sons, Ebenezer Harding and George Tryon Harding. Ebenezer did not plan to stay in Blooming Grove and sold his share to his brother, who, in 1831, bought an additional eighty acres to increase his total to 240.[1]

In 1856, George Tryon Harding Sr. built a two-story home, about 28 square feet on his property (the family had previously been living in a log cabin). In 1860, George died and the property was passed on to his wife, Elizabeth. By this point, her son, Charles, was living in the eventual birthplace home and she moved in with him. Two months later, she deeded the property to her son, William Oliver Perry Harding. However, only four days after that, William sold most of the property to his brother Charles Alexander Harding "for a consideration of $2,200."[2]

Charles and his wife, Mary Anne, had six children who survived past infancy. Their third child and only son, George Tyron Harding, had been born in 1844. In 1864, George married his sweetheart, Phoebe Elizabeth Dockerson, and then promptly went off to fight in the Civil War. After his brief, undistinguished service, he returned to Blooming Grove and along with his new bride, moved into the family homestead on what had become a 185.5-acre farm.[3]

On November 2, 1865, the couple had a child, Warren Gamaliel Harding, who would one day distinguish himself as the first President of the United States to be born after the Civil War. The young couple stayed in this home for sixteen months until late February 1867 when they moved into a newly constructed home on the property. The family continued to live on the farm, albeit not in the birth home, until Warren was seven years old. As a child, Warren enjoyed fishing on the creek that ran through the property and spent a lot of time at his birth home where his aunts continued to live.[4] In 1873, his family moved to Caledonia, about ten miles away, and Dr. George Tryon Harding, Sr. sold the farm to his sisters. The Harding sisters later sold to a distant relative, Charles Erickson of Pennsylvania, who sold to his son, Harry Erickson, in 1890. Harry, who had married the president's second cousin, owned the home for thirty-three years and throughout Warren G. Harding's presidency.[5]

On October 4, 1922, when he was still president, Warren decided to purchase his birth home and the neighboring farm so he could retire there when his term ended in 1925. His friend and Marion postmaster, French Crow, negotiated the purchase. The total land was 265.5 acres and he planned to build a golf course on the property. At the time, the house was still standing but in bad shape and was being used to store farm machinery.[6] However, perhaps feeling nostalgic for the old days after two difficult years in office, Harding had plans to restore the old home.[7] He kept the purchase a secret for six months until it finally made the papers the following April.[8] Unfortunately, President Harding never got the chance to enjoy retirement at his birthplace. He died in San Francisco after returning from a trip to Alaska several months later.

Upon his death, the home was passed to Warren's brother, George T. Harding, and was later deeded to George's three sons, Charles, George, and Warren. The three nephews operated the farm for thirty years, but were not successful at turning a profit and finally sold the home in December 1954. For the first time since the 1820s, a Harding family did not own the birthplace property when Mr. and Mrs. Everett Bash of Forest, Ohio, and their seven children purchased the home. The Bash's were purely interested in the farm, and didn't even realize that almost a century earlier, the nation's twenty-ninth president was born at the place. At the time, tourists were pouring in at a rate of one per day, even though the birth home was no longer in existence.[9]

Preservation

Considered one of the worst presidents in history, for years there was little desire to memorialize Harding's birthplace. In the 1950s, there was a small semi-circle of evergreens at the site, but no marker. In 1965, a major event was planned by the Harding Memorial Association, which was comprised of relatives and friends of the president, to coincide with what would have been his 100th birthday. The plans were derailed when a biography of the president was being researched called *Shadow of Blooming Grove* by Francis Russell (it was published in 1968). The book exposed several extramarital affairs on top of the known scandals and corruption surrounding President Harding. Due to this negative publicity, plans were muted; however, the Harding Memorial Association still unveiled a marker on his birth site on December 12, 1963. The money for the marker was donated to the Ohio Historical Society by Ralph Lewis, a Marion grocery store owner and friend of Harding's. Warren's nephew, Doctor George Harding, and seventy-five more members of the Harding family who made up the Harding Memorial Society were present for the dedication. Despite his failings, the people of Blooming Grove still acknowledged their small town hero.[10] On that cold day, speakers praised the former president, and after the ceremony, a modest banquet was held in his honor.[11]

In 1977, the Harding Memorial Library Association and The Ohio Historical Society placed a flag and a simple marker at the birth location, which still stands today.

Visitor Information

The Harding birthplace is not easy to find and the marker is not very informative, which was one of the reasons I was motivated to write this book. Good or bad, this man reached the highest office in the land and his birthplace deserves to be celebrated. The remote area is very scenic and one can only imagine how it appeared at the time of Warren's birth. When visiting the site of the birth home, please remember the home at the site is not the original. What is there now is a private residence and you should respect the privacy of the current owners.

30.
John Calvin Coolidge

The birthplace of Calvin Coolidge in Plymouth Notch, Vermont.

Vital Birthplace Information

Birthplace	Plymouth Notch, Vermont
President's birthday	July 4, 1872
How long in the home	4 years
Life of the home	Before 1835 to present
Style	General store
Still in existence	Yes
Commemoration	President Calvin Coolidge State Historic Site
Still in existence	Yes
Open to the public	Yes
Cost	$7.50 ($6.50 with AAA card)
For more information	www.historicvermont.org/coolidge/coolidge.html
Replica exists	No
Significance	First president to have his entire birthplace town commemorated
Closest birthplace	Franklin Pierce, 92 miles

What you will find there today:

The authentic birthplace is part of the President Calvin Coolidge State Historic Site. The site consists of eighteen buildings and comprises the entire village of Plymouth Notch, Vermont. Nearby, you can also visit "Silent Cal's" final resting place.

History

The town of Plymouth Notch sits nestled in the Green Mountains of Vermont. Coolidge's roots run deep in the town as one of his ancestors founded Plymouth Notch in 1780. The building that was the birthplace of the thirtieth president was first a country store built prior to 1835 – the main portion was 2 stories, and later a 1.5-story addition was added in the back. While the front portion continued to be used as a general store, the back served as a home for the proprietors and the upstairs was used for meetings and dances.

Colonel John Calvin Coolidge, future father of the president, began operating the store and moved into the rear living quarters in 1868. That same year he married Victoria Josephine Moor. The Colonel was a good businessman; he paid $40 a year rent and pulled in $100 a month in profit.[1] Soon afterwards, John Coolidge purchased the store and the family moved into the home in the rear. On July 4, 1872, John Calvin Coolidge, later to be known as Calvin, was born in the downstairs bedroom. Starting in this

Address/Directions:

3780 Route 100A
Plymouth Notch, Vermont 05056

From the east, take Interstate I-91 to Exit 8. Follow Route 131 west for nineteen miles to Ludlow. Go north on Route 100 for eleven miles, then right on Route 100A. Plymouth Notch is approximately one mile north.

From the west, take either Route 7 or Route 4 to Rutland. Follow Route 4 east for 23 miles until it meets Route 100A. Take Route 100A South for six miles until you reach Plymouth Notch.

small town, one day he would become the thirtieth President of the United States of America. Three years later his sister, Abigail, was also born in the home.

In 1876, the Coolidges were eager to upgrade to a larger home; however, they were not willing to give up the small-town lifestyle. So they packed up and moved across the street to the home where Calvin's father remained until his death in 1926. Later in his life, Calvin described his fond memories of growing up in Plymouth Notch when he said:

It would be hard to imagine better settings for a boy than I had.[2]

Colonel John Coolidge retained ownership of the store, including the birthplace addition; however, he later sold his share of the business, and after 1877, the store was run by Josephine's brother, Franklin C. Moor.

In 1917, Florence V. Cilley purchased the store from Colonel John and renamed the establishment "Cilley's Store." In 1924, when Calvin Coolidge was elected president, he chose to keep close ties with his roots in Plymouth Notch. He transformed the upper floor of his birth home into his "Summer White House Office" to use for official business when he was visiting his hometown. At the time, the room was being used as a community hall.[3] Another change in Plymouth Notch after Coolidge was president was the tourists. By 1925, over 50,000 people had come to visit Plymouth Notch at a time when there were less than thirty full-time residents.[4]

Florence Cilley remained the owner of the store until 1945 when she sold it to her daughter, Violet, and her son-in-law, Herman Pelkey. In memory of Plymouth Notch's most famous son, the Pelkeys restored the store to how it looked twenty-two years earlier on August 3, 1923. On that day, at 2:47 a.m., Calvin Coolidge's father, a notary republic, swore in his son, Calvin Coolidge, as president after learning of Warren G. Harding's death a day earlier. After Harding died, Calvin Coolidge could not be reached by phone, because the only telephone in Plymouth Notch was in the birthplace store and the call came at night after the store had closed.[5]

Over the following decades, the state made several offers to purchase the birthplace building, but the Pelkeys always refused. Throughout the years, the rear home was modernized; however, the store retained its 1923 appearance including the name "Florence V. Cilley" painted prominently above the entrance. In the front of the store was a post office that served Plymouth Notch until 1976, and when it was decommissioned, a new one was added onto the side of the store, which still serves the community today.

Preservation

About a year after becoming president, a sign was hung from the column by the entrance to the store to commemorate the famous building. The sign simply read:

BIRTHPLACE OF CALVIN COOLIDGE, PLYMOUTH VT. Home Town Coolidge Club.

The Home Town Coolidge Club was established in Plymouth Notch when Calvin Coolidge was running for President in 1924 and held their meetings in the hall above the birthplace room.[6]

In 1958, the Vermont Historic Sites Commission erected a more permanent marker in front of the birthplace that still stands today. It reads:

CALVIN COOLIDGE 1872-1933 Born July 4, 1872, in a house back of store, Calvin Coolidge from 4 years of age lived in the Homestead across the road, now owned by the State of Vermont. Here on Aug. 3, 1923, he was inaugurated president and here he spent many vacations. In the Notch Cemetery he rests beside his wife and son and 4 generations of forebears.

Additional recognition came seven years later when the home became a National Historic Landmark (National Register Number #66000794) on June 22, 1965, along with Herbert Hoover's birthplace and thirty-one other sites.[7]

In 1968, the Vermont Division For Historic Preservation finally was able to purchase the birth home. They promptly began a project to restore the home to how it looked in the 1870s when the Coolidges lived there. Structurally, the building had not changed much, but the far wall of the birthplace room (at the immediate left when you enter the home from the rear of the store) had been removed; it was replaced so the room appeared how it did in 1872. The Coolidge family donated original furnishings, and the state, in honor of Calvin Coolidge's infamous frugality, chose to restore the home in as thrifty a manner as possible.[8]

Visitor Information

The Calvin Coolidge birthplace may very well be the most scenic of all of the Presidential Birthplaces. I visited in summer 2010 as part of a New England Coolidge-Arthur-Pierce birthplace trifecta. The drive in on Route 100 from the west was absolutely beautiful – lush green trees and grass, cool lakes, and people everywhere biking, hiking, and swimming. The ride brought me past some very rustic homes and I could swear I passed an outhouse or two.

The tour of the historic village starts with a twenty-minute video presentation of Plymouth Notch and its favorite son. The most prominent building in the town is, of course, the general store, in which you can purchase an Ice Cold Moxie and a "Birthplace of Calvin Coolidge" pennant before walking to the rear to see the room in which Calvin was born. The guides and townsfolk are still very proud of their hometown hero and it's hard to not get swept up in the nostalgia. They laugh off the nickname "Silent Cal" saying he was the first president on radio and to those who were lucky enough to know him, he wasn't quiet at all. After the birthplace, you can visit his church, the cheese factory, and the home across the street where his father swore him in as president. Before departing Plymouth Notch to rejoin the twenty-first century, make sure you visit his final resting place across Route 100A. The site is open daily from late May through Mid-October from 9:30 a.m. to 5 p.m.

FROM SEA TO SHINING SEA

31.
Herbert Clark Hoover

The birthplace of Herbert Hoover in West Branch, Iowa. *Courtesy of Joseph F. Picone*

Vital Birthplace Information

Birthplace	West Branch, Iowa
President's birthday	August 10, 1874
How long in the home	5 years
Life of the home	1871 to present
Style	Cottage
Still in existence	Yes
Commemoration	Herbert Hoover National Historic Site
Open to the public	Yes
Cost	Free
For more information	www.nps.gov/heho
Replica exists	Not anymore
Significance	First president born outside of the Eastern time zone
Closest birthplace	Ronald Reagan, 81 miles

What you will find there today:

The authentic, restored birthplace cottage is part of the Herbert Hoover National Historic Site. The site is located on twenty-eight acres and includes many other significant buildings.

Address/Directions:

110 Parkside Drive
West Branch, Iowa 52358

The birth home is located a half-mile north of exit 254 off Route 80 in West Branch, Iowa.

History

On January 23, 1852, Aaron Baker from Baltimore, Maryland, was awarded 160 acres in what is now West Branch, Iowa. Baker had served in the Mexican War, and the land patent was issued to him as compensation for his service. The parcel of land bordered what would become the intersection of Main and Downey Streets. Apparently, Baker did not have much use for the property since within four months he sold the entire parcel to Samuel King and his wife, Constance, of Cedar County, Iowa. For the 160 acres, Baker would pocket barely a dollar an acre at $162.50. Like Baker, the Kings were also not interested in a long-term settlement. Less than a year later, on March 28, 1853, they turned a nice profit when they sold half of the acreage to Joseph Steer for $208. Steer continued

subdividing the property just as the Kings had done, only into much smaller parcels. In 1871, five acres in the southeast corner were sold to J. M. Werthell. Werthell in turn further subdivided these five acres into lots, selling two lots to Jesse Hoover, Herbert's great grandfather, for $90 on April 13, 1871. The two lots were numbered #42 and #43 and were both 30 by 99 feet.[1]

The lot on the corner of Downey and Penn Street was #42, and it was there that Jesse and his father, Eli, built a small two-room cottage in 1871. For building materials, they hauled stones by wagon from the open prairie to use for the foundation and the lumber was floated down the Mississippi River from Wisconsin or Minnesota. The home was only 14 by 20 feet and had a single bedroom and a combination living room, dining room, and kitchen. There was also an enclosed porch, which was used as a spare bedroom. This is why the house is listed as two or three rooms, depending on how the porch is counted. Regardless, any way you look at it, this was not a big home. A year earlier, Jesse had married Huldah Minthorn and the couple already had one son, Theodore, when they moved into their new home. The young devout couple occasionally held church gatherings in the home.[2]

On August 10, 1874, Herbert Clark Hoover was born, the family's second child and our thirty-first president. Years later, his older brother would recall his father coming into his room, lamp in hand, to announce, "You have a little baby brother."[3] Just as America had moved west, so had the presidential birthplaces. Hoover was the first president born west of the Mississippi and the first born outside of the Eastern time zone. From this humble birth home, he would one day have entire communities of "homes" named after him, as shanty towns known as "Hoovervilles" began to sprout all over the county after the stock market crash in October 1929, perhaps most notably in New York's Central Park.

Herbert Hoover spent his first five years in the home. In 1879, now with three kids in a two-room cottage, the family moved out. Like his predecessor, the Coolidges, the Hoovers did not go far, moving about a block south on Downey Street. Tragically, within five years, both Jesse and Huldah had died, leaving ten-year-old Herbert and his two siblings orphans. Young Herbert was sent to live with his maternal grandfather.[4]

As for the birthplace home, the title was passed to G.M.D. Hill and his wife, Martha, from Johnson County. Along with lot #43 and #41, on which Jesse had built a blacksmith shop, Hill paid $1,000. The Hills had been married sixteen months and had an infant daughter. In 1881, they welcomed their second daughter, Maggie, born in the same home as Herbert Hoover. Despite the birth, all was not well with the Hills and soon their marriage began to deteriorate. Martha claimed that eight months after moving into the birth home her husband became abusive. The Hills tried to sell the cottage shortly before moving in and again in 1883; finally on Christmas 1885, they sold all three lots to Z. Taylor McCaleb, a blacksmith from Oasis, Iowa, for only $500, losing half of their money. The McCalebs allowed the Hills to remain in the home until the spring of 1886, several months before their July divorce.[5]

The McCalebs held on to the property for less than two years, selling the birthplace lot #42 and lot #43 to Victoria Hill on September 17, 1887, for $250. Just like the McCalebs, Victoria Hill did not live long in the home, staying for only a few months until March 1888. Victoria Hill, a widow and mother of three young children, married a wealthy farmer from Springdale Township, Iowa, named Oliver C. Pennock. After her marriage, she put the birthplace home up for sale so she could move in with her new husband. On December 23, 1889, the birthplace lot #42 and lot #43 were sold to R. Portland Scellers and his wife, Jennie, for $250.[6]

The Scellers had been acquiring adjacent lots for several years and would continue to do so for the next decade. They had five children including a daughter that had died in infancy. With seven people, they needed the extra room so, in 1890, the Scellers shifted the cottage to face a different direction and also added a two-story structure on the side of the home. By 1900, they had begun to experience financial problems. By refinancing the properties several times in the early 1900s, the Scellers were able to weather the storm, and by 1911, they were again acquiring additional sites bringing their total to twelve lots.[7]

By 1914, Herbert Hoover had begun to gain fame as the head of Woodrow Wilson's American Relief Committee, which was formed to assist the 150,000 soldiers stranded in Europe (World War I had broken out, but the United States was still three years away from entering the conflict). People began to stop by to see the birthplace cottage and the Scellers enjoyed meeting people and showing off their historic home.[8]

As the home was seen more and more as an important historic structure, some people wanted to take a little souvenir from their visit. One such example occurred, in July 1917, when a cane was carved from wood from the birthplace home and presented to Alfred H. O'Connor, a principal speaker at the West Branch Chautauqua, an adult education movement popular in rural America in the early years of the twentieth century. Luckily "birthplace canes" would not become a popular commodity. The next time on record one was created was for Herbert Hoover himself in 1928.[9]

In 1916, R. Portland Scellers passed away; however, his wife, Jennie, continued to live on the property for another eighteen years. These were very exciting times for the birthplace – in 1921, Herbert's wife, Lou Henry Hoover, visited the cottage, and in 1923, Herbert saw his birth home for the first time in many years, noting the vast changes since he had last seen it, when he came to West Branch to speak to the League of Women Voters.

Five years later, on August 21, 1928, Herbert Hoover returned for a longer visit, this time as a candidate for the President of the United States. The event spurred the formation of the Hoover Birthplace Committee, organized by several people including the mayor of West Branch, N.P. Olsen. Jennie Scellers invited Herbert Hoover to the birthplace home for "an old fashioned Iowa breakfast" – ham and eggs, coffee, jam, peaches, and cream – before he delivered his speech to 18,000 people.[10] The breakfast would have been prepared in the actual room where the president was born since, at the time, the birthplace room was used as the kitchen.[11]

More notable events happened at the birthplace over the next few years. In 1929, the home hosted two weddings (the last on the premises until 1940) and the Better Homes Committee of Des Moines created a replica of the birth home for the state fair circuit. In 1930, both the U. S. Marine Corp band and the U.S. Army band visited the birthplace cottage, with the Marines playing a concert at the home.[12]

Several times Mrs. Scellers received attractive offers to sell, including $3,500 by Presidential Secretary Lawrence Richey on behalf of the Hoovers in 1930. She ultimately turned them all down. Her sentimental ties to the property were too strong and she truly enjoyed her notoriety as the "Hostess to the nation."[13] The Hoovers were comfortable that she was taking good care of the property and were showing the home in a dignified matter, so therefore did not pursue the matter while she was still alive.[14]

On June 26, 1934, after suffering a stroke, Mrs. Jennie Scellers passed away. After her death, the property was divided among her four children. Her son, Earl, lived in the birthplace cottage after her passing, but he did not share his mother's hospitality and did not open the home to visitors. The next year, on July 29, 1935, the children sold all twelve properties to Fred Albin for $4,500. Fred Albin, a local businessman and boyhood pal of Herbert Hoover, had purchased the home on behalf of Herbert Hoover's son Allan. After fifty-six years, the birthplace home was now back in the hands of the Hoover family with the intention of preserving the historic site.[15]

Preservation

Once Herbert Hoover was nominated for president, thousands of people stopped by to see "the little cottage under the maples." Mrs. Scellers was eternally patient and gracious to all. In one month, 1,750 people signed her guest book and by August 1928, over 5,000 people had registered. Many of the visitors were from outside of the United States, including guests from Rangoon, Burma (now Myanmar), and Canton, China.[16]

Of course, the popularity as a tourist attraction skyrocketed after he was elected the thirty-first President of the United States on November 6, 1928. Foreigners continued to visit the site, and six months later, after his election, a college basketball team from Japan took the tour. With the larger crowds, Mrs. Scellers finally began to seize upon the business opportunity and started to charge a dime for the tour. This may not sound like much, but with thousands of visitors each month, the extra income must have been a big help, especially during the depression years. One visitor was Mrs. Lillian Clark Casey, National President of the Ladies of the Grand Army of the Republic who was especially interested in the preservation of presidential birthplaces.[17] Much like Teddy Roosevelt's birthplace preservation efforts a quarter century earlier, the movement to commemorate a sitting president's birthplace had sprung up without state or federal support. This new pattern marks a permanent shift in regards to presidential birthplace preservation.

In early 1929, the Iowa Chapter of the Daughters of the American Revolution received approval from Mrs. Scellers to place a memorial marker at the home.[18] The commemoration ceremony was held on August 10, 1929, Herbert Hoover's 55th birthday. Professor Benjamin F. Shambaugh, superintendent of the Iowa State Historical Society, presided over the ceremony.[19] Behind him on the platform, in what must have seemed like an episode of *This Is Your Life*, were Hoover's first schoolteacher, Mrs. Mollie Carran, his family physician, Dr. L. J. Leach, and his childhood buddy, Newt Butler. Despite these guests, the most impressive speaker of the day was the founder of Boys Town, Father Flanagan, who called Hoover the most distinguished orphan in the world. Accompanying Father Flanagan were forty boys from his famous orphanage in Omaha, Nebraska.[20] The monument unveiled that day was a small bronze tablet affixed to a 3,000-pound granite boulder with the following inscription:

Birthplace of Herbert Hoover. First President of the United States born west of the Mississippi River.

Marked by the pilgrim chapter of the Daughters of the American Revolution.[21]

For the first years of his presidency, visitors continued to flock to the birthplace. By the middle of July 1931, Mrs. Scellers' guest book tallied 34,348 names and the list continued to grow until her death in June 1934.[22] In July 1935, Fred Albin, boyhood friend and schoolmate of Herbert Hoover, purchased the home for $4,500.[23] He later said, at the time, he got the home for a bargain because it "looked like a henhouse."[24] He bought the birthplace on behalf of Herbert's son, Allan Hoover, so the family could restore it and make it available to visitors; however, that information was not made public until five months later when on October 16, 1935,

Albin transferred the deed to Allan Hoover.[25] Before restorations could begin, the president first wanted to survey the property in person, but he could not make the trip until June 11, 1937. He tried to keep the reason for his visit private; however, when pressed, he did admit he would restore the birth home, although he credited, or perhaps blamed, the decision on his wife, Lou Henry. He walked around the house and methodically noted all of the changes with impressive detail. Hoover decided that the home would be restored to how it looked when he was a boy, which included reversing the changes from 1890, which relocated the home and added an additional structure.[26]

Mrs. Hoover had taken a particular interest in restoring the birthplace, interviewing anyone who knew anything about its appearance when her husband lived there, including Herbert's older brother, Theodore "Tad" Hoover. In addition to the restoration, she was also working on a book about the birthplace entitled *Memories of a Little House* that provided extensive information about each room, how it looked and what it what used for.[27]

As seen many times, women's organizations have led the charge to restore the presidential birthplaces. In the case of Herbert Hoover, it was not an organization, but rather one woman who would be the driving force, Lou Henry Hoover. Since there was no organization leading the efforts towards preservation, Mrs. Hoover created one. In June 1938, she began to derive plans for the Herbert Hoover Birthplace Society, working with Harrison Spangler, an Iowa delegate and member of the Republican National Committee. The purpose of the society was to take ownership of the birthplace once the restorations were completed.[28]

The following year, on March 22, 1939, the initial meeting was held at the caretaker's home on the birthplace property; about thirty people attended, including friends of the Hoovers, local historians, and Bruce McKay from the McKay Construction Company, contracted by the Hoovers to complete the restorations. The first president of the birthplace society was Fred Albin, the Hoover's friend and agent who handled the birthplace purchase. The local newspaper reported on the progress and many curious locals stopped by to watch the work. By late October 1938, the structural changes were completed and Mrs. Hoover began efforts to authentically furnish the home. She started by contacting relatives and friends to locate original furnishings, but met with limited success since many were sold at auction when Herbert's mother passed away. So what she couldn't locate, she authorized the birthplace society President Fred Albin to purchase. By April 1941, the birthplace had been "refurnished to bring back the atmosphere of the days when the family occupied it and during which time the three Hoover children were born."[29] As promised, the home was turned over to the Herbert Hoover Birthplace Society after it was completed and the Herbert Hoover Birthplace Park was formed. The society continued to exist under several presidents until 1957 when it was merged with a similar organization from Oregon to form the Herbert Hoover Birthplace Foundation, and then finally the Herbert Hoover Presidential Library Association. The main focus of the new organization was the formation of the Presidential Library, completed in 1962.[30]

When the cottage was finally opened to the public, the Hoovers and residents of West Branch were thrilled. Herbert, a strong proponent of pulling oneself up by the bootstraps called the home "physical proof of the unbounded opportunity of American life."[31] In those first months, the home logged thousands of visitors, including several notable guests like the wife of famed author Jack London and Iowa's Governor George Wilson on September 3, 1941.[32]

By a unanimous vote of 45-0, the Iowa legislature appropriated funds for the maintenance of the birthplace site starting in 1941 at $1,200 annually. Funding increased throughout the 1940s and 1950s, but despite the money, maintenance on the birthplace cottage was minimal during these years. In the 1960s, the home had deteriorated and a number of repairs were made to the floor joists, foundation, and roof, and modern amenities were added such as heating and a fire alarm system.[33]

Obviously, the war years greatly reduced the number of visitors; however, in 1946, attendance quickly rebounded. In 1948, the Herbert Hoover Birthplace Society and funeral director Bill Anderson invited President Hoover to his birthplace for his 74th birthday:

We have long cherished the hope that you may again find it convenient to visit the place of your birth and we would like if it is agreeable for you and your family on the occasion of your birthday on August 10, 1948...It would please us immensely to observe this day, making it an occasion upon which all might unite in honoring Iowa's most distinguished citizen.[34]

Several weeks later, Anderson was delighted to receive a reply from Hoover of acceptance. Hoover, now living in Palo Alto, California, journeyed hundreds of miles and many hours for the celebration. On that day, Harrison Spangler welcomed the president and the town came out in full force to greet their favorite son. The streets were lined with well-wishers and over 25,000 people attended the celebration. This was his first visit in over a decade and he was candid as usual when he was asked if he recognized the birthplace:

I left this house when I was four years old, and we moved across the street. I don't remember anything about this house.[35]

Six years later, an invitation was once again extended for the president's 80th birthday. The previous year, Herbert's son, Allan, told Bill Anderson, "You people in Iowa don't realize how much that Cottage means to dad."[36] As a testament to integrity of the man, again he accepted. Still living in California, one can imagine how arduous a journey this must have been for him in 1954. At the time, only 750 people lived in West Branch; however, a crowd of 50,000 people came out to greet their "favorite barefoot boy."[37] There was a parade in his honor and speeches were delivered by Governor William Beadsley, University of Iowa president, Dr. Virgil

M. Hancher, and most notably, Vice President Richard Nixon. After the ceremony, a dinner for 200 was served in his honor.[38] On the menu was country fried chicken, potatoes, corn on the cob, salad, apple sauce, pickled beets, Amana bread, and pickles followed by coffee, ice cream, and a six-tier cake with eighty candles.[39]

Later that year, in December 1954, the Herbert Hoover Foundation was incorporated in West Branch, with the mission to preserve "the President's birthplace at West Branch, Iowa, and to aid in the advancement of the principles for which he has stood in education and scientific and public welfare activity".[40] They also hoped to one day take over the management of the birthplace; however, this never did happen. Lewis L. Strauss was the first chairman of the foundation. Strauss was a personal secretary to President Hoover during his presidency and, in 1954, served as chairman of the Atomic Energy Commission. Five years later, Strauss would also serve on the Woodrow Wilson Birthplace Foundation. The vice chairmen of the foundation were the president's two sons, Allan and Herbert Jr. The group met for the first time on February 11, 1955 to officially name all leadership posts.[41]

In the 1960s, there was a proposal to enclose the home within another structure similar to the Abraham Lincoln and Ulysses Grant birthplaces, but Herbert Hoover wisely opposed the suggestion. In 1962, the Herbert Hoover Presidential Library was completed in West Branch near the birthplace. Herbert Hoover had chosen the spot himself and the Herbert Hoover Foundation was critical in its formation. Never one to miss a day in his honor, Herbert Hoover was of course on hand on August 10, 1962, his 88th birthday, for the dedication of the Herbert Hoover Presidential Library. Accompanied by former President Harry S Truman, Hoover visited his birthplace for the last time. On October 20, 1964, shortly after his 90th birthday, he died and was buried on a grassy knoll overlooking his birthplace home.[42]

The next year on June 22, 1965, along with thirty-two other sites, the birthplace home was designated a National Historic Landmark (National Register Number #66000110).[43] Later that year, on August 10, on what would have been Hoover's 91st birthday, two presidents, one past and one future, visited the birthplace when General Dwight D. Eisenhower and Richard M. Nixon toured the cottage. Less than three months after being designated a National Historic Landmark, the birthplace was on its way to bigger and better accolades. On August 12, 1965, legislation was approved to make the home a National Historic Site.[44] It took three years for the process to run its course, but finally, in 1968, the birthplace home, the Presidential Library and several other structures were established as the Herbert Hoover National Historic Site. The site was officially dedicated four years later on August 10, 1972 or what would have been the president's 98th birthday. President Richard Nixon's daughter, Julie Nixon Eisenhower, made the dedication.[45] In February 1969, President Lyndon B. Johnson and his wife, Lady Bird, also visited the home.

Visitor Information

In the 1970s, about 400,000 people were visiting annually. That number dwindled to about 220,000 annually in the 1980s, and today, attendance is about 150,000 per year.[46] When visiting the home, make sure you take in all of the structures that make up the Herbert Hoover National Historic Site, including the Herbert Hoover Presidential Library and Museum. In addition to the birthplace are the graves of Herbert Hoover and his parents, Jesse and Huldah, who died so young. You can also visit the re-created blacksmith shop in which his father worked and the Quaker meeting house, built in 1857, and frequented by the Hoovers. The Herbert Hoover National Historic Site is open year round except Christmas, Thanksgiving, and New Year's Day from 9 a.m. to 5 p.m.

32.
Franklin Delano Roosevelt

Vital Birthplace Information

Birthplace	Hyde Park, New York
Name	Springwood, Crum Elbow
President's birthday	January 30, 1882
How long in the home	62 years (his entire life)
Life of the home	Approximately 1800 to present
Style	Mansion
Still in existence	Yes
Commemoration	The Franklin D. Roosevelt National Historic Site
Open to the public	Yes
Cost	$14.00 (includes Presidential Library)
For more information	www.nps.gov/hofr
Replica exists	No
Significance	Only president to live in his birthplace his entire life
Closest birthplace	Martin Van Buren, 45.7 miles

The birthplace of Franklin Delano Roosevelt in Hyde Park, New York. FDR is the only president to live in his birthplace home for his entire life. *Courtesy of the Roosevelt-Vanderbilt NHS, WD Urbin*

What you will find there today:

The birth home at Hyde Park is preserved as the Franklin D. Roosevelt National Historic Site. The site includes the home, his Presidential Library and a museum to perhaps the greatest president of the twentieth century. Included in the presidential memorabilia located at Hyde Park is the walnut bed in which the president was born.

History

Address/Directions:

519 Albany Post Road (Route 9)
Hyde Park, New York 12538

From the New York Thruway (Interstate 87), take Exit 17. Follow Interstate 84 East for about 3 miles and then turn left onto US-9W North/Albany Post Road/North Robinson Avenue. After about 14 miles, turn right onto NY-55/U.S. 44 for 2 miles. Then take U.S. 9 North/Albany Post Road for 5 miles until you arrive at the Franklin D. Roosevelt National Historic Site on the left.

On May 27, 1697, a parcel of land in upstate New York was granted by the English Crown to nine men. Known as the "Great Nine Partners Patent" or the "Lower Nine Partners Patent," the partners included New York businessmen John Aarston (or Jan Aarston), William Creed, James Emott (or James Emmot), Hendrick ten Eyck, Lieutenant Colonel Henry Filkin, Major Augustin Graham, Colonel Caleb Heathcote, David Johnstone and Jarvis Marshall.[1] The triangular property grant was approximately eight to ten miles wide on the Hudson River and encompassed all or parts of six Duchess County towns, including a portion of what is currently Hyde Park. This land was divided into thirty-six principal lots and nine water lots. Every partner owned one of the water lots, which were each about 3,400 acres and bordered the Hudson River. The FDR birth site is located on water lot 34, which was owned by William Creed.[2]

The original structure on the property was a farmhouse built sometime between 1790 and 1805. The two-story building measured 46 by 39 feet, had a full basement, and faced Albany Post Road. New York Merchant Josiah Wheeler purchased the estate in 1845 and remodeled the home, expanding it to fifteen rooms. James Roosevelt purchased the 116-acre estate from Josiah Wheeler in 1866 for $40,000. He named the home Springwood.[3]

On January 30, 1882, in a second-floor bedroom, Franklin Delano Roosevelt was born. He was the first and only child of James and Sara Delano Roosevelt and would one day become perhaps the greatest president of the twentieth century, leading America through its most difficult turmoil since the Civil War. With the expanded family, James made additions to the home, adding a two-story bay to the back of the house in 1887. He continued to enlarge the home in 1893 and again in 1900.[4]

By the time Franklin's father, James, passed away in 1900, the estate was 500 acres. Sara inherited the home and continued to live there for the rest of her life. In 1905, FDR married his fifth cousin, Eleanor Roosevelt, and the couple moved into the Springwood home after their marriage. Roosevelt affectionately called his home "Crum Elbow" after a nearby bend in the Hudson River, and throughout his rise in public life, the home served as both his retreat and his political headquarters.

Renovations continued into the twentieth century when electricity was added in 1908. In 1915, architect Francis L.V. Hoppin was hired to further expand the home. His design added north and south wings and a third floor to double the size of the home to its current thirty-five rooms and nine baths. To do the construction, Roosevelt chose Elliot Brown, who was a former center for the Princeton University football team and ironically nicknamed "Tiny." FDR was a prodigious collector, amassing thousands of coins, stamps, paintings, stuffed birds, and books. Once the work was completed in the summer of 1915, the additional space gave him plenty of room to store his collections.[5]

It served as his "Summer White House" during his presidency. His first visit home as president was on July 29, 1933, and in his twelve-plus years in office, he visited from Washington, D.C. almost two hundred times.[6] The home witnessed some of the most important historical events of his presidency. Its visitors included English royalty King George IV and Queen Elizabeth. Several of his infamous fireside chats were recorded at the library. In the summer of 1942, Winston Churchill visited the home and the world leaders jointly agreed to start the atomic program. From these seeds in Hyde Park, the project culminated with the bombings of Hiroshima and Nagasaki, leading to the end of World War II. More so than any other birthplace in presidential history, more historical occurrences related to the president born at the site occurred at Hyde Park.[7] In 1941, upon Sara's death, FDR inherited the estate.

Preservation

In 1938, Roosevelt donated his own home to the federal government. This donation was unprecedented in the annals of presidential birthplace history, since never before had a sitting president donated his own birthplace while still in office *and* still living in the home. His gesture included the stipulation that Eleanor and their children would live out their lives in the home and the scenic view of the Hudson was to be preserved. To satisfy the latter, the government acquired land through purchase and donations, which eventually grew the property to over 264 acres.

Starting in 1939, the Presidential Library was also built on the property. The next year the library and sixteen acres were donated to the federal government and in 1941, the museum was opened to the public. Roosevelt was deeply involved in the project, including designing the buildings. He used the library during his third and fourth terms of his presidency and several fireside chats were recorded there. Of the twelve presidential libraries run by the federal government, FDR's remains the only to be used during his presidency.

In 1944, the home was declared a National Historic Site, and the next year, FDR visited the home of his birth one final time in late March of 1945. Two weeks later, the president died in Warm Springs, Georgia, on April 12, 1945. His body was brought to New York for burial in the rose garden on the Hyde Park estate on April 15, 1945 (now joined by Eleanor and his Scottish Terrier, Fala). Upon his death, Eleanor waived the conditions of the donation, turning over full rights to the federal government on November 21, 1945. In 1946, the home was opened to the public.

Shortly before midnight on January 22, 1982, in the middle of a winter snowstorm, exactly a week before what would have been the former president's 100th birthday, a fire broke out in the home. For five weeks a contractor had been doing electrical work in the attic, and outmoded wiring was determined to have caused the blaze. Two hundred and fifty firemen converged upon the home to put out the fire while curators worked feverishly to save the invaluable contents located there. Tarps were thrown over furnishings while paintings, chairs and rugs were hauled into the cold of the night. To get to the burning insulation, they took an axe to the walls and ceiling. Dramatically a priceless chandelier was removed just as fireman evacuated the room fearing a collapse. When the fire was finally subdued about 4 a.m. the next morning, a seventy-five-foot section of the roof was destroyed and the home was soaked. While water streamed down the staircases, holes were drilled into the floor to drain the water into the basement where it was pumped out. In the end, due to the heroic efforts of the firefighters and curators, the home was saved and few items were damaged, and what did get damaged was more likely due to water, not fire. A week later, the home was opened on schedule for the 100th birthday celebration; however, a few rooms were still closed for repairs.[8]

Visitor Information

Attendance was strong following the president's death when over 430,000 people visited annually. The numbers have slowly dropped, and today, about 120,000 people visit Hyde Park each year.[9] Within the vicinity of Hyde Park, you can also visit two other National Park Sites, Eleanor's retreat Val-Kill and the Vanderbilt Mansion. Also plan on having dinner at one of the restaurants at the "other" CIA, the Culinary Institute of America, where students prepare the food. I visited Hyde Park (and the other two National Park Sites) on a crisp winter day in December 2007 along with my four-year-old son, Vincent. We arrived in time for the first tour at 10 a.m. and, not surprisingly, were the only two guests. My son, who had been on many of these tours before, was on his best behavior as the guide brought us around the home, but his favorite part was the barn where they had toys and crayons to keep his little hands busy. The home is open seven days a week from 9 a.m. to 5 p.m.

33.
Harry S Truman

The birthplace of Harry S Truman in Lamar, Missouri. *Courtesy of the Missouri Department of Natural Resources*

Vital Birthplace Information

Birthplace	Lamar, Missouri
President's birthday	May 8, 1884
How long in the home	10 months
Life of the home	1882 to present
Style	Small frame house
Still in existence	Yes
Commemoration	Harry S Truman Birthplace State Historic Site
Open to the public	Yes
Cost	Free
For more information	mostateparks.com/trumansite.htm
Replica exists	No
Significance	Only president born in Missouri
Closest birthplace	William Jefferson Clinton, 362 miles

Address/Directions:

1009 Truman Street
Lamar, Missouri 64759

From Route US-160 (12th Street East) turn north onto Truman Street. Drive about 500 feet to the home.

What you will find there today:

The thirty-third President's Birthplace is the centerpiece of the Harry S Truman Birthplace State Historic Site. The site is located in Lamar, Missouri, and is situated on 2.51 acres.

To the left of the home is a historic marker erected by the International Union, United Automobile, Aircraft and Agricultural Implement Workers of America and the U.A.W. Officers' Councils of St. Louis and Kansas City. While Truman would have undoubtedly been honored by the recognition, he would have also appreciated being correctly listed as the thirty-third president instead of the thirty-second. The full text reads:

This shrine is dedicated to Harry S. Truman *Thirty-second President* of the United States of America who was born at this location May 8, 1884 [died] Dec. 26, 1972

I ask only to be a good and faithful servant of my Lord and my People.

H.S.T. County Judge – 1923-1925
Presiding Judge – County Court - 1927-1935
United States Senator – 1935-1945
Vice-President of the United States of America – 1945
President of the United States of America – 1945-1953

This property is presented to the People of the State of Missouri by the International Union, United Automobile, Aircraft and Agricultural Implement Workers of America and the U.A.W. Officers' Councils of St. Louis and Kansas City as a token of our appreciation and respect for Harry S. Truman who served as the *32nd President* of the United States of America with honor and distinction and who gave our nation and the world courageous leadership in the search for peace, freedom and justice.

History

In 1880, Simon Bethrode purchased an 80- by 150-foot corner lot in Lamar, Missouri for $78.20, on which he built a small 20- by 28-foot two-story white frame house that he completed in 1882. The home had three rooms downstairs and two upstairs, and outside the home was a well, a smokehouse, and an outhouse. Later that year, on November 14, he sold it to newlyweds John Anderson Truman and Martha Ellen Young Truman for $685. John Truman was a mule salesman and had a quick walk to work to the lot across the street that he later purchased in 1883 for $200.[1]

On May 8, 1884, at about 4 p.m., Dr. W.L. Griffin delivered the couple's first child and future president, Harry S Truman in a small 6½- by 10¾-foot-bedroom in the southwest corner of the house. For his service to the Trumans and to our nation, Doctor Griffin charged just $15. The young couple named their son after Martha's brother, Harrison Young, but his middle name is not an initial, it is just the letter "S". Unsure whether to give him a middle name after his paternal grandfather Anderson Shipp Truman or his maternal grandfather Solomon Young, the couple chose a middle name of "S" as a compromise.[2] To mark the occasion of his son's birth, John nailed a mule shoe over the door of the birth room and planted an Austrian pine tree in the front yard.[3]

However, the mule business in Lamar was not as robust as John hoped, so ten months after Harry was born, on March 3, 1885, the Trumans moved to a farm in Harrisonville in Jackson County near Kansas City. They sold both the home and the livestock lot for $1,600.[4] Over the next thirty-five years, several people owned the home. In 1920, Walter and Emma Earp purchased the house. Walter's father, Jonathan, had a brother, Nicholas, whose son was the famous Wyatt Earp, making Walter and Wyatt first cousins (note the Wyatt Earp Birthplace is also a museum, located at 406 Third Street in Monmouth, Illinois).[5]

Emma died in 1923, but Walter lived long enough to see Harry Truman authorize the dropping of two atomic bombs to bring an end to World War II, passing away four months after the event on December 21, 1945. The president was friendly with the Earps and often stopped by when in Lamar and even sent a telegram from the White House when he learned of Walter's passing. Upon his death, the home passed to his son, Everett, and his wife Marie Earp. Everett was known as Big Chief, and like his famous cousin, Wyatt, he also served as chief constable, the first in Lamar history. Additionally, he was a real estate agent and tore down the outhouse to make room for an office. After Everett died in 1956, the United Auto Workers bought the home from his wife, Marie, for $6,000 and donated the home to the state of Missouri the following year.[6]

Preservation

When Walter Earp inherited the house from his father, he immediately understood the historical value of the birth home – the year was 1945 and Truman had ended the Second World War by forcing imperial Japan into unconditional surrender by dropping two atomic bombs. After four long years, the costliest war in the history of the world was over and Harry S Truman, picking up the gauntlet from FDR, was a national hero. As a cousin of Wyatt Earp, Walter also thought of himself as a hero, and was eager to capitalize on both associations. He petitioned the town to recognize the home, but apparently his position as town constable only held so much influence and no movement was made on his request. Finally, in August 1946, a year after V-J day, he decided to take matters into his own hands. After quarrelling with the Lamar City Council and the Chamber of Commerce to erect a sign to recognize the birthplace, Everett decided to do it himself. Earp explained to the reporters:

They've been doing a lot of talking about signs and markers but I got tired of waiting on them and went ahead myself. I've got Ernie Shaffer – he's my carpenter – building the sign right now. He's had a little trouble getting a piece of plyboard for the middle – that's hard stuff to find nowadays

– but he should be done in a day or so…. It's going to be a four-by-six-foot sign set in a lattice frame and I'm going to put it in the yard in front of the house by that tall pine tree – sixty feet high, it is – that the Trumans planted the day the President was born. Folks will be able to see it from highway 160 and from the Missouri Pacific depot both. The depot's just a block away.[7]

Earp was an astute businessman. Right beneath the birthplace sign he put up another sign for his real estate business. He also sold souvenir postcards and various other Wyatt Earp and Harry Truman novelties, and if a visitor spent fifty cents, he showed them the birth room for free.[8]

In June 1949, an effort was made by the state to buy the home. Missouri Representative T. Fred Cline introduced a bill to purchase the birth home from Everett Earp. An assessment valued the home at $600 and State Republican Floor Leader William Cruce described it as "a decrepit old house." Everett didn't flinch. His asking price was $20,000, but he was willing to knock $5,000 off that number if the state would put a bronze plaque in the living room to honor his famous cousin, Wyatt Earp.[9] The state declined.

Seven years later, when Everett passed away, his wife, Marie, settled for $6,000 from the United Auto Workers, who had been interested in buying the birthplace for several years. Russell Letner, regional director of the UAW said:

> **Mr. Truman was Missouri's only president and has a unique place in history because of his policies and doctrines he started and carried out.[10]**

Once the property went up for sale following Everett's death, local people from Lamar organized along with the Officers Councils of UAW to raise the $6,000 purchase price. The title was transferred from Mrs. Earp to the International Union, United Automobile, Aircraft and Agricultural Implement Workers of America (UAW-AFL-CIO), and its Officers Councils of Kansas City and Saint Louis on April 30, 1957.

Four days later, on May 3, 1957, the property was offered to the state. The only caveats were that the home had to be restored and remain as a birthplace site to honor President Truman and no admission fee would ever be charged. The state agreed to these terms and on June 24, 1957, the title was transferred to the Missouri State Park Board.[11] For the next two years, the birth home was faithfully restored and furnished in period style from when the Trumans occupied the residence at a cost of about $12,000, which included the removal of a front porch that was added about 1900.[12]

On April 19, 1959, there was a twenty-minute ceremony to commemorate the opening of the Harry S Truman Birthplace State Historic Site. The ceremony was at 4 p.m., to coincide with the approximate time of the president's birth almost seventy-five years earlier. It was a beautiful spring day and about 2,000 people were in attendance to view the formal acceptance of the property from the UAW, even though legally the transaction occurred two years earlier. The principal speaker for the afternoon was Missouri Senator Stuart Symington, who said:

> **The mission of Harry S Truman Birthplace State Historic Site is to preserve, restore and interpret the nationally significant birthplace of Harry S Truman, 33rd President of the United States of America, and to interpret the John A. Truman family within the context of life in Lamar, Missouri during the late 19th century.**

UAW First International Vice President Leonard Woodcock made the presentation of the deed, since President Walter Reuther was unable to attend due to illness. Governor James T. Blair formally accepted the deed.[13] The highlight of the ceremony was Harry S Truman being in attendance and presented with a 13- by 14-inch bronze plaque that was later placed above the door of the bedroom in which he was born. The plaque read:

> **In this room on May 8, 1884, was born Harry S Truman whose faith in the youth of this country has been an inspiration to all. In honest and sincere appreciation, the city of Lamar.**

After the ceremony, the doors were opened for visitors to see the famous birth home. Truman, never one to mince words, compared the experience to "being buried and dug up while still alive."[14]

This was the president's last visit to his birth home; he died thirteen years later on December 26, 1972. On May 6, 1984, two days before what would have been the president's 100th birthday, the 15th District of the American Legion Department of Missouri donated a monument to the birthplace.[15] The marker depicts a bust of the president as he looked in his years after the presidency. On his cap is the number 21. It reads:

> **In Memoriam Harry S Truman**
> **Born Lamar, Missouri May 8, 1884**
> **Died Kansas City, Missouri December 26, 1972**
> **Patriot – Statesman – Legionnaire**
> **First Legionnaire President of the United States**
>
> **This memorial was erected in May 1984 by Legionnaires and Friends of the American Legion Department of Missouri through efforts of the 15th District.**

Today, the birthplace attracts about 30,000 visitors every year.[16] In 2008, a bill was presented to add the birthplace to the Harry S Truman National Historic Site. The National Park Site consists of his home in Independence, Missouri, 125 miles north of the birthplace. The bill died in the Senate; however, in January 2009, United States Representative Ike Skelton had plans to re-introduce the bill.[17]

Another view of Truman's birthplace.

Visitor Information

The birthplace is open Wednesday through Sunday from March through October from 10 a.m. to 4 p.m. (open noon on Sunday) and Wednesday through Saturday from November through February. After the tour, continue your nostalgic blast from the past by taking in a movie at Barco Drive-In Theater, located only a mile and a half from the birthplace on East Highway 160. The theater was built in 1950, when Harry S Truman was midway through his second term as President of the United States of America.

34.
Dwight David Eisenhower

The birthplace of Dwight David Eisenhower in Denison, Texas. *Courtesy of Joseph F. Picone*

Vital Birthplace Information

Birthplace	Denison, Texas
President's birthday	October 14, 1890
How long in the home	18 months
Life of the home	1883 to present
Style	Modest frame house
Still in existence	Yes
Commemoration	Eisenhower Birthplace State Historic Site
Still in existence	Yes
Open to the public	Yes
Cost	$4.00
For more information	www. visiteisenhowerbirthplace.com
Replica exists	No
Significance	First president born in Texas
Closest birthplace	William Jefferson Clinton, 188 miles

What you will find there today:

The authentic birth home is the centerpiece of Eisenhower Birthplace State Historic Site, which sits on six acres. Much of the land is wooded and it includes a walking trail that was converted from an abandoned railroad.

Address/Directions:

**609 South Lamar Avenue
Denison, Texas 75021**

From Eisenhower Parkway (Route 69), turn onto Main Street heading east. Take Crockett Street south and then turn right onto East Shepherd Street for one block until you reach the birthplace at the intersection with Lamar Avenue.

History

The Texas town of Denison, a stop on the Missouri, Kansas, and Texas Railroad, was established in 1872. In 1883, when the town was still young, a two-story house with six rooms was built on the corner of South Lamar Avenue and Day Street.[1] In 1889, David and Ida Eisenhower and their two sons moved to Denison in search of work. Dwight had landed a job as an engine wiper on the Missouri, Kansas, and Texas Railroad Yards for $40 a month.[2] Just like today, when people look for a home, the most important thing in real estate is location, location, location, and the Eisenhowers were no different. The modest frame home at 609 South Lamar Avenue was close to Dwight's job on the railway, so the couple rented the small house from J.R. Rylander. At the time, this was considered the best part of town and one of their neighbors was the mayor of Denison.[3]

The next year, on October 14, 1890, the couple's third son, Dwight David Eisenhower, was born in the front downstairs bedroom. Dr. D.H. Bailey was the attending physician that brought the baby into the world who would grow to lead the allied forces on D-Day and become the thirty-fourth President of the United States of America. The family of five stayed in Denison until early 1892 at which time David secured a job as a refrigeration engineer with a creamery back in Hope, Kansas. Over the next fifty years, the home continued to be an undistinguished place of residence for over a dozen owners.[4] It was not until World War II that it began to gain notoriety as the birthplace of one of our nation's greatest military heroes.

Preservation

At the onset of World War II the public struggled to determine the birthplace of the famous general. Various sources incorrectly reported him as having been born in Abilene, Kansas, or one of the Texas towns of Tyler, Commerce, or Bug Tussle. The main confusion came from Eisenhower himself since he listed his birthplace as Tyler, Texas, when he entered West Point. As his fame grew during World War II, citizens of the town of Denison tried to prove their case as the true birthplace of the American hero. Miss Jennie Jackson, a retired schoolteacher who claimed in her younger years to have "bounced Eisenhower on her knee when he was a baby," contacted Eisenhower to have him verify the location of his birth.[5] Oddly enough, Eisenhower was not sure, so he directed Jackson to his mother. Jackson called Eisenhower's mother who confirmed by both phone and letter that her son was indeed born in the north Texas railroad town of Denison.

Now that the town was confirmed, Fred Conn, publisher of the Denison Herald, began a search for the birthplace home. From historical records, he found that the house in which Eisenhower was born was located at the corner of Day Street and South Lamar Avenue. Once the birthplace building was established, Conn and Miss Jennie Jackson led the effort to purchase and restore the home. The pair worked well together, Conn was the business side and Jackson was in charge of restorations. To help raise funds to purchase the home, they looked to the Denison residents. Locals donated what they could and school children gave their pennies and nickels, reminiscent of the "Lincoln League" donations from children who helped fund the commemoration of Abraham Lincoln's birthplace.[6] Soon, Conn and Jackson had raised $3,200, enough to purchase the home. Immediately, a sign was erected that simply stated "EISENHOWER BIRTHPLACE." Once the restorations were completed, Conn turned the home over to the city of Denison.

On April 20, 1946, the home had a distinguished guest when Ike himself visited and was greeted by 40,000 people, the first of three visits that he made to the scene of his nativity. The restorations were completed just in time for the visit and Miss Jennie Jackson proudly greeted the president at the home.[7] In 1952, running for president and in the middle of the Republican primaries, Eisenhower once again returned to the home where he was born. After Ike won the election that November, the preservation efforts completed six years earlier no longer seemed adequate for a United States President. Immediately after his victory, visitation doubled to about 300 people per month. The "Gold Star Mothers of Denison" took over as guardians and tour guides of the birthplace and had their hands full with the extra visitors.[8]

A letter sent by V.W. Fuller from Dallas to the Denison Herald called for a restoration more fitting of a U.S. President. Included in his letter was a dollar to get the project rolling. Once again, Fred Conn led the effort when the Denison Herald sponsored "a statewide collection 'for the proper development of the Eisenhower birthplace as a national shrine.'"[9]

The summer of 1953 was eventful for the birthplace – a routine fire inspection was made of the home in June and an antique stove was found to be leaking gas, causing the local papers to label the home a "firetrap."[10] Two months later, the problems were partially solved when the home entered the twentieth century and indoor plumbing was installed.[11]

In 1952, the Eisenhower Birthplace Foundation was organized by Sid Richardson to acquire and restore the birthplace home.[12] The next year, Fred Conn officially chartered the foundation in October 1953, and was in charge of the restoration along with a local architect named Donald Mayes.[13] As expected, the first order of business was to raise money to purchase additional land and pay for the restorations. In addition to a statewide campaign, they also once again looked to the school children to support their local hero with whatever change they could spare.[14]

In 1955, the city of Denison turned over the deed to the Eisenhower Birthplace Foundation. To determine what the home looked like almost three quarters of a century earlier, "exhaustive interviews with Denison old-timers who remember how the house looked when the future President was born" were undertaken.[15] Not much needed to be done, or at least the "old-timers" couldn't remember many differences. Structurally, only a small addition in the back of the home was removed. The foundation was able to purchase the entire block consisting of five acres and several homes were razed to allow the Eisenhower birthplace to stand on its own. In May 1956, the restorations were completed for a final cost of $50,000.[16] Afterwards, a photo album was sent to President Eisenhower to show him the restorations. In appreciation, Ike sent a wedding picture of his parents to Web Maddox, president of the Eisenhower Birthplace Foundation, who promptly hung the photograph at the birth home.[17]

In 1958, the Eisenhower Birthplace Foundation turned the home back over to the state and the Eisenhower Birthplace State Park was established. Originally operated by the Texas State Parks Board, the home was transferred to the Texas Historical Commission on January 1, 2008.[18]

In the later 1950s, the home fell victim to several acts of vandalism, but these incidents were as unique as the hero who was born in the home. The first unfortunate event occurred on August 15, 1956, when a cross was placed on the front lawn of the house and set on fire. Nowadays, this would justifiably cause an uproar, but this was 1956 and in the deep south, and the Supreme Court had only recently ruled on school integration. Even understanding that the fiery cross was a symbol of the Ku Klux Klan, the local authorities treated the incident as if some crazy kids threw toilet paper in the trees, chalking it up to the work of "pranksters or cranks."[19]

A year later, the house was again vandalized in a bizarre fashion reminiscent of *The Godfather's* Luca Brasi when "a package of fish heads and a small gold fish were found... on the front porch of President Eisenhower's birthplace" on September 26, 1957.[20] Finally, on January 8, 1958, bottles and eggs were pelted at the home. This defacement was in response to school integration in Arkansas, which was not going over well with some of the citizens of Denison.[21]

In the 1960s and 1970s, the vandalism subsided and several prominent visitors stopped by the birth home, including, on April 13,1965, Lady Bird Johnson, who visited the Eisenhower birthplace for thirty-six minutes accompanied by four secret servicemen. She had just spent several years working on the re-creation of Lyndon Johnson's birthplace and may have been checking out how the competition fared.[22]

On September 1,1965, Ike visited his birthplace for the third and final time. During his visit, he noted a quilt his mother had made:

You know, my brother and I helped cut the scraps that went into this quilt.

He also got a chance to meet the president of the Kansas and Texas Railroad Yards, John Barringer who said he "always wanted to come meet the son of one of our former employees."[23] On his visit, Dwight David Eisenhower was also introduced to Dwight David Gaines, a two-month-old baby from Dallas named in his honor.[24] However, the former president had more than babies, quilts, and trains on his mind. He was in town to dedicate the auditorium at Denison High School also named in his honor. At the dedication, he took a serious tone and spoke of the moral degradation occurring in society.

Several notable events occurred in the 1970s. In October 1971, Dwight's beloved wife, Mamie, visited the birth home.[25] The following year, in September 1972, a nine-foot bronze statue of Ike was erected in front of birthplace sculpted by artist Robert Dean.[26] On Monday July 9, 1973 at 2:00, Julie Nixon Eisenhower, daughter of then President Richard Nixon and granddaughter by marriage to Dwight Eisenhower, dedicated the statue. Thousands of visitors attended the ceremony.[27]

Visitor Information

The birthplace is open year round from Tuesday through Sunday and is closed on Mondays. The home is open 9 a.m. to 5 p.m., with shorter hours on Sundays (1 p.m. to 5 p.m.). After visiting the birthplace, you may want to drive the 6.5 miles to Loy Park to see a towering twenty-one-foot-tall bust of Dwight Eisenhower. This sculpture was unveiled, on February 21, 2011, at a Presidents Day celebration and was dedicated to our nation's true heroes, the military veterans who have kept our country safe and free throughout the generations. The sculpture was created by David Adickes for the cost of $120,000 and is inscribed with the words:

In appreciation for, and in honor of all veterans who have served to protect our freedom.[28]

35.
John Fitzgerald Kennedy

The birthplace of John F. Kennedy on Beals Street in Braintree, Massachusetts.

Birthplace	Brookline, Massachusetts
President's birthday	May 29, 1917
How long in the home	6 years
Life of the home	1909 to present
Style	Colonial Revival
Still in existence	Yes
Commemoration	John F. Kennedy National Historic Site
Still in existence	Yes
Open to the public	Yes
Cost	$3.00
For more information	www.nps.gov/jofi
Replica exists	No
Significance	Only authentic birthplace of an assassinated president still in existence
Closest birthplace	George Herbert Walker Bush, 8 miles

Address/Directions:

83 Beals Street
Brookline, Massachusetts 02446

From I-90/Massachusetts Turnpike take Exit 18 if driving eastbound or Exit 20 if driving westbound. Merge onto Cambridge Street and after about one mile turn left at the fourth traffic light onto Harvard Street. After one mile, turn left onto Beals Street.

From I-95, take Exit 20 and follow Route 9E/Boylston Street. After about five miles, turn right onto Walnut Street and then make a quick right onto Harvard Street. After one mile, turn left onto Beals Street.

What you will find there today:

The John F. Kennedy National Historic Site is one of twelve presidential birthplaces managed by the National Park Service.

History

English Puritans first populated the area where Kennedy was born shortly after they arrived at Massachusetts Bay in the 1630s, and in 1705, the town of Brookline was officially incorporated. The property, which would one day become the JFK birthplace, was part of a larger parcel of land first owned by Jacob Eliot in the 1600s. After Eliot's death, his heirs sold the land to a Frenchman named Edward Devotion in about 1700. Edward passed the land down to his son Edward Jr. who sold the property to Solomon Hill in 1739. The land changed hands several times over the next 100 years eventually falling into the hands of Israel and Augustus Thorndike, two merchants from Boston. On January 9,1835, they sold the seventy-six-acre property to George Babcock for $4,583.33.[1]

After George's death, his wife, Lucy Babcock, sold thirteen acres to James M. Beals for $13,020.70 on July 6, 1868. Beals owned the land for about two decades and passed it on to his son, James H. Beals Jr., after his death in the late 1890s. Taking advantage of an increased interest in the Boston suburbs, Beals worked with local real estate agent Benjamin B. Newhall to subdivide the land into individual housing lots. In 1897, Beals Street was laid out with seventy home sites. That same year, Benjamin B. Newhall purchased seven of the parcels for himself, including #47 for $9,794.95. Later, the lot #47 was sold to Oscar Johnson, a builder from Cambridge who owned the home according to a 1900 census. However, by 1902, after failing to pay his taxes, Johnson lost the home. Lot #47 continued to change hands and its new owners also experienced tax issues over the next several years. In 1906, Mary M. Poor of Andover purchased the site for $1,600.[2]

The next year in 1907, Mary M. Poor sold to Robert M. Goode, a real estate agent from Newton. Goode filed a builder's application on April 6, 1909, and promptly began construction on a house on the property. The structure was a three-story, nine-room house built in the Colonial Revival style and was one day to become the birthplace of our thirty-fifth president. Goode completed construction over the summer and on September 17, 1909, he sold it to Boston lawyer Daniel J. Kiley, who lived in the home for three years after it was built. On February 1, 1913, Kiley sold the home to Howard S. Kline, a buyer from Boston, and his wife, Laura B. Kline, from Manhattan, New York. The Klines only lived in the home for a year and a half.[3]

On August 20, 1914, Joseph P. Kennedy bought the home on 83 Beals Street in Brookline, Massachusetts, from the Klines for $6,500, which he had to borrow to cover the purchase price. Joseph was engaged, but not yet married, to Rose Elizabeth Fitzgerald; they wed later that year on October 7, and moved into 83 Beals Street after their honeymoon. At the time he bought the home, Joe Kennedy was the president of the Columbia Trust Company, making him the youngest person to hold that bank's title. Both Rose and Joseph were grandchildren of immigrants who left Ireland in the potato famine of the 1840s and settled in Boston, Massachusetts. The young couple felt the modest home on the Sycamore-lined street was an ideal place to start their family. Rose Kennedy later recalled, "Here we had light and air."[4]

When you visit, you will find the Kennedy birthplace in the middle of Beals Street with additional homes to both sides, but this was not the case in 1914. At that time, if you stood on the porch looking onto Beals Street to the right you would see open fields, as the Kennedy home was the last house on the block. An added bonus was that many of their neighbors were fellow Irishmen.

On May 29, 1917 at about 3:00 in the afternoon, their second child, John Fitzgerald Kennedy, was born in the second-floor master bedroom. The baby was born "in the bed nearest the window, so the doctor would have proper light," recalled Mrs. Kennedy.[5] John, or Jack as he was often called, would one day become the first (and only) Roman Catholic president, in addition to being the first born in the twentieth century. The Kennedy family doctor, Frederick Good, delivered the future president for the hefty sum of $150. Jack was the second child born to the family, but the first born in the home. His older brother, Joseph, who was later killed in World War II, was born while the family was on vacation.

Four years after John was born, and now with four children, the Kennedys decided 83 Beals Street was getting a little crowded. On September 13, 1920, they sold the home to their close friends, Edward and Mary Moore, and moved several blocks away to a larger home on the corner of Naples and Abbotsford Roads. The two families were such good friends that the Kennedys named their ninth and final child in their honor, Edward Moore Kennedy, or Teddy, as he was better known. The Moores remained in the home until 1928 when they sold to Lucy Myerson, wife of a Brookline physician Simon Myerson. The home was sold in 1944 to Sarah Pollack who owned the home until 1953. On January 20, 1953, the home was owned by Alice Farrell for only one day before it was transferred to Louis and Martha Pollack. Martha still owned the home ten years later when the president was assassinated.[6]

Preservation

After John F. Kennedy was inaugurated as the nation's thirty-fifth president, the town of Brookline knew they had to recognize the historic home, but deciding exactly how to commemorate the birthplace of the standing president took a few months to figure out. The first hurdle the town had to overcome was getting permission from the current owner, Mrs. Martha Pollack. She had purchased the home in 1953 and was not thrilled about the idea of a memorial plaque in her front yard and the gawkers it would attract. Finally, in February 1961, the town and Mrs. Pollack came to an agreement – she would allow a plaque to be placed on her home, but only after she received a free paint job in return.[7] On September 12,1961, twenty-five union painters volunteered their time and materials to give the home a fresh coat of light gray paint with white and blue trim.[8] When the paint dried and the home was appropriately presentable, the plaque was affixed to the home.[9]

The following year, on John F. Kennedy's 45th birthday, May 29,1962, the Brookline Board of Selectmen held a ceremony to formally dedicate the plaque. For the ceremony, the plaque was moved to a more permanent historic marker placed in front of the home. The plaque, which still stands today, reads:

BIRTHPLACE OF JOHN F. KENNEDY
35th President of the United States
Born May 29, 1917 on this site 83 Beals Street Brookline, Mass
This Commemorative plaque Erected by Town of Brookline,
Mass On September 12, 1961.[10]

Two months later, John F. Kennedy was gracious enough to take the time to send Mrs. Martha Pollack a letter in which he expressed his affection for the home and gratitude to its owner.

There is within each man a very special affection for the place of his birth, and I am deeply pleased to know you are living a full and enjoyable life at my birthplace. I hope you will continue to do so for many years to come.[11]

On November 22, 1963, the nation was shocked, saddened, and forever changed when President John F. Kennedy was shot in Dallas, Texas. On the morning after the president's death, Martha Pollack opened her door to find a sea of people that had come to pay their respects to the president. Mrs. Pollack took a picture of the crowd and, according to the park ranger when I went to visit, upon seeing the photograph, Rose Kennedy was inspired to repurchase the home to serve as a memorial to her slain son.

A month after the horrific killing, forty-three African-Americans calling themselves "Freedom Fighters" from Williamston, South Carolina, visited the birthplace on Christmas Eve. The group was from the Southern Christian Leadership Conference founded by Martin Luther King six years earlier. Standing outside the home in the snow, they joined hands and sang freedom songs such as "We Shall Overcome" and "The Lord Will Make Us Free." In the height of the Civil Rights movement, this group had come to pay homage to the fallen president. Sara Small, president of the Williamston unit of the Southern Christian Leadership Conference, said:

We have come to see the birthplace of the president who has done so much for our race[12]

Several days after the shooting, the town of Brookline began discussing plans to memorialize the slain President's birthplace, and they were prepared to use "any means necessary" to do it. On April 7, 1964, a proposal was made at a Brookline town meeting to "raise and appropriate a sum of money for the purchase, or taking by eminent domain, of the [JFK] birthplace."[13] Apparently, the other residents on Beals Street, including the owners of the eight homes threatened with eminent domain,

The John F. Kennedy birthplace marker located in front of the home in which he was born in Braintree, Massachusetts.

were not happy about the idea and objected loudly enough for the town to back off of the plan.

On May 7, 1964, the Federal Advisory Board on National Parks completed a brief explanatory statement and determined that the birthplace should be memorialized as a National Shrine. A year later, in May 1965, that declaration was made official when the birthplace was dedicated as a National Historic Landmark. Additional recognition came on May 26, 1967, when it was also added to the National Register of Historic Places (National Register Number #67000001).

In 1966, Mrs. Pollack put up the home for sale. Seeing it on the market, a Boston Lawyer, Merrill I. Hassenfeld, and a few of his friends purchased the home in September. They "decided it would be better to buy it and offer it to the Kennedys. It should be a shrine". Hassenfeld stated he was not "interested in making money on the resale," and was only motivated to ensure the home did not fall into the wrong hands.[14] Two months later, on November 1,1966, the Kennedy family re-purchased the home from Merrill Hassenfeld for $55,000. Working on behalf of the Kennedy family, Rose's nephew, Joseph Gargan, completed the purchase and then turned it over to his aunt, returning it to the family after forty-five years.[15]

Starting in 1967, Rose Fitzgerald Kennedy spent time restoring the house to how it looked in 1917, when her son John was born within its walls. Of course, a loving mother's memory can be a little biased, especially after fifty years, so her efforts were, according to the National Park Service, a little "nostalgic and subjective".[16] During the years since 1917, there were no structural changes to the home; however, a detached garage was added, which was promptly removed. Rose worked with Robert Luddington of the Jordan Marsh retail store to decorate the home. Using personal photographs, furniture, and other items from her current residence, the home was restored as to the best of her memory.

When I visited, the National Park Ranger mentioned that the kitchen was the most difficult room for her to recollect, explaining that Rose Kennedy would not have spent much time in the kitchen since her servants did the cooking for her family. Rose also chose not to restore the third floor, which were the servants' quarters. Rose recorded her thoughts to help add a voice to the experience, which can be heard throughout the tour. Especially poignant is the mention of the good times the family had in the home:

> We were very happy here, and although we did not know about the days ahead, we were enthusiastic and optimistic about the future.[17]

For over three years, Rose Kennedy was involved in this labor of love. During this time, the Kennedys once again encountered tragedy when Sirhan Sirhan assassinated Bobby Kennedy on June 5, 1968. Still, she labored on. Finally, in May 1969, the restoration was completed. Two years earlier, in March 1967, Democratic senator from Washington, Henry M. Jackson and Kentucky Republican John Sherman Cooper presented a bi-partisan bill for the federal government to accept the birthplace as a donation to create a National Historic Site. Massachusetts House Democrat Tom P. "Tip" O'Neill also presented a similar bill.[18] On May 26, 1969, the United States Congress passed Public Law 90-20, establishing the home as the John Fitzgerald Kennedy National Historic Site.

Three days later, on what would have been John F. Kennedy's 52nd birthday, May 29, 1969, Rose Kennedy turned over the deed to 83 Beals Street to the Department of the Interior, which manages the National Park Service. After a private mass at Saint Aidan's Church, the Kennedys gathered for a dedication ceremony at the home. Before 700 to 800 people, Undersecretary Russell Train accepted the deed for the home and property, as the Secretary Walter J. Hickel was unavailable due to illness.[19]

The home, said Rose, is a "gift of the Kennedy family to the people of the United States."[20] The birthplace was now officially a National Historic Site.

Over the next few years, about 30,000 people visited the birthplace annually. Strong compared to today's numbers, but far less than the National Park Service anticipated. The numbers remained steady until 1975 when tragedy struck the historic home.

On Monday, September 8 1975, the night before the Boston public schools opened for the year, tensions were running high on the eve of the second year of court-ordered bussing to combat the highly segregated conditions in the city school system. Shortly after 10 p.m., in a protest against Senator Ted Kennedy's support of the bussing program, the birth home was vandalized. Criminals threw a firebomb into the kitchen door in the back of the home and spray-painted "Bus Teddy" in large black letters on the sidewalk and graffiti on the walls of the home.[21] One of the neighbors, who saw two men running away, grabbed a garden hose to try his best to control the fire until the firemen arrived. Luckily, nobody was hurt and none of the authentic pieces were damaged. The home was immediately closed to the public so it could be repaired. The cost was originally estimated at $10,000; however, the final price tag for the repairs would come to $30,000.[22] Over twenty-five years later, in 2001, it was revealed that the notorious Boston gangster James "Whitey" Bulger was behind the attacks. Normally, when one says a crime kingpin is behind an attack, it means he made the orders, but did not actually do the deed. Not in this case. In 1975, Whitey Bulger, along with one of his crew members, were the ones who hurled the Molotov cocktail into the home and spray painted the sidewalk.[23]

The National Park Service used the opportunity to do a full assessment of the home and commissioned a professional analysis, placing Ranger John Heath in charge of the project. The results revealed a China hutch behind the walls that had been closed over between the kitchen and dining room. Another discovery was that the original plaster was made with horsehair. To restore the home as authentically as possible, a craftsman with horsehair experience was located in Boston. Using horsehair obtained from nearby Suffolk Downs Racetrack, the kitchen was replastered, although it is unknown how much this touch of authenticity cost the taxpayers.[24] The home was reopened over one year after the firebombing, on November 15, 1976.

Visitor Information

Although consistently ranked as one of our nation's most popular presidents, his birthplace ranks as the least visited of those administered by the National Park Service, with about 10,000 visitors each year.[25] Contributing to this low attendance are the seasonal hours beginning in May (most National Park Sites are open year round). Tours run on the hour from 10 a.m. to 3 p.m. and last about 30 minutes. When you visit, look for the photograph of John and his older brother, Joe, in their Sunday best standing on the front lawn. You'll see how much different the neighborhood looked in 1919 when the photograph was taken. Take time to see the remaining buildings that make up the John F. Kennedy National Historic Site, which includes their second home on Abbotsford Road, and Saint Aiden's Church where the Kennedy family had a private mass prior to donating the home in May 1969 and little John F. Kennedy served as an altar boy as a child. There are several other significant sites, including the Edward Devotion School, named after the owner of the birthplace property from the early 1700s.

36.
Lyndon Baines Johnson

The reconstructed birthplace of Lyndon Baines Johnson in Stonewall, Texas.
Courtesy of the Lyndon Baines Johnson National Historic Site

Vital Birthplace Information

Birthplace	Stonewall, Texas
President's birthday	August 27, 1908
How long in the home	5 years
Life of the home	1899 to 1940s
Style	Texas dogtrot house
Still in existence	No
Ultimate fate	Torn down
Commemoration	Recreation at the Lyndon Baines Johnson National Historic Site
Open to the public	Yes
Cost	Free
For more information	www.nps.gov/lyjo
Replica exists	Yes, at birthplace
Significance	Only birthplace replica built while the president was still in office
Closest birthplace	Dwight Eisenhower, 300 miles

Address/Directions:

Park Road 49
Stonewall, Texas 78671

Take Highway 49 east from Fredericksburg for 16 miles to the Lyndon B. Johnson National Historical Park. The birthplace is located behind the visitor center, across the Pedernales River on Park Road 49.

What you will find there today:

At the birthplace is a reconstructed home within the Lyndon Baines Johnson National Historic Site.

History

In 1845, the land on which eventually stood the birth home of Lyndon Baines Johnson was purchased by Rachael Means. The property was a part of a German area in Gillespie County, Texas on the banks of the Pedernales River.[1] In 1882, Eliza Bunton Johnson purchased 950 acres. Eliza and her husband, Sam Ealy Johnson Sr., had to find creative ways to help them pay for their new acquisition – to fund the down payment she sold a silver-mounted carriage and her horses (which had been a wedding gift from Sam's brother), and to cover the monthly payments, she taught school.[2] Seven years later, in 1889, Sam built a small home on the property.

The style of home was called Texas dogtrot because of a middle passageway that ran front to back to cool off the home from the Texas heat. Apparently, this breezeway was popular with the dogs in Texas at the turn of the century. To the right were a living room and a bedroom and to the left, another bedroom and a kitchen. Adjoining these two sides was the dogtrot, covered by a sagging, slanting roof.[3] The home was the smaller of two homes on the Johnson farm.[4]

Sam and Eliza's son was Sam Ealy Johnson Jr., who went on to have a prodigious political career of his own. In 1905, he was elected to the Texas House of Representatives where he served five terms. After marrying Rebekah Baines on August 20, 1907, the couple moved into the dogtrot house.

On August 27, 1908, a little over a year after they were married, their first son and our thirty-sixth president, Lyndon Baines Johnson was born in the home. According to his mother, on the night baby LBJ was born "lamps had burned all night" until finally there was "a sharp compelling cry of a newborn baby; the first child of Sam Ealy and Rebekah Johnson was 'discovering America'".[5]

The family stayed there five more years and went on to have two more children in the home, Rebekah Luruth and Josefa Hermine. In 1913, the Johnsons moved to nearby Johnson City; however, Eliza Johnson retained ownership of the property until her death in 1917. After she died, the land passed to her son, Sam Ealy Johnson.[6] Sam Ealy Johnson rented the home to tenants in 1920 and in 1922 he sold his share of the family ranch, including the birth home.

Over the next decade, the home and the nation fell on tough times. In the 1930s, the home became another casualty of the Great Depression when it was abandoned and fell into disrepair. In the 1940s, most of the home was torn down. The property was purchased by Harvey Jordan in 1944 for $1,500, by which time all that remained was the rock foundation, the two fireplaces, and one wall. Jordan owned the property for another twenty years. When Lyndon Baines Johnson became president under most unfortunate circumstances in 1963, Jordan was quoted as saying:

I think it's quite a distinction having the birthplace of a president on your property.[7]

Jordan was also aware that this distinction made his property much more valuable. In the spring of 1964, the Johnson family repurchased the two acres that included the birthplace from Jordan for what he called "a very fair price."[8] The actual purchase price was top-secret, but only several months earlier Jordan had said he wouldn't sell for under $100,000.[9]

Preservation

In 1963, shortly after Lyndon Johnson was sworn in as our nation's thirty-sixth president, people began to seek out historic landmarks associated with the famous Texan. The birthplace had been torn down two decades earlier, but the second smaller structure still stood, so people naturally assumed this was the birthplace home. Newspapers printed pictures of the dilapidated, but still-standing house, incorrectly calling it the "birthplace" home. When Alejandro Aleman, a pecan farmer, passed by and inquired about renting the home for his wife and six children, an *Associated Press* reporter was there to inform him, albeit incorrectly, that the home was the birthplace of LBJ. Aleman responded, "Really? Well I guess they'll probably want to keep it as an antique" before driving off in search of a place for his family to live.[10]

Perhaps more than any other man to serve the highest office, Lyndon Baines Johnson was proud of his birthplace. He saw himself as a rags-to-riches success story and wanted to show the world where he first saw the light of day. The problem was, by the time he became president, there was really nothing left of the birthplace to show off. However, as we have seen throughout birthplace history, starting with the very first president, a lack of a birthplace is not an insurmountable obstacle. One can always be built, and in LBJ's case, it could also be built a little better than the real thing. So in spring 1964, while serving the first year of his presidency after the assassination of his predecessor John F. Kennedy, the Johnson family purchased the historic birthplace property and donated it to the Johnson City Foundation, an organization created and funded by the Johnson family through tax-free contributions.[11] To rebuild the dogtrot home, they hired architect J. Roy White. First, he did an architectural investigation using photographs and family memories. For materials, he used logs from a nearby structure, which may have contained some of the original birthplace materials, to re-create the five-room cottage. Possibly to eliminate any confusion, the building, which had been mistaken for the birth home, was torn down.[12]

Despite all of the research and attention to detail, what was constructed was not an exact replica of the birthplace. Instead, according to the National Park Service, the re-created "house represents how Lyndon Johnson wanted us to see the birthplace".[13] Like many of us, Lyndon choose not to remember the imperfections and shabby exterior of his birth home, but instead what he presented to us was his idealized vision. As for the interior, the president's sister, Mrs. Birge Alexander, furnished the replica with authentic and period pieces.[14]

In April 1965, Claudia Alta "Lady Bird" Taylor Johnson visited the Eisenhower birthplace looking for insight as to how best memorialize the sitting President Lyndon Baines Johnson.[15] Later that same year, Lady Bird also visited the Johnson reconstruction. Much like Lou Henry Hoover was the driving force behind the Herbert Hoover birthplace restoration, so had Lady Bird Johnson become the force behind her husband's birthplace legacy. While her husband was still president, she immersed herself in his childhood history including not just his birthplace, but also other homes in the area that now comprise the Lyndon Baines Johnson National Historic Site.[16] Over the following years, the first lady would also visit the birthplace homes of John Adams, John Quincy Adams, James K. Polk, and Richard Nixon.

This purchase and reconstruction mark a seismic shift in the history of presidential birthplace preservation. For most presidents, birthplace recognition did not occur until years after their death, or at least until after their presidency. The exceptions were Teddy Roosevelt and Herbert Hoover; however, their preservation efforts were grass roots movements led by admirers of the men. Perhaps one other exception is Franklin Roosevelt who donated his birthplace to the federal government while he was still president; however, as his lifelong residence, Hyde Park was associated with national historic events and was not primarily associated with being his birthplace. In LBJ's case, it was not only that a sitting president was being honored, but also this time it was the president's family who was doing the honoring. Another major distinction was that in Teddy Roosevelt, Franklin Roosevelt, and Hoover's case, the actual birth homes still stood. Regardless of these outliers, Johnson's overt self-awareness and indulgence of one's own historic significance is unique to history at this point, and may only be rivaled by Jimmy Carter through all of the presidents.

The first tour of the home was held on Sunday July 10, 1966, and was open for reporters only. Lady Bird Johnson orchestrated the event and curated the first tour while President Johnson chatted with the newsmen. On that first tour, refreshments were served; however, photographs were not permitted. Lady Bird kept tight control over how the home was presented, even going so far as to write the eleven-page script that was used by subsequent guides.[17] Three days later, on Wednesday, July 13, the home was first opened to the public.

The home was initially open four days a week for a one-month trial basis, with the condition that "if enough tourists show[ed] up for a free-of-charge look" it would remain open year round.[18] The tourists did not disappoint. Before the doors even opened, seventy-five people were lined up like they were waiting for Bruce Springsteen tickets. After an hour, a hundred people had entered the re-created birth home.[19] In the first two days 2,225 people visited.[20] By the end of the month that number soared to 14,000.[21]

Later that year, in the midst of the 1968 presidential campaign, an election that Lyndon Johnson had refused to run, Republican candidate Richard Nixon and his running mate Spiro Agnew visited the president at his Texas White House. After spending two hours discussing the war in Vietnam, Johnson moved on to more pressing matters and showed Nixon his restored birthplace.[22]

In January 1970, Congress voted for the federal government to accept both the birthplace replica and Johnson's boyhood home in nearby Johnson City. The first attempt at a ceremony to formally accept the birthplace was postponed when Johnson was "hospitalized with symptoms of a heart attack."[23] On June 13, 1970, with Johnson feeling well enough, the ceremony was held in Johnson City in 100-degree Texas heat on what the president called a "good day for drying hay."[24] Lyndon Johnson and Texas Governor Preston Smith presented the titles to both the birth home and his boyhood home in nearby Johnson City to the Secretary of the Interior Walter J. Hickel.

In the first month that the National Park Service took over, 16,000 people took the efficient fourteen-minute tour. Much like the JFK home, recordings of Lady Bird could be heard throughout the visit. Some very fortunate tourists were even greeted by Lyndon Johnson himself. After serving in the White House, Johnson had retired to his ranch in Johnson City and he sometimes took a break from his farming to meet the birthplace visitors. He reportedly enjoyed talking livestock and the weather, and would gladly sign an autograph.[25]

The following year, in 1971, Congress authorized the establishment of the Lyndon Baines Johnson National Historic Site. On January 22, 1973, Lyndon Baines Johnson died after suffering a heart attack. As one last expression of love for his birthplace, he was buried just 100 yards away from the reconstructed home, as he had previously requested.

In April 1981, shortly after leaving office, Jimmy Carter and his wife, Rosalynn, visited with Lady Bird Johnson at the LBJ Ranch. Carter was looking for tips on how to preserve his own birthplace. If LBJ broke birthplace ground when he rebuilt his birthplace home for posterity while the Oval Office still smelled of JFK's cologne, Carter took it even one step further by memorializing his entire home town as a National Park Site… and then continuing to live in it for the next thirty years and counting![26]

Visitor Information

The home is open daily from 9 a.m. to 11:30 a.m. and then reopens from 1 p.m. to 4:30 p.m. The Lyndon Baines Johnson National Historic Site contains several buildings that celebrate the thirty-sixth President of the United States. The park is separated into the Johnson City District and the LBJ Ranch District. The two areas are fourteen miles apart and the reconstructed birthplace and family cemetery are located in the LBJ Ranch District. Also nestled within the LBJ Ranch District is the Lyndon B. Johnson State Park and Historic Site. Here, you will also find the working Sauer-Beckmann Farm, which is not historically significant to the Johnson family.

As usual, your best bet is to start with the Visitor Center in the LBJ Ranch District where you can pick up a permit and driving-tour audio CD to narrate your LBJ experience. After the birthplace became a National Park Site, visitation started off strong and quickly peaked to 579,000 in 1973. Since then, it has seen a slow decline, but still has strong attendance of about 80,000 people per year since the year 2000.[27]

37.
Richard Milhous Nixon

The home in which Richard Nixon was born in Yorba Linda, California. *Courtesy of Joseph F. Picone*

Vital Birthplace Information

Birthplace	Yorba Linda, California
President's birthday	January 9, 1913
How long in the home	9 years
Life of the home	1912 to present
Style	Clapboard kit house
Still in existence	Yes
Commemoration	Richard Nixon Birthplace and Presidential Library
Open to the public	Yes
Cost	$9.95 (includes Presidential Library)
For more information	www.nixonlibraryfoundation.org
Replica exists	No
Significance	Earliest birthplace recognition (nine years before he was president)
Closest birthplace	Lyndon Baines Johnson, 1,292 miles

What you will find there today:

The Richard Nixon birthplace is located on the same property as his Presidential Library in Yorba Linda, California. The nine-acre site is managed by the Richard Nixon Library and Birthplace foundation. Placed in front of the birthplace are three markers that were erected after he was elected vice president, after his impeachment, and after his death. Curiously, no markers were placed at the home during the five years, six months, and twenty days he served as President of the United States (January 20, 1969 - August 9, 1974).

Address/Directions:

18001 Yorba Linda Boulevard
Yorba Linda, California 92686

From the Richard M. Nixon Freeway (Route 90), take the Yorba Linda Boulevard exit. In .3 miles the Richard Nixon Birthplace and Presidential Library will be on the right.

History

The land that was to become the town of Yorba Linda, was first settled by Bernando Yorba, a rancher and son of one of the early settlers of California. On August 1, 1834, the Mexican government granted him 13,328 acres, referred to as Rancho Cañon de Santa Ana. After the Mexican War and California gained its statehood in 1850, Bernando Yorba "fell prey to various frauds" and lost his land. The property changed hands over the years, and in 1908, it was taken over by the Janns Investment Company, a Los Angeles real estate firm founded by Dr. Peter Janns, a physician from Nebraska. The land was subdivided into ten-acre plots, selling for $250 an acre of what was, perhaps disingenuously, advertised as "the richest land in California." Janns named the town "Yorba Linda," Yorba for the original settler and Linda being the Spanish word for "beautiful." In this new town, Janns prohibited the sale of alcohol, a rule which would attract many Quaker settlers, such as the Nixons.

One of these ten-acre plots was purchased by Frank Milhous, who used his land to grow barley. In the winter of 1911, he sold the land to his daughter Hannah Milhous and her husband, Francis Anthony Nixon, for them to farm citrus fruit.

On his newly acquired land, Frank used a catalog kit to build a one and a half story white clapboard-sided home. He completed the home, located on a hill near the Anaheim ditch off of Yorba Linda Boulevard, in January 1912. [1]

Richard Nixon later recalled proudly:

My father built this house himself. My father wasn't trained as an architect but he taught himself to become a highly skilled mason and carpenter. He was particularly proud of the living room fireplace, and apparently others admired it as well because I am told that in addition to ours, he built the fireplaces of several of the neighboring houses.[2]

In this new home, the Nixons farmed oranges and lemons and kept a cow, a horse, chickens, and rabbits.

A year after the home was built, at 9:35 p.m. on January 9, 1913, Dr. Horace Wilson and his assistant nurse, Henrietta Shockney, delivered an eleven-pound Richard Milhous Nixon, who would grow up to become the last president born in a home built by his ancestors. President Nixon later said about that day,

I was born on January 9, 1913, in my parent's bedroom, which is located off the main living room. It was the coldest day of one of the coldest winters in California's history. Our family doctor, who had driven out to Yorba Linda in a horse and buggy from Whittier twelve miles away, wrapped me in a blanket after delivering me and put me in a laundry basket to keep warm. Years later, he told me that his main recollection was that I had the strongest and loudest voice of any baby he had ever delivered.[3]

Today you can still see the original bed on which he was born.

At this home, Richard Nixon grew into a young boy. He first shared a room with his brothers in the back of the home. Later, the boys moved into a bedroom in the attic, sharing it with his father's helper, Ollie Burgh. Burgh had started working for the Nixons in 1913 and would later say the future president "was a very good kid, very quiet, never a crybaby at least around his father."[4] However, Frank was not successful as a farmer. By 1919, he had given up on the lemon grove, and by 1922, they decided to leave Yorba Linda, so in May of that year he sold the farm at a loss and moved to Whittier, California.

Over the next twenty-six years, several different people owned the birthplace home. In the 1920s, the property was purchased by the Yorba Linda School District and an elementary school was built in front of the home.[5] In 1945, the school's janitor and bus driver Mr. Jesse F. Waldron, his wife, and their children moved into the historic house.[6] During the twenty-four years that the Waldrons lived in the home, Richard Nixon visited his birthplace several times. According to Jesse's daughter, Linda Waldron Bugbee, "It was a wonderful place to grow up!"[7] Of course, that was not during the Watergate years. After Jesse Waldron retired in 1969, the school's next janitor, Vincent Ellingson, along with his wife, Dodie, and three children, moved into the home. They rented the home from the Yorba Linda School District for $80 a month.[8] Throughout these years, the home faced destruction several times. Luckily, none of these plans were successful.

Preservation

In 1959, while Richard Nixon was serving as vice president under Dwight D. Eisenhower, the Yorba Linda School Board and local citizens banded together to designate the green-trimmed white framed home as a historic site.[9] A dedication ceremony was held on Nixon's 46th birthday on January 9, 1959, with honorary mayor Hoyt Corbit, serving as the master of ceremonies. The Fullerton Junior College Orchestra entertained the crowd of between 800 and 1,000 people, which included about 400 school children who were excused from their classes. Honored guests included Nixon's mother, his brother Don, three of his aunts, and his first secretary Mrs. Evelyn Dorn. The dedication was made by County School Superintendent Linton T. Simmons who spoke of the value of education. The main event was when Mrs. R.C. Cochran, one of Richard Nixon's first school teachers, removed the cover from the plaque that read:

The birthplace of Richard Millhous Nixon who, through devotion to his country, rose to become Vice President of the United States of America.[10]

Despite what was written on the plaque, Nixon's mother shocked those in attendance when she blurted out:

He was born in a hospital, but we lived here until Richard was 7![11]

For starters, Richard Nixon lived at the home for nine years, not seven, but that's obviously not the blockbuster here. Was this an elderly mother's senior moment or a slip up in a birthplace conspiracy? Nixon was already preparing for the run at the White House in 1960, so perhaps he was laying the groundwork for the cliché "humble beginnings" storyline. Local residents were astonished and distraught over the comments. The next day, Mrs. Nixon began damage control in what may be the original Nixon cover-up. She quickly retracted her statements from the previous day, "He was not [born in a hospital]. He was born in the front bedroom of that very house."[12] While it's difficult to see how a mother could make that kind of error, it is also very unlikely that in 1913 in rural California a child of fruit farmers would have been born in a hospital. The chairman of the birthplace marker committee, W.H. Barton, also corroborated the story. He said that he was "sure of Nixon's nativity when they had a plaque made up to mark the house as a historical shrine."[13] Nativity? Shrine? We are talking about Richard Nixon still, aren't we?

Still, the controversy would not end. It was not until Richard Nixon himself chimed in on the matter from Washington, D.C. to confirm that he "always believed [he] was born in the front bedroom of the white house" that matters began to settle down. Despite the uncertain tone of his declaration, the controversy seemed to have run its course.[14] Unfortunately for Richard Nixon, this would not be the last alleged cover-up in which he was involved. Unique to presidential birthplace history, this honor made almost a decade prior to him taking office is significant as the earliest a presidential birthplace was officially recognized.[15]

Since Richard Nixon was unable to attend in January, he returned to his hometown several months later in June 1959. He visited the home, which was, at the time, occupied by the school janitor, Jesse F. Waldron, and his family. Upon seeing the plaque erected five months earlier, Nixon graciously said:

I don't know of anything that has moved me more than this action.[16]

In addition to the stone marker, another sign was placed at the home, this one "adorned with gold-leaf embellishments" announcing the birthplace of Richard Nixon. Unfortunately, in the summer of 1960 when Richard Nixon was running for president, the sign was stolen.[17] Mrs. Mildred Corbit, president of the Yorba Linda Republican Club for Nixon was undeterred. Not only did she have a replacement sign quickly erected, she also had a few extra made just in case the replacements were stolen, although she said:

If he loses, there won't be much of a threat from souvenir hunters.[18]

She must not have been too disappointed when Nixon was defeated by Kennedy in 1960.

In December 1968, after Richard Nixon was elected president, the Nixon Birthplace Foundation was founded by a group of six people including Yorba Linda's first mayor, Roland Bigonger, and Chamber of Commerce president Dr. Robert Meador; however, they quickly ceded control to W.H. Hurless Barton, second cousin to the president.[19] The group was formed "for one purpose, and one purpose only – to acquire, preserve and perpetuate the birthplace of our thirty-seventh president."[20] Nixon had personally requested that fundraising was not done publicly, but instead by word of mouth.[21] He also mentioned that if the group needed money, they should reach out to the chairman of the Nixon Foundation and tire magnate, Harvey F. Firestone.[22]

The next year, only two weeks after Neil Armstrong took his "one small step for [a] man, one giant leap for mankind" when he landed on the moon, Ronald Reagan, then governor of California, proposed federal intervention to preserve the birthplace. As seen over and over, this particular strategy rarely works for birthplace preservation, but the Gipper gave it a shot anyway. In late July 1969, Governor Reagan said, "Preserving the Nixon home is in the national public interest" and requested that the National Park Service purchase the land for $500,000.[23] At the time, Dodie and Vince Ellingson and their three children lived in the home. In addition to the stone marker from 1959, a sign was also placed on the chain link fence that read:

Birthplace of Richard M. Nixon.

The couple reportedly enjoyed the attention, "except on Sundays [when] people come around and peek in the windows."[24] Tough to argue with the Ellingsons there.

On December 12, 1971, the home received an additional honor when it was listed in the National Register of Historic Places (National Register Number #71000171). On January 9, 1972, Nixon's 59th birthday, a ceremony was held at the birthplace. About 250 people were in attendance to witness the dedication of a flagpole as well as the unveiling of a historic marker erected by the Mojave Chapter of the Daughters of the Revolution. Mr. and Mrs. R.L. Fullerton, former residents of Yorba Linda, donated the flagpole and the Shell Oil Company and Pacific Telephone corporations helped fund the memorial. The Mojave Chapter of the Daughters of the Revolution arranged the ceremony, which included a concert by the Third Marine Aircraft Wing Band from El Toro and an invocation by Lawrence Lang who was a past president of the Los Ninos Society Children of the American Revolution. While not able to attend in person, President Nixon along with Governor Ronald Reagan sent their greetings, which were read aloud by the D.A.R. Chapter regent, Mrs. Vincent J. Musso. Several other members of the D.A.R. Chapter participated in the ceremony.[25]

From here things began to go downhill for both the president and the birthplace. Between Vietnam and Watergate, the 1970s were turbulent times and the birthplace was sometimes caught up in this maelstrom. On May 13, 1972, an anti-war protest was being held in front of the birthplace. About thirty demonstrators held a multi-day "end the war" vigil and even went so far as to raise a Viet Cong flag on the flag pole which only a few months earlier had been dedicated to the president. In the midst of the protest, two men approached the home and knocked at the door. At the time, the school janitor Vincent Ellingson, and his family lived in the home. The men told the Ellingsons:

We have been sent to tell you that you have an hour to get out before this place is blown up.[26]

The Ellingsons wisely left the home in a hurry. Police were called and searched the home; however, no explosives were found.

Despite incidents like this, the town of Yorba Linda was still strongly behind Richard Nixon and many residents were confident Watergate would blow over. In January 1972, a register was placed outside of the birth home on weekends. The comments over the next two years show mostly unwavering support throughout the difficult times along with the expected smattering demands to "impeach him."[27]

The Nixon Birthplace Foundation also forged ahead with their efforts to try to purchase the home. Hurless Barton, chairman of the Nixon Birthplace Foundation, said the birthplace "will be a memorial to his devotion to this county's finest ideals that will endure long after Watergate and its flashy headlines have been forgotten."[28] While this was wishful thinking on Hurless's part, initially there actually was a spike in donations after Watergate. However, after President Nixon resigned from office prior to an inevitable impeachment over the Watergate scandal, the tone of the preservation efforts changed drastically. Donations slowed to a trickle and even the local Yorba Linda newspaper disavowed Nixon when they changed their moniker from the "Birthplace of Richard Nixon" to a more generic "Birthplace of our 37th President."[29] Despite the trend, the Nixon Birthplace Foundation's support did not waiver. To demonstrate their loyalty, the organization erected a stone monument in front of the home, near the marker placed at the home in 1959 when Nixon was elected vice president. This new marker, emblazoned with a bronze plaque, used bold language to celebrate his abbreviated presidency:

BIRTHPLACE OF RICHARD MILHOUS NIXON, PRESIDENT OF THE UNITED STATES OF AMERICA
Inaugurated January 20, 1969
Inaugurated For Second Term January 20, 1973
We are Proud of Our Native Son
A Man Who Has Spared Nothing of Himself to Help Build a Great Nation.[30]

Around this time, work began on another birthplace memorial, this time by stonemason Robert Farrell. W.H. Hurless Barton had asked him to build a suitable birthplace memorial and Farrell came up with a unique design using a stone from all fifty states plus one for Washington, D.C. He solicited donations from stone dealers throughout the county and he quickly had twenty-two rocks. Then came Watergate and the stones stopped arriving. The project was restarted in 1976 when President Nixon's sister-in-law, Clara Jane Nixon (wife of Donald), joined the effort. She appealed to friends across the county for stones and by 1977 the monument was completed and placed in front of the birth home. Although not known for his sense of humor, when Richard Nixon was told that a stone was also sent from Washington D.C., he said he didn't know they sent stones from D.C.; he thought they only threw them. Despite his failings, Nixon still had many supporters in his hometown.[31] Unfortunately, the innovative monument is no longer in existence. In the years following its creation, it was relocated in 1989 and the stones were reconstructed to use as a walkway. In the mid 2000s, the walkway was removed to accommodate an expanding presidential library.[32]

Meanwhile, the prospects for the Birthplace Foundation to purchase the home looked grim in early 1977. Chairman of the Nixon Birthplace Foundation Hurless Barton was now much less optimistic:

Watergate and all that stuff has sort of slowed things up.[33]

However, the group persisted, and luckily for them, the school district was financially strapped and eager to sell. Finally, in the middle of October 1977, an agreement was reached and the Richard Nixon Birthplace Foundation purchased the home and 1.3 acres from the Yorba Linda School District for $125,000.[34] The transaction took almost a year to clear and was finally completed in July 1978. The purchase price was donated by several of Nixon's wealthy friends as well as proud and loyal supporters from Yorba Linda.[35] Also included in the donations was $44,000 from two Nixon supporters from New Jersey who had originally raised the money for the Watergate defense fund.[36] Cassius H. Daly, former mayor of Leonia, New Jersey, started the "Save the President" committee in 1973. The group raised about $150,000; however, after Nixon resigned, whatever was left remained in a bank account for five years until Daly decided the birthplace was a good cause for the remaining money.[37]

Despite the success in acquiring the birthplace, the ability to memorize a disgraced president continued to be an uphill battle for the years to come. In December 1985, perhaps hoping to cash in on the Christmas spirit, Republican California Congressmen William E. Dannemeyer sponsored a bill to purchase the birthplace and 7.2 acres for $1,000,000 and have it turned over to the National Park Service. He was not alone as he had bipartisan support from a thirty-member delegation from California. The bill was considered along with similar bills to also commemorate Jimmy Carter and

Gerald Ford's birthplaces. Dannemeyer claimed, "time heals all wounds and Mr. Nixon has earned himself a place in history."[38] He may have been right, but he would also soon find out that many of his fellow congressmen did not agree that eleven years was enough time.

Despite the initial bi-partisan support, politicians soon retreated to their respective corners. Republican President Ronald Reagan endorsed the bill while Democrats fiercely opposed it. Minnesota Democratic Representative Bruce Vento said:

The memories are too vivid and the feelings are too strong.[39]

Less than four months later, in May 1986, the bill, along with the efforts to memorialize Jimmy Carter's Plains, Georgia birthplace were officially taken off the docket.

The next year, the residents of Yorba Linda took matters into their own hands. Discussions had been underway since 1983, led by the Richard Nixon Presidential Archives Foundation, to build a Presidential Library. Proposed locations were between Yorba Linda and San Clemente. Both cities were jockeying for the library, which would be a major tourist coup. In December 1987, the decision was made to go with Yorba Linda when they proposed to build the twenty-five million dollar Presidential Library. Yorba Linda Mayor Roland Bigonger announced that the birthplace had been acquired from the school district along with 6.1 acres for $1,300,000.[40]

The next year, the nearby school was demolished to make way for the Presidential Library. The Richard Nixon Presidential Archives Foundation restored the birthplace home and furnished it with authentic and period pieces from the years the Nixons resided there. In 1990, the restorations were completed at a cost of twenty-one million dollars, less than the original estimates. On July 19, 1990, a dedication ceremony was held with thirty to forty thousand people in attendance. Speaking at the ceremony were former Presidents Ronald Reagan and Gerald Ford and the current Commander In Chief George Herbert Walker Bush. Along with Richard Nixon, this historic gathering of the presidents was only the second time in history four presidents were at the same place at the same time (the previous time was at the White House after the death of Egyptian President Anwar Sadat in 1981). Jimmy Carter sent a note of congratulations, but was not in attendance denying the event the presidential record number five. Perhaps he was busy, or maybe this was payback for Richard Nixon skipping the opening of his Presidential Library. Also making history was the first time four first ladies were at the same public appearance. Neither Watergate

nor his resignation was mentioned at the ceremony and the crowd was mostly supportive of their former fallen hero. Only two people were ejected for unruly behavior.[41]

On April 22, 1994, President Nixon died and was buried at his birthplace along side his wife, Pat. President Bill Clinton attended the ceremony along with approximately 50,000 mourners. Upon his death, most of his estate went to the birthplace, including what remained from a $1,200,000 pledge Nixon had made to his birthplace and library a year earlier. He also left the birthplace and library any documents "which have had historical or commemorative significance."[42] Towards those final years, Nixon may have felt he had few friends and was grateful for the honor and support provided by the Richard Nixon Birthplace and Presidential Library.

On January 9, 1995 on what would have been Nixon's 82nd birthday, the site was officially recognized as California Historical Landmark (#1015). Perhaps now that Nixon had passed on, the state knew they would receive less resistance for the recognition. A ceremony was held at the birthplace and was presided over by California State Attorney General Dan Lundgren, who also had tenuous ties to the president, as his father was Nixon's physician.[43] At the dedication ceremony, a historic plaque was unveiled. The marker, which sits in the middle of a circular flower bed, reads:

RICHARD NIXON BIRTHPLACE
"I was born in a house my father built"
President Richard Nixon (1913-1994)

In 1912 Frank and Hannah Nixon built this modest farmhouse on their small citrus ranch. Here Richard Nixon was born, January 9, 1913, and spent his first nine years. He served his country as Congressman, U.S. Senator, Vice President, and 37th President of the United States (1969-1974). He was the first native-born Californian to hold the Presidency. President Nixon achieved significant advances in International Diplomacy by ending U.S. involvement in the Vietnam War, opening lines of communication with China and the Soviet Union, and initiating the Middle East Peace process.

California Registered Historical Landmark No. 1015

Plaque placed by the State Department of Parks and Recreation in cooperation with the Richard Nixon Library and Birthplace. Dedicated January 9, 1995

Visitor Information

Perhaps it's Watergate, or maybe it's because Yorba Linda is only fifteen minutes from Disneyland, but whatever the draw, 150,000 people visit Richard Nixon's birthplace each year.[44] The home is open every day except major holidays and hours are 10 a.m. to 5 p.m. except on Sundays (11 a.m. to 5 p.m.). You can take a docent-guided tour or save a few bucks and do it yourself on a self-guided tour.

When visiting the Presidential Library, look for the infamous photograph of Richard Nixon and Elvis Presley shaking hands in the oval office. On that historic day on December 21, 1970, the King of Rock and Roll showed up at the White House unannounced and requested to meet the president. This was an offer even the most powerful man in the free world could not refuse! Interesting note, the King of Rock and Roll and President Nixon's birthdays are only one day apart, Elvis on January 8, Nixon on January 9.

38.
Leslie Lynch King
(a.k.a. Gerald Rudolff Ford)

Vital Birthplace Information

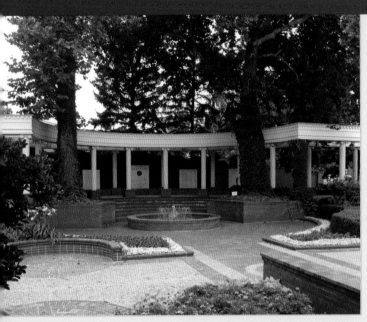

The Gerald R. Ford Birth Site and Gardens in Omaha, Nebraska. *Courtesy of Dave Rimington*

Birthplace	Omaha, Nebraska
President's birthday	July 14, 1913
How long in the home	16 days
Life of the home	1893 to 1971
Style	Victorian mansion
Still in existence	No
Ultimate fate	Destroyed by fire
Commemoration	Gerald R. Ford Birth Site and Gardens
Open to the public	Yes
Cost	Free
For more information	www.nebraskahistory.org/ conserve/brthsite.htm
Replica exists	No
Significance	Shortest time lived in birthplace (16 days)
Closest birthplace	Herbert Hoover, 259 miles

What you will find there today:

At the birthplace location is the Gerald R. Ford Birth Site and Gardens. Within the gardens is a commemorative marble tablet that reads:

BIRTH SITE OF GERALD FORD
38th President of the United States
My fellow Americans, our long national nightmare is over. Our Constitution works; our great Republic is a government of laws and not of men. Here the people rule….

President Ford's Inaugural Address
August 9, 1974

President Gerald Ford visited this site during construction May 7, 1976 and personally dedicated it to the people of Omaha Sept 21, 1977

Address/Directions:

3202 Woolworth Avenue
Omaha, Nebraska 68103

From the Gerald R. Ford Expressway (Route 480W) take Exit 1A. Turn right onto Martha Street and then make a quick right onto Park Avenue. After .4 miles, make the first left onto Woolworth Avenue. In .2 miles you will arrive at the Gerald R. Ford Birth Site and Gardens.

History

The three-story, fourteen-room Victorian style mansion that stood on 3202 Woolworth Avenue was once one of the finest homes in Omaha. It was built in 1893 for about $10,000, which at the time was very expensive.[1] In 1913, the home was owned by Charles Henry King and his wife, Martha Alicia Porter, who were in the wool business and were worth millions of dollars. Their son, Leslie Lynch King, married Dorothy Ayer Gardner on September 7, 1912, and the couple moved into a small apartment. Almost immediately, the relationship soured and Leslie became abusive to his new bride. However, also almost as quickly, Dorothy became pregnant. The couple moved into Leslie's parents' home for the birth, where her first son, Leslie Lynch King Jr., was born on a hot night on July 14, 1913. Leslie Jr. would one day become the only man to become President of the United States of America that was neither elected president nor vice president.

Unfortunately, having a newborn baby did not stop Leslie's abusive behavior. Only sixteen days after Leslie Lynch King Jr. was born, Dorothy had had enough. She took her son, and nothing else, and left her husband and 3202 Woolworth Avenue for good. Later in life, when asked about his father, Gerald Ford simply stated, "my father was a bad man." [2] Three years after leaving King, Dorothy married a good man, Gerald Rudolff Ford in 1916. Soon after their marriage, her new husband adopted the young boy who was renamed from Leslie to Gerald Rudolff Ford. His stepfather would always hold a special place in President Ford's heart.[3]

In 1971, a fire destroyed the home and tragically, a resident was killed in the blaze. The next year, whatever was left of the home was razed. The land went up for sale and remained unsold for three years. During that time, the plot became overgrown with weeds and littered with beer cans and other assorted trash.

Preservation

In the midst of the Watergate scandal, Richard Nixon's Vice President Spiro Agnew resigned on October 10, 1973. About two months later, on December 6, 1973, Gerald Ford was sworn in as our nation's vice president. Now that his birth site, which had devolved into a weed-ridden trash heap since the home was razed the previous year, had become a vice-presidential birthplace, locals took note and began to take care of the site.

On February 15, 1974, Vice President Gerald Ford was in Omaha and stopped by his birth site. Earlier in the day, a group of middle school children had cleaned the garbage from the vacant lot. Ford, the consummate nice-guy stopped by their classroom to thank them personally, commenting:

It looks better than my yard at home.[4]

Later on, Ford was more frank, although still diplomatic, when he stated, "the land was in a very difficult situation."[5]

After Ford's visit, the novelty of having a famous birthplace in town wore off quickly and again the site began to deteriorate, becoming overrun with weeds and littered with trash. However, all that changed on August 9, 1974. Now this weedy, trashy parcel of land was a presidential birthplace and locals again began to take notice. The property was cleared of weeds and several makeshift

signs popped up on the property, including a large hand painted placard that simply stated:

BIRTHPLACE OF PRES FORD.

Locals by the handful began to visit the famous birth site.[6]

Ten days after becoming president, on August 19, members of the Omaha Boy Scout Troop #388 cleaned the vacant lot. As if he did not have enough on his plate, Ford, again proving that his previous gesture was no fluke, still found time to send a telegram to the Boy Scouts to thank them.[7]

Back when Ford was still vice president, local businessman James M. Paxson, President of the Standard Chemical Company in Omaha, recognized the historic value of the birthplace property. At the time, the property was still for sale, so in 1973, he purchased the land for $17,250. Paxson also purchased a neighboring lot with the intentions of donating both properties to the city of Omaha to use as a memorial. The city declined citing a lack of funds required to maintain and memorialize the property. Without the support of the city, Paxson decided that since he'd started this effort, he would finish it. He established the Paxson Foundation and took it upon himself to raise the money, donating over $200,000 himself. Paxson, a true patriot, said:

I didn't do this for Gerald Ford personally. I did it for the office of the presidency. [President Ford] doesn't owe me anything.[8]

Not sure exactly how to mark the property, Paxson offered a $500 reward for whoever could come up with the best memorial design. The winner was Gary Dubas, a University of Nebraska architecture student, who included elements from both the birth home and the White House. Using this concept, Omaha architecture firm Schlott-Farrington and Associates created the final design, which was unveiled to the public on August 27, 1975.[9]

In May 1976, Gerald Ford was in the middle of a heated primary race. Normally, an incumbent president could sit this one out, but Ronald Reagan had pulled the unusual move of challenging the sitting president from his own party and Ford was struggling. The Nebraska primary was May 11 and Ford came to Omaha to drum up support. A few days before the primary, on May 7, 1976, Ford made a detour from the campaign trail to visit his birthplace to see how the memorial was coming along. Later in life, he recalled the visit:

We were on our way to the Republican National Convention in Detroit, we stopped in Omaha, and for the first time saw the gardens in full bloom. There's no question about it, Betty and I both were thrilled.[10]

This would be his first and only birthplace visit during his brief presidency. Ford went on to lose the primary in his birth state, getting 45% of the vote to the Gipper's 54%; however, he did take Ward 3, which included his birthplace, by a two to one margin.

Throughout the construction of the birthplace memorial, Paxson kept in contact with the Fords. Included in the memorial was a gazebo, and bricks from the original birth home foundation were encased in glass. On September 21, 1977, with Jerry Ford in attendance, the memorial was officially dedicated as the Gerald Ford Birth Site Park. The quick half hour ceremony included speeches by Omaha Mayor Al Veys, Nebraska Governor J.J. Exon and of course, the guest of honor, Gerald Ford.[11] Until the birth site memorial, Ford had only bad memories of his life in Omaha. His father was an abusive drunk who beat his mother. The idea for the memorial took him by surprise. However, throughout the years the birthplace memorial was being developed, Ford found a deeper affection for his Omaha birthplace.[12]

Over the years, Ford's sentiment for his birthplace grew. On July 12, 1980, a couple of days before Ford's 67th birthday, the memorial rose garden that Betty Ford herself helped plan was dedicated. Jerry Ford returned again for the ceremonies. Speaking before about 2,000 people, Ford said:

Let me say, it's awfully nice to be home. Omaha is my home. I'm proud of it and deeply grateful for all of you turning out on a Saturday afternoon.[13]

In September 1995, Gerald Ford once again visited for the dedication of the Gerald R. Ford Exhibit as part of the state historical society's Gerald R. Ford Conservation Center, located across the street from the birthplace gardens. Gerald Ford passed away on December 26, 2006, and immediately after his death, people flocked to his birthplace park to leave flowers and to feel a connection with the man that saw our nation through a very difficult period. While maybe not a great president, he was the right man for the right time.

Today, the site includes busts of the former president and first lady. Engraved beneath his bust are the words:

PRESIDENT GERALD R. FORD
The 35th President of the United States revisited this site July 12, 1980.

The site's flower gardens and picturesque fountain make it a popular location for weddings.

Visitor Information

The Gerald Ford birthplace is one of the few presidential birthplaces where you can see more than a historic marker, but do not need to worry about visitor hours. Located across the street from the birthplace is the Gerald R. Ford Conservation Center, which is part of the Nebraska State Historical Society. The center includes an exhibit dedicated to the president, which can be seen by appointment only (call 402-595-1180).

One other tour you can take when in Omaha is the Village of Boys Town, located only ten miles away from the Gerald Ford birthplace. Started by Father Edward J. Flanagan, the first boys' home was opened in an old Victorian home on December 12, 1917. Boys Town was incorporated as a village in 1936, and it was designated a National Historic Landmark in 1985. After stopping at the visitor center, you can take a driving tour of the campus. On the tour, you will see the Father Flanagan House Museum and the Boys Town Hall of History Museum. You can attend mass at the Dowd Memorial Chapel or the Herbert B. Chambers Protestant Chapel of the Nativity of Our Lord or spend a few tranquil moments in the Garden of the Bible, which is maintained by the residents of Boys Town.[14] Not only is this a wonderful way to spend a few hours while in Omaha, but it also has ties to presidential birthplaces. On August 10, 1929, Father Flanagan attended the dedication at the Herbert Hoover birthplace in West Branch, Iowa. Accompanied by forty of his boys, he praised Hoover the most famous orphan in the world.[15]

39.
James Earl Carter

The Lillian G. Carter Health Nursing Center where Jimmy Carter was born in Plains, Georgia. (*Used by permission from Mary Baldwin from the Lillian G. Carter Health Nursing Center*)

Vital Birthplace Information

Birthplace	Plains, Georgia
President's birthday	October 1, 1924
Location of birth	Wise Sanitarium (currently Lillian G. Carter Nursing Center)
Still in existence	HOSPITAL: yes
How long in the home	2 years
Life of the home	1910 to present
Style	Ground-floor apartment
Still in existence	APARTMENT: yes (currently the Plains Bed and Breakfast Inn)
Commemoration	Jimmy Carter National Historic Site
Open to the public	Yes
Cost	Free
For more information	HOSPITAL: www.lilliangcarterhealth.org HOME: www.nps.gov/jica
Replica exists	No
Significance	First president born in a hospital
Closest birthplace	Herbert Hoover, 257 miles

What you will find there today:

HOSPITAL

The hospital where Jimmy Carter was born is still an active hospital and is today known as the Lillian G. Carter Nursing Center. It is named after Jimmy Carter's mother who was a registered nurse at the hospital when her son was born on October 1, 1924.

In front of the hospital is an undated historic marker erected by the Plains Historical Preservation Trust that reads:

Wise Sanitarium
1921-1936

Built in 1921 by Doctors Samuel, Thaddeus, and Bowman Wise, sons of Dr. Burr T. and Laura Addy Wise, early settlers of Plains, this innovative hospital was known as "the Mayo Clinic of the South." Originally opening above Plains Pharmacy in 1912 with 15 beds, it moved to the second floor of the A. C. Wellons building on Main Street in 1917 with 20 beds. In 1921, this building was built with 60 beds, an operating room, and an X-Ray room with radium treatment capability. Black patients were treated in a separate building to the rear of the main building. It was one of the first small hospitals in the state to be accredited by the American College of Surgeons and the American Medical and Hospital Association and also served as an accredited training school for nurses. It was here that Lillian Gordy Carter received her nurse training. Jimmy Carter, son of Earl and Lillian Carter, was born here on October 1, 1924. He was the first President of the United States to be born in a hospital.

On January 21, 1936 a fire damaged this building. Dr. Sam and Dr. Thad relocated their practice to Americus and Dr. Bowman opened an office in Plains.

Marker funded by Plains Historical Preservation Trust.

Address/Directions:

HOSPITAL
Lillian G. Carter Nursing Center
225 Hospital Street
Plains, Georgia 31780

HOME
100 Church Street (Routes 280/27)
Plains, Georgia 31780

The hospital and first home site are both right around the corner from the visitor center of the Jimmy Carter National Historic Site.

HOME
The first home where Jimmy Carter lived is currently operated as the Plains Bed and Breakfast Inn. However, perhaps to highlight the fact that Carter was the first president born in a hospital, there is no sign to mark the spot even though the location is within the grounds of the Jimmy Carter National Historic Site. The home sits across from both the Plains police station and City Hall. As of this writing, the home is up for sale.

History

HOSPITAL

The area where Jimmy Carter was born was originally inhabited by Creek Indians. The town of Plains, Georgia, originally known as the "Plains of Dura" was first established in 1827; but back then, it was located about a mile away. When a railroad was established, the town picked up and moved to be closer to the tracks so they could better market their farming crops. Plains was officially incorporated in 1896.

In 1921, brothers Samuel, Burr Thaddeus, and Bowman J. Wise built the Wise Sanitarium, a prestigious medical center with sixty hospital beds that would become known as the "Mayo Clinic of the South." On October 1, 1924 at 7 a.m., James Earl Carter Jr. was born within the walls of the Wise Sanitarium, delivered by Doctor Samuel Wise with assistance from nurse Gassie Abrams. Jimmy Carter would one day become the thirty-ninth President of the United States and the first born in a hospital, forever changing the landscape of presidential birthplace history.[1] Twelve years later, the hospital was damaged in a fire on January 21, 1936. The hospital was rebuilt, but the Wise brothers did not return. Samuel and Burr Thaddeus relocated to Americus and Bowman opened a practice in Plains. In the following years, the hospital has changed names several times. When Jimmy Carter was elected, it was known as the Plains Convalescent Home and today, the birthplace hospital is known as the Lillian G. Carter Nursing Center.

HOME

When Lillian Gordy Carter was pregnant, she was living with her husband, James, in an upstairs apartment with an outdoor bathroom in Plains, Georgia. Given her condition, her doctor, Sam Wise, suggested she move to a ground-floor apartment. The Carters took his advice and relocated to a ground floor room at Emmett and Bessie Cook's house.[2] The home was built fourteen years earlier in 1910. Sometime around the years the Carters resided in the home, the Carter's landlord, Emmett Cook, served as mayor of Plains.

The Cook's house was on 100 Church Street, around the corner from the Wise Sanitarium, which made a short commute for Lillian to get to work.[3] Even though Lillian was a nurse, she planned to have her first child at home, but when the time came, there was an empty room at the hospital. In addition, Dr. Wise thought that she would recover faster if the baby were born in the hospital. Being her boss, perhaps he had ulterior motives and was also concerned with how quickly she would return to work.[4]

After being born in the Wise Sanitarium on October 1, 1924, the Carters returned to their room at the Cook's house. The couple stayed in the home for two years until the birth of their next child, Gloria. With the growing family, the Carters were getting a little crowded in the Cook's house, so they moved out to a larger rental on South Bond Street owned by Cora Lunsford. However, according to Jimmy Carter himself, the crowded conditions were not the only reason for the move. When Jimmy Carter was born, someone gave the family a dog as a gift. The canine became a point of contention between the Carters and Cooks that apparently turned pretty heated. Eventually, the Cooks decided that both the dog and the Carters needed to leave, so the new baby may have been the perfect opportunity for both families to part gracefully.[5] Sometime later the home was converted to a Bed and Breakfast, one of the few lodging opportunities available in Plains.

Preservation

HOSPITAL

On October 18, 2001, the hospital was renamed the Lillian G. Carter Nursing Center in honor of the president's mother who worked there at the time of Jimmy Carter's birth. There was a ceremony marking the occasion and Jimmy Carter himself gave the dedication to his mother, who had died in 1983.

On October 17, 2009, the hospital was dedicated by descendents of the three Wise doctors who founded the home. Speaking at the ceremony that day were Annette Wise and Georgia Representative Mike Cheoka. However, the most important man that stood up to the dais that day was the most famous person born in the hospital, Jimmy Carter himself.[6]

HOME

The site of the first home is within the boundaries of the Jimmy Carter National Historic Site. Despite the historic significance of the home, there is no historic marker at the location.

Visitor Information

The Jimmy Carter birthplace is unique in that if you visit, you have an outside chance of actually meeting the former president, or "Mr. Jimmy," as locals affectionately call him. When I visited in 2012, I had the good fortune of meeting President Carter and the first lady after Easter Sunday service and the first couple could not have been more warm and friendly to my wife and children. My advice is don't rush your visit to this charming little town. A perfect place to stay (and possibly your only option) is the Plains Historic Inn. Located at 106 West Main Street, it is in the heart of the historic district. From the balcony you can sit in one of the creaky rocking chairs and gaze across the street and see the first home, Billy Carter's gas station, and the train depot that doubled as his 1976 campaign office. The spacious rooms are named and decorated after the decades from the 1920s (Jimmy Carter is born) to the 1980s (Jimmy Carter loses his re-election bid). Ask for the 1970s room; not only is it the decade of disco and when Jimmy Carter was our nation's leader, but it is also the room in which the president and Rosalynn once stayed for a night. Along with tracking down his birthplace locations, you can also visit his former high school, which now serves as the National Historic Site Visitor Center and the farm home where his family moved when he was four. The Lillian G. Carter Nursing Center is a working hospital and is not open to visitors. When Jimmy Carter was first elected president in 1976, crowds flocked to this little town. During his term about 30,000 people a day visited Plains. By the middle of the 1980s, that number had dwindled to about 300 daily. Today, about 75,000 people visit his hometown each year.[7]

40.
Ronald Wilson Reagan

Vital Birthplace Information

Birthplace	Tampico, Illinois
President's birthday	February 6, 1911
How long in the home	2 months, 29 days
Life of the home	1895 to present
Style	Second-floor apartment
Still in existence	Yes
Commemoration	Ronald Reagan Birthplace and Museum
Open to the public	Yes
Cost	Free
For more information	www.tampicohistoricalsociety. com/R_Reagan_Birthplace_ Museum.html
Replica exists	No
Significance	Only president born in Illinois
Closest birthplace	Herbert Hoover, 81 miles

Address/Directions:

111 South Main Street
Tampico, Illinois 61283

From the Ronald Reagan Memorial Highway (Interstate 88), take the IL-40 South/Hoover Road exit. In about four and a half miles, turn right onto IL-172 South/Star Road. Stay on IL-172 until it becomes South Main Street and you arrive at the Ronald Reagan Birthplace and Museum.

The birthplace of Ronald Reagan, Tampico, Illinois. *Courtesy of Joan Johnson, Ronald Reagan Birthplace & Museum*

What you will find there today:

The apartment where Ronald Reagan was born is open to the public as the Ronald Reagan Birthplace and Museum.

History

The town of Tampico was first settled in 1861 when Ohio native John W. Glassburn purchased 160 acres in Northwestern Illinois. Glassburn built a home and farm on his land. Things remained pretty quiet for Glassburn until 1872 when the Chicago, Burlington and Quincy Railroad built a station on his property. The railroad led to rapid growth; however, Tampico was also plagued by troubles in those early years: fires in 1872, 1874 and 1876 and a tornado that nearly destroyed the young town in 1874. Despite these setbacks, the town of Tampico persevered to be officially incorporated on February 26, 1875. A boom started in 1896 when buildings began to spring up all over Main Street.[1]

The building in which President Reagan was born was built in 1895. Fred Harvey Seymour completed the construction for George W. Stauffer, a commercial entrepreneur. On the first floor were commercial space and twenty-one steps that brought you upstairs to a 1,700 square-foot second-floor apartment. For the first nineteen years, from 1896 through 1915, there was a tavern on the first floor.[2] The Stouffers owned the home for seven of those years until selling to William Walter of Mendota, Illinois, on May 8, 1903.

During the time William Walter owned the home, he welcomed new tenants, Jack and Nelle Reagan, on October 1, 1906. Jack was a salesman and ironically, he had very liberal political views. When they moved in, the young couple had no children; however, two years later, they had their first son, John Neil, on September 16, 1908. Three years later, just before 6 a.m. on February 6, 1911, the couple welcomed their second son and future President of the United States, Ronald Wilson Reagan. Family legend has it that when Jack first saw his ten-pound baby son, he said:

> He looks like a fat little Dutchman. But who knows, he might grow up to be president some day.[3]

In a small town like Tampico in 1911, a new baby was big news, so four days after the birth, the *Tampico Tornado* newspaper printed the rather unusual birth announcement that read:

> February 10, 1911 John REAGAN has been calling thirty-seven inches a yard and giving seventeen ounces for a pound this week at PITNEY's store, he has been feeling so jubilant over the arrival of a ten pound boy Monday.

The Reagans soon came to realize that the apartment was too small for the family of four so they packed up and moved out on May 5, 1911 for a two-story house. Just like the Coolidges and Hoovers, the Reagans did not go far. They stayed in the same town, moving about a half-mile away into a home at 104 Glassburn Street.

Over the next seven years, the birthplace property and tenants changed hands many times. On May 8, 1912, a year after the Reagans moved out, William Walter sold to James M. Graham. Graham held the home for only nineteen days before selling to F. L. Pitney, who held the property for about a year and a half until selling to Harry Whitver on December 22, 1913. The following year, on July 14, 1914, Whitver sold to John G. Kinneman. A little less than a year later, Kinneman defaulted on the property; it went into foreclosure and the tavern closed, but by August 1915, it was reopened and owned by Harry Dunn. After their daughter became sick, the Dunns sold the business to Mr. and Mrs. John H. Cooley, who converted the tavern into a bakery. The Cooleys owned the bakery for two years before selling to Mr. and Mrs. I.J. Booz on March 1917, who renamed the establishment Booz's Bakery. During these years, F. L. Pitney repurchased the building, which he had owned three years earlier, on October 11, 1915. He kept the building for four years, until selling on June 16, 1919 to Willis L. Brown.[4]

At that time, the First National Bank was located across the street on the west side. In March 1920, the stockholders voted to move the bank across the street. The birthplace building was purchased for $5,000, and four months later, in early July 1920, the bank and bakery traded places – the First National Bank moved into 111 South Main Street and Booz's Bakery moved across the street.[5] In 1929, when the stock market crashed and the nation sunk into a Great Depression, banks began dropping like flies. The First National Bank bucked the trend and survived independently until 1931, when it merged with the Tampico State Bank. The building was transferred to the Tampico State Bank, and R.F. Woods was made trustee. By 1937, the merged bank finally succumbed to the hard times and became another depression casualty when they shut their doors for good. During the next thirty years, there were no businesses on the first floor; however, the town did occasionally rent out the space for use as the village hall.

In 1948, R.F. Woods became the buildings sole owner. His son, R.S. Woods, bought the building from his father in 1956.[6] The building stayed in the Woods family, and in 1968, Helen Woods Nicely purchased the building from her brother, R.S. Woods. She lived there with her husband and schoolteacher, Paul Nicely.

Preservation

Besides being a schoolteacher, Paul Nicely was a Reagan historian and Helen was also an expert on Tampico 's favorite son. At the time, Ronald Reagan was already a huge movie star, as well as the recently elected Governor of California. In 1976, when the Gipper ran for president against incumbent Gerald Ford, he visited his hometown of Tampico to launch his campaign. To welcome him back, the Nicelys opened the first floor for President Reagan to use as his "National Honorary Headquarters" and two years later, they began to restore the birthplace.

Ronald Reagan did not win the Republican nomination in 1976, but after four years of the Carter administration, change was imminent, so Reagan put his name on the ticket again in 1980. With another run at the presidency, there became a renewed interest in the birthplace. A few months before the election, there was a brief dispute of the actual birthplace of Ronald Reagan. Nobody disputed it was Tampico and people even agreed that it was on Main Street; however, the point of contention was whether he was born on the east or west side. In the end, all agreed that Reagan was born on the east side at 111 South Main Street.[7] As Reagan campaigned for the presidency, the Nicelys and the town of Tampico braced themselves for the pros and cons of being the birthplace to a president. Tampico, like Plains, is a small town with a population of under a thousand residents. After seeing what happened to Jimmy Carter's birthplace, Tampico residents understandably had mixed feelings. They dreaded the onslaught of tourists ("we don't want a carnival atmosphere here" said the Tampico commissioner in 1980), but eagerly awaited the tourist dollars.[8] The Nicelys even invested $25,000 to fix up the building, adding a new furnace and rest rooms, with hopes that one day the state may take over the site.[9] At the time, the apartment where Ronald Reagan was born was being rented by Bernie Staelens, a truck driver and, perhaps unfortunately for him, a Democrat! In anticipation of a Reagan victory, the Nicelys, hopefully politely, "told him he has to get out."[10] Ronald Reagan did win the election by a landslide, but the crowds never did come as anticipated. Even the Gipper himself stayed away. Throughout the full two terms, the town of Tampico never did experience the tourism boom that was rightfully expected.[11]

Regardless of the sparse crowds, accolades were received on June 2, 1982, when the Tampico Main Street historic district was added to the U.S. National Register of Historic Places (National Register Number #82002602). Included in the district, of course, was the birthplace of Ronald Reagan. That same year, the Nicelys officially opened the doors to the Ronald Reagan Birthplace and Museum.[12]

Unfortunately, in August 1989, several months after Ronald Reagan completed his second term of office, the home was hit with a rash of vandalism. Criminals broke an outside light, a flagpole, and threw eggs at the home. Commenting on the incidents, the Nicelys said, "The kids in town have really become a problem."[13] This would have never happened when the Gipper was in charge!

In 1976, when he kicked off his campaign, Ronald Reagan swore to locals that one day he would return. Reagan was a man of his word; however, Tampico had to wait sixteen years for him to make good on that promise. Ronald and Nancy Reagan finally did visit the birthplace on May 10, 1992. The first couple ate at Dutch Diner, attended church, and stopped by his birthplace. At the time, the apartment was again being restored and the Reagans were able to check in on the progress.[14]

The Nicely family owned the property until Helen's death in 2003. At the time of her death, dedicated volunteers Amy and Lloyd McElhiney were managing the museum and tours. For seven days a week, the couple ran tours "when visitors trickle into Tampico."[15] In 2003, Wayne Whalen, an attorney for WPW Partners of Chicago, purchased the birthplace. Newspapers delighted in pointing out that the new owner of the Reagan birthplace was a Democrat.[16] After Mr. Whalen purchased the buildings, he restored the bank with the original fixtures, which he found stored in the basement. He also located the original floor plans that he used to return the bank to how it appeared in the 1920s. The next year Ronald Reagan passed away at the age of 93 and hundreds flocked to visit the birthplace to pay their respects to the man who many consider the greatest president of their generation. In 2011, as the Museum curators prepared for a 100th birthday celebration, Newt Gingrich stopped by the birthplace two days before the big event. Commenting about President Reagan, Gingrich said:

He may have left Illinois, but Illinois never left him.[17]

Visitor Information

In 2009, over 2,000 people came to visit the birthplace of one of the last century's greatest presidents. The home is opened April through October daily from 10 a.m. to 4 p.m., with shorter hours on Sunday (1 p.m. to 4 p.m.) and there are also limited openings in March. After visiting where Ronald Reagan was born, make sure to see his second home on Glassburn Street. It is marked as the Ronald Reagan Boyhood Home; however, it is privately owned and not open to visitors.

For a bite to eat, stop at Dutch Diner where Ronnie and Nancy ate in 1992. Their special is the Tampico Tornado, "an open faced Texas toast sandwich with your choice of a beef patty, chicken, tenderloin, ham, or fish topped with a mound of fries and covered with creamy cheese sauce".[18] The restaurant is not so pretentious that they would mark the seat where the Reagans ate, but the man behind the counter may wave a hand in the direction if you ask politely.

41.
George Herbert Walker Bush

The marker that stands before the birthplace of George Herbert Walker Bush in Milton, Massachusetts.

What you will find there today:

The home has remained a private residence and is not open to visitors. There are several large trees in the front of the home, making it difficult to get a good look during foliage season. At the corner is a Massachusetts historic marker with the following inscription:

173 Adams Street
Milton, Massachusetts
Birthplace of GEORGE HERBERT WALKER BUSH
June 12, 1924
Forty-first President of The United States of America

Vital Birthplace Information

Birthplace	Milton, Massachusetts
President's birthday	June 12, 1924
How long in the home	6 months
Life of the home	Approximately 1890 to present
Style	Victorian style
Still in existence	Yes
Commemoration	Historic marker
Open to the public	No
Cost	Free
For more information	www.miltonhistoricalsociety.org
Replica exists	No
Significance	Last president born in a home
Closest birthplace	John Adams and John Quincy Adams, 4.3 miles

Address/Directions:

173 Adams Street
Milton, Massachusetts 02187

The home where President George Bush was born is located in a quaint neighborhood a few hundred feet south of the Milton border on Adams Street. This is a historic road, as several miles away in Quincy is also John Adams' retirement home, Peacefield.

History

Thomas Hutchinson originally owned the land where the birthplace home now stands. His summer home (not the birth home) was built on forty-eight acres he dubbed "Unquety" in 1743.

After 1765, this home became his primary year-round residence. Hutchinson would later serve as the British Royal Governor of Colonial Massachusetts from 1771 to 1774.

By the nineteenth century, the home and property were owned by Lydia S. Russell, which she passed on to her children upon her death. On August 28, 1888, civil engineers surveyed the land and subdivided it into smaller parcels. One of these properties sized at 1.11 acres, became 173 Adams Street. Joseph Hall, a Dorchester saloon owner, and his wife, Eliza, both from Boston, purchased this parcel. Circa 1890, a Victorian style three-story, fifteen-room home was built with Queen Anne details. While the home is a very stylized home of the period, it is not ostentatious and did not stand out among the other homes in the neighborhood, nor does it now. The Halls owned the home for thirty-two years until 1922. Due to the Halls association with the home, historical records list the home as the Hall/Bush House.[1]

In 1923, Prescott Bush, his wife, Dorothy, and their son, Prescott Jr., rented the home. Prescott worked at nearby Steadman Products in South Braintree and the location gave him a quick commute.

Prescott had an illustrious political career of his own, including service as a United States Senator from Connecticut from 1952 to 1963. On June 12, 1924, in a room on the second floor, they had their second child and future president, George Herbert Walker Bush. George H. W. Bush is the last U.S. President to be born in a home; all of his successors have been born in hospitals. Perhaps this is symbolic, as many people view George Bush Sr. as a throwback to a more dignified era of United States presidents (consider that every president since George Bush Sr. has admitted to drug use to some extent).

In 1924, the Bush family left Milton and moved to Greenwich, Connecticut. Over the next four decades, the home had several owners and residents until 1965, when Nina and Dean Graves purchased the home. The couple still resided in the home thirty-two years later in 1997 when a historical plaque was dedicated to President Bush in their front yard.

Preservation

The Milton Historical Commission first recognized the home for its historical significance in May 1985, when George Bush was beginning his second term as vice president under Ronald Reagan. The home was originally listed as the "Hall house;" however, this was later changed to the "Hall/Bush house."[2]

Throughout the twelve years George Bush served as vice president and as president, the home was not memorialized. However, in the final year of his presidency, in 1992, his hometown finally began to take note. The first idea to commemorate his birthplace came from Kathleen Conlon, a young resident of Milton. Having worked for his reelection campaign, she felt that it was about time Milton recognized its most famous son. Amazingly, it took five more years for this plan to culminate.[3] One of the reasons for the delay was the owner of the home at the time was not happy with the idea, or the former president for that matter. She said:

Usually they don't do something like this until the person dies.... I have a lot of respect for the man, but I wouldn't call myself a fan.[4]

Bush in his typical self-deprecating good humor understood:

I must confess I sympathize with her feelings. We have tourists driving by our houses in Houston and Maine all the time and it can be annoying. Somehow, though, I don't think she'll get too much business.[5]

Finally, in 1997 town officials and the current owners came to an agreement to erect a modest plaque to mark the birthplace. On August 12, 1997, the former president returned to the home of his birth for a half hour to join the 1,000-strong celebration hosted by then-acting Governor Paul Cellucci. George Bush – WWII hero, director of the CIA, vice president and president of the free world – was apparently humbled by the celebration. He said:

One great problem when you're President is that you never adequately get to say thanks to the people who helped get you there.[6]

Visitor Information

In July 2009, I hit the grand slam of presidential birthplaces when I visited Milton, sandwiched between the two Adams and the JFK birthplace. All four were born in Norfolk County, Massachusetts, which is a record for a single county. As I stopped to admire the home, I chatted with a mailman walking his route. He asked, "Do you know that's a famous house you're looking at there?" "Yes", I replied, "George Bush was born there". A simple exchange of mutual recognition of a great man. Nearby is the Milton Public Library at 476 Canton Avenue. Not only is it a very large and impressive library, but it is also the location of the extremely helpful Milton Historical Society. Please remember the home is a private residence and you should respect the privacy of the current owners.

42.
William Jefferson Blythe
(a.k.a. William Jefferson Clinton)

The site where the Julia Chester Hospital once stood where Bill Clinton was born. Now at the location is the Brazzel-Oakcrest Funeral Home. *Courtesy of Joseph F. Picone*

Vital Birthplace Information

Birthplace	Hope, Arkansas
President's birthday	August 19, 1946
Location of birth	The Julia Chester Hospital
Still in existence	No
How long in first home	4 years
Life of the home	1917 to present
Style	American four-square
Still in existence	Yes
Commemoration	HOSPITAL: historic marker HOME: President William Jefferson Clinton Birthplace Home National Historic Site
Open to the public	Yes
Cost	Free
For more information	www.nps.gov/wicl
Replica exists	Yes, in Japan
Significance	Only president born in a hospital that is no longer in existence
Closest birthplace	Dwight David Eisenhower, 189 miles

What you will find there today:

HOSPITAL

The Julia Chester Hospital is no longer in existence and the Brazzel-Oakcrest Funeral Home now stands at the site. In front of the funeral home, at the base of a flagpole, is a stone historic marker affixed with a bronze plaque that reads:

William Jefferson Clinton 42nd President of the United States Was Born On This Site August 19th 1946.

Below the plaque the marker also states:
Brazzel Oakcrest Funeral Home Established April 21, 1954
Built on this site August 1, 1993. Site of Julia Chester Hospital 1932-1955.

HOME

Bill Clinton's first home is open to the public and in 2010 became a National Historic Site under the auspices of the National Park System. In his post-presidential autobiography, *My Life*, Bill wrote that his birthplace still holds deep memories "and it certainly is the place I associate with awakening to life."[1]

Address/Directions:

HOSPITAL
1001 South Main Street
Hope, Arkansas 71801

HOME
117 South Hervey Street
Hope, Arkansas 71801

Take I-30 take Exit 30 (US-278 East). The road changes from North Hervey Street to South Hervey Street, and after 1.5 miles, you will arrive at the first home. Continue on South Hervey Street for .1 mile and turn left on to West 3rd Street. After .3 miles, turn right onto South Main Street, and after a half mile, you'll arrive at the Brazzel-Oakcrest Funeral Home (former location of the Julia Chester Hospital).

History

HOSPITAL

The town of Hope, Arkansas was first settled in 1852 and was incorporated in 1875. It began as a railroad stop and was first mapped by James Loughborough, a land commissioner for the Cairo and Fulton Railroad. He named the town after his daughter.[2]

The Julia Chester Hospital was built at 1001 South Main Street in 1932 and stood for twenty-three years. In 1955, nine years after Bill Clinton's birth, the hospital closed its doors for good. In the following years the building was converted into apartments and was later destroyed by a fire. The burnt remains were later demolished, making Bill Clinton the only president born in a hospital that is no longer in existence.[3] By 1992, the location was an overgrown vacant lot; however, it would not remain that way for long.[4]

On April 21, 1954, a year before the hospital closed its doors, the Oakcrest Chapel Funeral Home was established. In 1993, they expanded their business and built a new funeral home on the same site where the Julia Chester Hospital had stood thirty-eight years earlier. On August 1, 1993, the Brazzel Oakcrest Funeral Home opened its doors and it remains open for business at this writing. Four years later, on June 25, 1997, Bill Clinton paid an unexpected visit to his birthplace when his Uncle Henry Oren "Buddy" Grisham passed away. Clinton had often spoken about his Uncle Buddy and the two had a close relationship since Bill was a boy. The viewing was held at the Brazzel Oakcrest Funeral Home and Bill Clinton eulogized his uncle at the somber gathering.[5]

HOME

In the early 1900s, Dr. Hosea S. Garrett, a physician known to be very generous with his time and talents, purchased an entire block on Giles Avenue in the town of Hope. There was already a home and huge pecan trees on the parcel, but he envisioned one day that his three children would also build homes on his property. His oldest son, also named Hosea Garrett, was a soldier in World War I and stationed in France. While there, he was briefly billetted in a home which he liked so much that when he returned from the war in 1917, he and his brother, Charles, had a home built in the same design on his father's estate. The home was two and a half stories with six rooms and a large front yard that extended to Giles Avenue, later renamed Hervey Street in tribute to a local boy killed in World War I. Despite the French inspiration, the design is similar enough to the typical American four-square style.[6]

Hosea Garrett lived in the home for a short period after, until approximately 1920, when he left the home so his recently married brother, Charles, could move in. Their marriage was not a happy one and did not last. After the couple divorced in approximately 1924, the home became the property of Charles' wife. By 1925, she had turned it into rental property. A few years later, in the late 1920s, the home was purchased by a Mr. Barlow, who owned the home until 1946. Barlow continued to rent the home throughout the 1930s as the nation suffered through the Great Depression. During these years, two or three families lived in the home until 1938, when new tenants Eldridge and Edith Grisham Cassidy, the couple that would one day become the maternal grandparents to the forty-second President of the United States, moved in.

The Cassidys had previously owned a home on Foster Street, but in the midst of the Great Depression, they had fallen on hard times and were unable to keep up with their payments. So, along with their daughter Virginia, they were forced to move.[7] Their daughter, and Bill's mother, met William Jefferson Blythe II in 1943, a traveling salesman from Texas. After a brief courtship, they were married on September 3, 1943, and two months later, William was shipped off to Italy to serve in World War II. Upon returning from service in 1945, the couple briefly lived with the Cassidy family before moving to Chicago where William had found work as a salesman for a heavy equipment company. Almost as soon as they arrived, Virginia discovered she was pregnant and returned to Hope to live with her parents while William remained in Chicago to continue to work to support his growing family. Three months before her due date, on May 17, 1946, William Blythe was driving from Chicago to Hope to see his wife, when he was in a car accident and tragically killed. This gives Bill Clinton the sad distinction as the third President whose father died before his birth, the other two being Andrew Jackson and Rutherford B. Hayes.

Three months later on August 19, 1946, just an hour past dawn following a violent storm, the young widow had a six and a half-pound baby boy by cesarean birth. She named him William Jefferson Blythe III, after his father. Bill Clinton would one day become the first "Baby Boomer" president born after World War II and the only president born in Arkansas. Young Bill Clinton continued to live with his grandparents for another four years. Years later, in his 2004 biography *My Life,* Bill Clinton would write, "that old house seemed massive and mysterious to me then and still holds deep memories today."[8] South Hervey Street, when Bill Clinton was born, was much different than it appears today. The large front yard from the time Hosea Garrett built the home was where young Billy played in the family-oriented neighborhood. In the 1970s, the road was changed from a quaint tree-lined street when it was widened into a feeder street to the I-30 highway.[9] Today, the home, as the *Lawrence Journal-World* newspaper described, "sits between a railway and a super-market on a busy four-lane, divided road where trucks rumble by."[10]

In 1949, Virginia moved to New Orleans to attend school to become an anesthetist, leaving Bill with his grandparents. She kept her room at her parent's home and returned for holidays and in-between semesters to spend time with young Bill. Returning to Hope in 1950, shortly after she met and married Roger Clinton from Hot Springs, Arkansas. The couple moved out of 117 South Hervey Street in 1950 to a house of their own at 321 East 13th Street, also in Hope. Young Bill Blythe took his stepfather's name and became Bill Clinton.

The first home where Bill Clinton lived in Hope, Arkansas. The sign attached to the front gate reads: "The First Home of William Jefferson Clinton 42nd President of the United States" *Courtesy of Joseph F. Picone*

Seven months before Bill Clinton was born, the Cassidy family had graduated from renters to homeowners after purchasing the home in January 1946. After Virginia and Bill moved out, they continued to live at 117 South Hervey Street for another six years. The Clintons often visited the birthplace home on weekends and summers until 1956, when Eldridge Cassidy, Bill's grandfather, passed away after suffering his second massive heart attack. Following his death, his widow, Edith, sold the home.[11]

The home then changed hands four times, the last to the Burton family in the 1980s. In June 1992, a fire broke out, damaging part of the house. Nobody was home at the time and the cause was determined to be electrical, but with the presidential election in full swing, the historical significance was becoming understood and the fire helped bring attention to the home.[12] When Bill Clinton won the 1992 election and became our forty-second president, newspapers reported that the "sad little tumble-down house at 117 S. Hervey Street" was "occupied by Arthur and Anna Mae Burton, parents of 11 kids, five of whom still live[ed] at home."[13] Arthur worked at the local Hudson Processing Plant, but in the lean years of the late 1990s, could not afford to spruce up the house to show the strangers that periodically stopped by to see the historic home.[14]

After Bill Clinton became the president, the home was purchased by Sammy and Mary Crabtree in the spring of 1993. Their motivation was to hold the home temporarily until a preservation group was able to purchase it. The Crabtrees made sure they first helped the Burtons resolve insurance issues resulting from the fire and found them alternate housing. The home had changed little in the seventy-six years since it was first built in 1917. The house was never altered or remodeled and still had the original floors.[15]

Preservation

HOSPITAL

When Bill Clinton was victorious in 1992, proud locals erected a patriotic hand-painted sign at the site where the hospital once stood that read:

THIS IS THE BIRTH SPOT of Bill Clinton NEXT PRESIDENT of the USA.

After the funeral home was built in 1993, a historic marker was erected to commemorate both the president's birth and the history of the funeral home. Due to the nature of the business, the Brazzel-Oakcrest Funeral Home is understandably discreet about the historic location, perhaps to discourage gawkers while a funeral is in progress.

HOME

Like Plains and Tampico before it, the residents of Hope anticipated the opportunity to cash in on their most famous son Bill Clinton when he was running for president in 1992. The town leaders banded together and tried to figure a way to find synergy with their other claim to fame as home to the largest watermelon in the world. A tourist map was printed to hand out to visitors at the annual "watermelon festival" held that August. Significant sites were numbered, with #8 being the birthplace home. The townsfolk braced themselves as they anticipated "yesterday's trickle of visitors to Hope… rapidly swelling into tomorrow's tidal wave."[16]

Friends and supporters of President Clinton founded the Clinton Birthplace Foundation in 1993 with the goal of raising $1,500,000 to purchase and restore 117 South Hervey Street. The foundation was able to purchase the home from Sammy Crabtree in 1994 for about $300,000. Over the next three years, the foundation, led by his boyhood friend and President of the Clinton Birthplace Foundation, Joe Purvis, restored and decorated the home.[17] Restorations included new roofing and siding. For furnishings, the foundation chose 1940s style and décor to remind visitors of the years young Bill resided in the home with his mother and grandparents. Bill Clinton's mother was consulted early on in the process; however, her input was limited when she unfortunately passed away in 1994. That same year, on May 19, the home was listed on the National Register of Historic Places (National Register Number #94000472). Normally, to qualify for this designation, the significant event that occurred at the structure needed to have happened at least fifty years prior. However, for the Clinton home, that rule was bypassed since Bill Clinton was only forty-eight years old at the time. This exemption was not unfounded, as approximately 2,000 of the more than 80,000 sites listed on the register at the time had been granted similar exemption.

On Sunday, June 1, 1997, the home was opened to the public.[18] Just a few months before the planned opening, the foundation had its records subpoenaed twice by Congress as part of a broader investigation into campaign financing. The gifts, which included $50,000 from Hong Kong businesswoman Nina Wang, were made as private donations, and after the records were subpoenaed,

donations dropped off substantially. Joe Purvis said the accusations of wrongdoing had a "chilling affect on [their] ability to raise money."[19] The dark cloud of impropriety also put a damper on the grand opening ceremonies, so the doors were opened to the public with "little fanfare."[20]

Perhaps to provide distance from the congressional activity, the dedication was planned the following year in the fall of 1998. However, the rescheduled date became a problem when it landed right in the middle of the Monica Lewinsky scandal, which led up to the impeachment hearings. Bill Clinton was invited, but with other pressing matters, like holding on to his presidency, he could not attend. The ceremony was moved, this time to the following year. Finally, scandal or not, the date was set for Friday, March 12, 1999. It was a cold and rainy day and a small crowd of only 100 to 200 people sat on aluminum chairs for the festivities. Obviously, the weather did not help, but more likely, the recent Monica Lewinsky scandal and impeachment hearings kept the crowds at home. Joe Purvis spoke about Clinton's ties to ordinary Americans. Hitting a familiar note, Purvis said:

He didn't come from a mansion. He came from a very simple, humble home.[21]

However, the feature speaker was Bill Clinton himself who graciously made time for this small ceremony. Standing next to his brother, Roger, President Clinton reminisced:

In this house, I learned to walk and talk; I learned to pray; I learned to read; I learned to count from the playing cards my grandparents tacked up on the kitchen windows.[22]

After the ceremony, the president headed for his mother's grave to pay his respects before leaving Hope.[23]

For the first eight years of operation, the birthplace did not turn a profit and the future of the museum was bleak. Finally, in the 2003-2004 season, the home entered the black with a windfall profit of $806![24] More sizable profits continued to evade the birthplace museum, but the foundation felt if they could hang in there a few more years, they would soon benefit from the Bill Clinton Presidential Library in nearby Little Rock, scheduled to be completed in 2004. When it was completed, there was a noticeable spike in birthplace visitation, but it was still not the windfall that the foundation had hoped for and the future looked uncertain. So as so often seen in birthplace history, the Clinton Birthplace Foundation looked to Plan B, turning it over to the federal government.

Starting in the mid 2000s, efforts were made to donate the home to the National Park Service. The proposal was made and on March 8, 2006 H.R. 4192 passed in the house by an overwhelming vote of 409-12. The Senate introduced their version of the bill S. 245 on January 10, 2007, and a month later, a study was published on February 15 that supported accepting the site as a donation from the Clinton Birthplace Foundation and estimated the costs to be about a million dollars per year. Curiously, nowhere in this study was it stated that the home was not really the birthplace and there was no mention of the hospital.[25]

Two years later, as the bureaucratic journey continued, the proposal to add the Bill Clinton birthplace as a National Historic Site was bundled into HR 146, the Omnibus Public Land Management Act of 2009 under section 7002. In the midst of an economic meltdown that started three months earlier, the entire bill came with an estimated price tag of six billion dollars over five years. The bill passed the Senate on January 15, 2009 by a vote of 73-21 and then went to the House of Representatives for consideration. Arkansas Representative Mike Ross was in favor of the bill and showed strong support for all Presidential Birthplaces when he said, albeit inaccurately:

> There have only been 43 presidents, I believe all of those, whether Democrat or Republican, where their birthplace homes are still standing, I believe they should be a national historic site. And, over half of them are already.[26]

Actually there are twenty-three original birth or first homes that are still standing and only seven are National Historic Sites, but who's counting?

On March 25, 2009, the House of Representatives passed the bill with an overwhelming majority 285 to 140. A little over two months after his inauguration, Barack Obama signed into law a declaration adding 117 South Hervey Street as a National Historic Site on March 30, 2009. On December 14, 2010, the Clinton Birthplace Foundation donated the home to the federal government, officially establishing the William Jefferson Clinton Birthplace Home National Historic Site.[27]

On Saturday, April 16, 2011, Bill Clinton returned to 117 South Hervey Street for a ceremony to mark the home's designation as a National Historic Site. The Hope High School Band, the Jazz Cats, entertained the audience and also in attendance were Secretary of the Interior Ken Salazar and Arkansas Congressman Mike Ross. Before a crowd of 400 people, Clinton addressed the partisan atmosphere in Washington, D.C.:

> One thing I learned in this home was arithmetic, evidence and aspirations of ordinary people are more important than anyone's ideology.[28]

Today, a third of the visitors are from outside the U.S. and people from 159 countries have seen the famous home; by the time of this writing, over 83,000 people have visited Bill Clinton's first home. Just like Plains and Tampico before it, Hope is eagerly awaiting the crowds now that the National Park status is official.[29]

An interesting side note:

One does not need to travel to Hope to see the birthplace of President Clinton. In fact, you do not even need to travel to Arkansas or even the United States of America for that matter. In July 2000, Takeharu Shiraishi, a Japanese Tycoon, opened the doors on a nearly identical replica of the Bill Clinton birthplace home constructed at his Kanucha Bay Resort in Okinawa, Japan. Shiraishi had visited America many times and is a self-proclaimed fan of the American presidents, especially Lincoln, FDR, and Clinton. He had visited the real birthplace in the fall of 1999 and became inspired to re-create the home on the other side of the world. The following year the G-8 summit was scheduled to take place on Okinawa in July 2000. Shiraishi figured that if he built the birthplace and invited President Clinton to visit while he was in Japan, he had an excellent chance the president would accept. After returning home, he contacted Beckie Moore, executive director of the actual birthplace in Hope, to share his concept. She assisted him with the interior furnishings, leading a "10-member Japanese shopping contingent" on an antique shopping spree in Arkansas and Texas.[30] The price tag came to eighty million yen or about $730,000. When it was completed, Shiraishi flew Beckie Moore out to Japan to inspect the results in person. Reportedly, she was brought to tears by the tribute. Mr. Shiraishi did invite President Clinton to see his creation, although unfortunately the president was not able to accept, but was gracious enough to meet Mr. Shiraishi at the airport to express his gratitude.

When the replica opened, there was no charge to enter the home; however, as is Japanese custom, guests are expected to remove their shoes. The home still resides at the resort; however, since Clinton left office in 2000, visitation dropped off so the resort sought a more practical purpose for the home. It was originally transformed into a daycare center and, as of this writing, the replica is being used as a glass craft workshop for resort guests to enjoy.[31]

Visitor Information

The birthplace marker at the Brazzel-Oakcrest Funeral Home may be difficult to locate because it is at the base of the flagpole and facing the funeral home. When you are visiting, please use tact, especially if a funeral is in process. At the time of this writing, the transition to the National Park Service was still in process and the website did not yet list visitors' hours, so it is recommended to contact the site for updated information. You can also visit President Clinton's second home at 321 East 13th Street, operated by the Clinton Birthplace Foundation since they purchased it in 2005.

43.
George Walker Bush

Yale-New Haven Hospital in New Haven, Connecticut, where George Walker Bush was born.

Vital Birthplace Information

Birthplace	New Haven, Connecticut
President's birthday	July 6, 1946
Location of birth	Grace-New Haven Hospital (currently Yale-New Haven Hospital)
How long in first home	2 years
Life of the home	1866 to present
Style	Victorian Italian Villa
Still in existence	Yes
Commemoration	None
Open to the public	No
For more information	HOSPITAL: www.ynhh.org HOME: www.econ.yale.edu
Replica exists	No
Significance	Least recognized Presidential Birthplace
Closest birthplace	Theodore Roosevelt, 81 miles

Address/Directions:

HOSPITAL
Yale-New Haven Hospital
20 York Street
New Haven, Connecticut 06511

From I-95, take exit 47 to Route 34 west to Exit 2 or 3 and then follow signs, which will take you to the main entrance at 20 York Street. There are many building for the current hospital complex, but the original Grace-New Haven Hospital was located at the same site of the main entrance to the current Yale -New Haven Hospital. The delivery room was located in a brick building now on the corner.

HOME
37 Hillhouse Avenue
New Haven, Connecticut 06511

From Route 95, which runs east to west through the state, take I-91 North towards Hartford. After one mile, take Exit 3 to merge onto Trumbull Street. After .8 miles, turn right at Hillhouse Avenue (this will be your fourth light). Hillhouse is a tree-lined street, and to the left are administrative buildings for Yale University and to the right is a row of homes. In about .1 mile, 37 Hillhouse Avenue will be on your right directly across from the Yale Admissions building.

What you will find there today:

HOSPITAL
The Yale-New Haven Hospital is a working hospital. There is not a historic marker at the site to commemorate the historic birth.

HOUSE
The Yale School of Economics now occupies the former Bush residence. Despite the fact two presidents once lived in this building, there is no indication to notify passersby of its historic residents. This oversight is even more perplexing considering that both Bush presidents are also Yale alumni.

History

HOSPITAL

In 1833, the General Hospital Society of Connecticut opened its doors. The hospital contained thirteen beds and was located between Cedar Street, Howard Street, Davenport Avenue, and Congress Avenue in New Haven (today this same hospital now has 944 beds). In 1884, the hospital's name was changed to New Haven Hospital, and by that time, it was the primary teaching hospital for the Yale Medical School. This relationship was made official in 1917. Twenty-eight years later, in 1945, another affiliation, this time with Grace Hospital, also in New Haven, resulted in the name change to Grace-New Haven Hospital.[1]

In July 1946, Barbara Pierce Bush was admitted to Grace-New Haven Hospital in labor with her first child. On July 6, Dr. Margaret Tyler delivered the future President of the United States, George Walker Bush. This was a unique time to have a baby at Grace-New Haven Hospital – in 1946, the hospital was pioneering a controversial program called "rooming-in" which permitted the newborn baby to sleep in the same room with the mother. Today, this does not seem unusual, but in 1946, the concept was revolutionary. When baby Bush was born, the delivery was done in a brick building known as the Private Pavilion on the corner of Cedar Street and Davenport Avenue (now York Street). In 1954, the Private Pavilion was remodeled and renamed the William Wirt Winchester Pavilion.[2] Today, the hospital and the Yale University School of Medicine share this building and the actual birth room is now the Yale Medical School Laboratory.[3]

In 1965, the hospital was renamed to Yale-New Haven Hospital. This is the fourth name for those keeping count, and as of today, the current name.

HOME

In 1866, John S. Graves, secretary and treasurer of the New Haven Gas Company, began construction on a Victorian Italian villa on Hillhouse Avenue. Before it was completed, it was sold to Tredwell Ketcham. Tredwell gave it to his daughter, Mary Van Winker Ketcham, wife of Daniel Coit Gilman, Yale graduate and professor of geography and librarian at the Sheffield Scientific School.

This historic structure was later known as the Graves-Gilman House. In 1876, the home was purchased by George B. Farnam, M.D. It remained with the Farman family until it was sold to Yale University in 1921. For the next twenty-five years, the house was leased to Mrs. Anna W. Whitecomb. Then came

1946, a year after the end of World War II and hundreds of thousands of heroic American soldiers were returning home and many of them were enrolling in college. This caused a housing shortage on many college campuses and Yale University was no exception. One of the ways they dealt with the issue was to convert the house at 37 Hillhouse Avenue into ten two-bedroom apartments for married students.

One of those married students was George H. W. Bush, who moved into the home with his wife, Barbara Pierce Bush, in 1946. The couple had married on January 6, 1945, exactly eighteen

The first home where George Walker Bush lived in New Haven, Connecticut.

months before the birth of George Walker Bush. Several days after his birth at Grace-New Haven Hospital, he was brought home to 37 Hillhouse Avenue to live his first years.[4] In 1948, George H. W. Bush graduated and moved out of the apartment to relocate to Texas. The home remained as apartments for students until 1957 when it was converted into the Yale Department of Economics. As of this writing, the Yale Department of Economics still occupies the building.

In 1964, George Walker Bush returned to the location of his birth when he attended Yale University. He graduated in 1968 with a bachelor's degree in history. It is unknown if he visited the hospital or his first home during his four years as a student.

Preservation

Today you will not find any recognition at either the hospital or first home. There was some talk that the home may become a National Historic Landmark when he was first elected; however, this did not occur. This omission is extremely unusual. Prior to Bush, you have to go all the way back to #14, Franklin Pierce, to find an unmarked birthplace and at least the lake that submerges Pierce's birth cabin has been named in his honor. This may not be a simple oversight as the state of Connecticut may still be holding a grudge. When the former president was campaigning in 2000, his official website made no mention of his birthplace, instead he skirted the issue by stating he was "born July 1946 and grew up in Midland and Houston, Texas."[5] Like his father, he identified more with his Texas heritage than his New England roots. When asked about the significance in an interview in 2004, as George Bush was wrapping up his first term, a hospital staff member said, "I don't know how important it is."[6]

Visitor Information

If you are out to visit all of the presidential birthplaces, you may find, as I have, that once you get started, the habit can be a tough one to break. For that reason, visiting the George Bush birthplace has turned into an annual pilgrimage for me. My father-in-law rents a cottage on Cape Cod each year and generously invites the whole family up, and the drive from New Jersey on Route 95 goes right past New Haven. I never set out to stop in New Haven, but the birthplace seems to mysteriously draw me in each year. I usually stop by the hospital entrance and take a self portrait in front of the historic building. I always get a few strange looks from the visitors and the workers in their scrubs, but so far nobody has had the temerity to ask me what exactly I was doing.

After visiting the hospital and first home, make sure to have a thematic dinner at Louis Lunch, which claims to be the "birthplace of the hamburger" by having served the first one back in 1900. The restaurant is located in downtown New Haven at 261-263 Crown Street.

44.
Barack Hussein Obama

The Kapi'olani Maternity and Gynecological Hospital in Honolulu, Hawaii, birthplace of Barack Obama. *Courtesy of E. Elanie Pichay and Alvin Fejarang*

Vital Birthplace Information

Birthplace	Honolulu, Hawaii
President's birthday	August 4, 1961
Location of Birth	Kapiolani Maternity and Gynecological Hospital (currently Kapi'olani Medical Center for Women and Children)
Still in existence	Yes
How long in first home	2 years or less
Life of the home	1848 to present
Style	Ranch
Still in existence	Yes
Commemoration	None
Open to the public	No
For more information	www.kapiolani.org/women-and-children/default.aspx
Replica exists	No
Significance	First president born outside of the continental 48 states
Closest birthplace	Richard Nixon, approximately 2,500 miles

What you will find there today:

HOSPITAL

The Kapi'olani Medical Center for Women and Children is a working hospital. There is no historic marker at the birthplace.

HOME

The home is a private residence. Just like the hospital, there are no monuments or plaques to commemorate Barack Obama's first home.

Address/Directions:

HOSPITAL
Kapi'olani Medical Center for Women and Children
1319 Punahou Street
Honolulu, Hawaii 96826

HOME
6085 Kalaniana'ole Highway (Route 72), in the Kuli'ou'ou area between 'Aina Haina and Hawai'i Kai.
Honolulu, Hawaii 96821

Both the home and the hospital are located on the same stretch of road. The hospital is to the west on H1. About eight miles east is President Obama's first home. The road changes to HI-72 when you are about half way there.

History

HOSPITAL

The birthplace of Barack Obama has the shortest history of human settlement of any of the presidential birthplaces. Polynesians were the first people to colonize Hawaii in approximately 300 A.D., long after Native American Indians settled the American mainland. It was not until 1778 that a British captain, James Cook, was credited as the first European to discover the islands (it's possible the Spanish beat him to it by 200 years).[1] Over a century later, and still sixty years before Hawaii would gain its statehood, the hospital where our forty-forth president was born was built. In 1890, Queen Kapi'olani, ruler of Hawaii, was concerned about the mothers on her native island. By organizing luaus and bazaars, she was able to raise $8,000 to build a maternity hospital on the island of Oahu.[2] In 1961, at the time of Obama's birth, the hospital was called Kapi'olani Maternity and Gynecological Hospital. The facility is now known as The Kapi'olani Medical Center for Women and Children.

After his parents divorced, Barack Obama's father returned to his ancestral home in Kenya, but came back to visit Hawaii several years later. Barack Obama was still a young boy and he recalled touring Oahu with his father in his book, *Dreams from My Father*, where he saw, among other places, "the remodeled hospital where I had been born."[3] Written thirteen years before he was elected our forty-fourth president, this recollection makes an inconvenient truth for "birthers," or conspiracy theorists that doubt that Barack Obama was not born in America, claiming he was instead born in his father's home country of Kenya. Barack Obama chose to take the high road and stay above the argument, but in the spring of 2011, pressure began to mount when Donald Trump, real estate mogul and possible presidential candidate, reignited the question of the president's legitimacy and sent a team of lawyers to Hawaii to investigate the true story of the president's nativity. On April 27, 2011, President Obama succumbed to political pressure and authorized the release of his birth certificate, proving once and for all his constitutional qualifications for holding the office of President of the United States.

HOME

Conspiracy theories aside, Hawaiian newspaper announcements from 1961 cite his parents' residence at 6085 Kalaniana'ole Highway. The home is a yellow ranch home with four bedrooms built in 1948. On the property there is also a 450-square-foot bungalow, which was built five years later in 1953.[4]

In 1960, Stan and Madelyn Dunham moved from Kansas to the home in Hawaii along with their daughter, Stanley Ann Dunham, who for obvious reasons preferred to go by her middle name, Ann. She met Barack Obama Sr. and they soon married. The next year on August 4, 1961 at 7:24 p.m., they had an eight-pound, two-ounce son, Barack Hussein Obama, who would one day become the first Hawaiian-born President of the United States.[5] The next week, the local paper printed a simple birth announcement:

Mr. And Mrs. Barack H. Obama, 6085 Kalanianaole Highway, son, Aug. 4.[6]

After the birth, Barack Obama Sr. and Ann Dunham brought baby Barack Obama to Ann's parents' home. It is possible the young couple and their new son may have lived in the detached bungalow. At the time Barack Obama Sr. also had another residence at 625 11th Avenue in Kaimuki. By 1963, the Dunhams left the home and moved into an apartment at #110 1427 Alexander Street. By this time, the young couple had separated and were divorced the following year in 1964.

The current owner purchased the home in 1979. He is an architect and has made some minor changes, but "claims the place is essentially the same as it was when it was built" in 1948.[7] Given Barack Obama's meteoric rise from State Senator to United States President, it is not surprising that the current owner did not learn that he was living in a presidential birthplace until shortly before the November 2008 elections. However, if the current resident didn't realize in 2008, he would have found out in 2009 when the home value rose sharply to over one million dollars in the middle of the housing market crash![8]

Preservation

The home has been thrust into the spotlight so recently that it remains a private residence with no monument or plaque at the site. As for the hospital, when asked shortly after the 2008 election about plans to memorialize the historic building, a Kapi'olani Medical Center spokeswoman responded, "We don't have plans to do anything."[9]

While there are no plans to commemorate the birth home at 6085 Kalaniana'ole Highway, the adjacent land at 6091 Kalaniana'ole Highway may be used to serve the purpose. The 4,124 square foot parcel of land is owned by the Department of Transportation, which purchased the lot as part of an effort to widen the state highway. As of this writing, the land is overgrown with weeds and industrial machinery. The effort to convert the parcel of land to the President Barack Obama Beach Park is being led by Republican State Representative Gene Ward. Regarding the effort, Ward has said:

> We're all Americans first and then we're Republicans and then we're Democrats...It's bare, except for two big HECO transformers and a big rock. It's there just kind of growing weeds.[10]

This effort is coupled with several other initiatives to honor the first president born in Hawaii.

Visitor Information

Please remember the home is a private residence and you should respect the privacy of the current owners. Excluding four years in Indonesia from 1967 through 1971, Barack Obama spent the years from birth through high school graduation in Hawaii, and during that time, he lived at several addresses. In 1963, his family moved to Apartment 110 at 1427 Alexander Street and then again moved in 1964 to a four-bedroom home at 2234 University Avenue. After returning from Indonesia in 1971, Barack Obama lived at Apartment 1206 at 1617 South Beretania and then his family moved one more time in 1973, this time to Apartment 1008 in the same building, which is where he stayed until leaving Hawaii in 1979.[11]

Checklist

President & Location	Date Visited	Notes
#1 George Washington Westmoreland County, Virginia		
#2 John Adams Quincy, Massachusetts		
#3 Thomas Jefferson Albemarle County, Virginia		
#4 James Madison Port Conway, Virginia		
#5 James Monroe Westmoreland County, Virginia		
#6 John Quincy Adams Quincy, Massachusetts		
#7 Andrew Jackson Waxhaws, South Carolina		
#8 Martin Van Buren Kinderhook, New York		
# 9 William Henry Harrison Charles City County, Virginia		
#10 John Tyler Charles City County, Virginia		
#11 James Knox Polk Pineville, North Carolina		
#12 Zachary Taylor Barboursville, Virginia		
#13 Millard Fillmore Summerhill, New York		

President & Location	Date Visited	Notes
#14 Franklin Pierce Hillsborough, New Hampshire		
#15 James Buchanan Cove Gap, Pennsylvania		
#16 Abraham Lincoln Hodgenville, Kentucky		
#1 CSA Jefferson Finis Davis Fairview, Kentucky		
#17 Andrew Johnson Raleigh, North Carolina		
#18 Hiram Ulysses Simpson Grant Point Pleasant, Ohio		
#19 Rutherford Birchard Hayes Delaware, Ohio		
#20 James Abram Garfield Moreland Hills, Ohio		
#21 Chester Alan Arthur Fairfield, Vermont		
#22/#24 Stephen Grover Cleveland Caldwell, New Jersey		
#23 Benjamin Harrison North Bend, Ohio		
#25 William McKinley Niles, Ohio		
#26 Theodore Roosevelt New York City, New York		

President & Location	Date Visited	Notes
#27 William Howard Taft Cincinnati, Ohio		
#28 Thomas Woodrow Wilson Staunton, Virginia		
#29 Warren Gamaliel Harding Blooming Grove, Ohio		
#30 John Calvin Coolidge Plymouth Notch, Vermont		
#31 Herbert Clark Hoover West Branch, Iowa		
#32 Franklin Delano Roosevelt Hyde Park, New York		
#33 Harry S Truman Lamar, Missouri		
#34 Dwight David Eisenhower Denison, Texas		
#35 John Fitzgerald Kennedy Brookline, Massachusetts		
#36 Lyndon Baines Johnson Stonewall, Texas		
#37 Richard Milhous Nixon Yorba Linda, California		
#38 Gerald Rudolff Ford Omaha, Nebraska		

President & Location	Date Visited	Notes
#39 James Earl Carter Plains, Georgia		
#40 Ronald Wilson Reagan Tampico, Illinois		
#41 George Herbert Walker Bush Milton, Massachusetts		
#42 William Jefferson Clinton Hope, Arkansas		
#43 George Walker Bush New Haven, Connecticut		
#44 Barack Hussein Obama Honolulu, Hawaii		
#45		
#46		
#47		
#48		
#49		
#50		

End Notes

Introduction

[1] *The New York Times.* 5/25/1997. "Reliving Myth of the Presidential Log Cabin"

#1 George Washington

[1] *George Washington Birthplace National Monument Administrative History* by Seth C. Bruggeman. College of William & Mary 2006

[2] *Popes Creek Plantation Birthplace of George Washington* by Charles E. Hatch Jr. (Washington's Birthplace, Virginia: Wakefield National Memorial Association, 1979) p. 18, map p 169

[3] *Popes Creek Plantation Birthplace of George Washington* by Charles E. Hatch Jr. (Washington's Birthplace, Virginia: Wakefield National Memorial Association, 1979) p. 18, map p. 169

[4] National Park Service George Washington Birthplace National Monument

[5] *George Washington Birthplace National Monument Administrative History* by Seth C. Bruggeman, College of William & Mary 2006

[6] National Park Service, George Washington Birthplace National Monument

[7] National Park Service, George Washington Birthplace National Monument

[8] National Park Service, George Washington Birthplace National Monument

[9] National Park Service, George Washington Birthplace National Monument

[10] *The New York Times* 7/19/1931" Wakefield Washington Shrine Was Begun After Long Study"

[11] *The New York Times.* 7/19/1931. "Wakefield Washington Shrine Was Begun After Long Study"

[12] *The New York Times.* 2/18/1856. "The Birth-Place of Washington"

[13] *The New York Times.* 7/19/1931. "Wakefield Washington Shrine Was Begun After Long Study"

[14] *The New York Times.* 2/11/1894. "Of Good Old Virginia Blood"

[15] *The New York Times.* 7/19/1931. "Wakefield Washington Shrine Was Begun After Long Study"

[16] *Here, George Washington Was Born: Memory, Material Culture, and the Public History of a National Monument* by Seth C. Bruggeman. (Athens, Georgia: University of Georgia Press, 2008), p. 26

[17] *Here, George Washington Was Born: Memory, Material Culture, and the Public History of a National Monument* by Seth C. Bruggeman. (Athens, Georgia: University of Georgia Press, 2008), p. 51

[18] *Here, George Washington Was Born: Memory, Material Culture, and the Public History of a National Monument* by Seth C. Bruggeman. (Athens, Georgia: University of Georgia Press, 2008), p. 26

[19] *The New York Times.* 6/11/1879. "House of Representatives"

[20] *The New York Times.* 2/23/1881. "Congress Hard at Work"

[21] National Park Service, George Washington Birthplace National Monument

[22] *The Miami News.* 1/30/1926. "Shrine Planned At Birthplace of Washington"

[23] *Here, George Washington Was Born: Memory, Material Culture, and the Public History of a National Monument* by Seth C. Bruggeman. (Athens, Georgia: University of Georgia Press, 2008), p. 69

[24] *Here, George Washington Was Born: Memory, Material Culture, and the Public History of a National Monument* by Seth C. Bruggeman. (Athens, Georgia: University of Georgia Press, 2008), p. 67

[25] *Here, George Washington Was Born: Memory, Material Culture, and the Public History of a National Monument* by Seth C. Bruggeman. (Athens, Georgia: University of Georgia Press, 2008), p. 72

[26] *Here, George Washington Was Born: Memory, Material Culture, and the Public History of a National Monument* by Seth C. Bruggeman. (Athens, Georgia: University of Georgia Press, 2008), p. 75

[27] *The New York Times.* 7/19/1931. "Wakefield Washington Shrine Was Begun After Long Study"

[28] *The New York Times.* 1/6/1930. "Disputes Birthplace of Washington"

[29] *Here, George Washington Was Born: Memory, Material Culture, and the Public History of a National Monument* by Seth C. Bruggeman. (Athens, Georgia: University of Georgia Press, 2008), p. 97-99

[30] *The Free-Lance Star.* Fredericksburg, VA. 2/23/1966. "Washington's Birthplace Said 30 Yards off" *The New York Times.* 2/23/1966. "Washington's Birthplace"

[31] *Here, George Washington Was Born: Memory, Material Culture, and the Public History of a National Monument* by Seth C. Bruggeman. (Athens, Georgia: University of Georgia Press, 2008), p. 168

[32] National Park Service Public Use Statistics Office

#2 John Adams

[1] *The Quincy Sun.* 6/25/2009. "Birthplaces Of John And John Quincy Adams"

[2] *The Quincy Sun.* 6/25/2009. "Birthplaces Of John And John Quincy Adams"

[3] *Boston Journal.* 8/11/1895. "Where the Adams Were Born"

[4] *Adams National Historical Park* by Caroline Keinath. (Lawrenceburg, Indiana: R.L. Ruehrwein, 2008), p. 4-6

[5] National Register of Historic Places Registration Form. "John Adams Birthplace"

[6] National Register of Historic Places Registration Form. "John Adams Birthplace"

[7] *The New York Times.* 6/18/1897. "Adams Houses Restored"

[8] *The Quincy Sun.* 6/25/2009. "Birthplaces Of John And John Quincy Adams"

[9] *The Lewiston Daily Sun.* 2/13/1951. "Adams' Birthplace Damaged By Vandals"

[10] *The New York Times.* 5/12/1963. "Where John and John Quincy Adams Were Born"

[11] *The New York Times.* 7/16/1925. "Coolidge Visits Home of Adamses"

[12] *The Toledo Blade.* 6/10/1967. "Mrs. Johnson Visits Home Of Two Former Presidents"

[13] Historic Furnishings Report: The Birthplaces of Presidents John Adams and John Quincy Adams. National Park Service

[14] *The Quincy Sun.* 6/25/2009. "Birthplaces of John and John Quincy Adams"

#3 Thomas Jefferson

[1] *The New York Times.* 1/7/1962. "A New Jefferson Shrine In Virginia"

[2] *Middlesboro Daily News.* 6/22/1964. "'Arrack Punch' Give[sic]

Trouble To Forefathers"

[3]*The Sumter Daily Item.* 5/10/1961. "Jefferson's Home New Tourist Spot"

[4]*The Century* magazine. September 1887 p. 647

[5]Monticello.org. "The Jefferson Encyclopedia."

[6]*The New York Times.* 10/12/1912. "Levy for Sulzer's Place"

[7]*The New York Times.* 1/7/1962. "A New Jefferson Shrine In Virginia"

[8]Monticello.org. "The Jefferson Encyclopedia." With help from Anna Berkes, Monticello Research Librarian

[9]Monticello.org. "The Jefferson Encyclopedia."

[10]*The Free-Lance Star.* Fredericksburg, VA. 9/17/1991. "Archeologists dig Jefferson"

[11]Monticello.org. "The Jefferson Encyclopedia."

[12]*The Free-Lance Star.* Fredericksburg, VA. 9/17/1991. "Archeologists dig Jefferson"

[13]*The New York Times.* 11/7/1945. "Letters to The Times"

[14]Monticello.org. "The Jefferson Encyclopedia."

[15]Sarasota Herald-Tribune. 5/8/1955. "Steel Fingers To Seek Jefferson Birthplace"

[16]*The Free-Lance Star.* Fredericksburg, VA. 9/17/1991. "Archeologists dig Jefferson"

[17]*The New York Times.* 1/7/1962. "A New Jefferson Shrine In Virginia"

[18]Monticello.org. "The Jefferson Encyclopedia."

[19]*The New York Times.* 1/7/1962. "A New Jefferson Shrine In Virginia"

[20]*The New York Times.* 1/7/1962. "A New Jefferson Shrine In Virginia"

[21]Monticello.org. "The Jefferson Encyclopedia." With help from Anna Berkes, Monticello Research Librarian

[22]Ray Crider, Concierge at The Boar's Head Inn, Charlottesville, Virginia

[23]*The Free-Lance Star.* Fredericksburg, VA. 9/17/1991. "Archeologists dig Jefferson"

[24]Historical rankings of Presidents of the United States, Schlesinger 1948, Schlesinger 1962, Murray-Blessing 1982, *The Chicago Tribune* 1982, Siena 1982, Siena 1990, Siena 1994, Ridings-McIver 1996, Schlesinger 1996, CSPAN 1999, *Wall Street Journal* 2000, Siena 2002, *Wall Street Journal* 2005, *The New York Times*, CSPAN 2009, Siena 2010

#4 James Madison

[1]*The Free-Lance Star.* Fredericksburg, VA. 4/20/1971. "Five-unit House, Formal Gardens"

[2]*The Free Lance-Star.* Fredericksburg, VA. 1/7/2005. "Lots To Do In Winter Garden. History And Trees At Mount Sion"

[3]*The Free-Lance Star.* Fredericksburg, VA. 4/20/1971. "Five-unit House, Formal Gardens"

[4]*The Bryan Times.* 8/4/1892

[5]*Gettysburg Compiler.* 3/12/1901. "Birth Places of presidents that should be preserved as National landmarks"

[6]*The Free-Lance Star.* Fredericksburg, VA. 5/17/1929. "Caroline Chamber Wants New Bridge"

[7]*The Free-Lance Star.* Fredericksburg, VA. 10/5/1956. "Madison Birthplace Claim Signals 2 – County Dispute"

[8]*The Free-Lance Star.* Fredericksburg, VA. 5/7/1973. "Belle Grove is chosen as a landmark"

[9]*The Free-Lance Star.* Fredericksburg, VA. 5/29/1987. Mount Vernon Realty Advertisement

[10]*The Free-Lance-Star.* Fredericksburg, VA. 8/10/2003. "BELLE GROVE, BIRTHPLACE OF MADISON, IS REVIVED." Franz Haas Machinery A Company History (available on www.haasusa.com) with help from Michael Fleetwood

[11]*The Free-Lance Star.* Fredericksburg, VA House and Home. 7/25/2003. "Southern Belle"

[12]Horne's Restaurant & Gift Shop. website www.hornes.com

#5 James Monroe

[1]National Register of Historic Places Registration Form. "Monroe, James, Birthplace Updated Nomination"

[2]*Genealogies of Virginia Families from Tyler's Quarterly Historical and Genealogical Magazine.* (Baltimore, Maryland: Genealogical Publishing Company, 1981). p 704

[3]*Genealogies of Virginia Families from Tyler's Quarterly Historical and Genealogical Magazine* (Baltimore, Maryland: Genealogical Publishing Company, 1981). p 704

[4]National Register of Historic Places Registration Form. "Monroe, James, Birthplace Updated Nomination"

[5]National Register of Historic Places Registration Form. "Monroe, James, Birthplace Updated Nomination"

[6]National Register of Historic Places Registration Form. "Monroe, James, Birthplace Updated Nomination"

[7]National Register of Historic Places Registration Form. "Monroe, James, Birthplace Updated Nomination"

[8]National Register of Historic Places Registration Form. "Monroe, James, Birthplace Updated Nomination"

[9]National Register of Historic Places Registration Form. "Monroe, James, Birthplace Updated Nomination"

[10]"The Heiress of Washington City: Marcia Burnes Van Ness, 1782-1832." *Records of the Columbia Historical Society, Washington, D.C.* by Frances Carpenter Huntington (Washington, D.C.: *Columbia Historical Society,* 1971) p 80

[11]National Register of Historic Places Registration Form. "Monroe, James, Birthplace Updated Nomination"

[12]National Register of Historic Places Registration Form. "Monroe, James, Birthplace Updated Nomination"

[13]National Register of Historic Places Registration Form. "Monroe, James, Birthplace Updated Nomination"

[14]National Register of Historic Places Registration Form. "Monroe, James, Birthplace Updated Nomination"

[15]National Register of Historic Places Registration Form. "Monroe, James, Birthplace Updated Nomination"

[16]*The Free-Lance Star.* Fredericksburg, VA. 6/6/2005. "Conflicting plots"

[17]*The Reading Eagle.* 11/21/1923. "Monroe Descendants To Save His Birthplace"

[18]*The New York Times.* 11/21/1923. "Plan for Monroe Shrine"

[19]*The Free-Lance Star.* Fredericksburg, VA. 6/6/2005. "Conflicting plots"

[20]*The Free-Lance Star.* Fredericksburg, VA. 3/1/1929. "Seek To Locate Monroe Birthplace"

[21]Bill Thomas, president of the James Monroe Memorial Foundation interview 9/30/2009

[22]*The Free-Lance Star.* Fredericksburg, VA. 3/10/1937. "Appeals for the

Funds to Acquire Birthplace of James Monroe"

[23]*The New York Times.* 3/28/1937. "Drive for memorial to Monroe Is Pressed; contributions Sought in All Hemisphere"

[24]*The Free-Lance Star.* Fredericksburg, VA. 3/5/1938. "National Shrine To Monroe Closes"

[25]*The Free-Lance Star.* Fredericksburg, VA. 10/30/1951. "Two Groups of James Monroe Admirers to Go Own Ways, Birthplace Group Decides Here"

[26]*The Free-Lance Star.* Fredericksburg, VA. 5/7/1953. "Pan-American Park Envisioned At James Monroe Birthplace"

[27]*The Free-Lance Star.* Fredericksburg, VA. 5/18/1973. "Legal point ties up Monroe birthplace"

[28]National Register of Historic Places Registration Form. "Monroe, James, Birthplace Updated Nomination"

[29]*The Free-Lance Star.* Fredericksburg, VA. 11/29/1971. "Monroe birth site condition 'disgrace'"

[30]*The Free-Lance Star.* Fredericksburg, VA. 12/28/1972. "County seeks to get Monroe Birthplace"

[31]*The Free-Lance Star.* Fredericksburg, VA. 5/18/1973. "Legal point ties up Monroe birthplace"

[32]*The Free-Lance Star.* Fredericksburg, VA. 8/28/1973. "Monroe birthplace ownership assured." *The Free-Lance Star.* Fredericksburg, VA. 7/23/1974. "Monroe birth site sought. Excavation a step closer"

[33]*The Free-Lance Star.* Fredericksburg, VA. 1/25/1975. "Monroe's birthplace offer has had no U.S. response"

[34]*The Free-Lance Star.* Fredericksburg, VA. 1/25/1975. "Monroe's birthplace offer has had no U.S. response"

[35]*The Free-Lance Star.* Fredericksburg, VA. 1/22/1976. "In Westmoreland, team digs into James Monroe's past"

[36]*The Free-Lance Star.* Fredericksburg, VA. 3/17/1976. "Exposed Westmoreland home may be Monroe's birthplace"

[37]*The Free-Lance Star.* Fredericksburg, VA. 1/4/1977. "Landmarks register adds James Monroe home site"

[38]*The Free-Lance Star.* Fredericksburg, VA. 4/28/1984. "Monroe's birthplace offered to Uncle Sam"

[39]*The Free-Lance Star.* Fredericksburg, VA. 11/14/1985. "James Monroe Birthplace site may finally have found a home"

[40]*The Free-Lance Star.* Fredericksburg, VA. 2/23/1988. "Latest Monroe birthplace offer falls through in Westmoreland"

[41]*The Free-Lance Star.* Fredericksburg, VA. 2/13/2005. "Big Plan for James Monroe Birthplace"

[42]*The Free-Lance Star* Fredericksburg, VA 2/13/2005 "Big Plan for James Monroe Birthplace"

[43]Bill Thomas, president of the James Monroe Memorial Foundation interview 9/30/2009

[44]Fredricksburg.com. 7/16/2008. "A Visitors Center You Can't Visit" by Frank Delano

[45]Fredricksburg.com. 7/16/2008. "A Visitors Center You Can't Visit" by Frank Delano

[46]*The Shelton-Mason County Journal.* 12/19/2007. "New year hold promise for James Monroe Birthplace"

#6 John Quincy Adams

[1]National Register of Historic Places Registration Form. "John Quincy Adams Birthplace"

[2]*The Quincy Sun.* 6/25/2009. "Birthplaces Of John And John Quincy Adams"

[3]*The Quincy Sun.* 6/25/2009. "Birthplaces Of John And John Quincy Adams"

[4]*Boston Journal.* 8/11/1895. "Where the Adams were Born"

[5]Historic Furnishings Report: The Birthplaces of Presidents John Adams and John Quincy Adams. National Park Service

[6]*Adams National Historical Park* by Caroline Keinath (Lawrenceburg, Indiana: R.L. Ruehrwein, 2008), p 4-6

[7]*Gettysburg Compiler.* 3/12/1901. "Birth Places of presidents that should be preserved as National landmarks"

[8]National Register of Historic Places Registration Form. "John Quincy Adams Birthplace"

[9]National Register of Historic Places Registration Form. "John Quincy Adams Birthplace"

[10]*The New York Times.* 6/18/1897. "Adams Houses Restored"

[11]*The Quincy Sun.* 6/25/2009. "Birthplaces Of John And John Quincy Adams"

[12]*The Meriden Record.* 7/16/1925. "Coolidge Visitor At Ancient Quincy Predecessor's Home"

[13]*The Toledo Blade.* 6/10/1967. "Mrs. Johnson Visits Home Of Two Former Presidents"

[14]Historic Furnishings Report: The Birthplaces of Presidents John Adams and John Quincy Adams. National Park Service

[15]*The New York Times.* 5/12/1963. "Where John and John Quincy Adams Were Born"

[16]*The Quincy Sun.* 6/25/2009. "Birthplaces Of John And John Quincy Adams"

[17]*Discover Historic Quincy* Visitor Guide

#7 Andrew Jackson

[1]*Touring North Carolina's Revolutionary War Sites* by Daniel W. Barefoot (Winston-Salem, North Carolina: John F. Blair, 1998) p 145-148

[2]*The New York Times.* 9/3/1922. "Andrew Jackson, North or South Carolinian?"

[3]*The New York Times.* 9/3/1922. "Andrew Jackson, North or South Carolinian?"

[4]*New Zealand Tablet.* 12/9/1881. "Two Irish-American Presidents"

[5]*The New York Times.* 8/6/1858. "Andrew Jackson Claimed As Virginian." *A Genealogy of the Duke-Shepherd-Van Metre Family* edited by Samuel Gordon Smyth (Lancaster, Pennsylvania: Press of the New Era Printing Company, 1909) p 241

[6]*The Spartanburg Herald-Journal.* 3/15/1967. "Old Hickory's Glory Enough To Go Around." *The West Virginia Historical Magazine Quarterly.* October 1902. "Birthplace of Andrew Jackson." p 5-10

[7]*The Spartanburg Herald-Journal.* 5/2/1911. "Suggest Monument at Jackson's Birthplace"

[8]*The Rock Hill Herald* 7/1/1982 "Jackson's birthplace disputed"

[9]*Hornet's Nest The Story of Charlotte and Mecklenburg County* by LeGette Blythe and Charles Raven Brockmann (Public Library of Charlotte and Mecklenburg County, 1961)

[10]*The New York Times* 12/20/1902 "*The New York Times* Saturday Review of Books." *The New York Times* 12/27/1902 "Andrew Jackson's Birthplace"

[11]*History of Andrew Jackson, pioneer, patriot, soldier, politician, president Volume 1* by Augustus C. Buell (New York, New York: Scribner, 1904), p27

[12]*History of Andrew Jackson, pioneer, patriot, soldier, politician, president Volume 1* by Augustus C. Buell (New York, New York: Scribner, 1904), p28

[13]*The New York Times* 9/3/1922 "Andrew Jackson, North or South Carolinian?"

[14]*The New York Times* 9/3/1922 "Andrew Jackson, North or South Carolinian?"

[15]*The New York Times* 9/3/1922 "Andrew Jackson, North or South Carolinian?"

[16]*Jackson Birthplace Debated in Congress* by Louise Pettus (special thanks to the author)

[17]*The New York Times.* 8/16/1925. "Both Carolinas Claim Andrew Jackson; Congress Will Be Asked to Decide in Which State the President Was Born and End Sharp Controversy"

[18]*The Reading Beagle.* 11/4/1927. "Jackson Letter Found." *The New York Times* 11/4/1927. "Jackson Note Adds Data on Birthplace"

[19]*The New York Times.* 2/23/1929. "Congress Biography Evades Fixing Jackson Birthplace"

[20]*The New York Times.* 9/3/1922. "Andrew Jackson, North or South Carolinian?"

[21]*The Spartanburg Herald-Journal.* 5/2/1911. "Suggest Monument at Jackson's Birthplace"

[22]*The New York Times.* 9/3/1922. "Andrew Jackson, North or South Carolinian?"

[23]*Jackson Birthplace Debated in Congress* by Louise Pettus (special thanks to the author)

[24]*The Rock Hill Herald.* 5/11/1929. "Andrew Jackson." *The Rock Hill Herald.* 5/11/1929. "Unveiling of Marker to be Notable event"

[25]*Andrew Jackson Marker* by Louise Pettus (special thanks to the author)

[26]*Andrew Jackson Marker* by Louise Pettus (special thanks to the author)

[27]*The Rock Hill Herald.* 4/2/1951. "Lancaster County May Get New Park"

[28]*The Rock Hill Herald.* 12/24/1953. "Andrew Jackson was born on Lancaster Outskirts"

[29]*The Tuscaloosa News.* 3/12/1962. "Old Hickory's Birthplace: in North or South Carolina?"

[30]*Wilmington Morning Star.* 8/23/1991. "Carolinas feuding over Jackson Birthplace"

[31]*Touring North Carolina's Revolutionary War Sites* by Daniel W. Barefoot (Winston-Salem, North Carolina: John F. Blair, 1998) p145-148

[32]*Wilmington Morning Star.* 8/18/1979. "N.C. wins Jackson's birthplace"

[33]*Wilmington Morning Star.* 8/19/1983. "N.C. Calendar Filled With Activities"

[34]*Wilmington Morning Star.* 8/23/1991. "Carolinas feuding over Jackson Birthplace"

[35]*The Toledo Blade.* 8/26/1986. "Old Hickory's Birthplace A Knotty Postal problem"

[36]*The Spartanburg Herald-Journal.* 8/23/1991. "Andrew Jackson Memorial Revives Carolina Feud"

[37]*The Post and Courier.* 2/4/1992. "Tar Heel concedes Jackson born in S.C."

[38]*The Post and Courier.* 2/4/1992. "Tar Heel concedes Jackson born in S.C."

#8 Martin Van Buren

[1]*Cape Girardeau Bulletin Journal.* 11/27/1980. "Homes and Holidays linked through time"

[2]*Cape Girardeau Bulletin Journal.* 11/27/1980. "Homes and Holidays linked through time"

[3]Kinderhook Connection website

[4]*Daytona Beach Morning Journal.* 7/6/1974. "Van Buren to get Late Recognition," Martin Van Buren National Historic Site

[5]Zillow.com

[6]*The New York Times.* 6/4/1939. "Van Buren Home Copied in Jersey." *The New York Times.* 7/2/1939. "Big Building Year in Lake Resorts"

#9 William Henry Harrison

[1]*The cradle of the republic: Jamestown and James River* by Lyon Gardiner Tyler (Richmond, Virginia: The Hermitage Press, 1906) p 225 – 229

[2]*The Boston Phoenix.* 11/20/1984. "Virginia Real On Thanksgiving's Origins"

[3]*Some prominent Virginia families, Volume 2* by Louise Pecquet du Bellet, Edward Jaquelin, Martha Cary Jaquelin (Lynchburg, Virginia: J.P. Bell Company, 1907) p 380-383

[4]*The Boston Phoenix.* 11/20/1984. "Virginia Real On Thanksgiving's Origins"

[5]*The cradle of the republic: Jamestown and James River* by Lyon Gardiner Tyler (Richmond, Virginia: The Hermitage Press, 1906) p 225 – 229

[6]*The Boston Phoenix.* 11/20/1984. "Virginia Real On Thanksgiving's Origins"

[7]*The cradle of the republic: Jamestown and James River* by Lyon Gardiner Tyler (Richmond, Virginia: The Hermitage Press, 1906) p 225 – 229

[8]*The cradle of the republic: Jamestown and James River* by Lyon Gardiner Tyler (Richmond, Virginia: The Hermitage Press, 1906) p225 – 229

[9]*Washington Post.* 10/16/1987. "Their Owne Landes"

[10]*Visit Berkeley A James River Plantation* brochure

[11]National Register of Historic Places Nomination Form. "Berkeley – (Benjamin Harrison V Birthplace and Home)"

[12]National Register of Historic Places Nomination Form. "Berkeley – (Benjamin Harrison V Birthplace and Home)"

[13]*Lawrence Journal World.* 6/21/1999. "Gore goals call for big government."

[14]*The Evening Independent.* 8/8/1980. "Our National Political Conventions: Staged 'Quadrennial Blood-Lettings'?"

[15]Berkeley Plantation Tour, March 2010

[16]*1400 Days The Civil War Day By Day* by Chris Bishop, Ian Drury, and Tony Gibbons (New York, New York: Smithmark Publishers, 1990) p 88-92

[17]*The Toledo Blade.* 6/29/1969. "'Taps' Melody to be Honored With Monument"

[18]*1400 Days The Civil War Day By Day* by Chris Bishop, Ian Drury, and Tony Gibbons (New York, New York: Smithmark Publishers, 1990) p 88-92

[19]*The Rock Hill Herald.* 8/7/1995. "Berkeley Plantation now national treasure"

[20]*Boston Evening Transcript.* 10/29/1913. "Patriotic"

[21]*The Rock Hill Herald.* 8/7/1995. "Berkeley Plantation now national treasure"

[22]*The Rock Hill Herald.* 8/7/1995. "Berkeley Plantation now national treasure"

[23]*The Rock Hill Herald.* 8/7/1995. "Berkeley Plantation now national treasure"

[24]*The Toledo Blade.* 6/29/1969. "'Taps' Melody to be Honored With Monument"

[25]*The Rock Hill Herald.* 8/7/1995. "Berkeley Plantation now national treasure"

[26]*The New York Times.* 11/6/1988. "Quayle Role As Phantom Of Campaign." The *Washington Post.* 11/20/2007. "Bush Calls for More Community Service"

[27]Coinnews.net. 2/17/2009. "Harrison Presidential $1 Coins Launched in US Mint Ceremony"

[28]Berkeley Plantation Tour, March 2010

#10 John Tyler

[1]*John Tyler: The Accidental President* by Edward P. Crapol (Chapel Hill, North Carolina: The University of North Carolina Press, 2006) p 30-31

[2]*Historic Shrines of America* by John Thomson Faris (New York, New York: George H. Doran Company, 1918) p 257-262

[3]*The Letters and Times of the Tylers V1, Volume 1* by Lyon Gardiner Tyler (Richmond, Virginia: Whittet and Shepperson,1884) p 339

[4]*The Letters and Times of the Tylers V1, Volume 1* by Lyon Gardiner Tyler (Richmond, Virginia: Whittet and Shepperson,1884) p 188-190

[5]*The Letters and Times of the Tylers V1, Volume 1* by Lyon Gardiner Tyler (Richmond, Virginia: Whittet and Shepperson,1884) p 188-190

[6]*The Letters and Times of the Tylers V1, Volume 1* by Lyon Gardiner Tyler (Richmond, Virginia: Whittet and Shepperson,1884) p 188-190

[7]*The Letters and Times of the Tylers V1, Volume 1* by Lyon Gardiner Tyler (Richmond, Virginia: Whittet and Shepperson,1884) p 339

[8]*The Letters and Times of the Tylers V1, Volume 1* by Lyon Gardiner Tyler (Richmond, Virginia: Whittet and Shepperson,1884) p 339

[9]National Register of Historic Places Nomination Form. "Greenway"

[10]*The Florence (Alabama) Times Daily.* 5/31/1932. "Estate is Regained by President Tyler's Son"

[11]*The Free-Lance Star.* Fredericksburg, VA. 10/11/1933. "Tyler's Home to go under Hammer." *The New York Times.* 10/18/1933. "Tyler's birthplace auctioned"

[12]*Daily Press Newport News*, VA. 11/22/1989. "New Bill Would Ease Tax Bite Facing Heirs of Historic Places"

[13]*The Ocala Star-Banner.* 10/4/1979. "Foreigners Buy Two presidential Birthplaces"

[14]*The Ocala Star-Banner.* 10/4/1979. "Foreigners Buy Two presidential Birthplaces"

[15]*Boston Evening Transcript.* 10/29/1913. "Patriotic"

[16]*John Tyler Address Delivered before the Colonial Dames of American the State of Virginia at Greenway, Charles City County, VA on Monday October 27, 1913 at the unveiling of a memorial to Mark the birthplace of President Tyler* by Honorable George Christian of Richmond, VA. (Richmond, Virginia: Whittet and Shepperson,1913) p 6-7

[17]*The Virginia Landmarks Register* by Calder Loth, Virginia Department of Historic Resources (Charlottesville, Virginia: University Press of Virginia, 1999) p 96

#11 James Knox Polk

[1]President James K. Polk State Historic Site website and visitor information. Additional information provided by Scott Warren (Historic Site Manager II), Courtney Rounds (Site Interpreter II), Robert Dreher (Maintenance Mechanic II) and Sarah Allen (Intern, UNCC)

[2]President James K. Polk State Historic Site website and visitor information. Additional information provided by Scott Warren (Historic Site Manager II), Courtney Rounds (Site Interpreter II), Robert Dreher (Maintenance Mechanic II) and Sarah Allen (Intern, UNCC)

[3]President James K. Polk State Historic Site website and visitor information. Additional information provided by Scott Warren (Historic Site Manager II), Courtney Rounds (Site Interpreter II), Robert Dreher (Maintenance Mechanic II) and Sarah Allen (Intern, UNCC)

[4]Charlotte-Mecklenburg Historic Landmarks Commission

[5]President James K. Polk State Historic Site website and visitor information. Additional information provided by Scott Warren (Historic Site Manager II), Courtney Rounds (Site Interpreter II), Robert Dreher (Maintenance Mechanic II) and Sarah Allen (Intern, UNCC)

[6]President James K. Polk State Historic Site website and visitor information. Additional information provided by Scott Warren (Historic Site Manager II), Courtney Rounds (Site Interpreter II), Robert Dreher (Maintenance Mechanic II) and Sarah Allen (Intern, UNCC)

[7]*Literary and historical activities in North Carolina, 1900-1905* by North Carolina State Department of Archives and History, William Joseph Peale (Publications of the Historical Commission, 1907) p 526

[8]*The Knox Family a Genealogical and Biographical Sketch of the Descendens of John Knox* by Hattie S. Goodman (Richmond, Virginia: Whittet and Shepperson, 1905) p 124-125

[9]Information provided by Michael Hill, Research Branch Supervisor, NC Office of Archives and History

[10]*The Hendersonville Times-News* 6/18/1963 "Capital Square Chatter"

[11]President James K. Polk State Historic Site website and visitor information. Additional information provided by Scott Warren (Historic Site Manager II), Courtney Rounds (Site Interpreter II), Robert Dreher (Maintenance Mechanic II) and Sarah Allen (Intern, UNCC)

[12]Charlotte-Mecklenburg Historic Landmarks Commission

[13]*Rome News Tribune.* 5/21/1968. "Lady Bird presented with key to Carolina city." *The Times-News* Hendersonville, N.C. 5/18/1968. "Mrs. Johnson Speaks At Polk's Birthplace"

[14]President James K. Polk State Historic Site website and visitor information. Additional information provided by Scott Warren (Historic Site Manager II), Courtney Rounds (Site Interpreter II), Robert Dreher (Maintenance Mechanic II) and Sarah Allen (Intern, UNCC)

#12 Zachary Taylor

[1]*Zachary Taylor* by Jeremy Roberts (Minneapolis, Minnesota: Lerner Publishing Group, 2005) p 13

[2]National Register of Historic Places Nomination form. "Hare Forest Farm"

[3]*The New York Times.* 7/22/1934. "Virginians Plan Pageant"

[4]*The Free-Lance Star.* Fredericksburg, VA. 4/23/1976. "Homes relate to two presidents"

[5]*Tri-City Herald.* 3/27/1981. "Historic Place"

[6]*The Ocala Star-Banner.* 10/4/1979. "Foreigners Buy Two Presidential Birthplaces"

[7]*The Free-Lance Star.* Fredericksburg, VA. 4/20/1971. "Dolly Madison Tour In Orange"

[8]*The Free-Lance Star.* Fredericksburg, VA. 4/23/1976. "Homes relate to two presidents"

[9]*Virginia's Presidential Homes* by Patrick O'Neill (Charleston, South Carolina: Arcadia Publishing, 2010), p109

[10]*Daughters of the American Revolution Magazine, Volume 17* by The Daughters of the American Revolution p 277-278

#13 Millard Fillmore

[1]*The Remarkable Millard Fillmore: The Unbelievable Life of a Forgotten President* by George Pendle (New York, New York: Three Rivers Press, 2007)

[2]*Millard Fillmore* by Paul Finkelman (New York, New York: Times Books, 2011) p 4

[3]Fillmore Glen State Park historic marker

[4]*Berkeley Daily Gazette.* 5/14/1931. "President Fillmore's Birthplace Located"

[5]*The New York Times.* 7/5/1868

[6]*Chicago Sun-Times.* 7/13/1988. "It's time to haul out the anecdotes and trivia about veeps"

[7]*The New York Times.* 12/10/1929. "Bill Asks Memorial for Fillmore"

[8]*Berkeley Daily Gazette.* 5/14/1931. "President Fillmore's Birthplace Located"

#14 Franklin Pierce

[1]*The History of Hillsborough, New Hampshire, 1735-1921* by George Waldo Browne (Manchester, New Hampshire: Published by The Town, 1922) p 455

[2]*The History of Hillsborough, New Hampshire, 1735-1921* by George Waldo Browne (Manchester, New Hampshire: Published by The Town, 1922) p 455

[3]*The Pierce Homestead National Landmark* brochure

[4]*The Evening Journal.* 11/13/1968. "Franklin Pierce, 14th President,

Was Bowdoin Graduate"
[5]*The Pierce Homestead National Landmark* brochure
[6]*Boca Raton News.* 2/19/1984. "Few Remember the 14th President"
[7]The Franklin Pierce Bicentennial website. www.FranklinPierce.ws

#15 James Buchanan

[1]*Gettysburg Compiler.* 3/12/1901. "Birth Places of presidents that should be preserved as National landmarks"
[2]*Gettysburg Compiler.* 3/12/1901. "Birth Places of presidents that should be preserved as National landmarks"
[3]*Fulton County News.* 10/8/2009. "Buchanan Subject of Historical Society Program"
[4]*The Mercersburg Journal.* 9/19/1990. "Where there is a 'will', there is a way, eventually"
[5]*The New York Times.* 2/19/1893. "Buchanan's Birthplace"
[6]*The Mercersburg Journal.* 9/19/1990. "Where there is a 'will', there is a way, eventually"
[7]*The Pittsburgh Press.* 10/6/1907. "Monument to Buchanan." *The Reading Eagle.* 12/18/1907. "Monument Marks Buchanan's Old Home"
[8]*The History and Tradition of the James Buchanan's Birthplace Log Cabin,* A discussion paper by Dan Guzy (2011)
[9]*The Harrisburg Daily Patriot.* 2/11/1880. "The Birth-Place of James Buchanan." *Shippensburg Democratic Chronicle.* 2/13/1880. "Home In Which the Late President was Born"
[10]*Kentucky New Era.* 9/17/1953. "Cabin Recalls Early Leader"
[11]*The Harrisburg Daily Patriot.* 2/11/1880. "The Birth-Place of James Buchanan" *Shippensburg Democratic Chronicle.* 2/13/1880. "Home In Which the Late President was Born"
[12]*History of Franklin County* by Samuel Penniman Bates, Jacob Fraise Richard (Chicago, Illinois: Warner, Beers & Co., 1887) p 510
[13]*The New York Times.* 11/30/1902. "Buchanan's Birthplace in Decay." *The Reading Eagle.* 8/25/1925. "Now Negro Family Cabin, Buchanan Birthplace to become a Museum"
[14]*Hartford Courant.* 10/3/1925. "To Restore Natal Cabin of Buchanan." *The Reading Eagle.*11/23/1925. "Where Buchanan Was Born"'
[15]*The Log Cabin in America: From Pioneer Days to The Present* by Clinton Alfred Weslager (New Brunswick, New Jersey: Rutgers University Press, 1969) p285-286
[16]Deed #5020 from John M. Gelwix and Mary C. Gelwix, his wife and Frank A. Zimmerman and Florence D. Zimmerman, his wife To The Stony-Batter Antique Exchange, In. from November 4, 1925
[17]The Franklin County Historical Society – Kittochtinny research paper
[18]Deed The Stony-Batter Antique Exchange, Inc. with Arthur V. Rock from January 13, 1947
[19]*The Star and Sentinel.* 2/1/1947. "Gets Museum in Chambersburg"
[20]*Gettysburg Times.* 3/19/1947. "Lippy To Open Third Museum"
[21]*Kentucky New Era.* 9/17/1953. "Cabin Recalls Early Leader"
[22]*Gettysburg Times.* 4/29/1991. "Memorial rededicated at birthplace of James Buchanan"

#16 Abraham Lincoln

[1]Administrative History of the Abraham Lincoln Birthplace National Historic Site, ABLI-1 by Gloria Peterson, published September 20, 1968
[2]Administrative History of the Abraham Lincoln Birthplace National Historic Site, ABLI-1 by Gloria Peterson, published September 20, 1968. *The Toledo Blade.* 4/17/1913. "Wednesday, April, 9."
[3]Administrative History of the Abraham Lincoln Birthplace National Historic Site, ABLI-1 by Gloria Peterson, published September 20, 1968

[4]Administrative History of the Abraham Lincoln Birthplace National Historic Site, ABLI-1 by Gloria Peterson, published September 20, 1968
[5]Administrative History of the Abraham Lincoln Birthplace National Historic Site, ABLI-1 by Gloria Peterson, published September 20, 1968
[6]*Footprints of Abraham Lincoln: presenting many interesting facts* by Jonathan Todd Hobson (Dayton, Ohio: The Otterbein Press, 1909) p 13-16
[7]*The Weekly Guernsey Times.* 2/18/1909. "Full Address By President At Birthplac[sic] Of Lincoln"
[8]Administrative History of the Abraham Lincoln Birthplace National Historic Site, ABLI-1 by Gloria Peterson, published September 20, 1968
[9]Administrative History of the Abraham Lincoln Birthplace National Historic Site, ABLI-1 by Gloria Peterson, published September 20, 1968
[10]Administrative History of the Abraham Lincoln Birthplace National Historic Site, ABLI-1 by Gloria Peterson, published September 20, 1968
[11]*The New York Times.* 2/13/1904. "Lincoln's Birthplace for a Park"
[12]Administrative History of the Abraham Lincoln Birthplace National Historic Site, ABLI-1 by Gloria Peterson, published September 20, 1968
[13]*The New York Times.* 11/26/1901. "A.W. Dennett Bankrupt"
[14]*The Mt. Sterling Advocate.* 2/21/1906. "To Preserve the Lincoln Farm"
[15]*The New York Times.* 9/7/1895. "Abraham Lincoln's Birthplace"
[16]Administrative History of the Abraham Lincoln Birthplace National Historic Site, ABLI-1 by Gloria Peterson, published September 20, 1968
[17]*Bowling Green Daily News.* 5/23/1991. "Historian Questioning Cabin's Authenticity." *Lincoln Legends: Myths, Hoaxes, and Confabulations Associated With Our Greatest President* by Edward Steers (Lexington, Kentucky: The University Press of Kentucky, 2007)
[18]*Lincoln Legends: Myths, Hoaxes, and Confabulations Associated With Our Greatest President* by Edward Steers (Lexington, Kentucky: The University Press of Kentucky, 2007)
[19]*Official catalogue and guide book to the Pan-American Exposition* (Buffalo, New York: Charles Arhart, 1901) p 42
[20]*Boston Evening Transcript.* 4/23/1903. "The 'Lincoln Cabin' Fraud"
[21]*The Richmond Times Dispatch.* 3/29/1903. "Curious Mixup"
[22]*The New York Times.* 3/23/1903. "Lincoln and Davis Cabin." *The Reading Eagle.* 3/25/1903. "Historic Cabins mixed Up"
[23]*Boston Evening Transcript.* 4/23/1903. "The 'Lincoln Cabin' Fraud"
[24]*Lies Across America* by James W. Loewen (New York, New York: The New Press, 1999) p166-169
[25]*The New York Times.* 4/21/1899. "Abraham Lincoln's Birthplace Sold"
[26]*Boston Evening Transcript.* 6/14/1905. "Lincoln's Birthplace For Sale"
[27]*The New York Times.* 3/2/1902. "Lincoln's Birthplace"
[28]*The New York Times.* 3/9/1902. "Lincoln Homestead Saved"
[29]*The New York Times.* 11/26/1901. "A.W. Dennett Bankrupt"
[30]*Boston Evening Transcript.* 4/22/1904
[31]*Boston Evening Transcript.* 4/22/1904
[32]*The New York Times.* 1/25/1908. "Alfred W. Dennett Dead"
[33]Administrative History of the Abraham Lincoln Birthplace National Historic Site, ABLI-1 by Gloria Peterson, published September 20, 1968
[34]*Boston Evening Transcript.* 6/14/1905. "Lincoln's Birthplace For Sale"
[35]*Boston Evening Transcript.* 2/12/1909. "America's New Mecca"
[36]*Boston Evening Transcript.* 2/12/1909. "America's New Mecca." *The New York Times.* 8/29/1905. "Lincoln's Birthplace Sold"
[37]Abraham Lincoln Birthplace Memorial Building Historic Structure Report, 2001, National Park Service
[38]*The New York Times.* 1/13/1907. "A Lincoln Memorial. A Plea by Mark Twain for the Setting Apart of His Birthplace"

[39]*The New York Times.* 6/24/1907. "Sage Gift of $25,000 for Lincoln Cabin"

[40]Administrative History of the Abraham Lincoln Birthplace National Historic Site, ABLI-1 by Gloria Peterson, published September 20, 1968

[41]*The Mt. Sterling Advocate.* 2/21/1906. "To Preserve the Lincoln Farm"

[42]*The New York Times.* 2/21/1906. "Lincoln Logs in Storage"

[43]*Lies Across America* by James W. Loewen (New York, New York: The New Press, 1999) p166-169

[44]*The New York Times.* 6/1/1906. "To Show Lincoln's Birthplace"

[45]Administrative History of the Abraham Lincoln Birthplace National Historic Site, ABLI-1 by Gloria Peterson, published September 20, 1968

[46]Administrative History of the Abraham Lincoln Birthplace National Historic Site, ABLI-1 by Gloria Peterson, published September 20, 1968

[47]*The New York Times.* 2/14/1909. "Roosevelt Returns from Lincoln Farm"

[48]*Gettysburg Times.* 2/12/1909. "Lincoln Day At His Birthplace"

[49]*Gettysburg Times.* 2/12/1909. "Lincoln Day At His Birthplace"

[50]*Arizona Journal-Miner.* 2/13/1909. "Roosevelt Lays Cornerstone Memorial"

[51]*Arizona Journal-Miner.* 2/13/1909. "Roosevelt Lays Cornerstone Memorial"

[52]*The New York Times.* 5/23/1909. "Lincoln Cabin Removed"

[53]*Lies Across America* by James W. Loewen (New York, New York: The New Press, 1999) p166-169

[54]*Ithaca Chronicle.* 11/9/1911. "Lincoln Farm Now Property Of Nation"

[55]Administrative History of the Abraham Lincoln Birthplace National Historic Site, ABLI-1 by Gloria Peterson, published September 20, 1968

[56]*The Toledo Blade.* 4/17/1913. "Wednesday, April, 9"

[57]*The Evening Independent.* 9/4/1916. "Lincoln Birthplace In Kentucky Is Accepted By President Wilson"

[58]*The New York Times.* 9/5/1916. "Eulogizes Lincoln at his Birthplace"

[59]Administrative History of the Abraham Lincoln Birthplace National Historic Site, ABLI-1 by Gloria Peterson, published September 20, 1968

[60]Administrative History of the Abraham Lincoln Birthplace National Historic Site, ABLI-1 by Gloria Peterson, published September 20, 1968

[61]Administrative History of the Abraham Lincoln Birthplace National Historic Site, ABLI-1 by Gloria Peterson, published September 20, 1968

[62]Administrative History of the Abraham Lincoln Birthplace National Historic Site, ABLI-1 by Gloria Peterson, published September 20, 1968

[63]Administrative History of the Abraham Lincoln Birthplace National Historic Site, ABLI-1 by Gloria Peterson, published September 20, 1968

[64]*The New York Times.* 12/22/1923. "Lloyd George Goes To Lincoln Cabin"

[65]*The New York Times.* 6/15/1936. "Visits Lincoln Cabin"

[66]*Lewiston Morning Tribune.* 4/24/1954. "President Eisenhower Asserts Indochina Is Testing Ground Between Slavery And Freedom"

[67]*The Rock Hill Herald.* 2/11/1921. "Three Places Claim Honor Being Birthplace Lincoln"

[68]*The Tarheel Lincoln* by Jerry Goodnight (Hickory, North Carolina: Tarheel Press, 2003)

[69]The Forbes House Museum website. www.forbeshousemuseum.org

[70]*The New York Times.* 3/9/1930. "Abraham Lincoln"

[71]*The Chicago Tribune.* 2/4/1959. "GI's in Germany Build Lincoln Cabin Replica"

[72]Consulate general of the United States Frankfurt Germany website "History of the Amerika Haus"

[73]*The New York Times.* 12/2/1987. "The Toy Industry; Under the Tree, in Christmas Past"

[74]National Park Service Public Use Statistics Office

#1 Jefferson Finis Davis

[1]*The Pittsburgh Press.* 11/1/1903. "Jefferson Davis' Youth," *The Chicago Tribune.* 8/7/2005. "Kentucky remembers native son Jefferson Davis"

[2]*Weekly Kentucky New Era.* 5/27/1903. "By Private Marks 'Squire Brewer Could Identify Davis Cabin Logs," *The Register of the Kentucky Historical Society, Volume 7* by Kentucky Historical Society (Frankfort, Kentucky: The Globe Printing Company,1909) p 39-42

[3]*Proceedings of the Mississippi Valley Historical Association, Volume 9* by Mississippi Valley Historical Association (Cedar Rapids, Iowa: The Torch Press,1919) p 156-157

[4]*Miami Daily News and Metropolis.* 6/14/1924. "Southern Hopes Splendidly Realized in Dedication of Imposing Shaft In Memory of Jefferson Davis, Confederate Statesman, at Fairview, Kentucky"

[5]*Kentucky New Era.* 6/4/1900. "Anniversary of Jefferson Davis' Birth Observed With Fitting Ceremonies"

[6]*Kentucky New Era* 6/4/1900. "Anniversary of Jefferson Davis' Birth Observed With Fitting Ceremonies"

[7]*The New York Times.* 11/17/1886. "Jefferson Davis Growing Old"

[8]*The Register of the Kentucky Historical Society, Volume 7* by Kentucky Historical Society (Frankfort, Kentucky: The Globe Printing Company,1909) p 39-42

[9]*Miami Daily News and Metropolis.* 6/14/1924. "Southern Hopes Splendidly Realized in Dedication of Imposing Shaft In Memory of Jefferson Davis, Confederate Statesman, at Fairview, Kentucky"

[10]*The New York Times.* 6/4/1908

[11]*Jefferson Davis: Private Letters, 1823-1889 by Jefferson Davis*, edited by Hudson Strode (New York, New York: Harcourt, Brace & World,1966) p 544

[12]Weekly *Kentucky New Era.* 5/27/1903. "By Private Marks' Squire Brewer Could identify Davis Cabin Logs"

[13]*Bowling Green Daily News.* 5/23/1991. "Historian Questioning Cabin's Authenticity"

[14]*Official catalogue and guide book to the Pan-American Exposition* (Buffalo, New York: Charles Arhart, 1901) p 42

[15]*The Richmond Times. Dispatch* 3/29/1903. "Curious Mixup"

[16]*The New York Times.* 3/23/1903. "Lincoln and Davis Cabin"

[17]*Lies Across America* by James W. Loewen (New York, New York: The New Press, 1999) p166-169

[18]*Report Of The Monumental Committee Of The United Confederate Veterans* (Louisiana, New Orleans: Press of Schumert & Warfield, Ltd., 1910)

[19]*Todd County, Kentucky, Family History, Volume 1* (Paducah, Kentucky: Turner Publishing Company, 1995), p 69

[20]*The Pittsburgh Press.* 11/1/1903. "Jefferson Davis' Youth"

[21]*Miami Daily News and Metropolis.* 6/14/1924. "Southern Hopes Splendidly Realized in Dedication of Imposing Shaft In Memory of Jefferson Davis, Confederate Statesman, at Fairview, Kentucky." Kentucky State Parks, Jefferson Davis State Historic Site

[22]*Miami Daily News and Metropolis.* 6/14/1924. "Southern Hopes Splendidly Realized in Dedication of Imposing Shaft In Memory of Jefferson Davis, Confederate Statesman, at Fairview, Kentucky." *The New York Times.* 6/4/1909. "Dedicate Davis Park"

[23]*The New York Times.* 6/8/1924. "Dedicate Memorial To Jefferson Davis"

[24]*Weekly Kentucky New Era.* 5/27/1903. "By Private Marks' Squire Brewer Could identify Davis Cabin Logs"

[25]*The New York Times.* 6/8/1924. "Dedicate Memorial To Jefferson Davis"

[26]*The Lewiston Daily Sun.* 8/16/1921. "Monument To Jefferson Davis Nearly Completed"

[27]*The New York Times.* 8/28/1921. "To Finish Davis Obelisk"

[28]*The San Jose California Evening News.* 9/17/1921. "Jeff Davis Memorial Nearing Completion"

[29]*The New York Times.* 8/28/1921. "To Finish Davis Obelisk"

[30]*The Rock Hill Herald.* 11/2/1922. "Jefferson Davis Monument –

Present Height"

31*Kentucky New Era.* 11/20/1974. "Davis Monument is Tribute to Confederacy's President"

32*Jefferson Davis Gets his Citizenship Back* by Robert Penn Warren (Lexington, Kentucky: University Press of Kentucky Press, 1980) p .95

33*Miami Daily News and Metropolis.* 6/14/1924. "Southern Hopes Splendidly Realized in Dedication of Imposing Shaft In Memory of Jefferson Davis, Confederate Statesman, at Fairview, Kentucky"

34*Miami Daily News and Metropolis.* 6/3/1924. "Will Dedicate Shaft To Davis"

35*Weekly Kentucky New Era.* 5/27/1903. "By Private Marks' Squire Brewer Could identify Davis Cabin Logs"

36*Kentucky New Era.* 6/27/1924. "Reproduction of Davis Home Park At Fairview"

37*The Spartanburg Herald-Journal.* 8/4/1922. "Monument to Jefferson Davis"

38*Jefferson Davis Gets his Citizenship Back* by Robert Penn Warren (Lexington, Kentucky: University Press of Kentucky Press, 1980) p 95

39*The Cape Girardeau Southeast Missourian.* 5/7/1963. "Shrine To Civil War Leaders"

40*The Fort Scott Tribune.* 4/23/1984. "Who gave the Jefferson Davis Monument in Fairview, Kentucky a Face Lift? Mind-Continental Restoration Co. Of Fort Scott"

41FoxNews.com. 2/23/2008. "Remember Jefferson Davis? Many Say Forget It"

42*The Pittsburgh Press.* 11/1/1903. "Jefferson Davis' Youth"

43*Miami Daily News and Metropolis.* 6/14/1924. "Southern Hopes Splendidly Realized in Dedication of Imposing Shaft In Memory of Jefferson Davis, Confederate Statesman, at Fairview, Kentucky"

44*Park City Daily News.* 11/26/2005. "Kentucky's heritage crosses north, south"

#17 Andrew Johnson

1*Andrew Johnson A Biography* by Hans Louis Trefousse (Newton, Connecticut: W. W. Norton & Company, 1997) p 17

2*Historical Raleigh* by Moses Amis (Raleigh, North Carolina: Commercial Printing Company, 1913), p 105

3*A Mountaineer in Motion: The Memoir of Dr. Abraham Jobe, 1817-1906* by David C. Hsiung (Knoxville, Tennessee: University Tennessee Press, 2009) p87

4*Historical Raleigh from its foundation in 1792* by Moses Neal Amis (Raleigh, North Carolina: 1902)

5*The New York Times.* 5/10/1901. "Andrew Johnson's Home"

6*The Evening Post*, Volume CXXV, Issue 48. 2/26/1938. "The Roving Home of a President"

7*Berkeley Daily Gazette.* 10/9/1930. "Former President's Home is Restored"

8*The New York Times.* 11/7/1937. "Johnson's Home Moved"

9*Christian Science Monitor.* 7/5/1940. "Andrew Johnson's Home Moved Again"

10*The Evening Post*, Volume CXXV, Issue 48. 2/26/1938. "The Roving Home Of A President"

11*The Evening Post*, Volume CXXV, Issue 48. 2/26/1938. "The Roving Home Of A President"

12*The New York Times.* 6/16/1974. "A Peripatetic Presidential Pad"

13Andrew Johnson National Historic Site Administrative History by Cameron Binkley, 2001

#18 Hiram Ulysses Simpson Grant

1*The Cincinnati Enquirer.* 4/15/2011. "Grant is Clermont's greatest hero"

2*The True Story of U S Grant the American Soldier: Told for Boys and Girls* by Elbridge S. Brooks (Boston Massachusetts: Lothrop Publishing Company, 1897) p 17

3*The Cincinnati Enquirer.* 4/15/2011. "Grant is Clermont's greatest hero"

4*Personal Memoirs of U.S. Grant* by Hiram Ulysses Grant (Mineloa, New York: Dover, 1995), p 3

5*Harper's Weekly.* 11/25/1865

6*The New York Times.* 8/16/1885. "Gen. Grant's Birthplace"

7*The Numismatist Volume XXXV* (Federalsburg, Maryland: The American Numismatic Association, 1922) p 126, *Bush Advocate*, Volume IX, Issue 787, page 6, 6/3/1893 "The World's Fair."

8*Ohio Archeological and Historical Quarterly, Volume 31* by Ohio State Archaeological and Historical Society (Columbus, Ohio: A.H. Smythe, January 1922) p289, *The New York Times* 9/5/1896 "US Grant's Cottage Dedicated"

9*The True Story of U S Grant the American Soldier: Told for Boys and Girls* by Elbridge S. Brooks (Boston Massachusetts: Lothrop Publishing Company, 1897) p17

10*Ohio Archeological and Historical Quarterly, Volume 31* by Ohio State Archaeological and Historical Society (Columbus, Ohio: A.H. Smythe, January 1922) p 289. *The New York Times.* 9/5/1896. "US Grant's Cottage Dedicated"

11LaVon Shook, Official Ohio State Fair Historian interview and personal tour at the Ohio State Fairgrounds

12LaVon Shook, Official Ohio State Fair Historian interview and personal tour at the Ohio State Fairgrounds

13*The New York Times.* 10/3/1907. "Tables to Grant Dedicated"

14*Ohio Historical Society Timeline* publication v. 23 n. 2, April/June 2006. p 21

15*The Numismatist Volume XXXV* (Federalsburg, Maryland: The American Numismatic Association, 1922) p 126

16*The Miami News.* 4/26/1922. "Grant's Birthplace little changed in last ten years"

17*The New York Times.* 8/21/1926. "Grant's Birthplace Burns." *The New York Times.* 8/29/1926. "Grant Cabin Not Burned"

18*The New York Times.* 10/30/1927. "U.S. Grant Cabin and Bridge Dedicated at Point Pleasant"

19*The New York Times.* 8/24/1930. "Legions of The G.A.R. Are Gathering In Ohio"

20*The New York Times.* 7/27/1930. "General Grant's Birthplace"

21Ohio Memory Project. www.ohiomemory.org

22Ohio Historical Society *Timeline* publication v. 23 n. 2, April/June 2006. p 21

23Ohio Memory Project www.ohiomemory.org, *The Cape Girardeau Southeast Missourian* 10/5/1936 "Grant's Cabin Restored"

24LaVon Shook, Official Ohio State Fair Historian interview and personal tour at the Ohio State Fairgrounds

25*The Toledo Blade.* 4/6/1986. "Preservations Say U.S. Grant Birthplace is Deteriorating"

26*The Toledo Blade.* 9/23/1990. "Grant's neighbors tire of the potty calls"

27*The Toledo Blade.* 6/5/1994. "U.S. Grant's Ohio birthplace gets little respect"

28*The Cincinnati Enquirer.* 10/16/1998. "Grant birthplace celebrates designation to National Register"

#19 Rutherford Birchard Hayes

1City of Delaware, Ohio History

2*History of Delaware County and Ohio* by William Henry Perrin (Chicago, Illinois: O.L. Baskin & Co., 1882) p 313

3*The Birthplace of Rutherford Birchard Hayes Delaware, Ohio* compiled by Anna C. Smith Pabst, 1972 and researched by Sandy Wicker, Librarian from the Delaware County Historical Society

4*Clinton Mirror.* 8/13/1910. "Events Here and There"

5*The Daughters of the American Revolution* Magazine May 1963, Special thanks to Sandy Wicker, Librarian from the Delaware County Historical Society

#20 James Abram Garfield

1*James A. Garfield* by Ira M. Rutkow (New York, New York: Times

Books, 2006) p 4

[2]Village of Moreland Hills with special thanks to Katie Martin

[3]*The Life Speeches and Public Services of Gen. James A. Garfield Of Ohio* by Russell H. Conwell (Boston, Massachusetts: Russell H. Conwell & Co., 1880) p 40-46

[4]Village of Moreland Hills information provided by Katie Martin

[5]*The New York Times.* 6/20/1880. "Garfield Honored at Home"

[6]*The Milwaukee Journal.* 11/19/1931. "Native Town Pays Honors To Garfield On Birth Centennial"

[7]*Cape Girardeau Bulletin Journal.* 11/27/1980. "Homes And Holidays Linked Through Time."

[8]Village of Moreland Hills information provided by Katie Martin

#21 Chester Alan Arthur

[1]Chester A. Arthur State Historic Site website. www.historicvermont.org/sites/html/arthur.html

[2]Chester A. Arthur State Historic Site website. www.historicvermont.org/sites/html/arthur.html

[3]*The New York Times.* 11/20/1886. "Sorrow In His Native State"

[4]*Genealogical And Family History Of The State Of Vermont* edited by Hiram Carleton (New York, New York: The Lewis Publishing Company, 1903) p522

[5]*The New York Times.* 12/22/1880. "Material For A Democratic Lie"

[6]*Associated Press.* 8/17/2009. "Chester Arthur Rumor still lingers in Vermont"

[7]*How a British Subject Became President of the United States* by Arthur Hinman (New York, New York: 1884)

[8]*Associated Press.* 8/17/2009. "Chester Arthur Rumor still lingers in Vermont"

[9]*The Granby Leader-Mall.* 10/7/1937. "A Canadian Born U.S. President?"

[10]*Boston Evening Transcript.* 8/20/1903. "Appropriate Exercises Held at Fairfield, VT." The Clinton Morning Age 8/21/1903. "Monument to Arthur Dedicated"

[11]*Boston Evening Transcript.* 8/20/1903. "Appropriate Exercises Held at Fairfield, VT." *The Clinton Morning Age.* 8/21/1903. "Monument to Arthur Dedicated"

[12]Chester A. Arthur State Historic Site website. www.historicvermont.org/sites/html/arthur.html

#22 and #24 Stephen Grover Cleveland

[1]The First Presbyterian Church at Caldwell history website www.firstprescaldwell.org

[2]*Historic Shrines of America* by John Thomson Faris (New York, New York: George H. Doran Company, 1918) p 119-122

[3]The First Presbyterian Church at Caldwell history website www.firstprescaldwell.org

[4]The First Presbyterian Church at Caldwell history website www.firstprescaldwell.org

[5]The First Presbyterian Church at Caldwell history website www.firstprescaldwell.org

[6]*The Bryan Times.* 7/24/1884. "Cleveland's Birthplace"

[7]*The Grover Cleveland Birthplace State Historic Site* brochure

[8]*The New York Times.* 4/30/1907. "Cleveland's birthplace endangered"

[9]*The New York Times.* 2/25/1934. "New Jersey to Get Historic Dwelling"

[10]*The New York Times.* 4/30/1907. "Cleveland's birthplace endangered"

[11]*The New York Times.* 3/19/1913. "Old Cleveland home is taken for nation"

[12]*The New York Times.* 2/22/1913. "$18000 Fund To Buy Cleveland's Home"

[13]*The New York Times.* 2/22/1913. "$18000 Fund To Buy Cleveland's Home"

[14]*The New York Times.* 3/19/1913. "Old Cleveland home is taken for nation"

[15]*The New York Times.* 3/14/1913. "Wilson. Praises Cleveland"

[16]*The New York Times.* 3/9/1913. "T.R. praises Cleveland"

[17]*The New York Times.* 3/16/1914. "Meet to Honor Cleveland"

[18]*The New York Times.* 3/28/1916. "Aids Cleveland Memorial"

[19]*The New York Times.* 10/8/1916. "Cleveland Home Visited By Hughes"

[20]*The New York Times.* 9/16/1928. "Parade in Newark will greet Hoover"

[21]*The New York Times.* 3/16/1933. "Delay Action on Shrine"

[22]*The New York Times.* 2/13/1934. "Moore Names Board for Cleveland Home"

#23 Benjamin Harrison

[1]*Historical Collections of Ohio, Vol. I* by Henry Howe (Cincinnati, Ohio: C.J. Krihbiel & Co., Printers and Binders, 1902), p746

[2]*Historical Collections of Ohio, Vol. I* by Henry Howe (Cincinnati, Ohio: C.J. Krihbiel & Co., Printers and Binders, 1902), p748

[3]*The New York Times.* 7/29/1858. "Burning of General Harrison's Residence at North Bend – The Famous "Log Cabin"

[4]*The New York Times.* 7/29/1858. "Burning of General Harrison's Residence at North Bend – The Famous "Log Cabin"

[5]*Presidents Birthplaces, Homes and Burial Sites* by Rachel M. Kochmann (Osage, Minnesota: Osage Publishing, 1999) p 93

[6]*Youngstown Vindicator.* 10/10/1976. "Ohio Town Honors Harrison"

[7]Village of North Bend official website. www.northbendohio.org

#25 William McKinley

[1]William McKinley Birthplace Home and Research Center, information provided by Director Patrick Finan and volunteer Bill Jones

[2]William McKinley Birthplace Home and Research Center, information provided by Director Patrick Finan and volunteer Bill Jones

[3]William McKinley Birthplace Home and Research Center, information provided by Director Patrick Finan and volunteer Bill Jones

[4]William McKinley Birthplace Home and Research Center, information provided by Director Patrick Finan and volunteer Bill Jones

[5]Niles Historical Society website. www.nileshistoricalsociety.org

[6]William McKinley Birthplace Home and Research Center, information provided by Director Patrick Finan and volunteer Bill Jones

[7]William McKinley Birthplace Home and Research Center, information provided by Director Patrick Finan and volunteer Bill Jones

[8]Harris.com Company History. www.harris.com/company-history.html

[9]*The Buffalo News.* 8/1/2010. "Last of the trolley parks"

[10]*Mansfield Daily Shield.* 11/28/1909. "BUYS McKinley's BIRTHPLACE"

[11]*Mansfield Daily Shield.* 11/28/1909. "BUYS McKinley's BIRTHPLACE"

[12]William McKinley Birthplace Home and Research Center, information provided by Director Patrick Finan and volunteer Bill Jones

[13]*The Sunday Vindicator.* 11/28/1909. "McKinley's Birthplace a Neglected Ruin"

[14]Niles Historical Society website. www.nileshistoricalsociety.org

[15]William McKinley Birthplace Home and Research Center, information provided by Director Patrick Finan and volunteer Bill Jones

[16]William McKinley Birthplace Home and Research Center, information provided by Director Patrick Finan and volunteer Bill Jones

[17]*The New York Times.* 6/28/1914. "Want $100,000 For McKinley Memorial at his Birthplace"

[18]*The New York Times.* 1/171915. "New York Architects Win Award for McKinley Memorial"

[19]*The Evening Independent.* 10/5/1917. "M'Kinley's Birthplace Is Marked by Memorial"

[20]William McKinley Birthplace Home and Research Center, information provided by Director Patrick Finan and volunteer Bill Jones

[21]*Vindicator Correspondent.* 1/30/2006. "William McKinley's 163rd Birthday Noted"

[22]*The Evening Independent.* 10/5/1917. "M'Kinley's Birthplace Is Marked by Memorial"
[23]*Cabins, Cottages & Mansions: Homes of the Presidents of the United States* by Nancy D. Meyers Benbow and Christopher H. Benbow (Gettysburg, Pennsylvania: Thomas Publications,1993) p 108
[24]William McKinley Birthplace Home and Research Center, information provided by Director Patrick Finan and volunteer Bill Jones
[25]William McKinley Birthplace Home and Research Center, information provided by Director Patrick Finan and volunteer Bill Jones
[26]*Vindicator Correspondent.* 1/23/2002. "Niles McKinley research center groundbreaking cancelled"
[27]*The Bryan Times.* 5/3/2003. "Replica of McKinley home dedicated"

#26 Theodore Roosevelt

[1]Theodore Roosevelt Birthplace National Historic Site
[2]*The New York Times.* 10/21/1904. "Roosevelt Birthplace For Republican Meeting"
[3]*The New York Times.* 10/21/1904. "Roosevelt Birthplace For Republican Meeting"
[4]*The New York Times.* 10/21/1904. "Roosevelt Birthplace For Republican Meeting"
[5]*The New York Times.* 10/28/1905. "President's birthday Hailed at Birthplace"
[6]*The New York Times.* 12/24/1905. "Roosevelt Home Club Going To Investigate"
[7]*The New York Times.* 8/10/1906. "To Sell Roosevelt House"
[8]*The New York Times.* 1/16/1907. "End of Roosevelt Club"
[9]*The Evening Independent.* 11/24/1916. "Fail to Save Roosevelt Birthplace in New York"
[10]*The New York Times.* 10/6/1919. "General Wood to Speak"
[11]*The New York Times.* 10/6/1919. "General Wood to Speak"
[12]*The New York Times.* 1/3/1921. "To Mark Roosevelt Home"
[13]*The New York Times.* 4/25/1921. "Wants a Roosevelt Nation"
[14]*The New York Times.* 7/24/1921. "For Roosevelt's Birthplace"
[15]*The New York Times.* 3/22/1922. "Aid For Roosevelt Memorial House"
[16]*The New York Times.* 10/28/1919. "Nation in Tribute on Roosevelt Day"
[17]*The New York Times.* 4/24/1939. "Bridge To Assist Roosevelt House"
[18]*The New York Times.* 10/28/1923. "Roosevelt House Becomes A Shrine"
[19]*The New York Times.* 10/28/1923. "Roosevelt House Becomes A Shrine"
[20]*The New York Times.* 10/28/1923. "Roosevelt House Becomes A Shrine"
[21]*The New York Times.* 4/1/1929. "Roosevelt Memorial Soon To Be Erected"
[22]National Park Service Public Use Statistics Office
[23]Eisenberg's Sandwich Shop website. www.eisenbergsnyc.com

#27 William Howard Taft

[1]William Howard Taft National Historic Site Administrative History, National Park Service
[2]William Howard Taft National Historic Site Administrative History, National Park Service
[3]William Howard Taft National Historic Site Administrative History, National Park Service
[4]William Howard Taft National Historic Site Administrative History, National Park Service
[5]William Howard Taft National Historic Site Administrative History, National Park Service
[6]William Howard Taft National Historic Site Administrative History, National Park Service
[7]William Howard Taft National Historic Site Administrative History, National Park Service
[8]William Howard Taft National Historic Site Administrative History, National Park Service
[9]William Howard Taft National Historic Site Administrative History, National Park Service
[10]William Howard Taft National Historic Site Administrative History, National Park Service
[11]William Howard Taft National Historic Site Administrative History, National Park Service
[12]William Howard Taft National Historic Site Administrative History, National Park Service
[13]*The New York Times.* 6/25/1961. "Taft Data Sought"
[14]*The New York Times.* 7/15/1961. "Taft Museum Gains"
[15]William Howard Taft National Historic Site Administrative History, National Park Service
[16]*The Toledo Blade.* 12/3/1969. "Nixon Signs Bill Creating New Shrines"
[17]William Howard Taft National Historic Site Administrative History, National Park Service
[18]William Howard Taft National Historic Site Administrative History, National Park Service
[19]William Howard Taft National Historic Site Administrative History, National Park Service
[20]William Howard Taft National Historic Site Administrative History, National Park Service
[21]*The New York Times.* 9/22/1988. "The Home President Knew as a Boy"
[22]William Howard Taft National Historic Site Administrative History, National Park Service
[23]*The New York Times.* 9/22/1988. "The Home President Knew as a Boy"
[24]National Park Service Public Use Statistics Office

#28 Thomas Woodrow Wilson

[1]*Daughters of the American Revolution Magazine: Volume 8* (Washington, D.C.: National Society D.A.R., 1896) p339
[2]The Woodrow Wilson Presidential Library and website. "The Manse." www.woodrowwilson.org
[3]The Woodrow Wilson Presidential Library and website. "The Manse." www.woodrowwilson.org
[4]The Woodrow Wilson Presidential Library and website. "The Manse." www.woodrowwilson.org
[5]*Woodrow Wilson: A Biography* by August Heckscher (Newtown, Connecticut: American Political Biography Press, 2007), p10
[6]The Woodrow Wilson Presidential Library and website "The Manse" www.woodrowwilson.org
[7]The Woodrow Wilson Presidential Library and website. "The Manse." www.woodrowwilson.org
[8]*The New York Times.* 12/26/1912. "Staunton Ready for Wilson"
[9]*The Evening Independent.* 12/27/1912. "Big Camp Fires Welcome Wilson"
[10]*The New York Times.* 12/26/1912. "Staunton Ready for Wilson"
[11]*The News and Courier.* 7/5/1936. "Last Occupants of Woodrow Wilson Birthplace were South Carolinians"
[12]*The New York Times.* 2/3/1925. "College Seeks to Buy Manse in Which Wilson Was Born"
[13]*The Reading Eagle.* 10/7/1925. "To Buy Wilson Home As Memorial To President"
[14]*The Woodrow Wilson Presidential Library And Museum* (Staunton, Virginia: The Woodrow Wilson Presidential Library Foundation, 2009), p 20-21, *The Free-Lance-Star.* Fredericksburg, VA. 6/18/1929. "Shrine In Staunton To Honor Wilson"
[15]*The New York Times.* 6/28/1938. "Wilson's Old Home Will Be A Shrine"
[16]*Time* magazine. 7/11/1938. "National Affairs: The Manse"
[17]"The Woodrow Wilson Presidential Library And Museum" (The Woodrow Wilson Presidential Library Foundation, 2009), p 20-21.

Christian Science Monitor. 6/19/1940 ."Woodrow Wilson Home Is Restoration Project"

[18]*St. Petersburg Times.* 4/6/1941. "Wilson Birthplace to be Dedicated in Staunton May 4"

[19]*The New York Times.* 9/8/1944. "Mr. Wilson's Birthplace"

[20]*St. Petersburg Times.* 9/8/1944. "Money for Wilson Home Sought"

[21]*The New York Times.* 3/29/1956. "Fund Drive Set Up for Wilson Shrine"

[22]*The New York Times.* 12/30/1959. "Mrs. Wilson Gets Cake"

[23]*The New York Times.* 10/17/1960. "Discreet Political Strategy"

[24]*The Toledo Blade.* 10/28/1960. "President Visit's Wilson Birthplace"

[25]WHSV Amy Kehn 2/7/2005. "President's Birthplace gets a boost"

#29 Warren Gamaliel Harding

[1]*The Shadow of Blooming Grove: Warren G. Harding in His Times* by Francis Russell (New York, New York: McGraw-Hill, 1968) p 17-36

[2]*The Shadow of Blooming Grove: Warren G. Harding in His Times* by Francis Russell (New York, New York: McGraw-Hill, 1968) p 17-36

[3]*The Shadow of Blooming Grove: Warren G. Harding in His Times* by Francis Russell (New York, New York: McGraw-Hill, 1968) p 17-36

[4]*The Shadow of Blooming Grove: Warren G. Harding in His Times* by Francis Russell (New York, New York: McGraw-Hill, 1968) p 17-36

[5]*The New York Times.* 12/12/1954. "Nephews Selling Harding' Farm"

[6]*The New York Times.* 4/5/1923. "Harding Buys His Birthplace, Home of Barefoot Boyhood." *The Evening Independent.* 4/6/1923. "Harding Buys Home to Use after he Retires"

[7]*The Shadow of Blooming Grove: Warren G. Harding in His Times* by Francis Russell (New York, New York: McGraw-Hill, 1968) p554

[8]*The Evening Independent.* 4/6/1923. "Harding Buys Home to Use after he Retires"

[9]*Time* magazine. 12/20/1954. "People, Dec 20, 1954"

[10]*The Shadow of Blooming Grove: Warren G. Harding in His Times* by Francis Russell (New York, New York: McGraw-Hill, 1968) p659, *The Toledo Blade* 11/29/1963 "Plaque To Mark Harding Birthplace"

[11]*The Dessert News.* 8/5/1977. "Scandalous Presidency was among the worst"

#30 John Calvin Coolidge

[1]*The Day.* 9/19/1981. "The Vermont memorial to Coolidge"

[2]President Calvin Coolidge State Historic Site www.historicvermont.org/coolidge/coolidge.html

[3]President Calvin Coolidge State Historic Site www.historicvermont.org/coolidge/coolidge.html

[4]*The New York Times.* 2/15/1925. "President's father thinks of attending inauguration"

[5]President Calvin Coolidge State Historic Site www.historicvermont.org/coolidge/coolidge.html

[6]*The New York Times.* 4/24/1924. "Home Town Boosts Coolidge As Farmer"

[7]*The Ocala Star-Banner.* 6/23/1965. "Birthplace of Herbert Hoover Named Historic Site"

[8]*The New York Times.* 10/12/1969. "Thrifty Vermont Plans Repair Job In Coolidge Style"

#31 Herbert Clark Hoover

[1]Herbert Hoover The Hoover Houses and Community Structures by Edwin C. Bearss, Historic Structures Report, National Park Service, published November 30, 1971

[2]Herbert Hoover The Hoover Houses and Community Structures by Edwin C. Bearss, Historic Structures Report, National Park Service, published November 30, 1971

[3]Herbert Hoover The Hoover Houses and Community Structures by Edwin C. Bearss, Historic Structures Report, National Park Service, published November 30, 1971

[4]Herbert Hoover The Hoover Houses and Community Structures by Edwin C. Bearss, Historic Structures Report, National Park Service, published November 30, 1971

[5]Herbert Hoover The Hoover Houses and Community Structures by Edwin C. Bearss, Historic Structures Report, National Park Service, published November 30, 1971

[6]Herbert Hoover The Hoover Houses and Community Structures by Edwin C. Bearss, Historic Structures Report, National Park Service, published November 30, 1971

[7]Herbert Hoover The Hoover Houses and Community Structures by Edwin C. Bearss, Historic Structures Report, National Park Service, published November 30, 1971

[8]Herbert Hoover The Hoover Houses and Community Structures by Edwin C. Bearss, Historic Structures Report, National Park Service, published November 30, 1971

[9]Herbert Hoover The Hoover Houses and Community Structures by Edwin C. Bearss, Historic Structures Report, National Park Service, published November 30, 1971

[10]Herbert Hoover The Hoover Houses and Community Structures by Edwin C. Bearss, Historic Structures Report, National Park Service, published November 30, 1971

[11]*The Cape Girardeau Southeast Missourian.* 7/9/1928. "Hoover Soon To Revisit Old Iowa Home"

[12]Herbert Hoover The Hoover Houses and Community Structures by Edwin C. Bearss, Historic Structures Report, National Park Service, published November 30, 1971

[13]Herbert Hoover The Hoover Houses and Community Structures by Edwin C. Bearss, Historic Structures Report, National Park Service, published November 30, 1971

[14]Herbert Hoover The Hoover Houses and Community Structures by Edwin C. Bearss, Historic Structures Report, National Park Service, published November 30, 1971

[15]Herbert Hoover The Hoover Houses and Community Structures by Edwin C. Bearss, Historic Structures Report, National Park Service, published November 30, 1971

[16]*The New York Times* 8/18/1929 "Hoover Cottage A Mecca"

[17]Herbert Hoover The Hoover Houses and Community Structures by Edwin C. Bearss, Historic Structures Report, National Park Service, published November 30, 1971

[18]*The New York Times.* 1/16/1929. "To Mark Hoover Birthspot"

[19]*Ludington Daily News.* 8/9/1929. "To Place Markers beside Birthplace of Herbert Hoover"

[20]*The New York Times.* 8/11/1929. "West Branch Has Dedication"

[21]Herbert Hoover The Hoover Houses and Community Structures by Edwin C. Bearss, Historic Structures Report, National Park Service, published November 30, 1971

[22]Herbert Hoover The Hoover Houses and Community Structures by Edwin C. Bearss, Historic Structures Report, National Park Service, published November 30, 1971

[23]*The Reading Eagle.* 10/17/1935. "Young Hoover Buys Father's Birthplace"

[24]*Pittsburgh Post Gazette.* 8/10/1954. "Herbert Hoover at 'Home''

[25]*The New York Times.* 10/17/1935. "Allan Hoover Now Owns Father's Boyhood Home"

[26]Herbert Hoover The Hoover Houses and Community Structures by Edwin C. Bearss, Historic Structures Report, National Park Service, published November 30, 1971

[27]Herbert Hoover The Hoover Houses and Community Structures by Edwin C. Bearss, Historic Structures Report, National Park Service, published November 30, 1971

[28]Herbert Hoover The Hoover Houses and Community Structures by Edwin C. Bearss, Historic Structures Report, National Park

Service, published November 30, 1971

[29]Herbert Hoover The Hoover Houses and Community Structures by Edwin C. Bearss, Historic Structures Report, National Park Service, published November 30, 1971

[30]Herbert Hoover The Hoover Houses and Community Structures by Edwin C. Bearss, Historic Structures Report, National Park Service, published November 30, 1971

[31]Herbert Hoover The Hoover Houses and Community Structures by Edwin C. Bearss, Historic Structures Report, National Park Service, published November 30, 1971

[32]Herbert Hoover The Hoover Houses and Community Structures by Edwin C. Bearss, Historic Structures Report, National Park Service, published November 30, 1971

[33]Herbert Hoover The Hoover Houses and Community Structures by Edwin C. Bearss, Historic Structures Report, National Park Service, published November 30, 1971

[34]Herbert Hoover The Hoover Houses and Community Structures by Edwin C. Bearss, Historic Structures Report, National Park Service, published November 30, 1971

[35]Herbert Hoover The Hoover Houses and Community Structures by Edwin C. Bearss, Historic Structures Report, National Park Service, published November 30, 1971

[36]Herbert Hoover The Hoover Houses and Community Structures by Edwin C. Bearss, Historic Structures Report, National Park Service, published November 30, 1971

[37]*Pittsburgh Post Gazette.* 8/10/1954. "Herbert Hoover at 'Home''

[38]*The Free-Lance Star.* Fredericksburg, VA. 8/10/1954. "Ex-President Hoover Returns To Birthplace To New Honors"

[39]Herbert Hoover The Hoover Houses and Community Structures by Edwin C. Bearss, Historic Structures Report, National Park Service, published November 30, 1971

[40]*The Cape Girardeau Southeast Missourian.* 12/2/1954. "Hoover Foundation Formed in Iowa"

[41]*The Cape Girardeau Southeast Missourian.* 12/2/1954. "Hoover Foundation Formed in Iowa"

[42]Herbert Hoover The Hoover Houses and Community Structures by Edwin C. Bearss, Historic Structures Report, National Park Service, published November 30, 1971

[43]*The Ocala Star-Banner.* 6/23/1965. "Birthplace of Herbert Hoover Names Historic Site"

[44]*The Ocala Star-Banner.* 9/7/1965

[45]*The Free-Lance Star.* Fredericksburg, VA. 8/9/1972. "Julie to dedicate Hoover birthplace"

[46]National Park Service Public Use Statistics Office

#32 Franklin Delano Roosevelt

[1]Little Nine Partners Historical Society, New York

[2]*Early History of Amenia* by Newton Reed (Amenia, New York: DeLacy & Wiley, 1875) p 6

[3]Franklin D. Roosevelt National Historic Site, National Park Service

[4]Franklin D. Roosevelt National Historic Site, National Park Service

[5]National Register of Historic Places Nomination Form "Home of Franklin Delano Roosevelt National Historic Site," *An Untold Story: The Roosevelts of Hyde Park* by Elliot Roosevelt and James Brough (New York, New York: G.P. Putman's Sons, 1973) p 99-100

[6]*Gettysburg Times.* 7/29/1933. "Roosevelt Is Home For Rest"

[7]Franklin D Roosevelt National Historic Site, National Park Service

[8]*The Spokesman Review.* 1/24/1982. "Roosevelt's birthplace heavily damaged in Hyde Park fire"

[9]National Park Service Public Use Statistics Office

#33 Harry S Truman

[1]*Truman* by David McCullough (New York, New York: Simon & Schuster,1992) p 36-37

[2]Harry S Truman Library & Museum. "USE OF THE PERIOD AFTER THE "S" IN HARRY S Truman's NAME"

[3]*Time* magazine. 9/9/1946. "National Affairs: By The Tall Pine Tree." *Time* magazine. 6/13/1949. "National Affairs: A Question of Sentiment"

[4]Harry S Truman Library & Museum. "Birthplace of Harry S Truman"

[5]*Truman's Birthplace Lamar, Missouri* by Reba Earp Young (Gretna, Louisiana: Pelican Publishing, 2004)

[6]Harry S Truman Library & Museum "USE OF THE PERIOD AFTER THE "S." IN Harry S Truman's NAME"

[7]*Time* magazine. 9/9/1946. "National Affairs: By The Tall Pine Tree"

[8]*Time* magazine. 9/9/1946. "National Affairs: By The Tall Pine Tree"

[9]*Time* magazine. 6/13/1949 "National Affairs: A Question of Sentiment"

[10]*The New York Times.* 5/1/1957. "Buys Old Truman Home"

[11]Harry S Truman Birthplace State Historic Site Conceptual Development Plan, May 2002

[12]*The Tuscaloosa News.* 3/26/1959. "Truman Birthplace Will Be Dedicated"

[13]*The Tuscaloosa News.* 3/26/1959. "Truman Birthplace Will Be Dedicated"

[14]Harry S Truman Birthplace State Historic Site Conceptual Development Plan, May 2002

[15]Harry S Truman Birthplace State Historic Site Conceptual Development Plan, May 2002

[16]National Park Service Public Use Statistics Office

[17]*Associated Press.* 1/11/2009. "Truman birthplace gets second shot at National Park"

#34 Dwight David Eisenhower

[1]*The New York Times.* 1/12/1958. "House of Ike"

[2]Eisenhower Birthplace State Historic Site. www. visiteisenhowerbirthplace.com

[3]*The Victoria Advocate.* 2/16/1946 ."Five-star Shrine ***** Town Keeps General Ike's Birthplace"

[4]*The New York Times.* 1/12/1958. "House of Ike"

[5]*The New York Times.* 9/9/1956. "4 Towns in Texas Claim President"

[6]*The Victoria Advocate.* 2/16/1946. "Five-star Shrine ***** Town Keeps General Ike's Birthplace"

[7]*The Reading Eagle.* 4/21/1946 "Gen. Ike Says Food Important Peace to Peace"

[8]*The Victoria Advocate.* 3/4/1953. "Birthplace Of President draws crowds"

[9]*The Victoria Advocate.* 11/12/1952. "Denison Offers Birthplace of Ike as National Shrine"

[10]*The Reading Eagle.* 6/7/1953. "Ike's Birthplace Called Firetrap"

[11]*Gettysburg Times.* 8/26/1953. "Ike's birthplace gets inside water"

[12]*Denison: Birth Place of a President* by Archie P. McDonald, PhD

[13]The Dispatch (Lexington, NC). 5/23/1956. "Eisenhower's Birthplace Restored By Texas Town"

[14]*The New York Times.* 10/15/1953. "Texas Honors President"

[15]*The Florence (Alabama) Times Daily.* 5/13/1956. "Ike's Birthplace Restored To Way It Looked In 1890."

[16]*The Florence (Alabama) Times Daily.* 5/13/1956. "Ike's Birthplace Restored To Way It Looked In 1890."

[17]*The New York Times.* 4/30/1958. "Eisenhower Album"

[18]Eisenhower Birthplace State Historic Site www. visiteisenhowerbirthplace.com

[19]*The Victoria Advocate.* 8/15/1956. "Ike's Birthplace Gets Fiery Cross"

[20]*Chicago Daily Tribune.* 9/27/1957. "Find Fish Heads on Front Porch of Ike's Birthplace"

[21]*The New York Times.* 1/9/1958. "Dennison Shrine Pelted"

[22]*The Toledo Blade.* 4/14/1965. "Lady Bird Visits"

[23]*St. Petersburg Times.* 9/2/1965. "Ike Returns To Birthplace For Dedication"

[24]*The Tuscaloosa News.* 9/2/1965. "Ike meets namesake"

[25]*The Reading Eagle.* 10/25/1971. "Visiting Friends"

[26]*Beaver Country Times.* 9/14/1972. "Ike's status at his birthplace"

[27]*The Victoria Advocate.* 7/9/1973. "Julie Due To Appear In Texas"

[28]*The Herald Democrat.* 2/21/2011. 'Denison dedicates Eisenhower Veterans Monument'

#35 John Fitzgerald Kennedy

[1]*John F. Kennedy's Birthplace A Presidential Home In History And Memory*. A Historic Resource Study by Alexander von Hoffman (National Park Service U.S. Department of the Interior, 2004)

[2]*John F. Kennedy's Birthplace A Presidential Home In History And Memory*. A Historic Resource Study by Alexander von Hoffman (National Park Service U.S. Department of the Interior, 2004)

[3]*John F. Kennedy's Birthplace A Presidential Home In History And Memory*. A Historic Resource Study by Alexander von Hoffman (National Park Service U.S. Department of the Interior, 2004)

[4]*John F. Kennedy's Birthplace A Presidential Home In History And Memory*. A Historic Resource Study by Alexander von Hoffman (National Park Service U.S. Department of the Interior, 2004)

[5]*John F. Kennedy's Birthplace A Presidential Home In History And Memory*. A Historic Resource Study by Alexander von Hoffman (National Park Service U.S. Department of the Interior, 2004)

[6]*John F. Kennedy's Birthplace A Presidential Home In History And Memory*. A Historic Resource Study by Alexander von Hoffman (National Park Service U.S. Department of the Interior, 2004)

[7]*The Baltimore Sun.* 2/22/1961. "Plaque All Right, Now She Wants Paint for House"

[8]*The Spokane Daily Chronicle.* 9/14/1961. "Presidential Birthplace Painted"

[9]*Meriden Journal.* 9/14/1961. "A New Frontier Paint Job"

[10]*The New York Times* 5/30/1962 "Birthplace to be Marked"

[11]*The New York Times* 11/24/1963 "In South Boston, Angry Silence Reflects the Passing of a Hero"

[12]*The Washington Observer.* 12/26/1963. "'Freedom Fighters' Sing AT[sic] Kennedy's Birthplace"

[13]*John F. Kennedy's Birthplace A Presidential Home In History And Memory*. A Historic Resource Study by Alexander von Hoffman (National Park Service U.S. Department of the Interior, 2004)

[14]*The New York Times.* 9/9/1966. "Group in Boston Buys Kennedy's Birthplace"

[15]*The Free-Lance Star.* Fredericksburg, VA. 11/4/1966. "JFK Birthplace Taken Over By His Family"

[16]*John F. Kennedy's Birthplace A Presidential Home In History And Memory*. A Historic Resource Study by Alexander von Hoffman (National Park Service U.S. Department of the Interior, 2004)

[17]*The New York Times.* 5/30/1969. "Kennedy Birthplace Made a National Shrine"

[18]*The New York Times.* 3/22/1967. "Senate Votes a Bill to Make Kennedy Birthplace U.S. Site"

[19]*The New York Times.* 5/30/1969. "Kennedy Birthplace Made a National Shrine"

[20]*Eugene Register-Guard.* 5/29/1969. "JFK Birthplace Becomes Historic Site"

[21]*Eugene Register-Guard.* 9/9/1975. "Fire Bomb Damages Birthplace of JFK"

[22]*The Ocala Star-Banner.* 9/9/1975. "JFK's Birthplace in Brookline, Mass. Damaged By Fire"

[23]*The Boston Globe.* 4/22/2001. "Bulger Linked to 70s Antibusing Attacks"

[24]*The Free-Lance Star.* Fredericksburg, VA. 11/4/1976. "JFK Birthplace Gets new look"

[25]National Park Service Public Use Statistics Office

#36 Lyndon Baines Johnson

[1]National Register of Historic Places Registration Form. "Lyndon B. Johnson National Historic Park"

[2]*The New York Times.* 6/14/1970. "Two Johnson Homes Dedicated As Historic Sites"

[3]*Lone Star Rising: Lyndon Johnson and His Times, 1908-1960 Volume 1* by Robert Dallek (New York, New York: Oxford University Press, 1991)

[4]Lyndon Baines Johnson National Historic Site National Park Service www.nps.gov/lyjo

[5]*The New York Times.* 7/11/1966. "President Opens His Birthplace"

[6]National Register of Historic Places Registration Form. "Lyndon B. Johnson National Historic Park"

[7]*The Tuscaloosa News.* 12/7/1963. "Johnson Not Just a President in Stonewall, He's a Friend"

[8]*The Victoria Advocate.* 5/24/1964. "LBJ Birthplace Due Rebuilding"

[9]*The Tuscaloosa News.* 12/7/1963. "Johnson Not Just a President in Stonewall, He's a Friend"

[10]*The Spartanburg Herald-Journal.* 12/12/1963. "Pecan Picker Asked About Cabin, Then Just Kept on Going"

[11]*The New York Times.* 7/11/1966. "President Opens His Birthplace"

[12]*The Victoria Advocate.* 5/24/1964. "LBJ Birthplace Due Rebuilding"

[13]Lyndon Baines Johnson National Historic Site

[14]*The Victoria Advocate.* 7/14/1966. "LBJ Birthplace Opened to Public"

[15]*The New York Times.* 4/14/1965. "First Lady at Denison, Tex."

[16]*St. Petersburg Times.* 7/14/1965. "Mrs. Johnson Digs Into Ranch History"

[17]*The Harper Herald.* 7/15/1966. "Peace and Quiet of By-Gone Days prevail at President Johnson's Birthplace"

[18]*The New York Times.* 7/11/1966. "President Opens His Birthplace"

[19]*The Victoria Advocate.* 7/14/1966. "LBJ Birthplace Opened to Public"

[20]*St. Petersburg Times.* 11/17/1968. "Heart of Texas It Carries the LBJ Brand"

[21]*The New York Times.* 1/4/1967. "Work Started on Johnson Park As New Fund Head Takes Over"

[22]*The Milwaukee Journal.* 8/11/1968. "Nixon, Agnew Briefed at LBJ Ranch"

[23]*The New York Times.* 6/14/1970. "Two Johnson Homes Dedicated As Historic Sites"

[24]*The New York Times.* 6/14/1970. "Two Johnson Homes Dedicated As Historic Sites"

[25]*Time* magazine. 7/27/1970. "A Visit to Lyndon Johnson's Birthplace"

[26]*Rome News-Tribune.* 4/2/1981. "Carter is visiting LBJ library"

[27]National Park Service Public Use Statistics Office

#37 Richard Milhous Nixon

[1]*Richard Milhous Nixon The Rise of an American Politician* by Roger Morris (New York, New York: Henry Holt and Company, 1990) p 39-67

[2]Richard Nixon foundation website. "Museum Tour: The Birthplace." www.nixonlibraryfoundation.org/index.php?submenu = museuma ndsrc = gendocsandlink = TheBirthplace

[3]Richard Nixon foundation website. "Museum Tour: The Birthplace." www.nixonlibraryfoundation.org/index.php?submenu = museuma ndsrc = gendocsandlink = TheBirthplace

[4]*Richard Milhous Nixon The Rise of an American Politician* by Roger Morris (New York, New York: Henry Holt and Company, 1990) p 42

[5]*The Yorba Linda Star.* 7/15/1978. "10-year effort ends with sale of Nixon home"

[6]*The New York Times.* 8/15/1960. "One Will Become a U.S. Shrine"

[7]Correspondence with Linda Bugbee, daughter of Mr. Jesse F. Waldron who lived in the Nixon birthplace from 1945 – 1969

[8]*The Free-Lance Star.* Fredericksburg, VA. 8/14/1973. "Scandal Touches

Nixon Birthplace"

[9]National Survey of Historic Sites and Buildings. "Nixon Birthplace"

[10]*The Yorba Linda Star.* 1/15/1959. "Many Yorba Lindans, Many Guests Pay Tribute to the Vice President"

[11]*The Los Angeles Times.* 1/10/1959. "Yorba Lindans Dedicate Nixon Home." *The Owosso Argus Press.* 1/10/1959. "Marker Placed at Nixon Birthplace"

[12]Times Washington Bureau. 1/14/1959. "Nixon Affirms Yorba Linda Birthplace"

[13]*The Los Angeles Times.* 1/11/1959. "Nixon's Mother has Last Word in Birthplace Row"

[14]Times Washington Bureau. 1/14/1959. "Nixon Affirms Yorba Linda Birthplace"

[15]The Owosso Argus Press. 1/7/1959. "Marker Placed at Nixon Birthplace"

[16]*The Yorba Linda Star.* 6/18/1959. "Big day for Yorba Lindans when the vice-president visits"

[17]*The Los Angeles Times.* 8/4/1960. "Nixon Birthplace Sign Replaced"

[18]*The Los Angeles Times.* 8/4/1960. "Nixon Birthplace Sign Replaced"

[19]*The Yorba Linda Star.* 12/4/1968. "Nixon Birthplace Foundation organized here." *The Los Angeles Times.* 11/17/1989. "These Nixon Fans Make Their Feelings Perfectly Clear"

[20]The *Eugene Register-Guard.* 10/15/1977. "School district sells Nixon site"

[21]*The Free-Lance Star.* Fredericksburg, VA. 8/24/1974. "Birthplace of our 37th President"

[22]*The New York Times.* 5/7/1973. "Coast Town, Undeterred by Watergate, Pushes for National Shrine at Nixon Birthplace"

[23]*The New York Times.* 7/31/1969. "U.S. Urged to Buy Nixon Birthplace"

[24]*The Reading Eagle.* 3/16/1969. "Changes *Come Slowly Out In Nixon Country*"

[25]*The Yorba Linda Star.* 12/4/1968. "Nixon Birthplace Foundation organized here"

[26]*The New York Times.* 5/14/1972. "Bomb Hoax at Birthplace"

[27]*The Victoria Advocate.* 8/16/1973. "Nixon Birthplace Register Shows Watergate Effect"

[28]*The New York Times.* 5/7/1973. "Coast Town, Undeterred by Watergate, Pushes for National Shrine at Nixon Birthplace"

[29]*The Free-Lance Star.* Fredericksburg, VA. 8/24/1974. "Birthplace of our 37th President"

[30]*Orange Coast* magazine. January 1988. "Nixon Takes The Cake" by Elizabeth Pike

[31]*The Milwaukee Journal.* 5/17/1977. "Nixon Tribute took a while"

[32]The New Nixon Blog by the Nixon Foundation. 6/22/2007. "Stately Mosaic Was Early Marker for RN Birthplace: Master brick layer Robert Farrell created 50-state stonework"

[33]*The Modesto Bee.* 4/20/1977. "Nixon monument appears far off"

[34]*The Eugene Register-Guard.* 10/15/1977. "School district sells Nixon site"

[35]*The Yorba Linda Star.* 7/15/1978

[36]*The Free-Lance Star.* Fredericksburg, VA. 7/15/1978. "Watergate defense funds may restore Nixon birthplace"

[37]*The New York Times.* 3/26/1978. "Quandary on Funds for Nixon"

[38]*St. Petersburg Times.* 12/21/1985. "Bill would make Nixon's birthplace a monument." *The New York Times.* 12/17/1985. "Nixon Tribute proposed"

[39]*The Toledo Blade.* 3/10/1986. "Complaints Derail Plan to Honor Nixon's Birthplace"

[40]*The Yorba Linda Star.* 12/10/1987

[41]*The New York Times.* 7/20/1990. "Another Nixon Summit, at his Library"

[42]Richard Milhous Nixon Last Will and Testament

[43]*Associated Press.* 1/10/1995. "Nixon Library and Birthplace Now A Historic Landmark"

[44]*The Times.* 11/1/2008. "Top 10 US presidential addresses"

#38 Leslie Lynch King (a.k.a. Gerald Rudolff Ford)

[1]*The Los Angeles Times.* 7/2/1989. "Fourth Right Visiting Presidential Birthplaces can Remind us that All Men are Created Equal"

[2]*Write It When I'm Gone* by Thomas M. DeFrank (New York, New York G. P. Putnam's Sons, 2007), p 193

[3]*Nebraska Life* magazine. *July/August 2001 issue* "From Woolworth Ave. to the White House"

[4]*The New York Times.* 2/16/1974. "Ford opposed Election Financing Bill"

[5]*The Tuscaloosa News.* 5/2/1976. "Ford goes home in search of votes"

[6]*Rome News-Tribune.* 8/11/1974. "Youngsters visit President's Birthplace"

[7]*Times Daily.* 9/17/1974. "Omaha's Troop Scout 388"

[8]*The Toledo Blade.* 8/27/1975. "$200,000 Project To Mark Ford's Birthplace in Omaha"

[9]*The Argus Press.* 8/28/1975. "$200,000 Memorial Planned At Site of Ford's Birth"

[10]*Nebraska Life* magazine. July/August 2001 issue. "From Woolworth Ave. to the White House"

[11]*Spokane Daily Chronicle.* 9/16/1977. "Ford's Home Site Of Park"

[12]KETV.com 12/27/2006 "Former Mayor Recalls Ford's feelings Towards Omaha"

[13]*The Calgary Herald.* 7/14/1980. "People"

[14]Boys Town official website www.boystown.org

[15]*The New York Times.* 8/11/1929. "West Branch Has Dedication"

#39 James Earl Carter

[1]*Jimmy Carter: A Comprehensive Biography from Plains to Post-Presidency* by Peter G. Bourne (New York, New York: Scribner, 1997), p 18-22

[2]*An Hour Before Daylight* by Jimmy Carter (New York, New York: Simon & Schuster, 2001) p 119

[3]*Jimmy Carter: A Comprehensive Biography from Plains to Post-Presidency* by Peter G. Bourne (New York, New York: Scribner, 1997), p 18-22

[4]*An Hour Before Daylight* by Jimmy Carter (New York, New York: Simon & Schuster, 2001) p 119

[5]*An Hour Before Daylight* by Jimmy Carter (New York, New York: Simon & Schuster, 2001) p 119

[6]*The Americus Times-Recorder.* 10/17/2009

[7]National Park Service Public Use Statistics Office

#40 Ronald Wilson Reagan

[1]National Register of Historic Places Nomination Form. "Main Street Historic District (Tampico)"

[2]National Register of Historic Places Nomination Form. "Main Street Historic District (Tampico)"

[3]*An American Life* by Ronald Reagan (New York, New York: Simon & Schuster, 1999) p21

[4]National Register of Historic Places Nomination Form. "Main Street Historic District (Tampico)"

[5]*Tampico Tornado.* 3/18/1920. "Bank to have new quarters"

[6]Tampico Area Historical Society with assistance from Denise Wranik McLoughlin (Family History Coordinator) and Joan Johnson (Volunteer Coordinator), Ronald Reagan Birthplace/Museum

[7]*St. Petersburg Times.* 7/16/1980. "Town argues Reagan's birthplace"

[8]*The Miami News.* 8/19/1980. "Welcome to Tampico, Ill., birthplace of Ronald Reagan"

[9]*The Milwaukee Journal.* 2/13/1980. "Ronald Reagan's birthplace hopes to be another Plains"

[10]*The Pittsburgh Press.* 8/19/1980. "They Remember 'Dutch' Reagan"

[11]*The Free-Lance Star.* Fredericksburg, VA. 1/16/1989. "Tourists bypassing Reagan's hometown"

[12]Newsmax.com. 2/6/2004

[13]*Spokane Chronicle.* 8/23/1989. "Vandalism closes Reagan museum"

[14]*The Tuscaloosa News.* 5/10/1992. "Reagan returns to birthplace"

[15]*Jewish World Review.* 9/2003

[16]*The Chicago Tribune.* 9/17/2003. "Democrat buys, preserves Ronald

Reagan birthplace in Ill."

[17]*Quad City Times.* 2/5/2011. "Reagan remembered as a man of 'destiny'"

[18]R&B's Dutch Diner menu

#41 George Herbert Walker Bush

[1]Milton Historical Commission

[2]Milton Historical Commission

[3]*The Boston Globe.* 8/10/1997. "George Bush's birthplace getting recognition in Milton"

[4]*The New London Day.* 7/17/1994. "Owner opposes plans for plaque on house where Bush was born"

[5]*The New London Day.* 7/17/1994. "Owner opposes plans for plaque on house where Bush was born"

[6]*The Boston Globe.* 8/13/1997. "Bush shows he can go home again"

#42 William Jefferson Blythe (a.k.a. William Jefferson Clinton)

[1]*My Life* by Bill Clinton (New York, New York: Alfred A. Knopf, 2004) p 8

[2]City of Hope, Arkansas official website. www.hopearkansas.net

[3]*The Hour.* (Norwalk, CT) 11/24/1992. "Visit Clintons Birthplace"

[4]*The Complete Book of U.S. Presidents* by William A. DeGregorio (New York, New York: W.W. Norton, 1984)

[5]*The Free-Lance Star.* Fredericksburg, VA. 6/26/1997. "Clinton attends uncle's funeral"

[6]1997-2011 Clinton Birthplace Foundation, Inc., Hope AR, and Martha Berryman, Museum ED. 2006-2011

[7]1997-2011 Clinton Birthplace Foundation, Inc., Hope AR, and Martha Berryman, Museum ED. 2006-2011

[8]*My Life* by Bill Clinton (New York, New York: Alfred A. Knopf, 2004) p 8

[9]1997-2011 Clinton Birthplace Foundation, Inc., Hope AR, and Martha Berryman, Museum ED. 2006-2011

[10]*Lawrence Journal-World.* 5/26/1997. "Clinton birthplace to open as museum"

[11]1997-2011 Clinton Birthplace Foundation, Inc., Hope AR, and Martha Berryman, Museum ED. 2006-2011

[12]1997-2011 Clinton Birthplace Foundation, Inc., Hope AR, and Martha Berryman, Museum ED. 2006-2011

[13]*The Hour.* (Norwalk, CT) 11/24/1992. "Visit Clintons Birthplace"

[14]*The Hour.* (Norwalk, CT) 11/24/1992. "Visit Clintons Birthplace"

[15]1997-2011 Clinton Birthplace Foundation, Inc., Hope AR, and Martha Berryman, Museum ED. 2006-2011

[16]*The Hour.* (Norwalk, CT) 11/24/1992. "Visit Clintons Birthplace"

[17]*Lakeland Register.* 3/13/1999. "Clinton Dedicates Arkansas Birthplace"

[18]*The New York Times.* 3/13/1999. "Wistful Clinton Dedicates Boyhood Home"

[19]*Lawrence Journal-World.* 5/26/1997. "Clinton birthplace to open as museum"

[20]*Lawrence Journal-World.* 5/26/1997. "Clinton birthplace to open as museum"

[21]*Milwaukee Journal Sentinel.* 3/13/1999. "Clinton Boyhood home dedicated"

[22]*Milwaukee Journal Sentinel.* 3/13/1999. "Clinton Boyhood home dedicated"

[23]*Milwaukee Journal Sentinel.* 3/13/1999. "Clinton Boyhood home dedicated"

[24]*The Guelph Mercury.* 8/27/2005. "Clinton fans make Billgrimage to Arkansas birthplace, library"

[25]William Jefferson Clinton Birthplace Home National Historic Site Report submitted by Mr. Bingaman, from the Committee on Energy and Natural Resources. 2/15/2007

[26]*Hope Star.* 2/11/2009. "Quick action on birthplace change likely"

[27]*The Federal Register*, The Daily Journal of the United States Government. 12/28/2010. "President William Jefferson Clinton Birthplace Home National Historic Site, A Notice by the National Park Service"

[28]*Associated Press.* 4/15/2011. "Clinton hometown Hope-ing for tourism boost." OnlineJournal.com. 4/17/2011. "Bill Clinton Historic Site Designated at Boyhood home"

[29]*The Newark Star Ledger.* 11/15/2009. "Clinton's other white house"

[30]*The Los Angeles Times.* 7/23/2000. ABC News Reporters' Notebook by Josh Gerstein and Chika Nakayama

[31]Correspondence with David Coleman, Manager

#43 George Walker Bush

[1]"When George W. Bush was born at Grace-New Haven community Hospital" provided by the Yale-New Haven Hospital Archivist. 7/2009

[2]"When George W. Bush was born at Grace-New Haven community Hospital" provided by the Yale-New Haven Hospital Archivist. 7/2009

[3]*Hartford Courant.* 10/20/2004. "The Birth Of A President; Historical Footnote? Bush Delivery Not Exactly Special To New Haven"

[4]*Record Journal.* 12/15/2000. "Bush has many ties to New Haven"

[5]*The New York Times.* 12/24/2000. "Bush's Birthplace? It's Deep in the Heart of...New Haven"

[6]*Hartford Courant.* 10/20/2004. "The Birth Of A President; Historical Footnote? Bush Delivery Not Exactly Special To New Haven"

#44 Barack Hussein Obama

[1]*Hawaii* (London, England: Dorling Kindersley Publishing, Inc. 1998)

[2]The Kapi'olani Medical Center for Women and Children website. "A Century of Care for Hawaii's Women and Children"

[3]*Dreams from My Father* by Barack Obama (New York, New York: Three Rivers Press, 2004), p66

[4]Honoluluadvertiser.com. 11/9/2008. "Obama's Hawaii boyhood homes drawing gawkers"

[5]Birth Certificate, State of Hawaii Department of Health (61 10641)

[6]*The Honolulu Advertiser.* 8/13/1961

[7]Honoluluadvertiser.com. 11/9/2008. "Obama's Hawaii boyhood homes drawing gawkers"

[8]Zillow.com. 12/2/2009

[9]Honoluluadvertiser.com. 11/9/2008. "Obama's Hawaii boyhood homes drawing gawkers"

[10]Honoluluadvertiser.com. 1/2/2010. "Hawaii considering new holidays, parks to honor Obama

[11]Honoluluadvertiser.com. 11/9/2008. "Obama's Hawaii boyhood homes drawing gawkers"

Bibliography

Books

Amis, Moses. *Historical Raleigh*. Raleigh, North Carolina: Commercial Printing Company, 1913

Amis, Moses Neal. *Historical Raleigh from its foundation in 1792*. Raleigh, North Carolina: 1902

Barefoot, Daniel W. *Touring North Carolina's Revolutionary War Sites*. Winston-Salem, North Carolina: John F. Blair, 1998

Bates, Samuel Penniman and Richard, Jacob Fraise. *History of Franklin County*. Chicago, Illinois: Warner, Beers & Co., 1887

Benbow, Nancy D. & Christopher H. *Cabins, Cottages & Mansions: Homes of the Presidents of the United States*. Gettysburg, Pennsylvania: Thomas Publications,1993

Bishop, Chris and Drury, Ian and Gibbons, Tony. *1400 Days The Civil War Day By Day*. New York, New York: Smithmark Publishers, 1990

Blythe, LeGette and Brockmann, Charles Raven. *Hornet's Nest The Story of Charlotte and Mecklenburg County*. Public Library of Charlotte and Mecklenburg County, 1961

Bourne, Peter G. *Jimmy Carter: A Comprehensive Biography from Plains to Post-Presidency*. New York, New York: Scribner, 1997

Brooks, Elbridge S. *The True Story of U S Grant the American Soldier: Told for Boys and Girls*. Boston Massachusetts: Lothrop Publishing Company, 1897

Browne, George Waldo. *The History of Hillsborough, New Hampshire, 1735-1921*. Manchester, New Hampshire: Published by The Town, 1922

Bruggeman, Seth C. *Here, George Washington Was Born: Memory, Material Culture, and the Public History of a National Monument*. Athens, Georgia: University of Georgia Press, 2008

Buell, Augustus C. *History of Andrew Jackson, pioneer, patriot, soldier, politician, president Volume 1*.New York, New York: Scribner, 1904

Carleton, Hiram. *Genealogical And Family History Of The State Of Vermont*. New York, New York: The Lewis Publishing Company, 1903

Carr, Howie. *The Brothers Bulger*. New York, New York: Warner Books, 2006

Carter, Jimmy. *An Hour Before Daylight*. New York, New York: Simon & Schuster, 2001

Christian, Honorable George. *John Tyler Address Delivered before the Colonial Dames of American the State of Virginia at Greenway, Charles City County, VA on Monday October 27, 1913 at the unveiling of a memorial to Mark the birthplace of President Tyler*. Richmond, Virginia: Whittet and Shepperson,1913

Clinton, Bill. *My Life*. New York, New York: Alfred A. Knopf, 2004

Conwell, Russell H. *The Life Speeches and Public Services of Gen. James A. Garfield Of Ohio*. Boston, Massachusetts: Russell H. Conwell & Co., 1880

Crapol, Edward P. *John Tyler: The Accidental President*. Chapel Hill, North Carolina: The University of North Carolina Press, 2006

Dallek, Robert. *Lone Star Rising: Lyndon Johnson and His Times, 1908-1960 Volume 1*. New York, New York: Oxford University Press, 1991

DeFrank, Thomas M. *Write It When I'm Gone*. New York, New York G. P. Putnam's Sons, 2007

DeGregorio, William A. *The Complete Book of U.S. Presidents*. New York, New York: W.W. Norton, 1984

Donald, Aida D. *Lion in the White House: A Life of Theodore Roosevelt*. New York, New York: MJF Books, 2007

Faris, John Thomson. *Historic Shrines of America*. New York, New York: George H. Doran Company, 1918

Finkelman, Paul. *Millard Fillmore*. New York, New York: Times Books, 2011

Goodman, Hattie S. *The Knox Family a Genealogical and Biographical Sketch of the Descendents of John Knox*. Richmond, Virginia: Whittet and Shepperson, 1905

Goodnight, Jerry. *The Tarheel Lincoln*. Hickory, North Carolina: Tarheel Press, 2003

Grant, Hiram Ulysses. *Personal Memoirs of U.S. Grant*. Mineloa, New York: Dover, 1995

Hatch Jr., Charles E. *Popes Creek Plantation Birthplace of George Washington*. Washington's Birthplace, Virginia: Wakefield National Memorial Association, 1979

Heckscher, August. *Woodrow Wilson: A Biography*. Newtown, Connecticut: American Political Biography Press, 2007

Hinman, Arthur. *How a British Subject Became President of the United States*. New York, New York: 1884

Hobson, Jonathan Todd. *Footprints of Abraham Lincoln: presenting many interesting facts*. Dayton, Ohio: The Otterbein Press,1909

Howe, Henry. *Historical Collections of Ohio, Vol. I*. Cincinnati, Ohio: C.J. Krihbiel & Co., Printers and Binders, 1902

Hsiung, David C. *A Mountaineer in Motion: The Memoir of Dr. Abraham Jobe, 1817-1906*. Knoxville, Tennessee: University Tennessee Press, 2009

Huntington, Frances Carpenter. *Records of the Columbia Historical Society, Washington, D.C.* Washington, D.C.: *Columbia Historical Society, 1971*

Keinath, Caroline. *Adams National Historical Park*. Lawrenceburg, Indiana: R.L. Ruehrwein, 2008

Kochmann, Rachel M. *Presidents Birthplaces, Homes and Burial Sites*. Osage, Minnesota: Osage Publishing, 1999

Loewen, James W. *Lies Across America*. New York, New York: The New Press, 1999

Loth, Calder. *The Virginia Landmarks Register*. Charlottesville, Virginia: University Press of Virginia, 1999

McCullough, David. *John Adams*. New York, New York: Simon & Schuster, 1992

McCullough, David. *Truman*. New York, New York: Simon & Schuster, 2001

Morris, Roger. *Richard Milhous Nixon The Rise of an American Politician*. New York, New York: Henry Holt and Company, 1990

O'Neill, Patrick. *Virginia's Presidential Homes*. Charleston, South Carolina: Arcadia Publishing, 2010

Obama, Barack. *Dreams from My Father*. New York, New York: Three Rivers Press, 2004

Pecquet du Bellet, Louise, Edward & Jaquelin and Cary, Martha. *Some prominent Virginia families, Volume 2*. Lynchburg, Virginia: J.P. Bell Company, 1907

Pendle, George. *The Remarkable Millard Fillmore: The Unbelievable Life of a Forgotten President*. New York, New York: Three Rivers Press, 2007

Perrin, William Henry. *History of Delaware County and Ohio*. Chicago, Illinois: O.L. Baskin & Co., 1882

Reagan, Ronald. *An American Life*. New York, New York: Simon & Schuster, 1999

Reed, Newton. *Early History of Amenia*. Amenia, New York: DeLacy & Wiley, 1875

Roberts, Jeremy. *Zachary Taylor*. Minneapolis, Minnesota: Lerner Publishing Group, 2005

Roosevelt, Elliot and Brough, James. *An Untold Story: The Roosevelts of Hyde Park*. New York, New York: G.P. Putman's Sons, 1973

Russell, Francis. *The Shadow of Blooming Grove: Warren G. Harding in His Times*. New York, New York: McGraw-Hill, 1968

Rutkow, Ira M. *James A. Garfield*. New York, New York: Times Books, 2006

Steers, Edward. *Lincoln Legends: Myths, Hoaxes, and Confabulations Associated With Our Greatest President*. Lexington, Kentucky: The University Press of Kentucky, 2007

Strode, Hudson. *Jefferson Davis: Private letters, 1823-1889 by Jefferson Davis*. New York, New York: Harcourt, Brace & World,1966

Trefousse, Hans Louis. *Andrew Johnson A Biography*. Newton, Connecticut: W. W. Norton & Company, 1997

Tyler, Lyon Gardiner. *The cradle of the republic: Jamestown and James River*. Richmond, Virginia: The Hermitage Press, 1906

Tyler, Lyon Gardiner. *The Letters and Times of the Tylers V1, Volume 1*. Richmond, Virginia: Whittet and Shepperson,1884

Warren, Robert Penn. *Jefferson Davis Gets his Citizenship Back*. Lexington, Kentucky: University Press of Kentucky Press, 1980

Weslager, Clinton Alfred. *The Log Cabin in America: From Pioneer Days to The Present*. New Brunswick, New Jersey: Rutgers University Press, 1969

Young, Reba Earp. *Truman's Birthplace Lamar, Missouri*. Gretna, Louisiana: Pelican Publishing, 2004

Historical Publications

Abraham Lincoln Birthplace Memorial Building Historic Structure Report, 2001, National Park Service

Administrative History of the Abraham Lincoln Birthplace National Historic Site, ABLI-1 by Gloria Peterson, published September 20, 1968

Andrew Johnson National Historic Site Administrative History by Cameron Binkley, 2001

Architectural Data Form "Herbert Hoover Birthplace Home," National Park Service

George Washington Birthplace National Monument Administrative History by Seth C. Bruggeman, College of William & Mary 2006

Grover Cleveland Birthplace Historic American Buildings Survey, Photographs Written Historical and Descriptive Data

Herbert Hoover The Hoover Houses and Community Structures by Edwin C. Bearss, Historic Structures Report, National Park Service, published November 30, 1971

Historic Furnishings Report: The Birthplaces of Presidents John Adams and John Quincy Adams, National Park Service

John F. Kennedy's Birthplace A Presidential Home In History And Memory, A Historic Resource Study by Alexander von Hoffman (National Park Service U.S. Department of the Interior, 2004)

National Register of Historic Places Nomination Form. "Berkeley – (Benjamin Harrison V Birthplace and Home)"

National Register of Historic Places Nomination Form. "Calvin Coolidge Homestead District"

National Register of Historic Places Nomination Form. "Greenway"

National Register of Historic Places Nomination Form. "Home of Franklin Delano Roosevelt National Historic Site"

National Register of Historic Places Nomination Form. "Franklin Pierce Homestead"

National Register of Historic Places Nomination Form. "Hare Forest Farm"

National Register of Historic Places Nomination Form. "Main Street Historic District (Tampico)"

National Register of Historic Places Property Photograph Form. "Calvin Coolidge Homestead District"

National Register of Historic Places Property Photograph Form. "Theodore Roosevelt Birthplace"

National Register of Historic Places Registration Form. "John Adams Birthplace"

National Register of Historic Places Registration Form. "John Quincy Adams Birthplace"

National Register of Historic Places Registration Form. "Lyndon B. Johnson National Historic Park"

National Register of Historic Places Registration Form. "Monroe, James, Birthplace Updated Nomination"

National Survey of Historic Sites and Buildings. "Nixon Birthplace"

National Survey of Historic Sites and Buildings. "Woodrow Wilson Birthplace"

William Howard Taft National Historic Site Administrative History. National Park Service

William Jefferson Clinton Birthplace Home National Historic Site Report submitted by Mr. Bingaman, from the Committee on Energy and Natural Resources 2/15/2007

Index